THE VEST-POCKET CPA

Nicky A. Dauber, MS, CPA
Joel G. Siegel, Ph.D., CPA
Jae K. Shim, Ph.D.

PRENTICE HALL
Englewood Cliffs, New Jersey 07632

Prentice-Hall International (UK) Limited, *London*
Prentice-Hall of Australia Pty. Limited, *Sydney*
Prentice-Hall Canada, Inc., *Toronto*
Prentice-Hall Hispanoamericana, S.A., *Mexico*
Prentice-Hall of India Private Limited, *New Delhi*
Prentice-Hall of Japan, Inc., *Tokyo*
Simon & Schuster Asia Pte. Ltd., *Singapore*
Editora Prentice-Hall do Brasil, Ltda., *Rio de Janeiro*

© 1988 *by*

PRENTICE-HALL, Inc.
Englewood Cliffs, NJ

10 9 8 7 6

Library of Congress Cataloging-in-Publication Data

Dauber, Nicky A.
  The vest-pocket CPA / Nicky A. Dauber, Joel G. Siegel,
Jae K. Shim.
    p.   cm.
  Includes index.
  ISBN 0-13-942293-5
  1. Accounting—Handbooks, manuals, etc.   I. Siegel,
Joel G.   II. Shim, Jae K.   III. Title.
HF5635.D226   1988
657'.076—dc19   88-22406
                                                    CIP

ISBN 0-13-942293-5
ISBN 0-13-942137-8 PBK

PRENTICE HALL
BUSINESS & PROFESSIONAL DIVISION
A division of Simon & Schuster
Englewood Cliffs, New Jersey 07632

Printed in the United States of America

About the Authors

NICKY ANDREW DAUBER, MS, CPA, is an accounting practitioner with client responsibilities primarily in auditing and taxation. His prior experience includes service as an audit and tax manager at a CPA firm. He is also an Instructor of Auditing and Tax at Queens College of the City University of New York, as well as a lecturer and writer in auditing and taxation for Person-Wolinsky Associates. Mr. Dauber has also served as an instructor in auditing for the Foundation for Accounting Education of the New York State Society of CPAs. In addition to serving as a book reviewer for major book publishers, Mr. Dauber has had articles published in many professional accounting journals including *The CPA Journal*, *Massachusetts CPA*, *Virginia Accountant Quarterly*, and the *National Public Accountant*.

JOEL G. SIEGEL, Ph.D., CPA, is Professor of Accounting at Queens College of the City University of New York. He is also an accounting practitioner to various clients.

Dr. Siegel was previously a member of the audit staff of Coopers and Lybrand, CPAs, and a faculty resident with Arthur Andersen, CPAs. Dr. Siegel has acted as a consultant in accounting issues to many organizations, including International Telephone & Telegraph, Person-Wolinsky Associates, and Citicorp.

Dr. Siegel is the author of 19 books and approximately 135 articles on accounting topics. His books have been published by Prentice Hall, McGraw-Hill, John Wiley, Barron's, and the AICPA.

He has been published in numerous accounting and financial journals including *Massachusetts CPA*, *Ohio CPA*, *Michigan CPA*, *Virginia Accountant Quarterly*, *Delaware CPA*, *The CPA Journal*, *National Public Accountant*, *Financial Executive*, and *The Financial Analysts Journal*.

In 1972, he was the recipient of the Outstanding

Educator of America Award. He is listed in Who's Where Among Writers and Who's Who in the World.

JAE K. SHIM is Professor of Accounting at California State University, Long Beach. He received his MBA and Ph.D. degrees from the University of California at Berkeley. He has published over 50 articles in accounting and finance; he has 14 books to his credit. Dr. Shim has been, over a period of 12 years, an industrial consultant on accounting matters. Dr. Shim was the recipient of the Credit Research Foundation Award.

Introduction

Here is a handy pocket reference and problem-solver for today's busy accountant. It will help you quickly pinpoint:

- What to look for
- What to watch out for
- What to do
- How to do it

It will guide you through in the complex, ever-changing world of accounting. You'll find financial measures, guidelines, ratios, procedures, techniques, and rules of thumb to help you analyze, evaluate, and solve most accounting-related problems that come up. Throughout, you'll find this book practical, quick, comprehensive, and useful. You'll want to carry it around for constant reference where ever you go—on a business trip, visiting a client's office, meeting corporate executives, and at your office. The content of the book applies to public and private accountants whether employed by large, medium, or small firms. The uses for this book are as varied as the topics presented.

The book is a practical reference that contains proven approaches and techniques for understanding and solving problems of:

- Financial accounting
- Financial statement analysis
- Financial planning
- Managerial accounting
- Quantitative analysis and modeling
- Auditing
- Taxation

Part 1 takes you through accounting principles, financial reporting requirements, disclosures, and specialized accounting topics, to keep you up to date with generally accepted accounting principles.

Part 2 examines the financial health and operating performance of an entity. You'll learn about:

- Analytical tools in appraising a company as a basis for determining the extent of audit testing, financial reliance thereon, and going concern problems
- The viability of a targeted company for a merger
- Means of corporate and personal financial planning
- Achieving optimal investment return while controlling risk
- Investment analysis techniques
- Adequacy of insurance for the viability of the entity
- Retirement and estate planning issues

Part 3 presents internal accounting applications to help you:

- Evaluate your own company's performance, profitability, effectiveness, efficiency, marketing, and budgeting processes
- Highlight problem areas with variance analysis
- Move your company toward greater profits through break-even analysis

Guidelines are presented for evaluating proposals, whether they be short- or long-term, for profit potential and risk-return comparison. Operations research, quantitative, and modeling techniques are clearly presented so the accountant can use up-to-date approaches in solving business problems.

Part 4 relates to audit planning, procedures, and reporting. Means of gathering audit evidence, evaluating internal control, appraisal of financial statement items, and preparation of audit workpapers are addressed. Review and compilation services are also discussed. The practitioner is provided with a handy guide for designing audit programs. Checklists are provided to assist the auditor in developing work programs for any client environment. The practitioner is guided through the many Statements on Auditing Standards. The practitioner is exposed to the many types of reports pertinent to various engagements. Given a standard report, the practitioner can prepare modifications with a minimum of effort. The AICPA Statements relevant to the various reporting situations have been streamlined for easier application.

Part 5 applies to conducting income tax research.

The content of the book is clear, concise, and to the point. It is a valuable reference tool with guidelines, checklists, illustrations, step-by-step instructions, practical applications, and "how-to's" for you, the up-to-date, knowledgeable accountant. Keep this book handy for easy reference and daily use.

Dedication

To

MARGIE, MARC, AND SUSAN DAUBER
Loving and wonderful mother, father, and sister

KAREN J. DAUBER
Loving wife and dear friend

and

ROBERTA SIEGEL
Loving wife and expert typist

PHILIP E. LEVINE
Dear and precious friend

and

CHUNG SHIM
Dedicated wife

Acknowledgments

We wish to express our deep gratitude to Bette Schwartzberg for her outstanding editorial assistance during the project. Her input and efforts are recognized and greatly appreciated.

Thanks also to Christina Burghard for managing the production process so efficiently, and to Jan Douglas for her constructive editorial suggestions.

Contents

PART 1

COMMONLY USED GENERALLY ACCEPTED ACCOUNTING PRINCIPLES

CHAPTER 1

FINANCIAL STATEMENT REPORTING: THE INCOME STATEMENT

The reporting requirements of the income statement, balance sheet, statement of changes in cash flows, and interim reporting guidelines must be carefully examined. Individuals preparing personal financial statements have to follow certain unique reporting requirements, also true in accounting for a partnership. Points to note are:

- Income statement preparation involves proper revenue and expense recognition. The income statement format is highlighted along with the earnings per share computation.

- Balance sheet reporting covers accounting requirements for the various types of assets, liabilities, and stockholders' equity.

- The Statement of Cash Flows presents cash receipts and cash payments classified according to investing, financing, and operating activities. Disclosure is also provided for certain noncash investment and financial transactions. A reconciliation is provided between reported earnings and cash flow from operations.

- Interim financial reporting allows for some departures from annual reporting such as the gross profit method to estimate inventory. The tax provision is based on the effective tax rate expected for the year.

- Personal financial statements show the worth

3

of the individual. Assets and liabilities are reflected at current value in the order of maturity.

This chapter will deal with the reporting requirements on the income statement. Chapter 2 will deal with the balance sheet, and Chapter 3 will cover the remaining statements.

INCOME STATEMENT FORMAT

With respect to the income statement, the CPA's attention is addressed to:

- Income statement format
- Comprehensive income
- Extraordinary items
- Nonrecurring items
- Discontinued operations
- Revenue recognition methods
- Accounting for research and development costs
- Presentation of earnings per share

How are items on the income statement arranged?

In the preparation of the income statement, continuing operations are presented before discontinued operations.

Starting with income from continuing operations, the format of the income statement is as follows:

Income from continuing operations before tax

Less: Taxes

Income from continuing operations after tax

Discontinued operations:

Income from discontinued operations (net of tax)

Loss or gain on disposal of a division (net of tax)

Income before extraordinary items

Extraordinary items (net of tax)

Cumulative effect of a change in accounting principle (net of tax)

Net income

NOTE: Earnings per share is shown on the above items as well.

COMPREHENSIVE INCOME

What is comprehensive income?

Comprehensive income is the change in equity occurring from transactions and other events with nonowners. It excludes investment (disinvestment) by owners. Items included in comprehensive income but excluded from net income are:

- Cumulative effect of a change in accounting principle.
- Unrealized losses and gains on long-term investments.
- Foreign currency translation gains and losses.

Comprehensive income is subdivided into revenues and gains, as well as expenses and losses. These are further classified as either recurring or extraordinary.

EXTRAORDINARY ITEMS

What are extraordinary items?

Extraordinary items are those that are *both* unusual in nature and infrequent in occurrence.

- "Unusual in nature" means the event is abnormal and not related to the typical operations of the entity.
- "Infrequent in occurrence" means the transaction is not anticipated to take place in the foreseeable future taking into account the corporate environment.
- The environment of a company includes consideration of industry characteristics, geographic location of operations, and extent of government regulation.

• Materiality is considered by judging the items individually and not in the aggregate. However, if arising from a single specific event or plan they should be aggregated.

Extraordinary items are shown net of tax between income from discontinued operations and cumulative effect of a change in accounting principle.

What are some typical extraordinary items?

Extraordinary items include:

• Casualty losses.

• Losses on expropriation of property by a foreign government.

• Gain on life insurance proceeds.

• Loss or gain on the early extinguishment of debt.

• Gain on troubled debt restructuring.

• Loss from prohibition under a newly enacted law or regulation.

EXCEPTION: Losses on receivables and inventory occur in the normal course of business and therefore are not extraordinary. Losses on receivables and inventory are extraordinary, however, if they relate to a casualty loss (e.g., earthquake) or governmental expropriation (e.g., banning of product because of a health hazard).

NONRECURRING ITEMS

What are nonrecurring items?

Nonrecurring items are items that are *either* unusual in nature or infrequent in occurrence. They are shown as a separate line item before tax in arriving at income from continuing operations. EXAMPLE: The gain or loss on the sale of a fixed asset.

DISCONTINUED OPERATIONS

How is a discontinued operation defined?

A discontinued operation is an operation that has been discontinued during the year or will be discontinued shortly after year-end. A discontinued operation may be a business segment that has been sold, abandoned, or spun off.

The two components of discontinued operations are:

- income or loss from operations
- loss or gain on disposal of division.

What reporting requirements apply to a discontinued activity?

Footnote disclosure regarding the discontinued operation should include:

- an identification of the segment
- disposal date
- the manner of disposal
- description of remaining net assets of the segment at year-end.

(A business segment is a major line of business or customer class.) Even though it may be operating, a formal plan to dispose exists.

How is income or loss from operations handled?

In a year which includes the measurement date, it is the income from the beginning of the year to the measurement date. The measurement date is the date on which management commits itself to a formal plan of action. Applicable estimates may be required.

NOTE: If comparative financial statements are presented including periods before the measurement date, discontinued operations should be shown separately from continuing operations.

What are the requirements on a disposal of the division?

Income or loss from activities subsequent to the measurement date and before the disposal date is an element of the gain or loss on disposal.

- The disposal date is the date of closing by sale or the date activities cease because of abandonment.

• The gain or loss is shown in the disposal year. However, if losses are expected such losses are recorded in the year of the measurement date even if disposal is not completed in that year.

• Loss or gain should include estimated net losses from operations between the measurement date and the disposal date. If the loss cannot be estimated, a footnote is required.

• Loss on disposal includes the costs directly associated with the disposal decision. On the other hand, if a gain is expected, it should be recognized at the disposal date.

• The estimated gain or loss is determined at the measurement date and includes consideration of the net realizable value of the segment's assets.

• Loss or gain on disposal includes costs and expenses *directly* applicable to the disposal decision. These costs include severance pay, additional pension costs, employment relocation, and future rentals on long-term leases where subrentals are not possible.

NOTE: Normal business adjustments (e.g., routinely writing down accounts receivable) are *not* includable in the loss on disposal. These ordinary adjustments apply to the discontinued segment's operation rather than to the disposal of the segment. Typically, disposal is expected within one year of the measurement date.

EXAMPLE 1.1

On 6/15/19X8, ABC Company formulated a plan for disposal of segment X. The expectation is that the sale will take place on 3/1/19X9 for a selling price of $800,000. In 19X8, disposal costs were $100,000. Segment X's actual and estimated operating losses were:

1/1/19X8 to 6/14/19X8	$85,000
6/15/19X8 to 12/31/19X8	40,000
1/1/19X9 to 3/1/19X9	12,000

The carrying value of the segment on 3/1/19X9 is expected to be $900,000. The loss on disposal of segment X in the 19X8 income statement is:

Selling price		$800,000
Less: Disposal costs	$100,000	
Actual and expected operating losses after the measurement date	52,000	
Carrying value	900,000	
		$1,052,000
Loss on Disposal		$ 252,000

REVENUE RECOGNITION

What are the various ways of recording revenue?

Revenue, which is associated with a gross increase in assets or decrease in liabilities, may be recognized under different methods depending on the circumstances. (Special revenue recognition guidelines exist for franchisors and in sales involving a right of return. A product financing arrangement may also exist.) The basic methods of recognition include:

- Realization
- Completion of production
- During production
- Cash basis

1. Realization

When is revenue normally realized?

Revenue is recognized when goods are sold or services are performed. It results in an increase in net assets. This method is used almost all of the time. At realization, the earnings process is complete. Further, realization is consistent with the accrual basis, meaning that revenue is recognized when earned rather than when received. Realization should be used when:

- The selling price is determinable
- Future costs can be estimated
- An exchange has taken place that can be objectively measured

NOTE: There must be a reasonable basis for determining anticipated bad debts.

Three other methods of revenue recognition are used in exceptional situations, as discussed below.

2. At the Completion of Production

When can revenue be recognized upon completion of production?

Revenue is recognized prior to sale or exchange. *REQUIREMENTS:* There must be

- A stable selling price
- Absence of material marketing costs to complete the final transfer.
- Interchangeability in units

This approach is used:

- With agricultural products, by-products, and precious metals when the aforementioned criteria are met.
- In accounting for construction contracts under the completed contract method.

3. During Production

When can I recognize revenue during production?

In the case of long-term production situations, revenue recognition is made when:

- An assured price for the completed item exists by contractual agreement, and
- a reliable measure of the degree of completion at various stages of the production process is possible. EXAMPLE: The percentage of completion method used in accounting for long-term construction contracts.

Which is preferable—completed contract or percentage of completion method?

Under the completed contract method, revenue should not be recognized until completion of a contract. In general, the completed contract method should be used only when the use of the percentage of completion method is inappropriate.

How is revenue matched with costs in the percentage of completion method?

Under the percentage of completion method, revenue is recognized as production activity is occurring. The gradual recognition of revenue levels out earnings over the years and is more realistic since revenue is recognized as performance takes place.

RECOMMENDATION: This method is preferred over the completed contract method and should be used when reliable estimates of the extent of completion each period are possible. If not, the completed contract method should be used. Percentage of completion results in a matching of revenue against related expenses in the benefit period.

Using the cost-to-cost method, revenue recognized for the period equals:

$$\frac{\text{Actual Costs to Date}}{\text{Total Estimated Costs}} \times \text{Contract Price}$$
$$= \text{Cumulative Revenue}$$

Revenue recognized in prior years is deducted from the cumulative revenue to determine the revenue in the current period.

EXAMPLE 1.2

Cumulative Revenue (1–4 years)
Revenue Recognized (1–3 years)
Revenue (Year 4–current year)
Revenue less expenses equals profit.

In year 4 of a contract, the actual costs to date were $50,000. Total estimated costs are $200,000. The contract price is $1,000,000. Revenue recognized in the prior years (years 1–3) were $185,000.

$$\frac{\$50,000}{\$200,000} \times \$1,000,000$$
$$= \$250,000 \text{ Cumulative Revenue}$$

Cumulative Revenue	$250,000
Prior Year Revenue	185,000
Current Year Revenue	$ 65,000

Journal entries under the construction methods using assumed figures follow:

	Percentage of Completion		Completed Contract	
Construction-in-Progress	100,000		100,000	
Cash		100,000		100,000
Construction Costs				
Progress Billings Receivable	80,000		80,000	
Progress Billings on Construction-in-Progress		80,000		80,000
Periodic billings				
Construction-in-Progress	25,000		No Entry	
Profit		25,000		
Yearly profit recognition based on percentage of completion during the year				

In the last year when the construction project is completed, the following additional entry is made to record the profit in the final year:

	Percentage of Completion		Completed Contract	
Progress Billings on Construction-in-Progress	Total Billings		Total Billings	
Construction-in-Progress		Cost + Profit		Cost
Profit		Incremental Profit for Last Year		Profit for All the Years

Construction-in-Progress less Progress Billings is shown net. Usually, a debit figure results. This is shown as a current asset. Construction-in-Progress is an inventory account for a construction company. If a credit balance occurs, the net amount is shown as a current liability.

NOTE: Regardless of whether the percentage of completion method or the completed contract method is used, conservatism dictates that an obvious loss on a contract should immediately be recognized even before contract completion.

4. Cash Basis

When is cash basis, rather than accrual, preferable or required?

In the case of a company selling inventory, the accrual basis is used. However, the cash basis of revenue recognition is used under certain circumstances, namely, when revenue is recognized upon collection of the account. The cash basis instead of the accrual basis must be used when one or more of the following exist:

- Selling price is not objectively determinable at the time of sale
- Inability to estimate expenses at the time of sale
- Risk exists as to collections from customers
- Uncertain collection period.

How do I compute revenue under the installment method?

Revenue recognition under the installment method equals the cash collected times the gross profit percent. Any gross profit not collected is deferred on the balance sheet until collection occurs. When collections are received, realized gross profit is recognized by debiting the deferred gross profit account. The balance sheet presentation is:

Accounts Receivable (Cost + Profit)

Less: Deferred Gross Profit

Net Accounts Receivable (Cost)

NOTE: A service business that does not deal in inventory (e.g., accountant, doctor, lawyer) has the option of either using the accrual basis or cash basis.

How is revenue recognized if the buyer can return the goods?

When a buyer has a right to return the merchandise bought, the seller can only recognize revenue at the time of sale in accordance with FASB 48 provided that *all* of the following conditions are satisfied:

- Selling price is known.
- Buyer has to pay for the goods even if the buyer is unable to resell them. EXAMPLE: A sale of goods from a manufacturer to wholesaler. No provision must exist that the wholesaler has to be able to sell the items to the retailer.
- If the buyer loses the item or it is damaged in some way, the buyer still has to pay for it.
- Purchase by the buyer of the item has economic feasibility.
- Seller does not have to render future performance in order that the buyer will be able to resell the goods.
- Returns may be reasonably estimated.

If any of the above criteria are not met, revenue must be deferred along with deferral of related expenses until the criteria have been satisfied or the right of return provision has expired. As an alternative to deferring the revenue, record a memo entry as to the sale.

What factors affect the ability of a company to predict future returns?

The following considerations may be used in predicting returns:

- Predictability is detracted from when there is technological obsolescence risk of the product, uncertain product demand changes, or other material external factors.
- Predictability is lessened when there is a long-time period involved for returns.

- Predictability is enhanced when there exists a large volume of similar transactions.
- Weigh the seller's previous experience in estimating returns for similar products.
- Evaluate the nature of customer relationship and types of product involved.

CAUTION: FASB 48 does not apply to dealer leases, real estate transactions, or service industries.

What is the definition of a financing arrangement?

Per FASB 49, the arrangement involving the sale and repurchase of inventory is, in substance, a financing arrangement. It mandates that the product financing arrangement be accounted for as a borrowing instead of a sale. In many cases, the product is stored on the company's (sponsor's) premises. Further, often the sponsor will guarantee the debt of the other entity.

Typically, most of the product in the financing arrangement is eventually used or sold by the sponsor. However, in some cases, small amounts of the product may be sold by the financing entity to other parties.

The entity that gives financing to the sponsor is usually an existing creditor, nonbusiness entity, or trust. It is also possible that the finansor may have been established for the *only* purpose of providing financing for the sponsor.

NOTE: Footnote disclosure should be made of the particulars of the product financing arrangement.

What are some types of financing arrangements?

Types of product financing arrangements include:

• Sponsor sells a product to another business and agrees to reacquire the product or one basically identical to it. The established price to be paid by the sponsor typically includes financing and holding costs.

• Sponsor has another company buy the product for it and agrees to repurchase the product from the other entity.

• Sponsor controls the distribution of the product that has been bought by another company in accord with the aforementioned terms.

NOTE: In all situations, the company (sponsor) either agrees to repurchase the product at given prices over specified time periods, or guarantees resale prices to third parties.

How are financing arrangements reported?

• When the sponsor sells the product to the other firm and in a related transaction agrees to repurchase it, the sponsor should record a liability when the proceeds are received to the degree the product applies to the financing arrangement. CAUTION: A sale should *not* be recorded and the product should be retained as inventory on the sponsor's books.

• In the case where another firm buys the product for the sponsor, inventory is debited and liability credited at the time of purchase.

• Costs of the product, except for processing costs, in excess of sponsor's original production cost or acquisition cost or the other company's purchase cost constitute finance and holding costs. The sponsor accounts for these costs according to its typical accounting policies. Interest costs will also be incurred in connection with the financing arrangement. These should be shown separately and may be deferred.

EXAMPLE 1.3

On 1/1/19X1, a sponsor borrows $100,000 from another company and gives the inventory as collateral for the loan. The entry is:

Cash	100,000	
Liability		100,000

Note: A sale is *not* recorded here, and the inventory remains on the books of the sponsor. In effect, inventory serves as collateral for a loan.

On 12/31/19X1, the sponsor pays back the other company. The collateralized inventory item is returned. The interest rate on the loan was 8%. Storage costs were $2,000. The entry is:

Liability	100,000	
Interest Expense	8,000	
Storage Expense	2,000	
Cash		110,000

Recognition of Franchise Fee Revenue by the Franchisor

When can franchise fees be recognized?

According to FASB 45, the franchisor can record revenue from the initial sale of the franchise only when all significant services and obligations applicable to the sale have been substantially performed. Substantial performance is indicated by:

- Absence of intent to give cash refunds or relieve the accounts receivable due from the franchisee.
- Nothing material remains to be done by the franchisor.
- Initial services have been rendered.

The earliest date on which substantial performance can occur is the franchisee's commencement of operations unless special circumstances can be shown to exist. In the case where it is probable that the franchisor will ultimately repurchase the franchise, the initial fee must be deferred and treated as a reduction of the repurchase price.

How are deferred franchise fee revenues reported?

If revenue is deferred, the related expenses must be deferred for later matching in the year in which the revenue is recognized. This is illustrated below:

Year of initial fee:

Cash
   Deferred Revenue

Deferred Expenses
  Cash

Year when substantial performance takes place:

Deferred Revenue
  Revenue
Expenses
  Deferred Expenses

What are the requirements for initial franchise fees?

In the case where the initial fee includes both initial services and property (real or personal), there should be an appropriate allocation based on fair market values.

When part of the initial franchise fee applies to *tangible property* (e.g., equipment, signs, inventory), revenue recognition is based on the fair value of the assets. Revenue recognition may take place prior to or after recognizing the portion of the fee related to initial services. EXAMPLE: Part of the fee for equipment may be recognized at the time title passes with the balance of the fee being recorded as revenue when future services are performed.

How do I handle recurring franchise fees?

Recurring franchise fees are recognized as earned and receivable. Related costs are expensed. EXCEPTION: If the price charged for the continuing services or goods to the franchisee is below the price charged to third parties, it indicates that the initial franchise fee was in essence a partial *prepayment* for the recurring franchise fee. In this situation, part of the initial fee has to be deferred and recognized as an adjustment of the revenue from the sale of goods and services at bargain prices.

When *continuing franchise fees will probably not cover the cost of the continuing services and provide for a reasonable profit* to the franchisor, the part of the initial franchise fee should be deferred to satisfy the deficiency and amortized over the life of the franchise. SUGGESTION: The deferred amount should be adequate to meet future costs and generate an adequate profit on the recurring services. This situation may occur if the continuing fees are minimal relative to services provided or if the franchisee has the privilege of making bargain purchases for a particular time period.

What accounting requirements exist?

• *Unearned franchise fees* are recorded at present value. Where a part of the initial fee constitutes a nonrefundable amount for services already performed, revenue should be accordingly recognized.

• The *initial franchise fee is not typically allocated to specific franchisor services* before all services are performed. This practice can only be done if actual transaction prices are available for individual services.

• If the franchisor *sells equipment and inventory* to the franchisee *at no profit*, a receivable and payable is recorded. *No* revenue or expense recognition is given.

• In the case of *a repossessed franchise*, refunded amounts to the franchisee reduce current revenue. If there is no refund, the franchisor books additional revenue for the consideration retained which was not previously recorded. In either situation, *prospective* accounting treatment is given for the repossession. *Caution:* Do not adjust previously recorded revenue for the repossession.

• Indirect costs of an operating and recurring nature are expensed immediately. Future costs to be incurred are accrued no later than the period in which related revenue is recognized. Bad debts applicable to expected uncollectability of franchise fees should be recorded in the year of revenue recognition.

• Installment or cost recovery accounting may be employed to account for franchisee fee revenue *only* if a long collection period is involved and future uncollectability of receivables cannot be accurately predicted.

REQUIREMENTS: Footnote disclosure is required of:

• Outstanding obligations under agreement.
• Segregation of franchise fee revenue between initial and continuing.

RESEARCH AND DEVELOPMENT COSTS

How are research and development costs defined?

• *Research* is the testing done in search of a new product, service, process, or technique. Research can be aimed at deriving a material improvement to an existing product or process. Development is the translation of the research into a design for the new product or process.

• *Development* may also result in material improvement in an existing product or process.

How are R&D costs accounted for?

Per FASB 2, research and development costs are expensed as incurred.

NOTE: R&D costs incurred under contract for others that are reimbursable are charged to a receivable account rather than expensed. Further, materials, equipment, and intangibles purchased from others that have alternative future benefit in R&D activities are capitalized. The depreciation or amortization on such assets are classified as an R&D expense. If no alternative future use exists, the costs should be expensed.

What are R&D costs?

R&D costs include:

• the salaries of personnel involved in R&D activities
• a rational allocation of indirect (general and administrative) costs.

If a group of assets are acquired, allocation should be made to those that relate to R&D efforts. When a business combination is accounted for as a purchase, R&D costs are assigned their fair market value.

Expenditures paid to others to conduct R&D activities are expensed.

NOTE: FASB 2 does not apply to regulated industries and to the extractive industries (e.g., mining).

What are typical activities that may or may not be included as R&D?

R&D activities include:

- Formulation and design of product alternatives and testing thereof
- Laboratory research
- Engineering functions until the point the product satisfies operation requirements for manufacture
- Design of tools, molds, and dies involving new technology
- Pre-production prototypes and models
- Pilot plant costs.

Examples of activities that are not for R&D include:

- Quality control.
- Seasonal design changes.
- Legal costs of obtaining a patent.
- Market research.
- Identifying breakdowns during commercial production.
- Engineering follow-up in the initial stages of commercial production.
- Rearrangement and start-up activities including design and construction engineering.
- Recurring and continuous efforts to improve the product.
- Commercial use of the product.

NOTE: According to FASB 86, costs incurred for computer software to be sold, leased, or otherwise marketed are expensed as R&D costs until technological feasibility exists as indicated by the development of a detailed program or working model. After technological feasibility exists, software production costs should be deferred and recorded at the lower of unamortized cost or net realizable value. EXAMPLES: Debugging the software; improvements to subroutines; and adaptations for other uses.

Amortization begins when the product is available for customer release. The amortization expense should be based on the higher of:

- The percent of current revenue to total revenue from the product or
- The straight line amortization amount.

What are the requirements if another party funds R&D?

Per FASB 68, if a business enters into an arrangement with other parties to fund the R&D efforts, the nature of the obligation must be determined. In the case where the entity has an obligation to repay the funds irrespective of the R&D results, a liability has to be recognized with the related R&D expense. The journal entries are:

Cash

    Liability

Research and Development Expense

    Cash

A liability does not exist when the transfer of financial risk involved to the other party is substantive and genuine. If the financial risk applicable to R&D is transferred because repayment depends only on the R&D possessing future economic benefit, the company accounts for its obligation as a contract to conduct R&D for others. In this case R&D costs are capitalized and revenue is recognized as earned and becomes billable under the contract. REQUIREMENT: Footnote disclosure is made of the terms of the R&D agreement, the amount of compensation earned, and the costs incurred under the contract.

What if loans or advances are to be repaid depending on R&D results?

When repayment of loans or advances to the company depends *only* on R&D results, such amounts are deemed R&D costs incurred by the company and charged to expense.

How are warrants or other financial vehicles handled?

If warrants or other financial instruments are issued in an R&D arrangement, the company records part of the proceeds to be provided by the other parties as paid-in-capital based on their fair market value on the arrangement date.

EARNINGS PER SHARE (EPS)

Who must compute earnings per share?

APB 15 requires that earnings per share must be computed by publicly held companies. This is not required of nonpublic companies. In a simple capital structure, no potentially dilutive securities exist. Potentially dilutive means the security will be converted into common stock at a later date, reducing EPS. Thus, only one EPS figure is necessary. In a complex capital structure, dilutive securities exist requiring dual presentation.

What is the formula for EPS?

The dual presentation of EPS for all periods presented is:

$$\text{Primary EPS} = \frac{\text{Net Income} - \text{Preferred Dividend}}{\substack{\text{Weighted-Average Common Stock} \\ \text{Outstanding} + \text{Common Stock Equivalents}}}$$

$$\text{Fully Diluted EPS} = \frac{\text{Net Income} - \text{Preferred Dividend}}{\substack{\text{Weighted-Average Common Stock Outstanding} \\ + \text{Common Stock Equivalents} \\ + \text{Other Fully Diluted Securities}}}$$

NOTE: Fully diluted EPS reflects the *maximum* potential dilution per share on a prospective basis.

How do I calculate the weighted-average common stock outstanding?

Weighted-average common stock shares outstanding takes into account the number of months in which those shares were outstanding.

EXAMPLE 1.4

On 1/1/19X1, 10,000 shares were issued. On 4/1/19X1, 2,000 of those shares were bought back by the company. The weighted-average common stock outstanding is:

$$(10,000 \times \frac{3}{12}) + (8,000 \times \frac{9}{12})$$
$$= \underline{8,500} \text{ shares}$$

NOTE: When shares are issued because of a stock dividend or stock split, the computation of weighted-average common stock shares outstanding mandates retroactive adjustment as if the shares were outstanding at the beginning of the year.

What are common stock equivalents?

Common stock equivalents are securities which can become common stock at a later date and are shown in both primary EPS and fully diluted EPS.

Common stock equivalents include:

* Stock options.
* Stock warrants.
* Subscribed stock.
* Two-class common stock.
* Contingent shares only related to the passage of time.
* Convertible securities when the yield at the time of issuance is less than 2/3 of the average Aa bond yield at the time of issuance. Once a convertible security is defined as a common stock equivalent, it continues as such. For zero-coupon bonds, the effective yield is the interest rate necessary to discount the maturity value of the bond to its present value. This rate is then used to determine common stock equivalent by company by comparing it to the 2/3 average yield. In the situation where convertible securities are issued in a foreign country, we use the most comparable long-term yield in that country in performing the cash yield test.

NOTE: Although stock options are *always* deemed a common stock equivalent, they are only included in computing EPS if the market price of common stock is greater than the option price for substantially all of the last *three* months of the year. In this case, we assume the stock options were exercised at the *beginning* of the year (or at time of issuance, if later). While convertible securities are classified as common stock equivalents based on the circumstances at time of issue, warrants are classified according to the conditions at each period.

Why are common stock equivalents reflected in EPS calculations?

The inclusion of common stock equivalents in determining EPS is an example of theoretical substance over legal form. Although the common stock equivalent (e.g., stock option) is not *legally* common stock, it is treated as such since in theoretical substance the common stock equivalent is common stock.

When are common stock equivalents included in EPS?

In computing EPS, common stock equivalents are included if they have a dilutive effect. Dilutive effect means that the inclusion of a common stock equivalent reduced EPS by 3% or more in the aggregate and is applied by type of security. The 3% dilution also applies to presenting fully diluted EPS. Fully diluted EPS is also shown if it reduces primary EPS by 3% or more. Antidilutive securities that increase EPS are not shown in the EPS computation because they will increase EPS which violates conservatism.

How do I compute the common stock equivalent of options and warrants?

In computing the common stock equivalent in shares of options and warrants, the *treasury stock method* is used. Options and warrants are assumed to have been exercised at the beginning of the year (or at time of issuance, if later). The proceeds received from the options and warrants are assumed to:

- Buy back common stock at the average market price for the period not exceeding 20% of common stock outstanding at year-end

- Reduce long or short-term borrowing
- Invest in U.S. government securities or commercial paper

Assumption of exercise of options exists only when the market price of stock is greater than exercise price for three consecutive months ending with the year-end month.

In computing fully diluted EPS, the treasury stock method is modified in that the market price at the end of the accounting period is used if it is higher than the average market price for the period.

EXAMPLE 1.5

100 shares are under option at an option price of $10. The average market price of stock is $25. The common stock equivalent is 60 shares as calculated below:

Issued shares from option	100 shares × $10	= $1,000
Less: Treasury shares	40 shares × $25	= $1,000
Common Stock Equivalent	60 shares	

How do I find the common stock equivalent of convertible securities?

Convertible securities are accounted for using the "if converted method." The convertible securities are assumed converted at the beginning of the earliest year presented or date of security issuance. Interest or dividends on them are added back to net income since the securities are considered part of equity in the denominator of the EPS calculation.

What is the effect of including other fully diluted securities in EPS?

Fully diluted EPS is a pro forma presentation showing what EPS would be if *all* potential contingencies of common stock issuances having a dilutive effect took place. Other fully diluted securities are defined as convertible securities that did not meet the 2/3 test. They are included only in the calculation of fully diluted EPS. Thus, fully diluted EPS will be a lower figure than primary EPS because of the greater shares in the denominator. Contingent issuance of shares in computing fully diluted EPS is assumed to have occurred at the beginning of the year, or at the time of issuance if later.

To accomplish the fullest dilution in arriving at fully diluted EPS, an assumption is made that all common stock issuances on exercise of options or warrants during the period were made at the start of the year.

NOTE: The *higher* of the closing price or the average price of common stock is used in determining the number of shares of treasury stock to be purchased from the proceeds received upon issuance of the options. If the ending market price exceeds the average market price, the assumed treasury shares acquired will be lessened resulting in higher assumed outstanding shares with the resulting decrease in EPS.

What are the mechanics of the calculation of EPS?

In the numerator of the EPS fraction, net income less preferred dividends represents earnings available to common stockholders. On cumulative preferred stock, preferred dividends for the current year are subtracted out whether or not paid. Further, preferred dividends are only subtracted out for the current year. EXAMPLE: If preferred dividends in arrears were for 5 years, all of which were paid plus the 6th year dividend, only the 6th year dividend (current year) is deducted. Preferred dividends for each of the prior years would have been deducted in those years.

In computing EPS, preferred dividends are subtracted out only on preferred stock that was not included as a common stock equivalent. If the preferred stock is a common stock equivalent, the preferred divided would *not* be subtracted out since the equivalency of preferred shares into common shares is included in the denominator.

As for the denominator of EPS, if convertible bonds are included, they are considered as equivalent to common shares. Thus, interest expense (net of tax) has to be added back in the numerator.

What are the reporting requirements for EPS?

Disclosure of EPS should include:

- Information on the capital structure
- Explanation of the computation of EPS
- Identification of common stock equivalents
- Assumptions made
- Number of shares converted.

Rights and privileges of the securities should also be disclosed, including:

- Dividend and participation rights
- Call prices
- Conversion ratios
- Sinking fund requirements

Other points to remember are:

- A stock conversion occurring during the year or between year-end and the audit report date may have materially affected EPS if it had taken place at the beginning of the year. RECOMMENDATION: Supplementary footnote disclosure should be made reflecting on an "as if" basis what the effects of these conversions would have had on EPS if they were made at the start of the accounting period.

- If a subsidiary has been acquired under the *purchase accounting method* during the year, the weighted-average shares outstanding for the year are used from the purchase date. If a *pooling of interests* occurred, the weighted-average shares outstanding for all the years are presented.

- If common stock or a common stock equivalent is sold during the year and the proceeds are used to buy back debt or retire preferred stock, there should be a presentation of supplemental EPS figures.

- When comparative financial statements are presented, there is a retroactive adjustment for stock splits and stock dividends.

EXAMPLE 1.6

Assume in 19X5 a 10% stock dividend occurs. The weighted-average shares used for previous years' computations has to be increased by 10% to make EPS data comparable.

• When a prior period adjustment occurs that causes a restatement of previous years' earnings, EPS should also be restated.

EXAMPLE 1.7

The stockholders' equity section of ABC Company's balance sheet as of 12/31/19X3 appears below:

$1.20 cumulative preferred stock (par value of $10 per share, issued 1,200,000 shares, of which 500,000 were converted to common stock and 700,000 shares are outstanding)	$7,000,000
Common stock (par value of $2.50, issued and outstanding 6,000,000 shares)	15,000,000
Paid-in-capital	20,000,000
Retained earnings	32,000,000
Total stockholders' equity	$74,000,000

On 5/1/19X3, ABC Company acquired XYZ Company in a pooling of interest. For each of XYZ Company's 800,000 shares, ABC issued one of its own shares in the exchange.

On 4/1/19X3, ABC Company issued 500,000 shares of convertible preferred stock at $38 per share. The preferred stock is convertible to common stock at the exchange rate of 2 shares of common for each share of preferred. On 9/1/19X3, 300,000 shares and on 11/1/19X3 200,000 shares of preferred stock were converted into common stock. The market price of the convertible preferred stock is $38 per share.

During August, ABC Company granted stock options to executives to buy 100,000 shares of common stock at an option price of $15 per share. The market price of stock at year-end was $20.

ABC Company has 8%, $10,000,000 convertible bonds payable issued at fair value in 19X1. The conversion rate is 4 shares of common stock for each $100 bond. No conversions have occurred yet.

The Aa corporate bond yield is 10%. The tax rate is 34%. Net income for the year is $12,000,000.

The convertible bonds are not common stock equivalents because the interest rate of 8% is more than 2/3 of the Aa bond yield of 10%.

The convertible preferred stock is a common stock equivalent because its yield of 3.16% ($1.20/$38.00) is less than 2/3 of the Aa bond yield of 10%. NOTE: Stock options are always considered common stock equivalents.

Shares outstanding from 1/1/19X3 (including 800,000 shares issued upon acquisition of XYZ Company):		
6,000,000 − 1,000,000		5,000,000
Shares issued upon conversion of 500,000 shares of preferred stock to common stock:		
Issued 9/1/19X3 600,000 × 4/12	200,000	
Issued 11/1/19X3 400,000 × 2/12	66,667	266,667
Total shares of common stock		5,266,667
Common stock equivalents:		
Convertible preferred stock:		
500,000 shares of convertible preferred issued on 4/1/19X3		
500,000 × 2 × 9/12	750,000	
Less: Common shares applicable to 500,000 preferred shares converted during the year	266,667	
Common stock equivalents of convertible preferred stock		483,333
Common stock equivalents of stock options:		

Option   100,000 × $15 = $1,500,000

Less:

Treasury Stock <u>75,000</u> × $20 = 1,500,000

Common stock equivalent of stock options	25,000	25,000

Weighted-average common stock outstanding plus common stock equivalents for primary EPS 5,775,000

Convertible bonds payable assumed converted at 1/1/19X3 ($10,000,000/$100) = 100,000 bonds 100,000 bonds × 4 shares per bond 400,000

Weighted-average common stock outstanding plus common stock equivalents plus other fully diluted securities for fully diluted EPS 6,175,000

Primary EPS equals:

$$\frac{\$12,000,000}{5,775,000 \text{ shares}} = \$2.08$$

Fully Diluted EPS equals:

$$\frac{\$12,000,000 + \$528,000*}{6,175,000 \text{ shares}} = \$2.03$$

*$10,000,000 × 8% = $800,000 × 66% = 528,000

CHAPTER 2

FINANCIAL STATEMENT REPORTING: THE BALANCE SHEET

On the balance sheet, the CPA is concerned with the accounting for and reporting of assets, liabilities, and stockholders' equity.

ASSETS

What valuation is used for assets?

Assets are recorded at the price paid plus related incidental costs (e.g., insurance, freight). If an asset is acquired for the incurrence of a liability, the asset is recorded at the present value (discounted value) of the payments.

EXAMPLE 2.1

If a machine was acquired in exchange for making ten $10,000 payments at an interest rate of 10%, the asset would be recorded at:

$10,000 × 6.145* = $61,450

*Factor using the present value of annuity table for n = 10, i = 10%

NOTE: The asset is recorded at the principal amount excluding the interest payments. If an asset is acquired for stock, the asset is recorded at the fair value of the stock issued. If it is impossible to determine the fair market value of the stock (e.g., closely held corporation), the asset will be recorded at its appraised value.

Unearned discounts (except for cost or quantity), finance charges, and interest included in the face of receivables should be deducted therefrom to derive the net receivable.

Some of the major current and noncurrent assets include:

- accounts receivable
- inventory
- fixed assets
- intangibles

Accounts Receivable

What is the difference between an assignment and factoring?

The *assignment* of accounts receivable typically requires the incurrence of a financing charge as well as interest expense on the note.

EXAMPLE 2.2

In an assignment of accounts receivable, the entries are:

Accounts Receivable Assigned	50,000	
Accounts Receivable		50,000

To designate specific accounts for assignment and collateralization for the loan.

Cash	45,000	
Notes Payable		45,000

To recognize a liability for the advance received from the lending institution.

Allowance for Bad Debts	XX	
Accounts Receivable Assigned		XX

To write-off an uncollectible assigned accounts receivable.

At a particular date, the transferor's equity in the assigned receivables equals the difference between the accounts receivable assigned and the balance of the line ($5,000). When payments on the receivables are received, they are remitted by the company to the lending institution to reduce the liability. Assignment is on a non-notification basis to customers. It is made with recourse, where the company has to make good for uncollectible customer accounts.

In a *factoring* of accounts receivable, the receivables are in effect sold. Customers are typically notified. Factoring is usually done without recourse, where the risk of uncollectibility of the customer's account rests with the financing institution. Billing and collection is typically done by the factor. The difference between the factored receivable and the amount received represents a gain or loss as follows:

Cash

Loss (or Gain)

   Accounts Receivable

Receivables from officers and affiliates require disclosure.

When are transfers of receivables treated as sales?

According to FASB 77, a sale is recorded for the transfer of receivables with recourse if *all* of the following criteria are satisfied:

• The transferor gives up control of the future economic benefits applicable to the receivables (e.g., repurchase right).

• The liability of the transferor under the recourse provisions is estimable.

• The transferee cannot require the transferor to repurchase the receivables unless there is a recourse provision in the contract.

How are transfer sales disclosed?

When the transfer is treated as a sale, gain or loss is recognized for the difference between the selling price and the net receivables.

• The selling price includes normal servicing fees of the transferor and appropriate probable adjustments (e.g., debtor's failure to pay on time, effects of prepayment, and defects in the transferred receivable).

• Net receivables equals gross receivables plus finance and service charges minus unearned finance and service charges.

In the case where selling price varies during the term of the receivables due to a variable interest rate provision, the selling price is estimated with the use of an appropriate "going market interest rate" at the transfer date.

NOTE: Later changes in the rate cause a change in estimated selling price, *not* in interest income or interest expense.

If any one of the aforementioned criteria is not satisfied, a liability is recognized for the proceeds received.

The footnote disclosure includes:

• Amount received by transferor
• Balance of the receivables at the balance sheet date

Inventory

How may inventory be valued?

Inventory may be valued at the lower of cost or market value. Specialized inventory methods may be used such as:

• retail
• retail lower of cost or market
• retail LIFO
• dollar value LIFO

Losses on purchase commitments should be recognized in the accounts.

If ending inventory is overstated, cost of sales is understated, and net income is overstated. If beginning inventory is overstated, cost of sales is overstated, and net income is understated.

How does the lower of cost or market value method work?

Inventories are recorded at the lower of cost or market value for conservatism purposes applied on a total basis, category basis, or individual basis.

NOTE: The method used must be consistently applied.

If cost is below market value (replacement cost), cost is taken. If market value is below cost, we start with market value.

• Market value cannot exceed the ceiling which is net realizable value (selling price less costs to complete and dispose). If it does, the ceiling is chosen.

• Market value cannot be less than the floor which is net realizable value less a normal profit margin. If market value is less than the floor, the floor value is used.

• Market value is used when it lies between the ceiling and floor. The following diagram may be helpful:

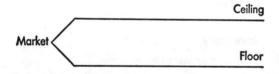

```
                                            Ceiling
         
Market <
                                            Floor
```

EXAMPLE 2.3

The lower of cost or market value method is being applied on an item-by-item basis. The circled figure is the appropriate valuation.

Product	Cost	Market	Ceiling	Floor
A	($5)	$7	$9	$6
B	14	12	(11)	7
C	18	(15)	16	12
D	20	12	18	(16)
E	(6)	5	12	7

In case E, market value of $5 was originally selected. The market value of $5 is less than the floor of $7, so the floor value would be used. However, if after applying the lower of cost or market value rule, the valuation derived ($7) exceeds the cost ($6), the cost figure is more conservative and thus is used.

NOTE: If market (replacement cost) is below the original cost but the selling price has not likewise declined, no loss should be recognized. To do so would create an abnormal profit margin in the future period.

The lower of cost or market value method is not used with LIFO since under LIFO current revenue is matched against current costs.

When and how should the retail method be applied?

The retail method is used by department stores and other large retail businesses that carry inventory items at retail selling price. The retail method is used to estimate the ending inventory at cost by employing a cost to retail (selling price) ratio. The ending inventory is first determined at selling price and then converted to cost. Markups and markdowns are both considered in arriving at the cost to retail ratio resulting in a higher ending inventory than the retail lower of cost or market value method.

How do I apply the retail lower of cost or market value method?

The "conventional retail" method is a modification of the retail method and is preferable to it. In computing the cost to retail ratio, markups but not markdowns are considered. This results in a lower inventory figure.

The following example illustrates the accounting difference between the retail method and the retail lower of cost or market value method.

EXAMPLE 2.4

	Cost	Retail
Inventory— 1/1	16,000	30,000
Purchases	30,000	60,000
Purchase returns	(5,000)	(10,000)

	Cost	Retail	
Purchase discount	(2,000)		
Freight In	1,000		
Markups	25,000		
Markup cancellations	(5,000)		
Net markups		20,000	
Total	40,000	100,000	(40%)
Markdowns	22,000		
Markdown cancellations	(2,000)		
Net markdowns		20,000	
Cost of goods available	40,000	80,000	(50%)
Deduct:			
Sales	55,000		
− Sales returns	(5,000)	50,000	
Inventory— Retail		30,000	
Retail method: At cost 50% × 30,000		15,000	
Retail lower of cost or market method: 40% × 30,000		12,000	

How does retail LIFO work?

In computing ending inventory, the mechanics of the retail method are basically followed. Beginning inventory is *excluded*, and both markups and markdowns are *included* in computing the cost to retail ratio. A decrease in inventory during the period is deducted from the most recently added layer and then subtracted from layers in the inverse order of addition. A retail price index is used in restating inventory.

EXAMPLE 2.5

Retail price indices follow:

19X7	100
19X8	104
19X9	110

	Cost	Retail
19X8		
Inventory–Jan. 1 (Base Inv.)	80,000	130,000
Purchases	240,000	410,000
Markups		10,000
Markdowns		(20,000)
Total (exclude Beg. Inv.)	240,000	400,000
Total (include Beg. Inv.)	320,000	530,000
Sales		389,600
19X8 Inv-End-Retail		140,400
Cost Basis		
19X8 Inventory in terms of 19X7 Prices		
$140,400 \div 1.04$		135,000
19X7 Base	80,000	130,000
19X8 Layer in 19X7 prices		5,000
19X8 Layer in 19X8 prices	3,120	5,200
	83,120	140,400
19X8 LIFO cost 60% × 5,200		

60%

$130,000 \times 1.04$ 135,200

5000×1.04 5,200

140,400

19X9

	Cost	Retail	
Inventory–Jan. 1	83,120	140,400	
Purchases	260,400	430,000	
Markups		20,000	
Markdowns		(30,000)	
Total (exclude Beg. Inv.)	260,400	420,000	
Total (include Beg. Inv.)	343,520	560,400	62%
Sales		408,600	
19X9 Inventory—End at Retail		151,800	

Cost Basis

	Cost	Retail	
19X9 Inventory in 19X7 prices 151,800 ÷ 1.10		138,000	
19X7 Base	80,000	130,000	130,000 × 1.10 143,000
Excess over base year		8,000	
19X8 Layer in 19X8 prices		5,000	
19X9 Layer in 19X7 prices	3,120	5,000	5,000 × 1.10 5,500
19X9 Layer in 19X9 prices		3,000	3,000 × 1.10 3,300
19X9 Increase in 19X9 prices		3,300	
LIFO cost 62% × 3,300	2,046		
	85,166	151,800	151,800

What are the steps in dollar value LIFO?

Dollar value LIFO is an extension of the historical cost principle. This method aggregates dollars instead of units into homogeneous groupings. The method assumes that an inventory decrease came from the last year.

The steps under dollar value LIFO are:

• Restate ending inventory in the current year into base dollars by applying a price index.

• Subtract the year zero inventory in base dollars from the current year's inventory in base dollars.

• Multiply the incremental inventory in the current year in base dollars by the price index to obtain the incremental inventory in current dollars.

• Obtain the reportable inventory for the current year by adding to the year zero inventory in base dollars the incremental inventory for the current year in current dollars.

EXAMPLE 2.6

At 12/31/19X1, the ending inventory is $130,000, and the price index is 1.30. The base inventory on 1/1/19X1 was $80,000. The 12/31/19X1 inventory is computed below:

12/31/19X1 inventory in base dollars $130,000/1.30	$100,000
1/1/19X1 beginning base inventory	80,000
19X1 Increment in base dollars	$ 20,000
19X1 Increment in current year dollars	× 1.3
	$ 26,000
Inventory in base dollars	$ 80,000
Increment in current year dollars	26,000
Reportable inventory	$106,000

What are some problems in determining inventory?

While the basics of inventory cost measurement are easily stated, difficulties arise because of cost allocation problems. EXAMPLES:

• Idle capacity costs and abnormal spoilage costs may have to be written off immediately in the current year instead of being allocated as an element of inventory valuation.

• General and administrative expenses are inventoriable when they specifically relate to production activity.

What if there is a loss on a prospective purchase?

Significant net losses on purchase commitments should be recognized at the end of the reporting period.

EXAMPLE 2.7

In 19X8, ABC Company committed itself to buy raw materials at $1.20 per pound. At the end of the year, before fulfilling the purchase commitment, the price of the materials dropped to $1.00 per pound. Conservatism dictates that a loss on purchase commitment of $.20 per pound be recognized in 19X8. Loss on Purchase Commitment is debited and Allowance for Purchase Commitment Loss is credited.

When can inventory be stated at market value in excess of cost?

Inventories may be stated in excess of cost under unusual circumstances when:

• there is no basis for cost apportionment (e.g. meat packing industry).

• immediate marketability exists at quoted prices (e.g. certain precious metals or agricultural products).

Disclosure is necessary when inventory is stated above cost.

Fixed Assets

How are fixed assets recorded?

A fixed asset is recorded at its fair market value or the fair market value of the consideration given, whichever is more clearly evident.

• The cost of *buying an asset* includes all costs necessary to put that asset into existing use and location, including freight, insurance, taxes, installation, and breaking-in costs (e.g., instruction).

• *Additions to an existing asset* (e.g., garage attached to a house) are capitalized and depreciated over the shorter of the life of the addition or the life of the house. Rearrangement and reinstallation costs should be capitalized if they have future benefit. If not, they should be expensed. RECOMMENDATION: Obsolete fixed assets should be reclassified from property, plant, and equipment to other assets and shown at salvage value reflecting a loss.

• When *two or more assets are bought for one price*, cost is allocated to the assets based on their relative fair market values. If an old building is demolished to make way for the construction of a new building, the costs of demolishing the old building are charged to the land account.

• Assets that are *self-constructed* are recorded at the incremental costs to build assuming idle capacity. However, they should not be reflected at more than the outside price.

EXAMPLE 2.8

Incremental costs to self-construct a machine is $15,000. The machine could have been purchased from outside at $10,000. The journal entry is:

Machine	10,000	
Loss	5,000	
Cash		15,000

• A fixed asset *donated to the company* should be recorded at fair market value. The entry is to debit fixed assets and credit paid-in-capital (donation).

NOTE: Fixed assets cannot be written-up except in the case of a discovery on a natural resource or in a purchase combination. In a discovery of a natural resource (e.g., oil), the land account is charged at appraised value and then depleted by the units of production method.

• *Land improvements* (e.g., sidewalks, driveways, fencing) are capitalized and depreciated over useful life. Land held for investment purposes or for a future plant site should be classified under investments and not fixed assets.

• *Ordinary repairs* to an asset (e.g., tune-up for a car) are expensed since they have a life of less than one year.

• *Extraordinary repairs* are capitalized since they benefit a period of one year or more (e.g., new motor for a car). Extraordinary repairs add to an asset's life or make the asset more useful. Capital expenditures improve the quality or quantity of services to be derived from the asset.

Depreciation

How do I calculate depreciation?

Fractional year depreciation is computing depreciation when the asset is acquired during the year. A proration is required.

EXAMPLE 2.9

On 10/1/19X7, a fixed asset costing $10,000 with a salvage value of $1,000 and a life of 5 years is acquired.

Depreciation expense for 19X8 using the sum-of-the-years' digits method is:

1/1/19X8–9/30/19X8	
$5/15 \times \$9,000 \times 9/12$	$2,250
10/1/19X8–12/31/19X8	
$4/15 \times \$9,000 \times 3/12$	600
	$2,850

Depreciation expense for 19X8 using double declining balance is:

Year	Computation	Depreciation	Book Value
0			$10,000
10/1/19X7–12/31/19X7	$3/12 \times \$10,000 \times 40\%$	$1,000	9,000
1/1/19X8–12/31/19X8	$\$9,000 \times 40\%$	⟨3,600⟩	5,400

How is depreciation calculated by group and composite methods?

Group and composite depreciation methods involve similar accounting. The group method is used for similar assets, while the composite method is used for dissimilar assets. Both methods are generally accepted. There is one accumulated depreciation account for the entire group.

$$\text{Depreciation rate} = \frac{\text{Depreciation}}{\text{Gross Cost}}$$

For a period:

Depreciation expense
$$= \text{Depreciation Rate} \times \text{Gross Cost}$$

$$\text{Depreciable life} = \frac{\text{Depreciable Cost}}{\text{Depreciation}}$$

When an asset is sold in the group, the entry is:

Cash (proceeds received)

Accumulated Depreciation (plug figure)

Fixed Asset (cost)

NOTE: Upon sale of a fixed asset in the group the difference between the proceeds received and the cost of the fixed asset is plugged to accumulated depreciation. No gain or loss is recognized upon the sale. The only time a gain or loss would be recognized is if the entire assets were sold.

EXAMPLE 2.10

Calculations for composite depreciation follow:

Asset	Cost	Salvage	Depreciable Cost	Life	Depreciation
A	$ 25,000	$ 5,000	$ 20,000	10	$ 2,000
B	40,000	2,000	38,000	5	7,600
C	52,000	4,000	48,000	6	8,000
	$117,000	$11,000	$106,000		$17,600

Composite Rate:

$$\frac{\$17,600}{\$117,000} = \underline{15.04\%}$$

Composite Life:

$$\frac{\$106,000}{\$17,600} = \underline{6.02} \text{ years}$$

The entry to record depreciation is:

Depreciation	17,600	
Accumulated Depreciation		17,600

The entry to sell asset B for $36,000 is:

Cash	36,000	
Accumulated Depreciation	4,000	
Fixed Asset		40,000

Capitalized Interest

When is interest expensed or capitalized?

Disclosure should be made of the interest capitalized and expensed. Interest incurred on borrowed funds is expensed.

However, interest on borrowed money is capitalized to the asset account and then amortized in the following instances:

- Self-constructed assets for the entity's own use. To justify interest capitalization, a time period must exist for assets to be prepared for use
- Assets purchased for the company's own use by arrangements mandating a down payment and/or progress payments
- Assets for sale or lease constructed as discrete, individual projects (e.g., real estate development)

Interest is *not* capitalized for:

- Assets produced in large volume or on a repetitive basis
- Assets in use or ready for use
- Assets not in use and not being prepared for use

What interest rate is used?

Interest capitalized is based on the average accumulated expenditures for that asset. The interest rate used is either:

- Weighted-average interest rate of corporate debt
- Interest rate on the specific borrowing

When does the capitalization period begin and end?

The interest capitalization period commences when the following exist:

- Expenditures have been incurred.
- Work is proceeding to make the asset ready for intended use. These activities are not limited to actual construction but may also include administrative and technical functions prior to the time of construction. Included are costs of unforeseen events taking place during construction. EXAMPLES: Labor problems and litigation.
- Interest is being incurred.

The capitalization period ceases when the asset is materially complete and usable. When an asset has individual parts (e.g., condominium units), the capitalization period of interest costs applicable to one of the separate units ends when the specific unit is materially finished and usable. Capitalization of interest is not continued when construction ends, except for brief or unexpected delays.

When the total asset must be finished to be useful, interest capitalization continues until the total asset is materially complete. EXAMPLE: A manufacturing plant where sequential production activities must take place.

Nonmonetary Transactions

How is an exchange of assets recorded?

Nonmonetary transactions covered under APB 29 deal primarily with exchanges or distributions of fixed assets.

In an exchange of *similar assets* (e.g., truck for truck), the new asset received is recorded at the book value of the old asset plus the cash paid. Since book value of the old asset is the basis to charge the new asset, no gain is possible. However, a loss is possible, because in no case can the new asset exceed the fair market value of the new asset.

In an exchange of *dissimilar assets* (e.g., truck for machine), the new asset is recorded at the fair market value of the old asset plus the cash paid. Thus, a gain or loss may arise because the fair market value of the old asset will be different than the book value of the old asset. However, the new asset cannot be shown at more than its fair market value.

Fair market value in a nonmonetary exchange may be based upon:

- Quoted market price
- Appraisal
- Cash transaction for similar items

EXAMPLE 2.11

An old fixed asset costing $10,000 with accumulated depreciation of $2,000 is traded in for a *similar*, new fixed asset having a fair market value of $22,000. Cash paid on the exchange is $4,000. The fair market value of the old asset is $5,000.

If a similar exchange is involved the entry is:

Fixed Asset (8,000 + 4,000)	12,000	
Accumulated Depreciation	2,000	
Fixed Asset		10,000
Cash		4,000

Assume instead that the fair market value of the new asset was $11,000, resulting in the exception where the new fixed asset must be recorded at $11,000. *Note:* The new fixed asset cannot be shown at more than its fair market value.

In this case, the entry is:

Fixed Asset	11,000	
Accumulated Depreciation	2,000	
Loss	1,000	
Fixed Asset		10,000
Cash		4,000

Assume the original facts except that a *dissimilar* exchange is involved. The entry is:

Fixed Asset (5,000 + 4,000)	9,000	
Accumulated Depreciation	2,000	
Fixed Asset		10,000
Gain		1,000

How is "boot" recorded?

In a nonmonetary exchange, the entity receiving the monetary payment ("boot") recognizes a gain to the degree the monetary receipt is greater than the proportionate share of the book value of the asset given up.

$$\text{Gain} = \text{Monetary Receipt}$$
$$- \left(\frac{\text{Monetary Receipt}}{\substack{\text{Fair Market Value of Total} \\ \text{Consideration Received}}} \right)$$
$$\times \left(\substack{\text{Book Value of Asset} \\ \text{Given Up}} \right)$$

• The company receiving the boot records the asset acquired at the carrying value of the asset surrendered minus the portion considered sold.

• The company paying the boot records the asset purchased at the carrying value of the asset surrendered plus the "boot" paid.

Involuntary Conversion

What is an involuntary conversion?

There may exist an involuntary conversion of nonmonetary assets into monetary assets, followed by replacement of the involuntarily converted assets. EXAMPLE: A warehouse is destroyed by a fire, and the insurance proceeds received are used to purchase a similar warehouse.

How is an involuntary conversion recorded?

Per Interpretation 30, gain or loss is recognized for the difference between the insurance recovery and the book value of the destroyed asset. EXAMPLE: The new warehouse (replacing the destroyed one) is recorded at its purchase price.

CAUTION: A contingency results if the old fixed asset is damaged in one period, but the insurance recovery is not received until a later period. A contingent gain or loss is reported in the period the old fixed asset was damaged. The gain or loss may be recognized for book and tax purposes in different years causing a temporary difference requiring interperiod income tax allocation.

Intangibles

What are intangible assets?

Intangible assets are assets having a life of one year or more and which lack physical substance (e.g., goodwill) or represent a right granted by the government (e.g., patent) or by another company (e.g., franchise fee). *Note:* "Goodwill" does not include identifiable assets.

How are intangible assets accounted for?

APB 17 covers accounting for intangible assets whether purchased or internally developed. The costs of intangibles *acquired* from others should be reported as assets. The cost equals the cash or fair market value of the consideration given.

Individual intangibles that can be separately identified must be costed separately. If not separately identified, the intangibles are assigned a cost equal to the difference between the total purchase price and the cost of identifiable tangible and intangible assets.

The cost of developing and maintaining intangibles should be charged against earnings if the assets are not specifically identifiable, have indeterminate lives, or are inherent in the continuing business (e.g., goodwill).

EXAMPLE: With respect to internally developed goodwill, the costs incurred in developing a name (e.g., "Burger King") are expensed.

How is useful life determined?

All intangible assets are amortized over the period benefitted using the straight-line method not exceeding a 40-year life. The factors in estimating useful lives include:

- Legal, contractual, and regulatory provisions
- Renewal or extension provisions (if a renewal occurs, the life of the intangible may be increased)

- Obsolescence and competitive factors
- Product demand
- Service lives of essential employees within the organization

EXAMPLE: An intangible may be enhanced because of good public relations staff.

NOTES:

- Intangibles on the books before 1970 need *not* be amortized.
- If the amortization expense of an intangible is not tax deductible (e.g., amortization of goodwill), a permanent difference arises. Thus, no interperiod tax allocation is involved.
- Footnote disclosure is made of the amortization period and method.

How is goodwill valued?

Goodwill is theoretically equal to the present value of future excess earnings of a company over other companies in the industry.

In buying a new business, a determination must often be made as to the estimated value of the goodwill. Two methods that can be used are:

- capitalization of earnings
- capitalization of excess earnings.

EXAMPLE 2.12

The following information is available for a business that we are contemplating acquiring:

Expected average annual earnings	$10,000
Expected future value of net assets exclusive of goodwill	$45,000
Normal rate of return	20%

Using the capitalization of earnings approach, goodwill is estimated at:

Total asset value implied ($10,000/ 20%)	$50,000
Estimated fair value of assets	45,000
Estimated goodwill	$ 5,000

Assuming the same facts as above except a capitalization rate of excess earnings of 22%, and using the capitalization of excess earnings method, goodwill is estimated at:

Expected average annual earnings	$10,000
Return on expected average assets ($45,000 × 20%)	9,000
Excess earnings	$1,000

Goodwill ($1,000/.22) = $4,545

EXAMPLE 2.13

The net worth of ABC Company excluding goodwill is $800,000, and profits for the last four years were $750,000. Included in the latter figure are extraordinary gains of $50,000 and nonrecurring losses of $30,000. It is desired to determine a selling price of the business. A 12% return on net worth is deemed typical for the industry. The capitalization of excess earnings is 45% in determining goodwill.

Net Income for 4 years	$750,000
Less: Extraordinary gains	50,000
Add: Nonrecurring losses	30,000
Adjusted 4 year earnings	$730,000
Average earnings ($730,000/4)	$182,500
Normal earnings ($800,000 × .12)	96,000
Excess annual earnings	$86,500

Excess earnings capitalized at 45%:

$$\frac{\$86,500}{.45} = \$192,222$$

How is goodwill accounted for?

If a firm buys, on a step-by-step basis, an investment using the equity method, the fair value of the acquired assets and the goodwill for each step purchased must be separately identified.

When the purchase of assets results in goodwill, later sale of a separable portion of the equity acquired mandates a proportionate reduction of the goodwill account. A portion of the unamortized goodwill is included in the cost of assets sold.

Goodwill is only recorded in a business combination accounted for under the purchase method when the cost to the acquirer exceeds the fair market value of the net assets acquired. Goodwill is then amortized using the straight-line method over the period benefitted not exceeding 40 years. If the cost to the acquirer is less than the fair market value of the net assets acquired, a credit arises. This reduces the noncurrent assets acquired on a proportionate basis (excluding long-term investments). If a credit still remains, it is treated as a deferred credit not to be amortized over more than 40 years under the straight line method.

How should I handle new product costs, organization costs, leaseholds?

Internally generated costs to derive a patented product are expensed (e.g., R&D incurred in developing a new product). The patent is recorded at the registration fees to secure and register it, legal fees in successfully defending it in court, and the cost of acquiring competing patents from outsiders. The patent account is amortized over its useful life not exceeding 17 years.

NOTE: If an intangible asset is deemed worthless, it should be written off, recognizing an extraordinary item.

Organization costs are the costs incurred to incorporate a business (e.g., legal fees). They are deferred and amortized.

Leaseholds are rent paid in advance and are amortized over the life of the lease.

Insurance

How is cash surrender value defined?

Cash surrender value of life insurance is the sum payable upon cancellation of the policy by the insured; the insured will of course receive less than the premiums paid in.

NOTE: Cash surrender value is classified under long-term investments.

How is possible reimbursement calculated?

Casualty insurance covers such items as fire loss and water damage. Casualty insurance reimburses the holder for the fair market value of property lost. Insurance companies typically have a coinsurance clause so that the insured bears part of the loss. The following insurance reimbursement formula assumes an 80% coinsurance clause:

$$\frac{\text{Face of Policy}}{.8 \times \text{Fair Market Value of Insured Property}} \times \begin{array}{c} \text{Fair Market Value} \\ \text{of Loss} \end{array}$$
$$= \text{Possible Reimbursement}$$

Insurance reimbursement is based on the lower of the face of the policy, fair market value of loss, or possible reimbursement.

EXAMPLE 2.14

Case	Face of Policy	Fair Market Value of Property	Fair Market Value of Loss
A	$4,000	$10,000	$6,000
B	6,000	10,000	10,000
C	10,000	10,000	4,000

Insurance reimbursement follows:

Case A:
$$\frac{\$4,000}{.8 \times \$10,000} \times \$6,000 = \boxed{\$3,000}$$
Case B:
$$\frac{\boxed{\$6,000}}{.8 \times \$10,000} \times \$10,000 = \$7,500$$
Case C:
$$\frac{\$10,000}{.8 \times \$10,000} \times \boxed{\$4,000} = \$5,000$$

What does a blanket policy cover?

A blanket policy covers several items of property. The face of the policy is allocated based upon the fair market values of the insured assets.

EXAMPLE 2.15

A blanket policy of $15,000 applies to equipment I and equipment II. The fair values of equipment I and II are $30,000 and $15,000, respectively. Equipment II is partially destroyed, resulting in a fire loss of $3,000.

The policy allocation to equipment II is computed below:

	Fair Market Value	Policy
Equipment I	$30,000	$10,000
Equipment II	15,000	5,000
	$45,000	$15,000

The insurance reimbursement is:

$$\frac{\$5,000}{.8 \times \$15,000} \times \$3,000 = \$1,500$$

How is a fire loss recorded?

When a fire loss occurs, the asset destroyed has to be removed from the accounts, with the resulting fire loss recorded based on book value. The insurance reimbursement reduces the fire loss. The fire loss is an extraordinary item (net of tax).

EXAMPLE 2.16

The following fire loss information applies to ABC Company. Merchandise costing $5,000 is fully destroyed. There is no insurance for it. Furniture costing $10,000 with accumulated depreciation of $1,000 and having a fair market value of $7,000 is entirely destroyed. The policy is for $10,000. A building costing $30,000 with accumulated depreciation of $3,000 and having a fair market value of $20,000 is 50% destroyed. The face of the policy is $15,000. The journal entries to record the book loss are:

Fire Loss	5,000	
Inventory		5,000
Fire Loss	9,000	

Accumulated Depreciation	1,000	
Furniture		10,000
Fire Loss	13,500	
Accumulated Depreciation	1,500	
Building		15,000

Insurance reimbursement totals $16,375 computed as follows:

Furniture:
$$\frac{\$10,000}{.8 \times \$7,000} \times \$7,000 = \$12,500$$

Building:
$$\frac{\$15,000}{.8 \times \$20,000} \times \$10,000 = \$9,375$$

The journal entry for the insurance reimbursement is:

Cash	16,375	
Fire Loss		16,375

The net fire loss is $11,125 ($27,500 − $16,375).

LIABILITIES

What types of liabilities must I focus on?

In accounting for liabilities, the CPA must consider numerous reporting and disclosure responsibilities:

• Bonds payable may be issued between interest dates at a discount or premium.

• Bonds may be amortized using the straight-line method or effective interest method.

• Debt may be retired before its maturity date, in cases where the company can issue new debt at a lower interest rate.

• Estimated liabilities must be booked when it is *probable* that an asset has been impaired or liability has been incurred by year-end, and the amount of loss is subject to reasonable estimation.

• An accrued liability may also be made for future absences, for example sick leave or vacation time.

• Special termination benefits such as early retirement may also be offered to and accepted by employees.

• Short-term debt may be rolled over to long-term debt, requiring special reporting.

• A callable obligation by the creditor may also exist.

• Long-term purchase obligations must be disclosed.

Bonds Payable

What is the effective cost of a bond?

The cost of a corporate bond is expressed in terms of yield. Two types of yield calculations are:

$$\text{Simple Yield} = \frac{\text{Nominal Interest}}{\text{Present Value of Bond}}$$

Yield to Maturity

$$= \frac{\text{Nominal Interest} + \dfrac{\text{Discount}}{\text{Years}} - \dfrac{\text{Premium}}{\text{Years}}}{\dfrac{\text{Present Value} + \text{Maturity Value}}{2}}$$

Simple yield is not as accurate as yield to maturity.

EXAMPLE 2.17

A $100,000, 10%, 5 year bond is issued at 96. The simple yield is:

$$\frac{\text{Nominal Interest}}{\text{Present Value of Bond}} = \frac{\$10,000}{\$96,000} = \underline{10.42\%}$$

The yield to maturity is:

$$\frac{\text{Nominal Interest} + \dfrac{\text{Discount}}{\text{Years}}}{\dfrac{\text{Present Value} + \text{Maturity Value}}{2}}$$

$$= \frac{\$10,000 + \dfrac{\$4,000}{5}}{\dfrac{\$96,000 + \$100,000}{2}} = \frac{\$10,800}{\$98,000} = \underline{11.02\%}$$

What is a discount or premium?

• When a bond is issued at a discount, the yield is greater than the nominal interest rate.

• When a bond is issued at a *premium*, the yield is less than the nominal interest rate.

How is a discount or premium amortized?

The two methods of amortizing bond discount or bond premium are:

• *Straight line method.* This results in a constant dollar amount of amortization but a different effective rate each period.

• *Effective interest method.* This results in a constant rate of interest but different dollar amounts each period.

RECOMMENDATION: The effective interest method is preferred over the straight line method.

The amortization entry is:

Interest Expense (Yield × Carrying Value of Bond at the beginning of the year)

    Discount

    Cash (Nominal Interest × Face Value of Bond)

In the early years, the amortization amount under the effective interest method is lower relative to the straight line method (either for discount or premium).

EXAMPLE 2.18

On 1/1/19X1, a $100,000 bond is issued at $95,624. The yield rate is 7% and the nominal interest rate is 6%. The following schedule is the basis for the journal entries to be made:

Date	Debit Interest Expense	Credit Cash	Credit Discount	Carrying Value
1/1/19X1				$95,624
12/31/19X1	$6,694	$6,000	$694	96,318
12/31/19X2	6,742	$6,000	742	97,060

The entry on 12/31/19X1 is:

Interest Expense	6694	
Cash		6000
Discount		694

At maturity, the bond will be worth its face value of $100,000.

How is a discount or premium amortized when bonds are issued between interest dates?

The entry is:

Cash

    Bonds Payable

    Premium (or debit Discount)

    Interest Expense

EXAMPLE 2.19

A $100,000, 5% bond having a life of 5 years is issued at 110 on 4/1/19X0. The bonds are dated 1/1/19X0. Interest is payable on 1/1 and 7/1. Straight line amortization is used. The journal entries are:

4/1/19X0 Cash		
(110,000 + 1,250)	111,250	
Bonds Payable		100,000
Premium on Bonds Payable		10,000
Bond Interest Expense (100,000 × 5% × 3/12)		1,250
7/1/19X0 Bond Interest Expense	2,500	
Cash		2,500
100,000 × 5% × 6/12		
Premium on Bonds Payable	526.50	
Bond Interest Expense		526.50

4/1/19X0–1/1/19X5 4 years, 9 months = 57 months

$$\frac{\$10,000}{57}$$

= $175.50 per month

$175.50 × 3 months =
$526.50

12/31/19X0 Bond Interest		
Expense	2,500	
Interest Payable		2,500
Premium on Bonds		
Payable	1,053	
Bond Interest Expense		1,053
1/1/19X1 Interest Payable	2,500	
Cash		2,500

How is bonds payable recorded?

Bonds Payable is shown on the balance sheet at its present value this way:

Bonds Payable

Add: Premium

Less: Discount

Carrying Value

Bond issue costs are the expenditures incurred in issuing the bonds such as legal, registration, and printing fees.

RECOMMENDATION: Preferably, bond issue costs are deferred and amortized over the life of the bond. They are shown as a Deferred Charge.

How do I compute the price of a bond?

The price of a bond is determined as follows:

• The face amount is discounted using the present value of $1 table.

• The interest payments are discounted using the present value of annuity of $1 table.

• The yield rate is used as the discount rate.

EXAMPLE 2.20

A $50,000, 10 year bond is issued with interest payable semiannually at an 8% nominal interest rate. The yield rate is 10%. The present value of $1 table factor for n = 20, i = 5% is .37689. The present value of annuity of $1 table factor for

$n = 20$, $i = 5\%$ is 12.46221. The price of the bond should be:

Present Value of Principal	
$50,000 × .37689	$18,844.50
Present Value of Interest	
Payments $20,000 × 12.46221	24,924.42
	$43,768.92

How do I handle a bond conversion?

In converting a bond into stock, three methods may be used:

- Book value of bond
- Market value of bond
- Market value of stock.

Book value of bond method: No gain or loss on bond conversion will result because the book value of the bond is the basis to credit equity.

Market value methods: Gain or loss will result because the book value of the bond will be different from the market value of bond or market value of stock which is the basis to credit the equity accounts.

EXAMPLE 2.21

A $100,000 bond with unamortized premium of $8,420.50 is converted to common stock. There are 100 bonds ($100,000/$1,000). Each bond is converted into 50 shares of stock. Thus, 5,000 shares of common stock are involved. Par value is $15 per share. The market value of the stock is $25 per share. The market value of the bond is 120. Using the book value method, the entry for the conversion is:

Bonds Payable	100,000.00	
Premium on Bonds		
Payable	8,420.50	
Common Stock		
(5,000 × 15)		75,000.00
Premium on		
Common Stock		33,420.50

Using the market value of stock method, the entry is:

Bonds Payable	100,000.00	
Premium on Bonds Payable	8,420.50	
Loss on Conversion	16,579.50	
Common Stock		75,000.00
Premium on Common Stock		50,000.00

5,000 × $25 = $125,000

Using the market value of the bond method, the entry is:

Bonds Payable	100,000.00	
Premium on Bonds Payable	8,420.50	
Loss on Conversion	11,579.50	
Common Stock		75,000.00
Premium on Common Stock		45,000.00

$100,000 × 120% = $120,000

Early Extinguishment of Debt

When can debt be retired early?

Long-term debt may be called back early when new debt can be issued at a lower interest rate. Or when the company has excess cash and wants to avoid paying interest charges and having the debt on its balance sheet.

How is early extinguishment handled?

The gain or loss on the early extinguishment of debt is an extraordinary item that should be shown net of tax. Extraordinary classification occurs whether the extinguishment is early, at scheduled maturity, or later.

EXCEPTION: The gain or loss on extinguishment is an ordinary item if it satisfies a sinking fund requirement that has to be met within one year of the date of extinguishment.

NOTE: Serial bonds do not have characteristics of sinking fund requirements.

Debt may be construed as being extinguished in the case where the debtor is relieved of the principal liability and will probably not have to make future payments.

EXAMPLE 2.22

A $100,000 bond payable with an unamortized premium of $10,000 is called at 85. The entry is:

Bonds Payable	100,000	
Premium on Bonds Payable	10,000	
Cash (85% × 100,000)		85,000
Extraordinary Gain		25,000

Footnote disclosures regarding extinguishment of debt include:

- Description of extinguishment transaction, including the source of funds used
- Per share gain or loss net of tax

How do I record the conversion of debt to equity?

If convertible debt is converted to stock in connection with an "inducement offer" where the debtor alters conversion privileges, the debtor recognizes an expense rather than an extraordinary item. The amount is the fair value of the securities transferred in excess of the fair value of securities issuable according to the original conversion terms. This fair market value is measured at the earlier of the conversion date or date of the agreement.

An inducement offer may be accomplished by giving debt holders:

- A higher conversion ratio
- Payment of additional consideration
- Other favorable changes in terms.

What if a trust is set up for payment of interest and principal?

According to FASB 76, if the debtor puts cash or other assets in an irrevocable trust to be used only for paying interest and principal on debt, disclosure should be made of the particulars, including a description of the transaction and the amount of debt considered to be extinguished.

Estimated Liabilities

How is a probable loss contingency defined?

A loss contingency should be accrued if *both* of the following criteria exist:

- At year-end, it is *probable* (likely to occur) that an asset was impaired or a liability was incurred.
- The amount of loss is subject to reasonable estimation.

What are some typical loss contingencies?

Examples of probable loss contingencies may be:

- Warranties.
- Lawsuits.
- Claims and assessments.
- Expropriation of property by a foreign government.
- Casualties and catastrophes (e.g., fire).

How is a probable loss contingency booked?

The loss contingency is booked because of the principle of conservatism. The entry for a probable loss is:

Expense (Loss)

    Estimated Liability

EXAMPLE 2.23

On 12/31/19X6, warranty expenses are estimated at $20,000. On 3/15/19X7, actual warranty costs paid for were $16,000. The journal entries are:

12/31/19X6	Warranty Expense	20,000	
	Estimated Liability		20,000
3/15/19X7	Estimated Liability	16,000	
	Cash		16,000

NOTE:

• A probable loss that cannot be estimated should be footnoted.

• If a loss contingency exists at year-end but no asset impairment or liability incurrence exists (e.g., uninsured equipment), footnote disclosure may be made.

• A probable loss occurring after year-end but before the audit report date requires only subsequent event disclosure.

• If the amount of loss is within a range, the accrual is based on the best estimate within that range. However, if no amount within the range is better than any other amount, the *minimum amount* (not maximum amount) of the range is booked. The exposure to additional losses should be disclosed.

Are there any other requirements on loss contingencies?

• In the case of a *reasonably possible loss* (more than remote but less than likely) no accrual is made, but footnote disclosure is required. The disclosure includes the nature of the contingency and the estimate of probable loss or range of loss. If an estimate of loss is not possible, that fact should be stated.

• A *remote contingency* (slight chance of occurring) is usually ignored and no disclosure is made. EXCEPTIONS: Guarantees of indebtedness, standby letters of credit, and agreements to repurchase receivables or properties are disclosed.

• *General (unspecified) contingencies* are not accrued. EXAMPLES: Self-insurance and possible hurricane losses. Disclosure and/or an appropriation of retained earnings can be made for general contingencies. To be booked as an estimated liability, the future loss must be *specific* and *measurable*, such as parcel post and freight losses.

• *Gain contingencies* cannot be booked. This violates conservatism. However, footnote disclosure can be made.

Accounting for Compensated Absences

What are compensated absences?

Compensated absences include:

• sick leave
• holiday
• vacation time

FASB 43 is *not* applicable to:

• Severance or termination pay
• Deferred compensation
• Post retirement benefits
• Stock option plans
• Other long-term fringe benefits (e.g., insurance, disability)

When should there be an accrual for compensated absences?

The employer shall accrue a liability for employee's compensation for future absences when *all* of these criteria are met:

• Employee services have already been performed
• Employee rights have vested
• Probable payment exists
• Amount of estimated liability can reasonably be determined

NOTE: If the criteria are satisfied except that the amount is not determinable, only a footnote can be made, since an accrual is not possible.

Accrual for sick leave is required only when the employer permits employees to take accumulated sick leave days off irrespective of actual illness. No accrual is required if employees may only take accumulated days off for actual illness, since losses for these are typically immaterial.

EXAMPLE 2.24

Estimated compensation for future absences is $30,000. The entry is:

| Expense | 30,000 | |
| Estimated Liability | | 30,000 |

If at a later date a payment of $28,000 is made, the entry is:

| Estimated Liability | 28,000 | |
| Cash | | 28,000 |

Accounting for Special Termination Benefits to Employees

What if employees leave early and take special benefits?

An expense should be accrued when an employer offers special termination benefits to an employee, he accepts the offer, and the amount is subject to reasonable estimation. The amount equals the current payment plus the discounted value of future payments.

When it can be objectively measured, the effect of changes on the employer's previously accrued expenses applicable to other employee benefits directly associated with employee termination should be included in measuring termination expense.

EXAMPLE 2.25

On 1/1/19X1, as an incentive for early retirement, the employee receives a lump sum payment of $50,000 today, plus payments of $10,000 for each of the next 10 years. The discount rate is 10%. The journal entry is:

| Expense | 111,450 | |
| Estimated Liability | | 111,450 |

Present value $10,000 ×		
6.145* =	$61,450	
Current payment	50,000	
Total	$111,450	

*Present value factor for n = 10, i = 10% is 6.145

Refinancing of Short-term Debt to Long-term Debt

When can a short-term obligation be considered long-term?

A short-term obligation shall be reclassified as a long-term obligation when *either* of the following conditions applies:

1. After the year-end of the financial statements but before the audit report is issued, the short-term debt is rolled over into a long-term obligation, or an equity security is issued in substitution.

2. Prior to the audit report date, the company enters into a contract for refinancing of the current obligation on a long-term basis and *all* of the following are met:

- Agreement does not expire within one year
- No violation of the agreement exists
- The parties are financially capable of meeting the requirements of the agreement

How do I book the reclassification of debt from short- to long-term?

The proper classification of the refinanced item is under long-term debt and *not* stockholders' equity, even if equity securities were issued in substitution of the debt.

RECOMMENDATION: When short-term debt is excluded from current liabilities, a footnote should describe the financing agreement and the terms of any new obligation to be incurred.

If the amounts under the agreement for refinancing vary, the amount of short-term debt excluded from current liabilities will be the *minimum* amount expected to be refinanced based on conservatism.

CAUTION: The exclusion from current liabilities cannot be greater than the net proceeds of debt or security issuances, or amounts available under the refinancing agreement.

Once cash is paid for the short-term debt, even if long-term debt of a similar amount is issued the next day, the short-term debt shall be shown under current liabilities since cash was disbursed.

Callable Obligations by the Creditor

What if the debtor violates the debt agreement?

If the debtor violates the debt agreement, and long-term therefore becomes callable, include the debt as a current liability, except if *one* of the following conditions exists:

• The creditor waives or loses his right to require repayment for a period in excess of one year from the balance sheet date.

• There is a grace period in the terms of the long-term debt issue during which the debtor may cure the violation and it is probable that the violation will be rectified within such grace period.

Disclosure of Long-term Purchase Obligations

What are unconditional purchase obligations?

An unconditional purchase obligation is an obligation to provide *funds* for goods or services at a determinable future date. EXAMPLE: A take-or-pay contract obligating the buyer to periodically pay specified amounts for products or services. Even in the case where the buyer does not take delivery of the goods, periodic payments must still be made.

How are unconditional purchase obligations disclosed?

When unconditional purchase obligations are recorded in the balance sheet, disclosure is still made of:

• Payments made for recorded unconditional purchase obligations.

• Maturities and sinking fund requirements for long-term borrowings.

Unconditional purchase obligations that are not reflected in the balance sheet should usually be disclosed if they meet these criteria:

- Noncancellable, except upon a remote contingency
- Negotiated to arrange financing to provide contracted goods or services
- A term in excess of one year

The disclosure needed for unconditional purchase obligations when not recorded in the accounts are:

- Nature and term
- Fixed and variable amounts
- Total amount for the current year and for the next five years
- Purchases made under the obligation for each year presented

Disclosure is optional for the amount of imputed interest required to reduce the unconditional purchase obligation to present value.

STOCKHOLDERS' EQUITY

In accounting for stockholders' equity, consideration is given to:

- Preferred stock characteristics
- Preferred stock conversion to common stock
- Stock retirement
- Appropriation of retained earnings
- Treasury stock
- Quasi-reorganization
- Dividends
- Fractional share warrants
- Stock options
- Stock warrants
- Stock splits

The stockholders' equity section of the balance sheet includes major categories for:

- Capital stock (stock issued and stock to be issued)
- Paid-in-capital

- Retained earnings
- Unrealized loss on long-term investments
- Gains or losses on foreign currency translation
- Treasury stock

NOTE: Disclosure should be made for required redemptions of capital stock redeemable at given prices on specific dates.

Preferred Stock

What are some characteristics of preferred stock?

Preferred stock may be fully or partially participating. *Participating preferred stock* is entitled to share in dividend distributions in excess of the preferred stock dividend rate on a proportionate basis using the total par value of the preferred stock and common stock.

Cumulative preferred stock means that if no dividends are paid in a given year, the dividends accumulate and must be paid before any dividends can be paid to noncumulative stock.

The *liquidation value of preferred stock* means that in corporate liquidation, preferred stockholders will receive the liquidation value (sometimes stated as par value) before any funds may be distributed to common stockholders.

NOTE: Disclosure for preferred stock includes liquidation preferences, call prices, and cumulative dividends in arrears.

How is preferred stock accounted for?

When preferred stock is converted to common stock, the preferred stock and paid-in-capital account are eliminated, and the common stock and paid-in-capital accounts are credited. If a deficit results, retained earnings would be charged.

Stock Retirement

What do I do if stock is retired?

A company may decide to retire its stock. If common stock is retired *at par value*, the entry is:

Common Stock $\Big\}$ Par Value
Cash

If common stock is retired for *less than par value*, the entry is:

Common Stock
  Cash
  Paid-in-capital

If common stock is retired for *more than par value*, the entry is:

Common Stock
Paid-in-capital (original premium per share)
Retained Earnings (excess over original premium per share)
  Cash

NOTE: In retirement of stock, retained earnings can only be debited, not credited.

Appropriation of Retained Earnings (Reserve)

What is a retained earnings appropriation?

Appropriation of retained earnings means setting aside retained earnings and making them unavailable for dividends. It indicates the need to stockholders to restrict asset disbursements because of expected major uses or contingencies. EXAMPLES: Appropriations for plant expansion, sinking fund, and contingencies.

How are retained earnings appropriations booked?

The entry to record an appropriation is:

Retained Earnings
  Appropriation of Retained Earnings

When the contingency occurs, the above entry is reversed.

Treasury Stock

How is treasury stock accounted for?

Treasury stock is issued shares that have been bought back by the company. There are two methods to account for treasury stock:

Cost Method. Treasury stock is recorded at the purchase cost and is shown as a reduction from total stockholders' equity.

If treasury stock is later *sold above cost*, the entry is:

Cash

    Treasury Stock

    Paid-in-capital

If treasury stock was *sold below cost*, the entry is:

Cash

Paid-in-capital—Treasury Stock (up to amount available)

Retained Earnings (if paid-in-capital is unavailable)

    Treasury Stock

If treasury stock is *donated*, only a memo entry is needed. When the treasury shares are later sold the entry based on the market price at that time is:

Cash

    Paid-in-capital—Donation

NOTE: An appropriation of retained earnings equal to the cost of treasury stock on hand is required.

Par Value Method. Treasury stock is recorded at its par value when bought. An appropriation of retained earnings equal to the cost of the treasury stock on hand is required. Treasury stock is shown as a contra account to the common stock it applies to under the capital stock section of stockholders' equity.

If treasury stock is *purchased at more than par value*, the entry is:

Treasury Stock—Par Value

> Paid-in-capital—original premium per share
> Retained Earnings—if necessary
> > Cash

If treasury stock is *purchased at less than par value*, the entry is:

Treasury Stock—Par Value
> Cash
> Paid-in-capital

If treasury stock is sold *above par value*, the entry is:

Cash
> Treasury Stock
> Paid-in-capital

If treasury stock is sold *under par value*, the entry is:

Cash
Paid-in-capital (amount available)
Retained Earnings (if paid-in-capital is insufficient)
> Treasury Stock

Quasi-Reorganization

What is a quasi-reorganization?

A quasi-reorganization gives a financially troubled company with a deficit in retained earnings a "fresh start." A quasi-reorganization is undertaken to avoid formal bankruptcy. There is a revaluation of assets and an elimination of the deficit by reducing paid-in-capital.

How do I handle a quasi-reorganization?

• Stockholders and creditors must agree to the quasi-reorganization.

• Net assets are written down to fair market value. If fair value is not readily available, then conservative estimates of such value may be made.

• Paid-in-capital is reduced to eliminate the deficit in retained earnings. If paid-in-capital is insufficient, then capital stock is charged.

• Retained earnings becomes a zero balance. Retained earnings will bear the date of the quasi-reorganization for 10 years subsequent to the reorganization.

The retained earnings account consists of the following components:

Retained Earnings—Unappropriated

Dividends	Net Income
Appropriations	
Prior Period Adjustments	
Quasi-reorganization	

The entry for the quasi-reorganization is:

Paid-in-capital

Capital Stock (if necessary)

    Assets

    Retained Earnings

CAUTION: If potential losses exist at the readjustment date but the amounts of losses cannot be determined, there should be a provision for the maximum probable loss. If estimates used are subsequently shown to be incorrect, the difference goes to the paid-in-capital account.

NOTE: New or additional common stock or preferred stock may be issued in exchange for existing *indebtedness*. Thus, the current liability account would be debited for the indebtedness and the capital account credited.

EXAMPLE 2.26

ABC Company shows the following balances before a quasi-reorganization:

	Capital Stock (80,000 shares, $10 par)	
Current Assets		
$100,000		$800,000

Fixed Assets	400,000	Paid-in-capital	200,000
		Retained Earnings	(500,000)
		Total Liabilities	
Total Assets	$500,000	and Capital	$500,000

Current assets are overvalued by $20,000 and fixed assets are overvalued by $100,000.

The entries for the quasi-reorganization are:

Quasi-reorganization	120,000	
Current Assets		20,000
Fixed Assets		100,000
Quasi-reorganization	500,000	
Retained Earnings		500,000
Paid-in-capital	200,000	
Quasi-reorganization		200,000
Common Stock	420,000	
Quasi-reorganization		420,000

Quasi-reorganization

120,000	200,000
500,000	420,000
620,000	620,000

Dividends

How is a cash dividend recognized?

A cash dividend is based on the outstanding shares (issued shares less treasury shares).

EXAMPLE 2.27

There are 5,000 issued shares and 1,000 treasury shares, a total of 4,000 outstanding shares. The par value of the stock is $10 per share. If a $.30 dividend per share is declared, the dividend is:

$$4,000 \times \$.30 = \underline{\$1,200}$$

If the dividend rate is 6%, the dividend is:

$$4,000 \text{ shares} \times \$10 \text{ par value} = \$40,000$$
$$\times .06$$
$$\overline{\$ 2,400}$$

Assuming a cash dividend of $2,400 is declared, the entry is:

Retained Earnings	2,400	
Cash Dividend Payable		2,400

No entry is made at the record date.
The entry at the payment date is:

Cash Dividend Payable	2,400	
Cash		2,400

Is a property dividend handled like a cash dividend?

Yes, but in the case of a property dividend, the entry at the declaration date at the fair market value of the asset is:

Retained Earnings

  Asset

Gain or loss arising between the carrying value and fair market value of the asset is recorded at the time of transfer.

How is a stock dividend handled?

A stock dividend is issued in the form of stock. Stock dividend distributable is shown in the capital stock section of stockholders' equity. It is *not* a liability.

• If the stock dividend is *less than 20%–25% of outstanding shares* at the declaration date, retained earnings is reduced at the market price of the shares.

• If the stock dividend is *in excess of 20%–25% of outstanding shares*, retained earnings is charged at par value. Between 20%–25% is a gray area.

EXAMPLE 2.28

A stock dividend of 10% is declared on 5,000 shares of $10 par value common stock having a market price of $12. The entry at the declaration and issuance dates follows:

Retained Earnings (500 shares	
× $12)	6,000

Stock Dividend Distributable		
(500 shares × $10)		5,000
Paid-in-Capital		1,000
Stock Dividend Distributable	5,000	
Common Stock		5,000

Assume instead that the stock dividend was 30%. The entries would be:

Retained Earnings (500 × $10)	5,000	
Stock Dividend Distributable		5,000
Stock Dividend Distributable	5,000	
Common Stock		5,000

How is a liability dividend accounted for?

A liability dividend (scrip dividend) is payable in the form of a liability (e.g., notes payable). A liability dividend sometimes occurs when a company has financial problems.

EXAMPLE 2.29

On 1/1/19X2, a liability dividend of $20,000 is declared in the form of a one year, 8% note. The entry at the declaration date is:

Retained Earnings	20,000	
Scrip Dividend Payable		20,000

When the scrip dividend is paid, the entry is:

Scrip Dividend Payable	20,000	
Interest Expense	1,600	
Cash		21,600

Stock Split

What is a stock split?

In a stock split, the shares are *increased* and the par value per share is *decreased*. However, total par value is the same.

How do I handle a stock split?

Only a memo entry is needed.

EXAMPLE 2.30

Before: 1,000 shares, $10 par value——
                         $10,000 total par value
2 for 1 stock split declared.
After: 2,000 shares, $5 par value——
                         $10,000 total par value
A reverse split would have the opposite effect.

Stock Options

What are non-compensatory and compensatory stock option plans?

Characteristics of non-compensatory plans are:

• Employees are offered stock on some basis (e.g., equally, percent of salary).

• Full-time employees may participate.

• A reasonable period of time exists to exercise the options.

• The price discount for employees on the stock is not better than that afforded to corporate stockholders if there was an additional issuance to the stockholders.

A compensatory plan exists if any one of the above four criteria is *not* met. Consideration received by the firm for the stock equals the cash, assets, or employee services obtained.

What is the purpose of a non-compensatory plan?

The purpose of a *non-compensatory plan* is to obtain funds and to reduce greater widespread ownership in the company among employees. It is not primarily designed to provide compensation for services rendered. Therefore, no compensation expense is recognized.

How are stock option plans recognized?

In a *compensatory* stock option plan for executives, compensation expense should be recognized in the year in which the services are performed. The deferred compensation is determined at the measurement date as the difference between the market price of the stock at that date and the option price. When there exists more than one option plan, compensation cost should be computed separately for each. If treasury stock is used in the stock option plan, its market value, *not* its cost should be used in measuring the compensation.

Deferred compensation is a contra account against stock options to derive the net amount under the capital stock section of the balance sheet.

EXAMPLE 2.31

On 1/1/19X1, 1,000 shares are granted under a stock option plan. At the measurement date, the market price of the stock is $10 and the option price is $6. The amount of the deferred compensation is:

Market price	$10
Option price	6
Deferred compensation	$ 4

Deferred compensation equals:
1,000 shares × $4 = $4,000

Assume the employees must perform services for four years before they can exercise the option.

On 1/1/19X1, the journal entry to record total deferred compensation cost is:

Deferred Compensation Cost	4,000	
Paid-in-capital—Stock Options		4,000

On 12/31/19X1, the entry to record the expense is:

Compensation Expense	1,000	
Deferred Compensation		1,000

$4,000/4 years = $1,000

The capital stock section on 12/31/19X1 would show stock options as follows:

Stock options	$4,000
Less Deferred compensation	1,000
Balance	$3,000

Compensation expense of $1,000 would be reflected for each of the next three years as well.

At the time the options are exercised when the market price of the stock at the exercise date exceeds the option price, an entry must be made for stock issuance.

Assuming a par value of $5 and a market price of $22, the journal entry for the exercise is:

Cash ($6 × 1,000)	6,000	
Paid-in-capital—Stock Options	4,000	
Common Stock		
($5 × 1,000)		5,000
Paid-in-capital		5,000

If the market price of the stock was below the option price, the options would lapse, requiring the following entry:

Paid-in-capital—Stock Options	4,000	
Paid-in-capital		4,000

Notes:

• When an employee *leaves after finishing the required service years*, no effect is given to recorded compensation and the nonexercised options are transferred to paid-in-capital.

• When the employee *leaves before the exercise period*, previously recognized compensation is adjusted currently.

• If the *grant date is prior to the measurement date*, estimate the deferred compensation costs until the measurement date so that compensation expense is recognized when services are performed. RECOMMENDATION: The difference between the actual figures and estimates is treated as a change in estimate during the year in which the actual cost is determined.

• When the *measurement date comes after the grant date*, compensation expense for each period from the date of award to the measurement date should be based on the market price of the stock at the close of the accounting period.

• In a *variable plan* granted for previous services, compensation should be expensed in the period the award is granted.

• When the *employee performs services for several years prior to the stock being issued*, an accrual should be made during these periods for compensation expense applicable to the stock issuance related thereto.

• When *employees receive cash in settlement* of a previous option, the cash paid is used to measure the compensation. If the ultimate compensation differs from the amount initially recorded, an adjustment should be made to the original compensation. It is accounted for as a change in estimate.

• The *accrual of compensation expense* may necessitate estimates which must later be revised. EXAMPLE: An employee resigns from the company and does not exercise his stock option. Compensation expense should be reduced when employee termination occurs. The adjustment is accounted for as a change in estimate.

• *Footnote disclosure* for a stock option plan includes the number of shares under option, option price, number of shares exercisable, and the number of shares issued under the option during the year.

• *Compensation expense is deductible for tax purposes when paid but deducted for book purposes when accrued.* This results in interperiod income tax allocation involving a deferred income tax credit. If for some reason reversal of the temporary difference does not occur, a permanent difference exists which does not affect profit. The difference should adjust paid-in-capital in the period the accrual takes place.

How is the measurement date determined?

The measurement date is the date upon which the number of shares to be issued and the option price are known.

• The measurement date cannot be changed by provisions that reduce the number of shares under option in the case of employee termination.

• A new measurement date occurs when an option renewal takes place.

• The measurement date is not altered when stock is transferred to a trustee or agent.

In the case of convertible stock being awarded to employees, the measurement date is the one upon which the conversion rate is known. Compensation is measured by the higher of the market price of the convertible stock or the market price of the securities into which the convertible stock is to be converted.

There may be a postponement in the measurement date to the end of the reporting year if *all* of these three conditions exist:

• A formal plan exists for the award.

• The factors determining the total dollar award are designated.

• The award relates to services performed by employees in the current year.

Debt Issued with Stock Warrants

How do I distinguish between detachable and undetachable warrants?

If bonds are issued along with *detachable* stock warrants, the portion of the proceeds applicable to the warrants is credited to paid-in-capital. The basis for allocation is the relative values of the securities at the time of issuance.

In the event that the warrants are *not detachable*, the bonds are accounted for solely as convertible debt. There is *no* allocation of the proceeds to the conversion feature.

EXAMPLE 2.32

A $20,000 convertible bond is issued at $21,000 with $1,000 applicable to stock warrants. If the warrants are not detachable, the entry is:

Cash	21,000	
Bonds Payable		20,000
Premium on Bonds Payable		1,000

If the warrants are detachable, the entry is:

Cash	21,000	
Bonds Payable		20,000
Paid-in-capital—		
Stock Warrants		1,000

In the event that the proceeds of the bond issue were only $20,000 instead of $21,000, and $1,000 could be attributable to the warrants, the entry is:

Cash	20,000	
Discount	1,000	
Bonds Payable		20,000
Paid-in-capital—		
Stock Warrants		1,000

Fractional Share Warrants

What recognition is given to fractional share warrants?

Let's see how fractional share warrants are handled in an example.

EXAMPLE 2.33

There are 1,000 shares of $10 par value common stock. The common stock has a market price of $15. A 20% dividend is declared resulting in 200 shares (20% × 1,000). Included in the 200 shares are fractional share warrants. Each warrant equals 1/5 of a share of stock. There are 100 warrants resulting in 20 shares of stock (100/5). Thus, 180 regular shares and 20 fractional shares are involved.

At the declaration date, the journal entries are:

Retained Earnings		
(200 shares × 15)	3,000	
Stock Dividends Distributable		
(180 shares × 10)		1,800
Fractional Share Warrants		
(20 shares × 10)		200
Paid-in-capital		1,000

At time of issuance, the journal entries are:

Stock Dividend Distributable	1,800	
Common Stock		1,800
Fractional Share Warrants	200	
Common Stock		200

If instead of all the fractional share warrants being turned in, only 80% were turned in the entry is:

Fractional Share Warrants	200	
Common Stock		160
Paid-in-capital		40

CHAPTER 3

FINANCIAL STATEMENT REPORTING: STATEMENT OF CASH FLOWS AND OTHER DISCLOSURES

In addition to the income statement and balance sheet, the CPA must be conversant with:

- Statement of cash flows
- Interim reporting
- Personal financial statements
- Partnerships

STATEMENT OF CASH FLOWS

According to FASB 95, a statement of cash flows is required in the annual report. In addition, separate reporting is mandated for certain information applicable to noncash investments and financing transactions.

What is the purpose of the statement of cash flows?

The statement of cash flows:

- Furnishes useful data regarding a company's cash receipts and cash payments for a period
- Reflects a reconciliation between net income and net cash flow from operations

• Shows the net effects of operating transactions on earnings and operating cash flow in different periods

• Explains the change in *cash and cash-equivalents* for the period

What is a cash-equivalent?

A cash-equivalent is a short-term very liquid investment satisfying these two criteria:

• Easily convertible into cash

• Very near the maturity date so there is hardly any chance of change in market value due to interest rate changes. (Typically, this criterion applies only to investments having original maturities of three months or less) EXAMPLES:

• Commercial paper
• Money market fund
• Treasury bills

How are cash-equivalents disclosed?

Disclosure of the company's policy for determining which items represent cash equivalents should be made. A change in such policy is accounted for as a change in accounting principle which requires the restatement of previous years' financial statements for comparative purposes.

How is the statement of cash flows structured?

The statement of cash flows classifies cash receipts and cash payments as arising from:

• Investing activities
• Financing activities
• Operating activities

The statement of cash flows presents the net source or application of cash by operating, investing, and financing activities. The net effect of these flows on cash and cash equivalents for the period shall be reported so that the beginning and ending balances of cash and cash equivalents may be reconciled.

What are investing activities?

Investing activities include making and collecting loans, buying and selling fixed assets, and purchasing debt and equity securities in other entities.

Cash inflows from investing:

- Collections or sales of loans made by a company and of another firm's debt instruments that were purchased by the company
- Receipts from sales of equity securities of other companies
- Amount received from disposing of fixed assets

Cash outflows for investing activities include:

- Disbursements for loans made by the company and payments to buy debt securities of other entities
- Disbursements to buy equity securities of other companies
- Payments to buy fixed assets

What are financing activities?

Financing activities include receiving equity funds and furnishing owners with a return on their investment, debt financing and repayment or settlement of debt, and obtaining and paying for other resources derived from creditors on noncurrent credit.

Cash inflows from financing activities:

- Funds received from the sale of stock
- Funds obtained from the incurrence of debt

Cash outflows for financing activities:

- Dividend payments
- Repurchase of stock
- Paying-off debt
- Other principal payments to long-term creditors

What are operating activities?

Operating activities relate to manufacturing and selling goods or the rendering of services, not to investing or financing functions. Cash flow derived from operating activities typically applies to the cash effects of transactions entering into profit computation.

Cash inflows from operating activities:

- Cash sales or collections on receivables arising from the initial sale of merchandise or rendering of service
- Cash receipts from returns on loans, debt securities, or equity securities of other entities (included are interest and dividends received)
- Receipt of a litigation settlement
- Reimbursement under an insurance policy

Cash outflows for operating activities:

- Cash paid for raw material or merchandise for resale
- Principal payments on accounts payable arising from the initial purchase of goods
- Cash payments to suppliers
- Employee payroll expenditures
- Payments to governmental agencies (e.g., taxes, penalties, fees)
- Interest payments to lenders and other creditors
- Lawsuit payment
- Charitable contributions
- Cash refund to customers for defective merchandise

NOTES: If a cash receipt or cash payment *applies to more than one classification* (investing, financing, operating), classification is made as to the activity which is the main source of that cash flow. EXAMPLE: The purchase and sale of equipment to be used by the company is typically construed as an investing activity.

In the case of *foreign currency cash flows*, use the exchange rate at the time of the cash flow in reporting its currency equivalent. The impact of changes in the exchange rate on cash balances held in foreign currencies is shown as a separate element of the reconciliation of the change in cash and cash equivalents for the period.

How are cash flows reconciled in the statement of cash flows?

Reconciliation is achieved by either the direct or indirect method.

The direct method is preferred, in that companies should report cash flows from operating activities by major classes of gross cash receipts and gross cash payments and the resulting net amount. A company using the direct method should present the following types of operating cash receipts and cash payments separately:

- Cash received from customers, licensees, and lessees
- Receipts from dividends and interest
- Other operating cash receipts
- Cash paid to employees and suppliers for goods or services
- Cash paid to advertising agencies and insurance companies
- Payment of interest
- Tax payments
- Other operating cash payments

Additional breakdowns of operating cash receipts and disbursements may be made to enhance financial reporting. EXAMPLE: A manufacturing company may divide cash paid to suppliers into payments applicable to inventory acquisition and payments for selling expenses.

The indirect reconciliation method may be used, although this is not the preferred practice. Under this method, the company reports net cash flow from operating activities indirectly, by adjusting profit to reconcile it to net cash from operating activities. The adjustment to reported earnings involves effects of:

- Deferrals of past operating cash receipts and cash payments (e.g., changes in inventory and deferred revenue)

- Accumulations of anticipated future operating cash receipts and cash payments (e.g., changes in receivables and payables)
- Items whose cash impact relates to investing or financing cash flows (e.g., depreciation expense, amortization expense, gain and loss on the sale of fixed assets, and gain or loss on the retirement of debt)

NOTES: Whether the direct or indirect method is used, there should be a reconciliation of net income to net cash flow from operating activities. The reconciliation shall identify the principal types of reconciling items. EXAMPLE: Major classes of deferrals and accruals affecting cash flows should be reported, including changes in receivables, inventory, and payables that apply to operating activities.

If the indirect method is employed, interest and income taxes paid during the period should be disclosed.

How are operating, financing, and investing activities distinguished on the statement of cash flows?

When the *direct method* of reporting cash flows from operating activities is used, the reconciliation of profit to cash flow from operations should be disclosed in a separate schedule. When the *indirect method* is followed, the reconciliation may appear within the body of the statement of cash flows or may be shown in a schedule.

There should be separate presentation within the statement of cash flows of cash inflows and cash outflows from investing and financing activities. EXAMPLE: The purchase of fixed assets is an application of cash, while the sale of a fixed asset is a source of cash. Both are shown separately to aid analysis by readers of the financial statements. Debt incurrence would be a source of cash, while debt payment would be an application of cash. Thus, cash received of $800,000 from debt incurrence would be shown as a source, while the payment of debt of $250,000 would be presented as an application. The net effect is $550,000.

NOTE: Separate disclosure shall be made of investing and financing activities that affect assets or liabilities but do *not* affect cash flow. This disclosure may be footnoted or shown in a schedule. Further, a transaction having cash and noncash elements should be discussed, but only the cash aspect will be shown in the statement of cash flows. EXAMPLES: Noncash activities of an investing and financing nature include:

- bond conversion,
- purchase of a fixed asset by the incurrence of a mortgage payable,
- capital lease, and
- nonmonetary exchange of assets.

Cash flow per share shall *not* be shown in the financial statements, since it will detract from the importance of the earnings per share statistic.

Who uses the statement of cash flows and why?

An analysis of the statement of cash flows helps creditors and investors:

- Evaluate the entity's ability to obtain positive future net cash flows
- Appraise the company's ability to satisfy debt
- Analyze the firm's dividend paying ability
- Establish an opinion regarding the company's capability to derive outside financing
- Notice a difference between net income and cash flow
- Evaluate the impact on the firm's financial position of cash and noncash investing and financing transactions

What financial information do I need to construct a statement of cash flows?

EXAMPLE 3.1*

Summarized on pages 93 and 94 is financial information for the current year for Company M, which provides the basis for the statements of cash flows.

COMPANY M
CONSOLIDATED STATEMENT
OF FINANCIAL POSITION

	1/1/X1	12/31/X1	Change
Assets:			
Cash and cash equivalents	$ 600	$ 1,665	$1,065
Accounts receivable (net of allowance for losses of $600 and $450)	1,770	1,940	170
Notes receivable	400	150	(250)
Inventory	1,230	1,375	145
Prepaid expenses	110	135	25
Investments	250	275	25
Property, plant, and equipment, at cost	6,460	8,460	2,000
Accumulated depreciation	(2,100)	(2,300)	(200)
Property, plant, and equipment, net	4,360	6,160	1,800
Intangible assets	40	175	135
Total assets	$8,760	$11,875	$3,115

Liabilities:			
Accounts payable and accrued expenses	$1,085	$ 1,090	$ 5
Interest payable	30	45	15
Income taxes payable	50	85	35
Short-term debt	450	750	300
Lease obligation	—	725	725
Long-term debt	2,150	2,425	275
Deferred taxes	375	525	150
Other liabilities	225	275	50
Total liabilities	4,365	5,920	1,555
Stockholders' equity:			
Capital stock	2,000	3,000	1,000
Retained earnings	2,395	2,955	560
Total stockholders' equity	4,395	5,955	1,560
Total liabilities and stockholders' equity	$8,760	$11,875	$3,115

*Source: Statement of Financial Accounting Standards No. 95, *Statement of Cash Flows*, 1987, Appendix C, Example 1, pp. 44–51. Reprinted with permission of the Financial Accounting Standards Board.

COMPANY M
CONSOLIDATED STATEMENT OF INCOME
FOR THE YEAR ENDED DECEMBER 31, 19X1

Sales	$13,965
Cost of sales	(10,290)
Depreciation and amortization	(445)
Selling, general, and administrative expenses	(1,890)
Interest expense	(235)
Equity in earnings of affiliate	45
Gain on sale of facility	80
Interest income	55
Insurance proceeds	15
Loss from patent infringement lawsuit	(30)
Income before income taxes	1,270
Provision for income taxes	(510)
Net income	$ 760

The following transactions were entered into by Company M during 19X1 and are reflected in the above financial statements:

a. Company M wrote off $350 of accounts receivable when a customer filed for bankruptcy. A provision for losses on accounts receivable of $200 was included in Company M's selling, general, and administrative expenses.

b. Company M collected the third and final annual installment payment of $100 on a note receivable for the sale of inventory and collected the third of four annual installment payments of $150 each on a note receivable for the sale of a plant. Interest on these notes through December 31 totaling $55 was also collected.

c. Company M received a dividend of $20 from an affiliate accounted for under the equity method of accounting.

d. Company M sold a facility with a book value of $520 and an original cost of $750 for $600 cash.

e. Company M constructed a new facility for

its own use and placed it in service. Accumulated expenditures during the year of $1,000 included capitalized interest of $10.

f. Company M entered into a capital lease for new equipment with a fair value of $850. Principal payments under the lease obligation totaled $125.

g. Company M purchased all of the capital stock of Company S for $950. The acquisition was recorded under the purchase method of accounting. The fair values of Company S's assets and liabilities at the date of acquisition are presented below:

Cash	$ 25
Accounts receivable	155
Inventory	350
Property, plant, and equipment	900
Patents	80
Goodwill	70
Accounts payable and accrued expenses	(255)
Long-term note payable	(375)
Net assets acquired	$950

h. Company M borrowed and repaid various amounts under a line-of-credit agreement in which borrowings are payable 30 days after demand. The net increase during the year in the amount borrowed against the line-of-credit totaled $300.

i. Company M issued $400 of long-term debt securities.

j. Company M's provision for income taxes included a deferred provision of $150.

k. Company M's depreciation totaled $430, and amortization of intangible assets totaled $15.

l. Company M's selling, general, and administrative expenses included an accrual for incentive compensation of $50 that has been deferred by executives until their retirement. The related obligation was included in other liabilities.

m. Company M collected insurance proceeds

of $15 from a business interruption claim that resulted when a storm precluded shipment of inventory for one week.

n. Company M paid $30 to settle a lawsuit for patent infringement.

o. Company M issued $1,000 of additional common stock of which $500 was issued for cash and $500 was issued upon conversion of long-term debt.

p. Company M paid dividends of $200.

Based on the financial data from the preceding example, the following computations illustrate a method of indirectly determining cash received from customers and cash paid to suppliers and employees for use in a statement of cash flows under the direct method:

Cash received from customers during the year:

Customer sales		$13,965
Collection of installment payment for sale of inventory		100
Gross accounts receivable at beginning of year	$2,370	
Accounts receivable acquired in purchase of Company S	155	
Accounts receivable written off	(350)	
Gross accounts receivable at end of year	(2,390)	
Excess of new accounts receivable over collections from customers		(215)
Cash received from customers during the year		$13,850

Cash paid to suppliers and employees during the year:

Cost of sales		$10,290
General and administrative expenses	$1,890	

Expenses not requiring cash outlay (provision for uncollectible accounts receivable)	(200)	
Net expenses requiring cash payments		1,690
Inventory at beginning of year	(1,230)	
Inventory acquired in purchase of Company S	(350)	
Inventory at end of year	1,375	
Net decrease in inventory from Company M's operations		(205)

Adjustments for changes in related accruals:

Account balances at beginning of year

Accounts payable and accrued expenses	$1,085	
Other liabilities	225	
Prepaid expenses	(110)	
Total		1,200
Accounts payable and accrued expenses acquired in purchase of Company S		255

Account balances at end of year

Accounts payable and accrued expenses	1,090	
Other liabilities	275	
Prepaid expenses	(135)	
Total		(1,230)
Additional cash payments not included in expense		225
Cash paid to suppliers and employees during the year		$12,000

Presented below is a statement of cash flows for the year ended December 31, 19X1 for Company M. This statement of cash flows illustrates the direct method of presenting cash flows from operating activities.

COMPANY M
CONSOLIDATED STATEMENT
OF CASH FLOWS
FOR THE YEAR
ENDED DECEMBER 31, 19X1
Increase (Decrease) in Cash
and Cash Equivalents

Cash flows from operating activities:		
Cash received from customers	$13,850	
Cash paid to suppliers and employees	(12,000)	
Dividend received from affiliate	20	
Interest received	55	
Interest paid (net of amout capitalized)	(220)	
Income taxes paid	(325)	
Insurance proceeds received	15	
Cash paid to settle lawsuit for patent infringement	(30)	
Net cash provided by operating activities		$1,365
Cash flows from investing activities:		
Proceeds from sale of facility	600	
Payment received on note for sale of plant	150	
Capital expenditures	(1,000)	
Payment for purchase of Company S, net of cash acquired	(925)	
Net cash used in investing activities		(1,175)

Cash flows from financing activities:		
Net borrowing under line-of-credit agreement	300	
Principal payments under capital lease obligation	(125)	
Proceeds from issuance of long-term debt	400	
Proceeds from issuance of common stock	500	
Dividends paid	(200)	
Net cash provided by financing activities		875
Net increase in cash and cash equivalents		1,065
Cash and cash equivalents at beginning of year		600
Cash and cash equivalents at end of year		$1,665

Reconciliation of net income to net cash provided by operating activities:

Net income		$ 760
Adjustments to reconcile net income to net cash provided by operating activities:		
Depreciation and amortization	445	
Provision for losses on accounts receivable	200	
Gain on sale of facility	(80)	
Undistributed earnings of affiliate	(25)	
Payment received on installment note receivable for sale of inventory	100	

Change in assets and liabilities net of effects from purchase of Company S:		
Increase in accounts receivable	(215)	
Decrease in inventory	205	
Increase in prepaid expenses	(25)	
Decrease in accounts payable and accrued expenses	(250)	
Increase in interest and income taxes payable	50	
Increase in deferred taxes	150	
Increase in other liabilities	50	
Total adjustments		605
Net cash provided by operating activities		$1,365

Supplemental schedule of noncash investing and financing activities:

The Company purchased all of the capital stock of Company S for $950. In conjunction with the acquisition, liabilities were assumed as follows:

Fair value of assets acquired	$1,580
Cash paid for the capital stock	(950)
Liabilities assumed	$ 630

A capital lease obligation of $850 was incurred when the Company entered into a lease for new equipment.

Additional common stock was issued upon the conversion of $500 of long-term debt.

Disclosure of accounting policy:

For purposes of the statement of cash flows, the Company considers all highly liquid debt instruments purchased with a maturity of three months or less to be cash equivalents.

Presented below is Company M's statement of cash flows for the year ended December 31, 19X1 prepared using the indirect method.

COMPANY M
CONSOLIDATED STATEMENT
OF CASH FLOWS
FOR THE YEAR
ENDED DECEMBER 31, 19X1
Increase (Decrease) in Cash
and Cash Equivalents

Cash flows from operating activities:		
Net income		$ 760
Adjustments to reconcile net income to net cash provided by operating activities:		
Depreciation and amortization	$ 445	
Provision for losses on accounts receivable	200	
Gain on sale of facility	(80)	
Undistributed earnings of affiliate	(25)	
Payment received on installment note receivable for sale of inventory	100	
Change in assets and liabilities net of effects from purchase of Company S:		
Increase in accounts receivable	(215)	
Decrease in inventory	205	
Increase in prepaid expenses	(25)	
Decrease in accounts payable and accrued expenses	(250)	

Increase in interest and income taxes payable	50	
Increase in deferred taxes	150	
Increase in other liabilities	50	
Total adjustments		605
Net cash provided by operating activities		1,365
Cash flows from investing activities:		
Proceeds from sale of facility	600	
Payment received on note for sale of plant	150	
Capital expenditures	(1,000)	
Payment for purchase of Company S, net of cash acquired	(925)	
Net cash used in investing activities		(1,175)
Cash flows from financing activities:		
Net borrowings under line-of-credit agreement	300	
Principal payments under capital lease obligation	(125)	
Proceeds from issuance of long-term debt	400	
Proceeds from issuance of common stock	500	
Dividends paid	(200)	
Net cash provided by financing activities		875
Net increase in cash and cash equivalents		1,065
Cash and cash equivalents at beginning of year		600
Cash and cash equivalents at end of year		$1,665

Supplemental disclosures of cash flow information:

Cash paid during the year for:

Interest (net of amount capitalized)	$ 220
Income taxes	325

Supplemental schedule of noncash investing and financing activities:

The Company purchased all of the capital stock of Company S for $950. In conjunction with the acquisition, liabilities were assumed as follows:

Fair value of assets acquired	$1,580
Cash paid for the capital stock	(950)
Liabilities assumed	$ 630

A capital lease obligation of $850 was incurred when the Company entered into a lease for new equipment.

Additional common stock was issued upon the conversion of $500 of long-term debt.

Disclosure of accounting policy:

For purposes of the statement of cash flows, the Company considers all highly liquid debt instruments purchased with a maturity of three months or less to be cash equivalents.

INTERIM REPORTING

How often should interim reports be given?

Interim reports may be issued at appropriate reporting intervals, for example quarterly or monthly. Complete financial statements or summarized data may be given, but interim financial statements do not have to be certified.

What type of report is appropriate for an interim period?

Interim balance sheets and cash flow data should be provided. If these statements are not presented, material changes in liquid assets, cash, long-term debt, and stockholders' equity should be disclosed. Usually, interim reports include results of the current interim period and the cumulative year-to-date figures. Typically, comparisons are made to results of comparable interim periods for the prior year.

What are some guidelines in preparing interim reports?

• Interim results should be based on the accounting principles used in the last year's annual report unless a change has been made in the current year.

• A gain or loss cannot be deferred to a later interim period except if such deferral would have been permissable for annual reporting.

• Revenue from merchandise sold and services performed should be accounted for as earned in the interim period in the same way as accounted for in annual reporting. If an advance is received in the first quarter and benefits the entire year, it should be allocated ratably to the interim periods affected.

• Costs and expenses should be matched to related revenue in the interim period. If a cost cannot be associated with revenue in a future interim period, it should be expensed in the current period. Yearly expenses such as administrative salaries, insurance, pension plan expense, and year-end bonuses should be allocated to the quarters. The allocation basis may be based on such factors as time expired, benefit obtained, and activity.

• The gross profit method can be used to estimate interim inventory and cost of sales. Disclosure should be made of the method, assumptions made, and material adjustments by reconciliations with the annual physical inventory.

• A permanent inventory loss should be reflected in the interim period during which it occurs. A subsequent recovery is treated as a gain in the later interim period. However, if the change in inventory value is temporary, no recognition is given in the accounts.

• When there is a temporary liquidation of the LIFO base with replacement expected by year-end, cost of sales should be based on replacement cost.

EXAMPLE 3.2

The historical cost of an inventory item is $10,000 with replacement cost expected at $15,000. The entry is:

Cost of Sales	15,000	
Inventory		10,000
Reserve for Liquidation of LIFO Base		5,000

Note: The Reserve for Liquidation of LIFO Base account is shown as a current liability.

When replenishment is made at year-end the entry is:

Reserve for Liquidation of LIFO Base	5,000	
Inventory	10,000	
Cash		15,000

• Volume discounts given to customers tied into annual purchases should be apportioned to the interim period base on the ratio of:

$$\frac{\text{Purchases for the interim period}}{\text{Total estimated purchases for the year}}$$

• When a standard cost system is used, variances expected to be reversed by year-end may be deferred to an asset or liability account.

How are taxes reflected in interim reports?

The income tax provision includes current and deferred taxes, both federal and local. The tax provision for an interim period should be cumulative. EXAMPLE: Total tax expense for a 9 month period is shown in the third quarter based on 9 month income.

The tax expense for the three month period based on 3 months' income may also be presented. EXAMPLE: Third quarter tax expense based on only the third quarter.

What tax rate do I use?

In computing tax expense, the estimated annual effective tax rate should be used. The effective tax rate should be based on income from continuing operations. If a reliable estimate is not practical, the actual year-to-date effective tax rate should be used.

SUGGESTION: At the end of each interim period, a revision to the effective tax rate may be necessary employing the best current estimates of the annual effective tax rate. The projected tax rate includes adjustment for net deferred credits. Adjustments should be contained in deriving the maximum tax benefit for year-to-date figures.

The estimated effective tax rate should incorporate:

- all available tax credits (e.g., foreign tax credit)
- all available alternative tax methods in determining ordinary earnings.

NOTE: A change in tax legislation is only reflected in the interim period affected.

How are income, losses, and carryforwards accounted for on interim reports?

Income statement items after income from continuing operations (e.g., income from discontinued operations, extraordinary items, cumulative effect of a change in accounting principle) should be presented net of the tax effect. Tax effect on these unusual line items should be reflected *only* in the interim period they actually occur.

CAUTION: Do not predict items before they occur. Prior period adjustments in the retained earnings statement are also shown net of tax when they take place.

The tax benefit of a previous year operating loss carryforward is recognized in each interim period to the extent that income is available to offset the loss carryforward.

What do I do about a change in principle?

When a change in principle is made *in the first interim period*, the cumulative effect of a change in principle account should be shown net of tax in the first interim period.

• If a change in principle is made *in a quarter other than the first* (e.g., third quarter), we assume the change was made at the beginning of the first quarter showing the cumulative effect in the first quarter. The interim periods will have to be *restated* using the new principle (e.g., first, second, and third quarters).

When *interim data for previous years* are presented for comparative purposes, data should be restated to conform with newly adopted policies. Alternatively, disclosure can be made of the effect on prior data, if the new practice had been applied to that period.

• *For a change in principle*, disclosure should be made of the nature and justification in the interim period of change. The effect of the change on per share amounts should be given.

What other factors affect interim results?

• Disclosure should be made of seasonality aspects affecting interim results and contingencies.

• A change in the estimated effective tax rate should be disclosed.

• If a 4th quarter is not presented, any material adjustments to that quarter must be commented upon in the footnotes to the annual report.

• If an event is immaterial on an annual basis but material in the interim period, it should be disclosed.

• Purchase or pooling transactions should be noted.

How do I present prior period adjustments?

The financial statement presentation for prior period adjustments:

- Net income for the current period should include the portion of the effect related to current operations.

- Restate earnings of impacted prior interim periods of the current year to include the portion related thereto.

- If the prior period adjustment affects prior years, include it in the earnings of the first interim period of the current year.

Criteria to be met for prior period adjustments in interim periods:

- Materiality
- Estimable
- Identified to a prior interim period

EXAMPLES: Prior period adjustments for interim reporting include:

- Error corrections
- Settlement of litigation or claims
- Adjustment of income taxes
- Renegotiation proceedings
- Utility revenue under rate making processes.

NOTES: Earnings per share is computed for interim purposes the same way as for annual purposes.

Segmental disposal is shown separately in the interim period during which it occurs.

PERSONAL FINANCIAL STATEMENTS

What are personal financial statements used for?

Personal financial statements may be prepared for an individual or family to show financial status. The accrual basis is followed. Some uses include:

- Obtaining credit
- Financial planning
- Compliance with disclosure requirements (for public officials).

What information should personal financial statements contain?

Disclosures in personal financial statements include:

- Individuals covered by the statement
- Methods used in determining current values

- Nature of joint ownership in property
- Identification of major investments
- Percentage of ownership in an identified closely-held business, including the nature of business activities consummated, and summarized financial data for the entity
- Identification of intangibles including estimated lives
- Amount of life insurance taken out
- Pension rights
- Methods and estimates employed in computing income taxes
- Particulars of receivables and payables, e.g., interest rates, pledged items, and maturities
- Noncapitalized commitments, e.g., rental agreements

What are the guidelines for preparing the statement of financial condition?

In the statement of financial condition:

• Assets are reflected at the estimated current value and are listed in the order of liquidity (maturity). Current value may be determined based on recent transactions of similar items, appraisals, present value of future cash flows from the asset, adjusting historical cost for inflation, etc.

• There is no breakdown between current and noncurrent classifications.

• Material business interests should be shown separately. EXAMPLE: A material interest in a closely held company should be shown separately from the equity investment in other companies.

• If assets are jointly owned, only the individual's beneficial interest should be reported.

• Liabilities should be shown at current amounts by order of maturity.

• Estimated current amounts is the lesser of the present value of the debt payments or the amount the liability could be currently paid off for. Usually, the liability equals the principal plus accrued interest due.

• Estimated taxes payable is shown as a liability, including provision for unpaid taxes of previous years and the estimated tax for the current year. The estimated tax for the present year should be based on the relationship of year-to-date taxable income to estimated taxable income for the year. The amount is reduced by any withholding and estimated tax payments.

• Net worth is the difference between assets and liabilities.

EXAMPLE 3.3

An illustrative statement of financial condition follows:

Mr. and Mrs. J. Smith
Statement of Financial Condition
December 31, 19X2

Assets

Cash	$ 5,000
Interest and Dividends Receivable	200
Marketable Securities	10,000
Interest in Closely Held Company	6,000
Cash Surrender Value of Life Insurance	1,000
Real Estate	100,000
Personal Property	30,000
Total	$152,200

Liabilities

Credit Cards	$ 6,000
Income Taxes Payable	3,000
Loans Payable	10,000
Mortgage Payable	60,000
	$79,000
Estimated taxes on the differences between the estimated current values of assets, the current amounts of liabilities and their tax bases	40,000
Net Worth	33,200
Total	$152,200

What role does cost basis play in the statement of financial condition?

The statement of financial condition includes another element for the tax provision based on the difference between the current estimated amounts of assets and liabilities and their respective bases.

EXAMPLE 3.4

An individual owns ABC stock that was bought five years ago for $8,000. The stock is currently worth $17,000. The individual is in the 38% tax bracket. If the individual sold the stock today, there would be a $9,000 gain, which would result in $3,420 in taxes. The $3,420 should be included in the "provision for estimated taxes on the difference between carrying amounts and tax bases of assets and liabilities." Since the $3,420 constitutes an amount of taxes that would be payable upon sale of the stock, it should be presented as a credit in the Statement of Financial Condition reducing the individual's net worth.

Is there another statement that can be prepared?

As an option, a statement of changes in net worth may be prepared. It is useful in showing the mix of business and personal items in personal financial statements. Increases and decreases in net worth are shown.

Items increasing net worth include:

- Income
- Increases in current value of assets
- Decreases in the current amounts of liabilities
- Decreases in estimated taxes on the difference between estimated current asset values and liability amounts and their tax bases.

Items decreasing net worth include:

- Expenses
- Decreases in current values of assets
- Increases in current amounts of liabilities

- Increases in estimated taxes on the difference between the current amount and the tax bases of assets and liabilities

Also optional are comparative financial statements.

INCORPORATION OF A BUSINESS

What accounting is needed when forming a corporation?

When an unincorporated entity (e.g., sole proprietorship, partnership) incorporates and issues stock or debt securities in exchange for the assets of the unincorporated business:

- The new corporation does not recognize the gain or loss on the issuance of stock in exchange for the unincorporated entity's assets
- Assets acquired are recorded at fair market value
- Current liabilities are recorded at face value
- Long-term liabilities are recorded at present value
- Stock issued is recorded at par value
- The excess of net fair market value of assets acquired over par value is credited to paid-in-capital

The journal entry is:

Cash
Current Assets
Fixed Assets
    Current Liabilities
    Long-term Liabilities
    Common Stock
    Paid-in-capital

PARTNERSHIPS

How do I account for a partnership?

When a partnership is formed:

- Assets are debited at fair market value

- Liabilities are credited for debt assumed, usually at the present value of future payments or fair value
- Capital is credited for the net difference

EXAMPLE 3.5

X and Y form a partnership. X transfers $10,000 cash, and B provides $30,000 of furniture with a loan thereon of $5,000. The journal entry is:

Cash	10,000	
Furniture	30,000	
Loans Payable		5,000
X Capital		10,000
Y Capital		25,000

What accounting changes are needed when a new partner is admitted?

A new partner may be admitted to the partnership by:

- *Buying the interest of an existing partner.* When an interest is purchased from an existing partner, it is a private transaction between the two parties not affecting the partnership's financial records. The new partner's capital account is recorded simply by re-labeling the old partner's capital account.
- *Contributing assets to the partnership* (e.g., new capital). In this case, the new partner may receive an interest in exchange for the contributed assets and/or goodwill (e.g., client following).

How is the new partner's admission accounted for?

The new partner's admission may be accounted for under either the bonus method or the goodwill method.

Bonus Method

The new partner's capital account is credited for an amount equal to his purchased share of the partnership's total capital. The total capital equals the net book value of assets before the new partner's contribution plus the fair value of net assets contributed by the new partner. A bonus arises for the difference between the fair market value of contributed assets and the credit to the new partner's capital account.

• If fair value of contributed assets *exceeds* the credit to the new partner's capital account, the excess increases the capital accounts of the old partners based on the profit and loss ratio.

• If fair value of contributed assets *is less than* the new partner's capital account, the new partner recognizes the bonus. RESULT: The bonus reduces the old partners' capital accounts based on the profit and loss ratio.

Goodwill Method

If the new partner's contribution *exceeds* the ownership interest obtained by him, the excess assets represent goodwill applicable to the old partners.

• When the new partner's asset contribution *is less than* the ownership interest received, the excess capital allowed to the new partner is construed as goodwill attributable to him.

How are profits and losses accounted for in a partnership?

Profit and loss of the partnership are divided equally unless stated otherwise in the partnership agreement. In dividing profits, the partnership may consider:

• Salary provision and interest on capital balances (interest based on the beginning, ending, or average capital)

• Time spent or capital invested

When interest and salary exceed profit, the resulting loss will be allocated based on the profit and loss ratio.

Partner drawing accounts exist to reflect cash withdrawals from the business. The drawing accounts are periodically closed to the capital accounts.

How do I treat partner withdrawals and liquidation of the partnership?

When the amount paid to a withdrawing or retiring partner exceeds his capital balance, the excess is either attributed to goodwill or charged against the remaining partners' capital balances based on the profit and loss ratio.

When a partnership is liquidated, gains or losses on sale of assets are divided among the partners based on the profit and loss ratio. The initial cash received is used to satisfy the liabilities.

NOTE: Before the cash can be distributed to a partner, liquidation losses and expenses must have been charged to the capital accounts.

CHAPTER 4

ACCOUNTING AND DISCLOSURES

Accounting changes include a change in:

• *Principle*, which requires a "cumulative effect of a change in principle" account to be shown in the current year's income statement.

• *Estimate*, which is accounted for prospectively over current and future years.

• *Reporting entity*, which mandates the restatement of previous years' financial statements as if both companies were always combined.

Corrections of errors adjust the beginning balance of retained earnings.

NOTE: Significant accounting policies must be disclosed.

Development stage companies must follow the same generally accepted accounting principles as established companies.

In a *troubled debt restructuring*, the debtor recognizes an extraordinary gain while the creditor recognizes an ordinary loss.

Segmental disclosures are required when a business segment comprises 10% or more of revenue, operating profit, or total assets of the entire company.

In the case of a noninterest bearing note, interest must be imputed based on the interest rate the borrower would normally pay for a note in an armslength transaction.

Accounting for futures contracts and oil and gas accounting problems are also addressed.

ACCOUNTING CHANGES

APB 20 provides for accounting changes in principle, estimate, and reporting entity. Correction of an error in a prior year is also briefly mentioned. Proper disclosure of accounting changes is necessary.

Change in Accounting Principle

May accounting principles be changed?

A change in principle should be made *only when necessary*. Once adopted, it is presumed that an accounting principle should not be changed for events or transactions of a similar nature. A method used for a transaction which is being terminated or was a single, nonrecurring event in the past should not be changed.

How is a change in accounting principle reflected?

A change in accounting principle is accounted for in the current year's income statement in an account called "cumulative effect of a change in accounting principle."

• The amount equals the difference between retained earnings at the beginning of the year with the old method, versus what retained earnings would have been at the beginning of the year if the new method had been used in prior years.

• The account is shown net of tax with EPS on it.

• The cumulative effect account is shown after extraordinary items and before net income in the income statement.

• The new principle is used in the current and future years. Consistency is needed for accurate user comparisons. NOTE: A change in depreciation method for a *new* fixed asset is *not* a change in principle.

NOTE: Footnote disclosure should be made of the nature of and justification for a change in principle including an explanation of why the new principle is preferred.

What justifies a change in principle?

A change in principle is justified by:

- A new FASB pronouncement
- A new tax law
- A new AICPA recommended practice
- A change in circumstances
- The need to more readily conform to industry practice

NOTES: According to FASB 32, specialized accounting practices and principles included in the AICPA Statements of Position (SOPs) and Guides are "preferable accounting principles" for the application of APB 20. Where summaries of financial data for several years are present in financial reports, APB 20 applies.

Indirect effects are included in the cumulative effect only if they are to be recorded on the books as a result of a change in accounting principle. The cumulative effect does *not* include nondiscretionary adjustments based on earnings (e.g., employee bonuses) which would have been recognized if the new principle had been used in prior years.

What about comparative financial statements?

If comparative financial statements are not shown, pro forma disclosures (recalculated figures) should be made between the body of the financial statements and the footnotes. Disclosures should show:

- What earnings would have been in prior years if the new principle was used in those prior years
- The actual amounts for those years

If income statements are presented for comparative purposes, they should reflect the change on a pro forma basis as if the change had been in effect in each of such years.

How do I present comparative financial statements?

Financial statements of prior years, presented for comparative purposes, are presented *as previously reported*. Income before extraordinary items, net income, and earnings per share for previous years presented are *recalculated* and disclosed on the face of the prior periods' income statements as if the new principle had been in use in those periods. This information may be presented in separate schedules showing both the original and recalculated figures.

NOTES: If only the current period's income statement is presented, the actual and pro forma figures for the immediately preceding period should be disclosed.

In exceptional cases, pro forma amounts are not determinable for prior years, even though the cumulative effect on the opening retained earnings balance can be computed. The cumulative effect of a change in principle is presented in the usual fashion with reasons given for omitting pro forma figures.

Similarly, when the cumulative effect of a change in principle is impossible to calculate, disclosure is given for the effect of the change on income data of the current period and explaining the reason for omitting the cumulative effect and pro forma amounts for prior periods. EXAMPLE: A switch from the FIFO to LIFO inventory pricing method.

If an accounting change in principle is deemed immaterial in the current year but is anticipated to be material in later years, disclosure is necessary.

When do I have to restate prior years after a change in principle?

Certain types of changes in accounting principle, instead of being shown in a cumulative effect account, require the restatement of prior years as if the new principle had been used in those years. These changes are:

• Change from LIFO to another inventory method

• Change in accounting for long-term construction contracts (e.g., changing from the completed contract method to the percentage of completion method)

• Change to or from the full cost method used in the extractive industry. (In the full cost method both successful and unsuccessful exploration costs are deferred to the asset account and amortized. In the alternative method only successful costs are deferred and unsuccessful ones are immediately expensed.)

Who is exempt from restating prior years after a change in principle?

A *closely held* business which for the *first time* registers securities, obtains equity capital, or effects a business combination is *exempt from the requirements of this opinion*. Such a company *may* restate prior year financial statements.

Not considered a change in accounting principle:

• A principle adopted for the first time on new or previously immaterial events or transactions.
• A principle adopted or changed due to events or transactions clearly different in substance.

What if I were to change a method, not a principle?

An *accounting principle* is not only an accounting principle or practice, but also includes the methods used to apply such principles and practices.

EXAMPLE: Changing the composition of the cost elements (e.g., material, labor, and overhead) of inventory qualifies as an accounting change. Changing the composition must be reported and justified as preferable.

The basis of preferability among the different accounting principles is established in terms of whether the new principle improves the financial reporting function. Preferability is not determinable by considering income tax effect alone.

EXAMPLE 4.1

X Company changed from double declining balance to straight-line depreciation in 19X7. It uses ACRS depreciation for tax purposes. This results in depreciation higher than the double declining balance method for each of the three years. The tax rate is 34%. Relevant data follow:

Year	Double Declining Balance Depreciation	Straight-Line Depreciation	Difference
19X5	$250,000	$150,000	$100,000
19X6	200,000	150,000	50,000
19X7	185,000	150,000	35,000

The entries to reflect the change in depreciation in 19X7 follow:

Depreciation	150,000	
Accumulated Depreciation		150,000

For current year depreciation under the straight-line method.

Accumulated Depreciation (100,000 + 50,000)	150,000	
Deferred Income Tax Credit (150,000 × .34)		51,000
Cumulative Effect of a Change in Accounting Principle		99,000

Change in Accounting Estimate

When do I change an accounting estimate?

A change in accounting estimate is caused by new circumstances or events requiring a revision in the estimates, such as a change in salvage value or in the life of an asset.

How is a change in estimate disclosed?

• A change in accounting estimate is accounted for prospectively over current and future years. There is *no* restatement of prior years.

• A footnote should describe the nature of the change.

• Disclosure is required in the period of the change for the effect on income before extraordinary items, net income, and earnings per share. Disclosure is *not* required for estimate changes in the ordinary course of business when immaterial. EXAMPLE: Revising estimates of uncollectible accounts or inventory obsolescence.

How is a change in estimate accounted for?

If a change in estimate is coupled with a change in principle and the effects cannot be distinguished, it is accounted for as a change in estimate. EXAMPLE: A change made from deferring and amortizing a cost to expensing it as incurred because of doubtful future benefits. This should be accounted for as a change in estimate.

EXAMPLE 4.2

Equipment was bought on 1/1/19X2 for $40,000, having an original estimated life of 10 years with a salvage value of $4,000. On 1/1/19X6, the estimated life was revised to 8 more years remaining with a new salvage value of $3,200. The journal entry on 12/31/19X6 for depreciation expense is:

| Depreciation | 2,800 | |
| Accumulated Depreciation | 2,800 | |

Computations follow:

Book value on 1/1/19X6:

Original cost		$40,000
Less: Accumulated Depreciation		
$\dfrac{\$40,000 - \$4,000}{10} = \$3,600 \times 4$		$14,400
Book value		$25,600

Depreciation for 19X6:

Book value	$25,600	
Less: New Salvage value	3,200	
Depreciable cost	$22,400	
$\dfrac{\text{Depreciable cost}}{\text{New Life}}$	$\dfrac{\$22,400}{8} = \$2,800$	

Change in Reporting Entity

How is a change in reporting entity treated?

A change in reporting entity (e.g., two previously separate companies combine) is accounted for by restating prior years' financial statements as if both companies were always combined.

• Restatement for a change in reporting entity is necessary to show proper trends in comparative financial statements and historical summaries.

• The effect of the change on income before extraordinary items, net income, and per share amounts is reported for all periods presented. The restatement process does not have to go back more than 5 years.

• Footnote disclosure should be made of the nature of and reason for the change in reporting entity only in the year of change.

EXAMPLES:

• Presenting consolidated statements instead of statements of individual companies

• Change in subsidiaries included in consolidated statements or those included in combined statements

• A business combination accounted for under the pooling-of-interests method

Correction of an Error

What do I do about a mistake?

A correction of an error is accounted for as a prior period adjustment. The retained earnings account absorbs the difference related to the error for previous years.

EXAMPLE 4.3

X Company acquired Y Company on 1/1/19X3, recording goodwill of $60,000. Goodwill was not amortized. The correcting entry on 12/31/19X5 follows:

Amortization Expense (1500 × 1 for 19X5)	1,500	
Retained Earnings (1500 × 2 for 19X3 and 19X4)	3,000	
Goodwill		4,500

EXAMPLE 4.4

At the end of 19X2, a company failed to accrue telephone expense which was paid at the beginning of 19X3. The correcting entry on 12/31/19X3 is:

Retained Earnings	16,000	
Telephone Expense		16,000

EXAMPLE 4.5

At the beginning of 19X5, a company bought equipment for $300,000, with a salvage value of $20,000 and an expected life of 10 years. Straight line depreciation is used. In error, salvage value was not deducted in computing depreciation. The correcting journal entries on 12/31/19X7 are:

19X5 and 19X6

Depreciation taken $300,000/10 × 2 years		$60,000
Depreciation correctly stated $280,000/10 × 2 years		$56,000 $ 4,000

Depreciation	28,000	
Accumulated Depreciation		28,000
Depreciation for current year		
Accumulated Depreciation	4,000	
Retained Earnings		4,000
Correct prior year depreciation misstatement		

PRIOR PERIOD ADJUSTMENTS

What are prior period adjustments?

The two types of prior period adjustments are:

- Recognition of a tax loss carryforward benefit arising from a purchased subsidiary.
- Correction of an error that was made in a prior year.

Errors may be due to mathematical mistakes, errors in applying accounting principles, or misuse of facts existing when the financial statements were prepared. Further, a change in principle from one that is not GAAP to one that is GAAP is an error correction.

Disclosure should be made of the nature of the error and the effect of correction on earnings.

How are prior period adjustments made?

When a single year is presented, prior period adjustments adjust the beginning balance of retained earnings. The presentation follows:

Retained Earnings—1/1 Unadjusted

Prior Period Adjustments (net of tax)

Retained Earnings—1/1 Adjusted

Add: Net Income

Less: Dividends

Retained Earnings—12/31

When comparative statements are prepared, a retroactive adjustment for the error is made insofar as it effects the prior years. The retroactive adjustment is disclosed by showing the effects of the adjustment on previous years' earnings and component items of net income.

EXAMPLE 4.6

On 1/1/19X2, an advance retainer fee of $50,000 was received covering a 5 year period. In error, revenue was credited for the full amount. The error was discovered on 12/31/19X4, before closing the books. The correcting entry is:

12/31/19X4 Retained		
Earnings	30,000	
Revenue		10,000
Deferred Revenue		20,000

EXAMPLE 4.7

A company bought a machine on January 1, 19X4, for $32,000 with a $2,000 salvage value and a five year life. Repairs expense was charged in error. The mistake was discovered on December 31, 19X7, before closing the books. The correcting entry is:

Depreciation Expense	6,000	
Machine	32,000	
Accumulated Depreciation		24,000
Retained Earnings		14,000

Accumulated depreciation of $24,000 is calculated below:

$$\frac{\$32,000 - \$2,000}{5} = \$6,000 \text{ per year} \times$$

4 years = $24,000

The credit to retained earnings reflects the difference between the erroneous repairs expense of $32,000 in 19X4 versus showing depreciation expense of $18,000 for three years (19X4–19X6).

DISCLOSURE OF ACCOUNTING POLICIES

What are accounting policies?

Accounting policies include accounting principles and methods of application in the presentation of financial statements, including:

- A selection from generally accepted accounting principles
- Practices unique to the given industry
- Unusual applications of generally accepted accounting principles

What should be described regarding accounting policies?

The first footnote or section preceding the notes to the financial statements should be a description of the accounting policies followed by the company.

EXAMPLES:

- The depreciation method used
- Consolidation bases
- Amortization period for goodwill
- Construction contract method
- Inventory pricing method

NOTES: Financial statement classification methods and qualitative data (e.g., litigation) are *not* accounting policies.

Non-profit entities should also disclose the accounting policies followed.

The application of GAAP requires the use of *judgment* where alternative acceptable principles exist and where varying methods of applying a principle to a given set of facts exist.

Disclosure of these principles and methods *is vital* to the full presentation of financial position and operations, so that rational economic decisions can be made.

Is disclosure of accounting policies always necessary?

Some types of financial statements do not need a description of the accounting policies followed.

EXAMPLES:

- Quarterly unaudited statements when there has not been a policy change since the last year-end
- Statements solely for internal use

DEVELOPMENT STAGE COMPANIES

What are development stage entities?

A development stage entity is one concentrating on establishing a new business, where major operations have not begun or operations have started but no significant revenue has been derived. Some activities of a development stage enterprise are:

- Establishing sources of supply
- Developing markets
- Obtaining financing
- Financial and production planning
- Research and development
- Buying capital assets
- Recruiting staff.

What are the requirements for a development stage company?

The *same* generally accepted accounting principles for an established company must be followed by a development stage enterprise. A balance sheet, income statement, and statement of cash flows are prepared.

• The balance sheet shows the accumulated net losses as a deficit.

• The income statement presents cumulative amounts of revenues and expenses since inception of the business.

• Similarly, the statement of cash flows presents the operating, investing, and financing cash receipts and cash payments.

• The stockholders' equity statement shows for each equity security from inception the date and number of shares issued and dollar figures per share applicable to cash and noncash consideration.

The nature and basis for determining amounts of noncash consideration must also be provided.

NOTES: Financial statements must be headed "development stage enterprise."

A footnote should describe the development stage activities.

In the first year that the entity is no longer in the development stage, it should disclose that in previous years it was.

TROUBLED DEBT RESTRUCTURING

What is a troubled debt restructuring?

In a troubled debt restructuring, a debtor in financial difficulty receives partial or complete forgiveness of the obligation by the creditor. The concession may be:

- By debtor-creditor agreement
- Imposed by law
- By foreclosure and repossession

Some types of troubled debt restructurings are:

• Debtor transfers to creditor receivables from third parties or other assets in part or full satisfaction of the debt.

• Debtor gives creditor equity securities to satisfy the debt.

• Modification of the debt terms including downwardly adjusting the interest rate, lengthening the maturity date, or reducing the face amount of the obligation.

The debtor recognizes an extraordinary gain (net of tax) on the restructuring, while the creditor recognizes a loss. The loss may be ordinary or extraordinary, depending on whether such arrangement by the creditor is unusual and infrequent. Typically, the loss is ordinary.

Debtor

How is the debtor's gain disclosed?

The gain to the debtor equals the difference between the fair value of assets exchanged and the book value of the debt including accrued interest. Further, there may be a gain on disposal of assets exchanged in the transaction equal to the difference between the fair market value and the book value of the transferred assets. The latter gain or loss is *not* a gain or loss on restructuring, but rather an ordinary gain or loss in connection with asset disposal.

EXAMPLE 4.8

A debtor transferred assets having a fair value of $80 and a book value of $60 in settlement of a payable with a carrying value of $90. The gain on restructuring is $10 ($90 − $80). The ordinary gain is $20 ($80 − $60).

What if the debtor transfers stock to the creditor?

A debtor may transfer an equity interest to the creditor. The debtor enters the equity securities issued on the basis of fair market value rather than the recorded value of the debt satisfied. The excess of the recorded payable satisfied over the fair market value of the securities issued is an extraordinary gain.

What must I do if the original debt agreement is changed?

When a modification in terms of an initial debt agreement exists, it is *accounted for prospectively*. There is a new interest rate computed based on the new terms. This interest rate is then employed to allocate future payments to reduce principal and interest. When the new terms of the agreement cause the sum of all the future payments to be *less* than the book value of the payable, the payable is reduced, and a restructuring gain is recognized for the difference. Future payments are construed as a reduction of principal only. No interest expense is recognized.

Is a transfer of assets the only way to restructure a debt?

A troubled debt restructuring may result in a *combination* of concessions to the debtor. This may occur when assets or an equity interest are transferred for *partial* satisfaction of the debt, and the balance is subject to a modification of terms. Two steps are involved:

- The payable is reduced by the fair market value of the assets or equity transferred

- The remaining part of the debt is accounted for as a "modification of terms" type restructuring

Direct costs (e.g., legal fees) incurred by the debtor in an equity transfer lower the fair value of the equity interest. All other costs reduce the gain on restructuring. If there is no gain involved, they are expensed.

Footnote disclosure by the debtor includes:

- Explaining the particulars of the restructuring agreement
- The aggregate and per share amounts of the gain on restructuring
- Amounts that are contingently payable including the contingency terms

Creditor

What is done if the creditor cannot collect?

The creditor's loss is the difference between the fair market value of assets received and the book value of the investment. In a modification of terms situation:

- The creditor recognizes interest income to the extent total future payments exceed the carrying value of the investment. Interest income is recognized using the effective interest method.
- Assets received are recorded at fair market value.
- When the carrying value of the receivable is greater than the aggregate payments, an ordinary loss is booked for the difference.
- All cash received in the future is accounted for as a recovery of the investment.
- Direct costs incurred by the creditor are expensed.

NOTES: The creditor does not recognize contingent interest until the contingency is removed and interest has been earned.

Future changes in the interest rate are accounted for as a change in estimate.

Footnote disclosure by the creditor includes:

- Commitments to lend additional funds to financially troubled debtors
- Loans and/or receivables by major class
- Debt agreements where the interest rate has been modified, explaining the particulars
- Description of terms of the restructuring

EXAMPLE 4.9

The debtor owes the creditor $100,000 and has indicated that because of financial problems there may be difficulty in meeting future payments. Footnote disclosure by the creditor and debtor are needed surrounding the financial problems.

EXAMPLE 4.10

The debtor owes the creditor $100,000. The creditor relieves the debtor of $20,000. The balance of the obligation will be paid at a later date. The journal entries are:

Debtor			*Creditor*		
Accounts					
Payable	20,000		Ordinary Loss	20,000	
Extraordinary			Accounts		
Gain		20,000	Receivable		20,000

EXAMPLE 4.11

The debtor owes the creditor $50,000. The creditor agrees to accept $45,000 in payment in full satisfaction of the debt. The journal entries are:

Debtor			*Creditor*		
Accounts					
Payable	5,000		Ordinary Loss	5,000	
Extraordinary			Accounts		
Gain		5,000	Receivable		5,000

SEGMENTAL REPORTING

What is segmental reporting?

Segmental data occurs when a company prepares a full set of financial statements (balance sheet, income statement, statement of cash flows, and related footnotes). The data are shown for each year presented. Information reported is a disaggregation of consolidated financial information.

Segmental information assists financial statement users in analyzing financial statements by allowing improved assessment of an enterprise's past performance and future prospects.

Financial reporting for business segments is useful in evaluating segmental performance, earning potential, and risk.

Segmental reporting may be by:

- Industry
- Foreign geographic area
- Export sales
- Major customers
- Governmental contracts

An industry segment sells merchandise or renders services to outside customers.

EXCEPTION: Segmental information is not required for nonpublic companies or in interim reports.

Do special principles apply to segmental reporting?

Accounting principles employed in preparing financial statements should be used for segment information, except that numerous intercompany transactions eliminated in consolidation are included in segmental reporting on a gross basis. The financial statement presentation for segments may appear in the body, footnotes, or in a separate schedule to the financial statements.

When must a segment be reported?

A segment must be reported if any of these criteria are met:

- Revenue is 10% or more of total revenue
- Operating income or loss is 10% or more of the combined operating profit
- Identifiable assets are 10% or more of the total identifiable assets

How are reportable segments established?

Reportable segments are determined by:

- Identifying specific products and services
- Grouping those products and services into segments by industry line
- Selecting material segments to the company as a whole

A number of approaches are possible in grouping products and services by industry lines. In many cases, management judgment is necessary to determine the industry segment.

A starting point in deriving the industry segment is by *profit center*. When the profit center crosses industry lines, it should be broken down into smaller groups. A company in an industry not accumulating financial information on a segregated basis must disaggregate its operations by industry line.

Although worldwide industry segmentation is recommended, it may not be practical. If foreign operations cannot be disaggregated, the firm should disaggregate domestic activities. Foreign operations should be disaggregated where possible and the remaining foreign operations treated as a single segment.

How do I determine whether a segment is significant?

According to FASB 14, a segment that was significant in the past, even though not meeting the 10% test in the current year, should still be reported if it is expected that the segment will be significant in the future.

Segments should constitute a substantial portion (75% or more) of the company's total revenue to outside customers. The 75% test is applied separately each year.

In order to derive 75%, no more than 10 segments should be shown for practical purposes. If more than 10 are identified, similar segments may be combined.

NOTES: Even though intersegment transfers are eliminated in the preparation of consolidated financial statements, they are includable for segmental disclosure in determining the 10% and 75% rules.

Disclosures are not required for 90% enterprises (i.e., a company that derives 90% or more of its revenue, operating profit, and total assets from one segment). In effect, that segment *is* the business. The dominant industry segment should be identified.

How is the 10% criterion applied?

In applying the 10% criterion, the accountant should note the following:

• *Revenue.* Revenue to unaffiliated customers and revenue to other business segments should be separated. Transfer prices are used for intersegmental transfers. Accounting bases followed should be disclosed.

• *Operating Profit or Loss.* Operating earnings of a segment excludes:

> • General corporate revenue and expenses that are not allocable
> • Interest expense (unless the segment is a financial type, such as one involved in banking)
> • Domestic and foreign income taxes
> • Income from unconsolidated subsidiaries or investees
> • Income from discontinued operations
> • Extraordinary items
> • Cumulative effect of a change in accounting principles
> • Minority interest.

Note: Directly traceable and allocable costs should be charged to segments when applicable thereto.

• *Identifiable Assets.* Assets of a segment include those directly in it and general corporate assets that can rationally be allocated to it. Allocation methods should be consistently applied. Identifiable assets include those consisting of a part of the company's investment in the segment (e.g., goodwill). Identifiable assets do not include advances or loans to other segments except for income therefrom that is used to compute the results of operations (e.g., a segment of a financial nature).

What disclosures do segments have to make?

Disclosures to be made by segments include:

- Aggregate depreciation, depletion and amortization expense
- Capital expenditures
- Company's equity in vertically integrated, unconsolidated subsidiaries and equity method investees (Note the geographic location of equity method investees)
- Effect of an accounting principle change on the operating profit of the reportable segment, including its effect on the company
- Material segmental accounting policies not already disclosed in the regular financial statements
- Transfer price used
- Allocation method for costs
- Unusual items affecting segmental profit
- Type of products

How does consolidation affect segmental reporting?

If a segment includes a *purchase method* consolidated subsidiary, the required segmental information is based on the consolidated value of the subsidiary (i.e., fair market value and goodwill recognized), *not* on the values recorded in the subsidiary's own financial statements. However, transactions between the segment and other segments, which are eliminated in consolidation, *are* reportable.

Segmental data are *not* required for *unconsoli-*

dated subsidiaries or other *unconsolidated investees*. NOTE: Each subsidiary or investee is subject to the rules of FASB 14 requiring that segment information be reported.

Some types of typical consolidation eliminations are *not* eliminated when reporting for segments. EXAMPLE: Revenue of a segment includes intersegmental sales and sales to unrelated customers.

A full set of financial statements for a foreign investee that is *not* a subsidiary does not have to disclose segmental information when presented in the same financial report of a primary reporting entity. EXCEPTION: The foreign investee's separately issued statements already disclose the required segmental data.

Are there other requirements that apply to segmental reporting?

The source of the segmental revenue should be disclosed, along with the percent so derived, when:

• 10% or more of revenue or assets is associated with a foreign area. Presentation must be made of revenue, operating profit or loss, and assets for foreign operations in the aggregate or by geographic area. (A foreign geographic area is a foreign country or group of homogeneous countries. Factors considered are geographical proximity, economic affinity, and similar business environments.)

• 10% or more of sales is to one customer. A group of customers under common control is construed as one customer.

• 10% or more of revenue is obtained from either domestic or foreign government contracts.

In some instances, *restatement* of prior period information is required for *comparative* reasons when:

• Financial statements of the company as a whole have been restated

• There is a pooling-of-interests

• A change has occurred in grouping products or services for segment determination

• A change has taken place in grouping of foreign activities into geographic segments

The nature and effect of restatement should be disclosed.

NOTE: Per FASB 24, segmental data that are presented in another company's financial report are not required in financial statements if those statements are:

- Combined in a complete set of statements, and both sets are presented in the same report
- Presented for a foreign investee (not a subsidiary of the primary enterprise) unless the financial statements disclose segment information (e.g., foreign investees for which such information is already required by the SEC)
- Presented in the report of a nonpublic company

NOTE: If an investee uses the cost or equity method and is not exempted by one of the above provisions, its full set of financial statements presented in another enterprise's report must present segment information if such data are significant to statements of the primary enterprise. Significance is determined by applying the percentage tests of FASB 14 (i.e., 10% tests) to the financial statements of the primary enterprise without adjustment for the investee's revenue, operating results, or identifiable assets.

IMPUTING INTEREST ON NOTES

What if a noninterest bearing note exists?

If the face amount of a note does not represent the present value of the consideration given or received in the exchange, imputation of interest is needed to avoid the misstatement of profit. Interest is imputed:

- On noninterest bearing notes
- On notes that provide for an unrealistically low interest rate
- When the face value of the note is significantly different from the "going" selling price of the property or market value of the note

NOTES: If a note is issued only for cash, the note should be recorded at the cash exchanged, irrespective of whether the interest rate is reasonable or of the amount of the face value of the note. The note has a present value at issuance equal to the cash transacted.

When a note is exchanged for property, goods, or services a presumption exists that the interest rate is fair and reasonable. Where the stipulated interest rate is not fair and adequate, the note has to be recorded at the fair value of the merchandise or services or at an amount that approximates fair value. If fair value is not determinable for the goods or services, the discounted present value of the note has to be used.

How do I determine the imputed interest rate?

The imputed interest rate is the one that would have resulted if an independent borrower or lender had negotiated a similar transaction. EXAMPLE: It is the prevailing interest rate the borrower would have paid for financing.

Factors to consider in deriving an appropriate discount rate:

- Prime interest rate
- "Going" market rate for similar quality instruments
- Issuer's credit standing
- Collateral
- Restrictive covenants and other terms in the note agreement
- Tax effects of the arrangement

For what kinds of instruments does imputed interest have to be determined?

APB 21 applies to long-term payables and receivables. Short-term payables and receivables are typically recorded at face value since the extra work of amortizing a discount or premium on a short-term note is not worth the information benefit obtained.

APB 21 is *not* applicable to:

- Security deposits
- Usual lending activities of banks
- Amounts that do not mandate repayment
- Receivables or payables occurring within the ordinary course of business
- Transactions between parent and subsidiary

How are premiums and discounts determined and handled?

The difference between the face value of the note and the present value of the note represents discount or premium. This must be accounted for as an element of interest over the life of the note. Present value of the payments of the note is based on an imputed interest rate.

The interest method is used to amortize the discount or premium on the note. The interest method results in a constant rate of interest.

Amortization = Interest Rate × Present Value of the Liability/Receivable at the beginning of the year

Interest expense is recorded for the borrower while interest revenue is recorded for the lender. Issuance costs are treated as a deferred charge.

The note payable and note receivable are presented in the balance sheet this way:

Notes Payable (principal plus interest)

Less: Discount (interest)

Present Value (principal)

Notes Receivable (principal plus interest)

Less: Premium (interest)

Present Value (principal)

EXAMPLE 4.12

On 1/1/19X1, a machine is bought for $10,000 cash and the incurrence of a $30,000, five year, noninterest bearing note payable. The imputed interest rate is 10%. The present value factor for n = 5, i = 10% is .62. Appropriate journal entries are:

1/1/19X1

Machine (10,000 + 18,600)	28,600	
Discount	11,400	
Notes Payable		30,000
Cash		10,000

Present value of note equals $30,000 × .62 = $18,600. On 1/1/19X1, the balance sheet shows:

Notes Payable	$30,000
Less: Discount	11,400
Present Value	$18,600

12/31/19X1

Interest Expense	1,860	
Discount		1,860

10% × $18,600 = $1,860

On 1/1/19X2, the balance sheet shows:

Notes Payable	$30,000
Less: Discount (11,400 − 1,860)	9,540
Present Value	$20,460

12/31/19X2

Interest Expense	2,046	
Discount		2,046

10% × $20,460 = $2,046

ACCOUNTING FOR FUTURES CONTRACTS

What are futures contracts?

A futures contract is a legal arrangement entered into by the purchaser or seller and a regulated futures exchange in the U.S. or overseas. FASB 80 does not apply to foreign currencies futures which are dealt with in FASB 82. Futures contracts involve:

• A buyer or seller receiving or making a delivery of a commodity or financial instrument (e.g., stocks, bonds, commercial paper, mortgages) at a given date. Cash settlement rather than delivery often exists (e.g., stock index future).

• A futures contract may be eliminated prior to the delivery date by engaging in an offsetting contract for the particular commodity or financial instrument involved. EXAMPLE: A futures contract to buy 100,000 pounds of a commodity by December 31, 19X1, may be cancelled by entering into another contract to sell 100,000 pounds of that same commodity on December 31, 19X1.

• Changes in value of open contracts are settled regularly (e.g., daily). The usual contract provides that when a decrease in the contract value occurs, the contract holder has to make a cash deposit for such decline with the clearinghouse. If the contract increases in value, the holder may withdraw the increased value.

When does a futures position constitute a hedge?

A *hedge* exists when both of the following criteria are met:

• The hedged item places price and interest rate risk on the firm. Risk means the sensitivity of corporate earnings to market price changes or rates of return of existing assets, liabilities, commitments, and expected transactions. NOTE: This criterion is *not* met where other assets, liabilities, commitments, and anticipated transactions *already* offset the risk.

• The contract lowers risk exposure and is entered into as a hedge. High correlation exists between the change in market value of the contract and the fair value of the hedged item. In effect, the market price change of the contract offsets the price and interest rate changes on the exposed item. EXAMPLE: When a futures contract exists to sell silver that offsets the changes in the price of silver.

How do I handle a change in the market value of the futures contract?

The change in market value of a futures contract involves a gain or loss that should be recognized in earnings. EXCEPTION: For certain contracts the timing of income statement recognition relates to the accounting for the applicable asset, liability, commitment, or transaction. This accounting exception applies when the contract is designed as a hedge against price and interest rate fluctuation. When the above criteria are met, the accounting for the contract relates to the accounting for the hedged item. Thus, a change in market value is recognized in the same accounting period during which the effects of related changes in price or interest rate of the hedged item are reflected in income.

What are the requirements for a "hedge-type" futures contract?

• A change in market value of a futures contract that meets the hedging criteria of the related asset or liability should adjust the carrying value of the hedged item. EXAMPLE: A company has an investment in a government bond that it anticipates selling at a later date. The company can reduce its susceptibility to changes in fair value of the bonds by engaging in a futures contract. The changes in the market value of the futures contract adjusts the book value of the bonds.

• A change in market value of a futures contract for the purpose of hedging a firm commitment is included in measuring the transaction satisfying the commitment. When the company hedges a firm purchase commitment by using a futures contract and the acquisition takes place thus satisfying the purchase commitment, the gain or loss on the futures contract is an element of the cost of the acquired item. EXAMPLE: Assume ABC Company has a purchase commitment for 30,000 pounds of a commodity at $2 per pound, totaling $60,000. At the time of the consummation of the transaction, the $60,000 cost is *decreased* by any gain (e.g., $5,000) arising from the hedged futures contract. The net cost is shown as the carrying value ($55,000).

• The accounting applicable for a hedged futures contract related to an expected asset acquisition or liability incurrence should be consistent with the company's accounting method employed for those assets and liabilities. EXAMPLE: The firm should book a loss for a futures contract that is a hedge of an expected inventory acquisition, if the amount will not be recovered from the sale of inventory.

• If a hedged futures contract is closed prior to

the expected transaction, the accumulated value change in the contract should be carried forward to be included in measuring the related transaction. If it is probable that the quantity of an expected transaction will be less than the amount initially hedged, recognize a gain or loss for a pro rata portion of futures results that would have been included in the measurement of the subsequent transaction.

NOTE: A "hedged" futures contract requires disclosure of:

- Firm commitments
- Nature of assets and liabilities
- Accounting method used for the contract, including a description of events or transactions resulting in recognizing changes in contract values
- Transactions expected to be hedged with futures contracts

How do I account for an anticipatory hedge contract?

A futures contract may apply to transactions the company *expects* to conduct in the ordinary course of business, but is not obligated to. These expected transactions do not involve existing assets or liabilities or transactions applicable to *existing* firm commitments. EXAMPLE: A company may *anticipate* buying a certain commodity in the future but has not made a formal purchase commitment. The company may minimize risk exposure to price changes by entering into a futures contract. The change in market value of this "anticipatory hedge" contract is included in measuring the subsequent transaction. The change in market value of the futures contract adjusts the cost of the acquired item.

Four criteria must be met for "anticipatory hedge" accounting:

- The first two are the same as the criteria for regular hedge contracts related to *existing* assets, liabilities, or firm commitments.
- Identification exists of the major terms of the contemplated transaction. Included are the type of

commodity or financial instrument, quantity, and expected transaction date. If the financial instrument carries interest, the maturity date should be given.

• It is probable that the expected transaction will take place. Probability of occurrence depends on

- Time period involved
- Monetary commitment for the activity
- Financial capability to conduct the transaction
- Frequency of previous transactions of a similar nature
- Possibility that other types of transactions may be undertaken to accomplish the desired goal
- Adverse operational effects of not engaging in the transaction

OIL- AND GAS-PRODUCING COMPANIES

What should I know about oil and gas accounting?

Under the successful efforts method used by oil and gas companies, *successful costs* of exploration are deferred and amortized. *Unsuccessful costs* of exploration are immediately expensed.

Capitalization should be made of these expenditures:

- Mineral interests in properties classified as proved or unproved
- Wells and related equipment
- Support equipment and facilities used in oil and gas producing activities
- Uncompleted wells, equipment, and facilities

These capitalized costs should be amortized as the oil and gas reserves are produced. Unproved properties should be assessed on a periodic basis and losses recognized. Costs not resulting in the acquisition of an asset should be expensed.

Disclosures include:

- Net quantities of proved reserves and changes during the year

- Capitalized costs
- Property acquisitions
- Exploration and development costs
- Results of operations
- A measure of discounted future net cash flows
- Production (lifting) costs

CHAPTER 5

KEY FINANCIAL ACCOUNTING AREAS

CONSOLIDATIONS

What is a consolidation?

Consolidation occurs when the parent owns more than 50% of the voting common stock of the subsidiary. The objective of consolidation is to present as one economic unit the financial position and operating results of a parent and subsidiaries. It shows the group as a single company with one or more branches or divisions, rather than as separate companies.

The companies making up the consolidated group keep their individual legal identities. Adjustments and eliminations are for the sole purpose of financial statement reporting.

NOTE: Consolidation is still appropriate even if the subsidiary has a material amount of debt. Disclosure should be made of the firm's consolidation policy in footnotes or by explanatory headings.

When is a consolidation not valid?

A consolidation is negated, even if more than 50% of voting common stock is owned by the parent, in these instances:

• Parent is not in actual control of subsidiary. *EXAMPLES:* Subsidiary is in receivership or in a politically unstable foreign country.

• Parent has sold or contracted to sell subsidiary shortly after year-end. The subsidiary is a temporary investment.

• Minority interest is very large in comparison to the parent's interest; individual financial statements are more appropriate.

How is a consolidation accounted for?

Intercompany eliminations include those for intercompany payables and receivables, advances, and profits. For certain regulated companies, intercompany profit does not have to be eliminated to the extent the profit represents a reasonable return on investment. Subsidiary investment in the parent's shares is not consolidated outstanding stock in the consolidated balance sheet.

NOTE: Consolidated statements *do not* reflect capitalized earnings in the form of stock dividends by subsidiaries subsequent to acquisition.

Minority interest in a subsidiary is the stockholders' equity in the partially owned subsidiaries outside of the parent's controlling interest. It should be shown as a separate component of stockholders' equity. When losses applicable to the minority interest in a subsidiary exceed the minority interest's equity capital, the excess and any subsequent losses related to the minority interest are charged to the parent. If profit subsequently occurs, the parent's interest is credited to the degree of prior losses absorbed.

NOTE: If a parent acquires a subsidiary in more than one block of stock, each purchase is on a step-by-step basis, and consolidation does not occur until control exists.

• *When the subsidiary is acquired within the year*, the subsidiary should be included in consolidation as if it had been bought at the beginning of the year with a subtraction for the preacquisition part of earnings applicable to each block of stock. ALTERNATIVE APPROACH: Include in consolidation the subsidiary's earnings subsequent to the acquisition date.

• *The retained earnings of a subsidiary* at the acquisition date are not included in the consolidated financial statements.

• When the *subsidiary is disposed of during the*

year, the parent should present its equity in the subsidiary's earnings prior to the sale date as a separate line item consistent with the equity method.

• A subsidiary whose *major business activity is leasing* to a parent should always be consolidated.

• Consolidation is still permissible without adjustments when the fiscal year-ends of the parent and subsidiary are 3 months or less apart. Footnote disclosure of material events occurring during the intervening period is needed.

What methods of accounting may be used?

The *equity method* of accounting is used for unconsolidated subsidiaries, unless there is a foreign investment or a temporary investment.

When the equity method is not used, the *cost method* is followed. The cost method recognizes the difference between the cost of the subsidiary and the equity in net assets at the acquisition date. Depreciation is adjusted for the difference as if consolidation of the subsidiary was made. There is an elimination of intercompany gain or loss for unconsolidated subsidiaries to the extent the gain or loss exceeds the unrecorded equity in undistributed earnings.

REQUIREMENT: Unconsolidated subsidiaries accounted for with the cost method should have adequate disclosure of assets, liabilities, and earnings. Such disclosure may be in footnote or supplementary schedule form.

Wouldn't combined statements sometimes be valid?

There are instances where combined financial statements are more appropriate than consolidated statements. EXAMPLE: A person owns a controlling interest in several related operating companies (brother-sister corporation).

NOTE: There are cases where parent company statements are required in addition to consolidated statements, in order to properly provide information to creditors and preferred stockholders. In this event, *dual columns* are needed—one column for the parent and other columns for subsidiaries.

BUSINESS COMBINATIONS

What is the distinction between pooling and purchase?

A business combination occurs before a consolidation. Business combinations may be accounted for under the pooling-of-interests method and the purchase method. Criteria for pooling and purchase, accounting and reporting requirements, and disclosures must be considered.

• *The purchase method:* Used when cash or other assets are given or liabilities incurred to effect the combination. An acquisition of a minority interest is always a purchase at a later date even if the original acquisition was accounted for as a pooling.

• *The pooling-of-interests method:* Used when there is an exchange of voting common stock and *all* the 12 criteria for a pooling are satisfied. In a pooling, it is assumed for accounting purposes that both companies were always combined. No purchase or sale is assumed to have taken place. A pooling is a union of the ownership interests of the two previously separated groups of stockholders.

Pooling-of-Interests Method

What is a pooling-of-interests?

A pooling-of-interests deals with:

• Independence of the combining companies
• Time period for consummation of the combination
• Voting rights
• Consideration given in the exchange
• Purchase of treasury stock
• Ownership interests
• Absence of planned transactions

The 12 criteria, *all of which must be met*, for a pooling are listed below. NOTE: When more than one company is acquired in a combination plan, all pooling criteria must be met by each company.

1. The combining companies are autonomous. A combining company must not have been a subsidiary or division of any other combining company within two years before the initiation date. NOTE: A new company incorporated within two years qualifies unless it is in any respect a successor to a company not considered autonomous.

2. The combining companies are independent. A combining company may not own 10% or more of another combining company's voting common stock at the initiation or consummation dates or at any time in between. NOTES: A change in the exchange ratio results in a new initiation date. The *consummation* date is the date on which the net assets are transferred to the acquiring company. However, temporary assets (e.g., cash, marketable securities) may be held to settle liabilities and contingent items.

3. The combining companies come together in a single transaction *or* within one year after the initiation date. A delay is allowed for litigation or governmental action. EXAMPLE: If the combination took 15 months, but 4 months resulted from a delay due to anti-trust litigation, this criterion is still satisfied.

4. The acquiring company issues voting common stock in exchange for 90% or more of the voting common stock of the acquired company. The following shares of the combiners are excluded from the 90% minimum:

- Shares owned by the issuing company or its subsidiaries prior to the initiation date
- Shares acquired by the initiating company other than by issuing its own common stock
- Shares outstanding subsequent to the consummation date

In determining if 90% of the stock of the combiner has been transferred to the issuing corporation, the number of shares transferred must be reduced by the equivalent number of shares of the issuing corporation owned by the combiner before combination. This reduced number of shares is then compared to 90% of the *total* outstanding shares of the combiner company, to determine if the requirement is satisfied.

An acquiring company may give cash or common stock for debt or preferred stock of an acquired business and qualify as a pooling, *only if* the debt securities and preferred stock were not issued in an exchange for voting common stock of the acquired business within two years before the initiation date.

A combination plan may not provide for a pro rata cash distribution, but may within certain restrictions have a cash distribution for fractional shares. Cash may also be used in a combination plan to retire or redeem callable debt and equity securities.

5. None of the combining companies alters the equity interest of voting common stock in anticipation of the combination in the two years preceding the combination. The voting interest is deemed changed for abnormal dividends based on taking into account profits and prior dividends.

6. Treasury stock is acquired by a combining company for reasons other than the business combination between the initiation and consummation dates. Treasury stock may be acquired for purposes of a stock option plan, compensation plan, or similar recurring transactions.

7. The relative ownership percentage of each stockholder in the combined entity remains the same as before. EXAMPLE: If Mr. A and Mr. B owned 2% of XYZ Company, they should still own the same percentage in the newly formed entity (e.g., 1.5%).

8. There is no restriction in voting rights among stockholders by the combined entity (e.g., delayed voting rights).

9. The combination is finalized at the consummation date with no pending provisions of any kind related to the combination. EXAMPLE: No contingently issuable shares or distribution of assets to the former stockholders of the combining companies are allowed.

10–12. There is an absence of planned or subsequent transactions related to the combination as follows:

10. Repurchase of stock issued to effect the combination.

11. Financial arrangements benefiting former stockholders of the combining companies. EXAMPLE: Guarantying loans secured by stock issued in the combination which in substance negates the exchange of equity securities.

12. Sale of a significant part of the combined entity's assets within two years subsequent to the combination, such as the disposal of a division. EXCEPTION: The disposal of a duplicate warehouse would be in the ordinary course of business.

How do I account for a pooling?

The accounting for a pooling is based on recognizing net assets at book value with earnings recognized for the entire year. The accounting under the pooling method is:

• Net assets of the acquired company are brought forth at book value.

• Retained earnings and paid-in-capital of the acquired company are brought forth at book value. NOTE: There is no change in *total* stockholders' equity but the equity components do change. Any necessary adjustments are made to paid-in-capital. In the event that paid-in-capital is insufficient to absorb the difference, retained earnings would be reduced next; retained earnings may not be increased. If there is a deficit in retained earnings for a combining entity, it is continued in the combined entity.

• Net income of the acquired company is brought forth for the entire year irrespective of the date of acquisition.

• Expenses of the pooling are charged against earnings as incurred. EXAMPLES: Registration fees, finders' fees, consultants' fees.

• A gain or loss from the sale of a major part of the assets of the acquired business within two years subsequent to combination is considered an extraordinary item.

EXAMPLE 5.1

The mechanics of a pooling follow:

	Company X	Company Y	Combined
Assets	$300	$100	$400
Liabilities	50	20	70
Equity	250	80	*

*Addition of:
- Capital stock of Company X before.
- Capital stock issued in the pooling.
- Retained earnings of both.
- Paid-in-capital absorbs the difference.

NOTE: There can be no new assets from a pooling. In the year of pooling, recurring intercompany transactions should be eliminated to the degree possible from the beginning of the period. Nonrecurring intercompany transactions relating to long-term assets and liabilities do not have to be eliminated.

What if different GAAPs are used by the combining companies?

Where one combining company employs a different GAAP than another (e.g., straight-line vs. double declining balance depreciation), the company is permitted to change to the GAAP used by the other combiner(s) and to record the cumulative effect of a change in accounting principle. REQUIREMENTS: Prior year financial statements, when issued on a pooled basis should be restated for accounting principle changes.

In what other ways may a pooling occur?

An issuing company may effect a pooling by distributing treasury stock (acquired prior to two years before combination). The transfer of this stock is accounted for as if the stock had been *retired* and then reissued to effect the combination. The reissuance of this stock is accounted for in the same way as the issuance of new shares.

Combining companies may hold investments in the common stock of each other. The accounting treatment is:

- Investment of a combiner in the common stock of the *issuing* corporation: The stock is in effect returned to the resulting combined entity and should be accounted for as treasury stock.

- Investments in the common stock of the *other* combining companies: This is an investment in the type of stock which is exchanged for the new shares issued. It should be accounted for as *retired* stock.

What should be said about a pooling in the footnotes?

Footnote disclosure describes the terms of the agreement and accounting adjustments made, including:

- Name and description of combined companies
- Statement that it is a pooling
- Description and number of shares issued to effect the pooling
- Net income of the previously separate companies
- Accounting method used for intercompany transactions
- Adjustments required to net assets so the combining companies are employing the same accounting methods, with related effects on earnings
- Particulars of changes in retained earnings due to a change in fiscal year of a combining company
- Reconciliation of profits previously reported by the issuing company

What are the advantages and disadvantages of pooling?

An advantage of pooling is the retention of historical cost. A disadvantage from a financial reader's perspective is the possible overstated earnings.

EXAMPLES:

- Picking up net income for the whole year regardless of acquisition date

- Lower depreciation charges related to purchase method
- Sale of low-cost basis assets at a gain

Purchase Method

When is there a purchase?

If any one of the 12 criteria is not satisfied for a pooling, the business combination is accounted for as a purchase. A purchase typically involves either the payment of assets or incurrence of liabilities for the other business. To effect a purchase, more than 50% of voting common stock has to be acquired.

How do I account for a purchase?

The accounting followed for a purchase is:

1. Net assets of the acquired company are brought forth at fair market value. Guidelines in assigning values to individual assets acquired and liabilities assumed (except goodwill) follow:

—*Marketable securities*—Current net realizable values.
—*Receivables*—Present value of net receivables using present interest rates.
—*Inventories—Finished goods* at estimated net realizable value *less* a reasonable profit allowance (lower limit). *Work-in-process* at estimated net realizable value of finished goods costs less costs to complete and profit allowance. *Raw materials* at current replacement cost.
—*Plants and equipment*—If to be employed in operations, show at replacement cost. If to be sold, reflect at net realizable value. If to be used temporarily, show at net realizable value, recognizing depreciation for the period.
—*Identifiable intangibles*—At appraisal value.
—*Other assets* (including land and noncurrent securities)—At appraised values.
—*Payables*—At estimated present value.
—*Liabilities and accruals*—At estimated present value.
—*Other liabilities and commitments*—At estimated present value. However, a deferred

income tax credit account of the acquired company is not brought forth.

2. The excess of cost paid over book value of assets acquired is attributed to the identifiable net assets. The remaining balance not attributable to specific assets is of an unidentifiable nature and is assigned to goodwill. The identifiable assets are depreciated. Goodwill is amortized over the period benefited, not exceeding 40 years. NOTE: Adjustments for fair value and amortization of goodwill are factors only in preparing consolidated financial statements.

REQUIREMENTS:

• Goodwill of the acquired company is not brought forth.

• None of the equity accounts of the acquired business (e.g., retained earnings) appear on the acquirer's books. Ownership interests of the acquired company stockholders are not continued subsequent to the merger.

• Net income of the acquired company is brought forth from the date of acquisition to year-end.

• Direct costs of the purchase are a deduction from the fair value of the securities issued; indirect costs are expensed as incurred.

—When stock is issued in a purchase transaction, quoted market price of stock is typically a clear indication of asset cost. Consideration should be given to price fluctuations, volume, and issue price of stock.

—If liabilities are assumed in a purchase, the difference between the fixed rate of the debt securities and the present yield rate for comparable securities is reflected as a premium or discount.

What if control is not established on the initial purchase?

The following step-by-step acquisition procedure is followed:

• If control is not accomplished on the initial purchase, the subsidiary is not includable in consolidation until control has been accomplished.

• Once the parent owns in excess of 50% of the subsidiary, a retroactive restatement should be made including all of the subsidiary's earnings in consolidated retained earnings in a "step-by-step" fashion commencing with the initial investment.

• The subsidiary's earnings are included for the ownership years at the appropriate ownership percentage.

• After control is accomplished, fair value and adjustments for goodwill will be applied retroactively on a "step-by-step" basis. Each acquisition is separately determined.

The acquiring company generally cannot record a net operating loss carryforward of the acquired company, since there is no assurance of realization. However, if realized in a later year, recognition will be a retroactive adjustment of the purchase transaction allocation causing the residual purchase cost to be reallocated to the other assets acquired. In effect, there will be a reduction of goodwill or the other assets.

What are preacquisition contingencies?

A preacquisition contingency is a contingency of a business that is acquired with the purchase method and that exists prior to the consummation date. EXAMPLES: A contingent asset, a contingent liability, or a contingent impairment of an asset.

How do I account for a preacquisition contingency?

FASB 38 provides guidelines for recording "preacquisition contingencies" during the "allocation period" as a part of allocating the cost of an investment in an enterprise acquired under the purchase method. The allocation period is the one required to identify and quantify the acquired assets and liabilities assumed. This period ceases when the acquiring company no longer needs information it has arranged to obtain and that is known to be available. Hence, the existence of a preacquisition contingency for which an asset, a liability, or an impairment of an asset cannot be estimated does not, of itself, extend the allocation period. Although the time required depends on the circumstances, the allocation period typically is not greater than one year from the consummation date.

Preacquisition contingencies (except for tax benefits of NOL carryforwards) must be included in the allocation of purchase cost. The allocation basis is determined by the *fair value* of the preacquisition contingency, assuming a fair value can be determined during the allocation period.

If *fair value* is *not determinable*, the following criteria are used:

• Information available before the termination of the *allocation* period indicates that it is probable that an asset existed, a liability had been incurred, or an asset had been impaired at the consummation date. It must be probable that one or more future events will occur confirming the existence of the asset, liability, or impairment.

• The amount of the asset or liability can be reasonably estimated.

Adjustments necessitated by a preacquisition contingency occurring after the end of the allocation period must be included in income in the year the adjustment is made.

What should I mention about a purchase in the footnotes?

Footnote disclosures under the purchase method include:

• Name and description of companies combined

• A statement that the purchase method is being used

• The period in which earnings of the acquired company is included

• Cost of the acquired company including the number and value of shares issued, if any

• Amortization period of goodwill

• Contingencies arising under the acquisition agreement

• Earnings for the current and prior periods as if the companies were combined at the beginning of the period (a pro forma disclosure to make the purchase method comparable to that of pooling)

What are the advantages and disadvantages of the purchase method?

ADVANTAGE: Fair value is used to recognize the acquired company's assets just as in the case of acquiring a separate asset.

DISADVANTAGES: Difficulty in determining fair value and amortization period; mixing fair value of acquired company's assets and historical cost for the acquiring company's assets.

INVESTMENTS IN STOCKS AND BONDS

Stock Investments

Investments in stock may be accounted for under the cost or equity method depending on the percentage of ownership involved in the voting common stock.

NOTES: Nonvoting stock (e.g., preferred stock) is always accounted for under the cost method.

FASB 12 does *not* apply to not-for-profit organizations, mutual life insurance companies, or employee benefit plans.

Cost Method

When is the cost method used?

Use the cost method of accounting for investments, when the holder owns less than 20% of the voting common stock of the company. However, the cost method could be used instead of the equity method when the holder owns between 20%–50% of the voting common stock but *lacks* significant influence (effective control).

When is "significant influence" indicated?

Significant influence may be indicated by:

- Involvement in decision making of owned company

- Material intercompany transactions
- Representation on the board of directors of the investee company
- Investor owns a high percentage of investee's shares relative to other stockholders
- Managerial personnel are interchanged between the investor and investee
- Investor provides investee with technological expertise

Indicators of a lack of significant influence are:

- Concentration of majority ownership of investee among a limited number of stockholders, especially when the group operates the investee in disregard of the investor's viewpoints
- Investor is unable to obtain the financial data needed from the investee to use the equity method
- Investor and investee sign an agreement ("standstill") in which the investor surrenders material shareholder rights ("Standstill" agreement typically employed to settle disputes between the investor and investee)
- Investee opposes the investment (e.g., a lawsuit or complaint is filed)

REQUIREMENT: The cost method must be used for equity securities. While it is not required for debt securities, debt securities in practice are usually reflected in the entire investment portfolio at the lower of cost or market value.

NOTE: The cost method is used to account for preferred stock, since it is nonvoting irrespective of the percentage of shares owned.

How do I account under the cost method?

The investment portfolio is broken down into current and noncurrent. Current securities are shown as marketable securities under current assets. Noncurrent securities are shown as noncurrent assets.

A security is usually classified as *current* if it is liquid and used for temporary excess cash.

A security is usually classified as *long-term* if:

- The intent is to hold for one year or more
- It is for capital appreciation purposes
- Dividend income is desired
- Possible eventual control is involved
- There is a lack of market price quotations
- Restricted marketability exists

NOTES: "Restricted" stock is noncurrent except if it qualifies for sale within one year of the balance sheet date and there are readily available price quotations.

The lower of cost or market value is applied to each portfolio separately.

- If market value is *in excess of cost*, the securities are shown at cost with market value either disclosed in parentheses or in a footnote.
- If market value is *less than cost*, the securities portfolio is written down to market value reflecting an unrealized loss due to conservatism.

Thus, a temporary decline in value of the portfolio is reflected. The portfolio is shown on the balance sheet at the lower of total cost or total market value. The following entry is made at the end of the year:

Unrealized Loss

Allowance to Reduce Securities from Cost to Market Value

- For *short-term* securities, the unrealized loss is shown in the income statement.
- For *long-term* securities, the unrealized loss is shown as a separate item in the stockholders' equity section. The allowance account is a contra account to Investments to derive the net amount. NOTE: The only time the allowance account is entered into is at the end of the year.

In the following year, if there is a partial or full recovery from cost to market value, the entry is:

Allowance to Reduce Securities from Cost to Market Value

Unrealized Gain

However, in recording the recovery from cost to market value, the portfolio can never be written up at an amount in excess of the original cost.

What if securities are sold during the year?

If securities are sold during the year, a realized loss or realized gain will occur. The realized loss or gain is shown in the income statement whether or not the portfolio is current or noncurrent. NOTE: The same realized loss or gain on sale is reflected for tax return preparation purposes.

If a balance sheet is unclassified, the investment security portfolio is considered to be noncurrent.

The entry to record the sale of securities is:

Cash (proceeds received)

Loss

    Securities (at cost)

    Gain

Either a loss or gain will be involved in the above entry.

CAUTION: A security cannot be recorded at more than cost, since that will lack conservatism. The only time market value can be used for valuation is in the case of a *permanent* increase in value. However, accountants are very reluctant to state that a permanent increase has occurred because of legal liability exposure.

When is a decline considered permanent?

A permanent decline in market price of stock may be indicated when the company has had several years of losses, is in a very weak financial condition, and has issued a liquidating dividend.

A permanent decline in value of a particular security is immediately recognized with a realized loss being booked shown in the income statement even if it is a noncurrent portfolio. The investment account is credited directly. The new market value becomes the new cost basis which means it cannot later be written up. EXAMPLE: If the company sells some of its major divisions and distributes the proceeds to stockholders, a writedown of the investment may be appropriate.

EXAMPLE 5.2

In a long-term investment portfolio, one stock in ABC Company has suffered a permanent decline in value from cost of $6,000 to market value of $5,000. The entry is:

Realized Loss	1,000	
Long-term Investment		1,000

The new cost now becomes $5,000 (the market value). If in a later period the market value increased above $5,000, the stock would *not* be written-up above $5,000.

What is the handling of a stock that changes classification?

If a particular stock is reclassified from noncurrent to current, or vice versa, it is transferred at the lower of cost or market value at the transfer date.

• If market value *exceeds cost*, it is transferred at cost intact with no unrealized gain being recorded.

• If market value is *below cost*, a realized loss in the income statement is booked and the investment account is credited.

• The new cost basis becomes the market value, which means the stock cannot be written up above cost.

EXAMPLE 5.3

XYZ stock is reclassified from noncurrent to current. If cost is $3,000 and market value is $2,700, the entry for the reclassification is:

Short-term Securities	2,700	
Realized Loss	300	
Long-term Investment		3,000

If a later recovery occurs and market value becomes $2,900, no entry will be made.

NOTE: If market value of a portfolio substantially drops below cost between year-end and the audit report date, subsequent event footnote disclosure is required.

What are the tax implications of stock investments?

Income tax allocation occurs with investments because of resulting temporary differences. A deferred tax credit will arise because unrealized losses and gains on securities are not reflected for tax return preparation purposes.

EXAMPLE 5.4

On 1/1/19X1, Company X purchases long-term securities of $480,000 plus brokerage commissions of $20,000. On 5/12/19X1, a cash dividend of $15,000 is received. On 12/31/19X1, the market value of the portfolio is $490,000. On 2/6/19X2 securities costing $50,000 are sold for $54,000. On 12/31/19X2, the market value of the portfolio is $447,000. The journal entries follow:

1/1/19X1 Long-term		
Investments	500,000	
Cash		500,000
5/12/19X1 Cash	15,000	
Dividend Revenue		15,000
12/31/19X1 Unrealized Loss	10,000	
Allowance		10,000

The balance sheet presentation of the long-term investments is:

Long-term Investments	$500,000
Less: Allowance	10,000
Net Balance	$490,000

If market value were $510,000 instead of $490,000, the securities portfolio would remain intact at $500,000, with the market value of $510,000 being disclosed.

2/2/19X2 Cash	54,000	
Long-term Investments		50,000
Gain		4,000
12/31/19X2 Allowance	7,000	
Unrealized Loss		7,000

The balance sheet presentation of the long-term securities is:

Long-term Investments	$450,000
Less: Allowance	3,000
Net Balance	$447,000

If instead market value was $435,000, the entry would have been:

Unrealized Loss	5,000	
Allowance		5,000

If instead market value was $452,000, the entry would have been:

Allowance	10,000	
Unrealized Loss		10,000

What if there is an exchange of stock?

If two or more securities are purchased at one price, the cost is allocated among the securities based on their relative fair market value. In the exchange of one security for another, the new security received in the exchange is valued at its fair market value.

EXAMPLE 5.5

Preferred stock costing $10,000 is exchanged for 1,000 shares of common stock having a market value of $15,000. The entry is:

Investment in Common Stock	15,000	
Investment in Preferred		
Stock		10,000
Gain		5,000

How is a stock dividend handled?

A stock dividend involves a memo entry reflecting more shares at no additional cost. As a result, the cost per share decreases.

EXAMPLE 5.6

50 shares at $12 per share for a total cost of $600 is owned. A 20% stock dividend is declared

amounting to 10 shares. A memo entry is made reflecting the additional shares as follows:

		Investment	
50	$12	$600	
10		0	
60	($10)	$600	

If 10 shares are later sold at $15, the entry is:

Cash	150	
Long-term Investment		100
Gain		50

What effect does a stock split have?

A stock split has the effect of increasing the shares and reducing the cost basis on a proportionate basis. A memo entry is made.

EXAMPLE 5.7

100 shares costing $20 per share was owned. A 2 for 1 split would result in 200 shares at a cost per share of $10. Total par value remains at $2,000.

Equity Method

When is the equity method used?

The investor company is the owner and the investee company is being owned. The equity method is used if:

- An investor owns between 20% to 50% of the voting common stock of an investee
- The holder owned less than 20% of the voting common stock but possessed significant influence (effective control)
- More than 50% of the voting common stock was owned but one of the negating factors for consolidation existed

NOTE: Investments in joint ventures have to be accounted for under the equity method.

How do I account when using the equity method?

The accounting under the equity method as per APB 18 is illustrated by the "T-accounts" shown in Figure 5.1.

• The cost of the investment includes brokerage fees. The investor recognizes his percentage ownership interest in the ordinary profit of the investee by debiting investment in investee and crediting equity in earnings of investee.

• The investor's share in investee's earnings is computed after deducting cumulative preferred dividends, whether or not declared. Investor's share of investee's profit should be based on the investee's most recent income statement applied on a consistent basis.

Investment In Investee

Cost	Dividends
Ordinary Profit	Amortization Expense on
Extraordinary Gain	Goodwill
	Depreciation on Excess
	of Fair Market Value
	less Book Value of
	Specific Assets
	Permanent Decline

Equity in Earnings of Investee

Amortization Expense	Ordinary Profit
Depreciation	

Loss

Permanent Decline	

Extraordinary Gain

	Extraordinary Gain

Figure 5.1

• Extraordinary gains or losses as well as prior period adjustments are also picked up as shown on the investee's books.

• Dividends reduce the carrying value of the investment account.

• The excess paid by the investor for the investee's net assets is first assigned to the specific assets and liabilities and is depreciated. The unidentifiable portion of the excess is considered goodwill which is amortized over the period benefited, not exceeding 40 years. The amortization expense on goodwill and depreciation on excess value of assets reduce the investment account and are charged to equity in earnings.

• *Temporary decline* in price of the investment in the investee is ignored. *Permanent decline* in value of the investment is reflected by debiting loss and crediting investment in investee.

• When the investor's share of the investee's losses is greater than the balance in the investment account, the equity method should be discontinued at the zero amount. EXCEPTIONS: The investor has guaranteed the investee's obligations or immediate profitability is assured. A return to the equity method is made only after offsetting subsequent profits against losses not recorded.

• When the investee's stock is sold, a realized gain or loss will arise for the difference between selling price and the cost of the investment account.

Isn't the equity method like a consolidation?

The mechanics of consolidation essentially apply to the equity method: For example, intercompany profits and losses are eliminated. Investee capital transactions impacting the investor's share of equity should be accounted for as in a consolidation. Investee's capital transactions should be accounted for as if the investee was a consolidated subsidiary. EXAMPLE: When the investee issues its common stock to third parties at a price in excess of book value, there will be an increase in the value of the investment and a related increase in the investor's paid-in-capital.

What else should I know about the equity method?

Interperiod income tax allocation will occur because the investor shows the investee's *profits* for book reporting but *dividends* for tax reporting. This results in a deferred income tax credit account.

If the ownership goes below 20%, or if the investor is unable to control the investee, the investor should cease recognizing the investee's earnings. The equity method is discontinued, but the balance in the investment account is maintained. The cost method should then be applied.

If the investor increases his ownership in the investee to 20% or more, the equity method should be used for current and future years. Further, the effect of using the equity method rather than the cost method on prior years at the old percentage (e.g., 15%) should be recognized as an adjustment to retained earnings and other accounts so affected (e.g., investment in investee). The retroactive adjustment on the investment, earnings, and retained earnings should be applied in the same manner as a step-by-step acquisition of a subsidiary.

What disclosures are necessary?

Disclosures of the following should be made by the investor in footnotes, separate schedules, or parenthetically:

- Percent owned
- Name of investee
- Investor's accounting policies
- Material effects of possible conversions and exercises of investee common stock
- Quoted market price (for investees not qualifying as subsidiaries)
- Summarized financial data as to assets, liabilities, and earnings for material investments in unconsolidated subsidiaries
- Material realized and unrealized gains and losses relating to the subsidiary's portfolio occurring between the dates of the financial statements of the subsidiary and parent

EXAMPLE 5.8

On 1/1/19X5, X Company bought 30,000 shares for a 40% interest in the common stock of AB Company at $25 per share. Brokerage commissions were $10,000. During 19X5, AB's net income was $140,000 and dividends received were $30,000. On 1/1/19X6, X Company received 15,000 shares of common stock as a result of a stock split by AB Company. On 1/4/19X6, X Company sold 2,000 shares at $16 per share of AB stock. The journal entries follow:

1/1/19X5 Investment in		
Investee	760,000	
Cash		760,000
12/31/19X5 Investment in		
Investee	56,000	
Equity in Earnings of		
Investee		56,000
40% × $140,000 = $56,000		
Cash	30,000	
Investment in Investee		30,000
1/1/19X6 Memo entry for		
stock split		
1/4/19X6 Cash (2,000 ×		
$16)	32,000	
Loss on Sale of		
Investment	2,940	
Investment in Investee		
(2,000 × $17.47)		34,940

$$\frac{\$786,000}{45,000} = \$17.47 \text{ per share}$$

Investment in Investee

1/1/19X5	760,000	12/31/19X5	30,000
12/31/19X5	56,000		
	816,000		
	786,000		

EXAMPLE 5.9

On 1/1/19X6, investor purchased 100,000 shares of investee's 400,000 shares outstanding for

$3,000,000. The book value of net assets acquired was $2,500,000. Of the $500,000 excess paid over book value, $300,000 is attributable to undervalued tangible assets and the remainder is attributable to unidentifiable assets. The depreciation period is 20 years and the maximum period is used to amortize goodwill. In 19X6, investee's net income was $800,000, including an extraordinary loss of $200,000. Dividends of $75,000 were paid on June 1, 19X6. The following journal entries are necessary for the acquisition of investee by investor accounted for under the equity method.

1/1/19X6 Investment in		
Investee	3,000,000	
Cash		3,000,000
6/1/19X6 Cash	18,750	
Investment in		
Investee		18,750
25% × $75,000 = $18,750		
12/31/19X6		
Investment in Investee	250,000	
Equity in Earnings		
of Investee		250,000
$1,000,000 × 25% =		
$250,000		
Extraordinary Loss		
from Investment	50,000	
Investment in		
Investee		50,000
$200,000 × 25% =		
$50,000		
Equity in Earnings of		
Investee	20,000	
Investment in		
Investee		20,000
Computation follows:		
Undervalued depreciable		
assets $300,000/20		
years		$15,000
Unrecorded goodwill		
$200,000/40 years		5,000
		$20,000

Bond Investments

How do I account for an investment in bonds?

The rules of FASB 12 do *not* require debt securities to be written down from cost to market value *for a temporary change.* A company has the option, which is often practiced, of retaining investments in debt securities (e.g., bonds) at cost. However, a *permanent* decline in the price of bonds requires loss recognition.

The difference between the cost of a bond and its face value represents discount or premium. Discount or premium is amortized over the life of the bond from the *acquisition date.*

The bond investment account is usually recorded *net* of the discount or premium. If bonds are acquired between interest dates, accrued interest should be recorded separately.

How is the market value of a bond determined?

The market price of the bond takes into account:

- The financial health of the issuer
- The maturity period
- Prevailing interest rates in the market

The market price is determined by discounting the principal and interest payments using the yield rate.

EXAMPLE 5.10

An investor purchases $100,000, 6%, 20 year bonds on 3/1/19X5. Interest is payable on 1/1 and 6/30. The bonds are bought at face value.

3/1/19X5 Investment in		
Bonds	100,000	
Accrued Bond Interest		
Receivable	1,000	
Cash		101,000

$100,000 × 6% = $6,000
per year

$6,000 × 2/12 = $1,000

6/30/19X5 Cash	3,000	
Accrued Bond Interest Receivable (2 months)		1,000
Bond Interest Earned (4 months)		2,000

$6,000 × 6/12 = $3,000

12/31/19X5		
Accrued Bond Interest Receivable	3,000	
Bond Interest Earned		3,000
1/1/19X6 Cash	3,000	
Accrued Bond Interest Receivable		3,000
6/30/19X6		
Cash	3,000	
Bond Interest Earned		3,000

EXAMPLE 5.11

On 1/19X5, $10,000 of ABC Company 6%, 10 year bonds are purchased for $12,000. Interest is payable 1/1 and 6/30. On 4/1/19X6, the bonds are sold for $11,000. A commission charge on the bonds of $100 is required. Appropriate journal entries follow:

1/1/19X5 Investment in Bonds	12,000	
Cash		12,000
6/30/19X5		
Bond Interest Earned	100	
Investment in Bonds		100

Amortization of premium computed as follows:
$2,000/10 years = $200 per year × 6/12 = $100

| Cash | 300 | |
| Bond Interest Earned | | 300 |

6% × $10,000 = $600 × 6/12 = $300

12/31/19X5		
Accrued Bond Interest Receivable	300	
Bond Interest Earned		300

Bond Interest Earned	100	
Investment in Bonds		100

4/1/19X6

Accrued Bond Interest		
Receivable	150	
Bond Interest Earned		150

$6\% \times \$10,000 \times 3/12 = \$150$

Bond Interest Earned	50	
Investment in Bonds		50

Amortization of premium
computed as follows:
$200 per year × 3/12 = $50

Cash (11,000 + 150 − 100)	11,050	
Loss on Sale of Investments	850	
Investment in Bonds		
(12,000 − 100 − 100 − 50)		11,750
Accrued Bond Interest		
Receivable		150

LEASES

How are leases defined?

Leases are typically long-term, noncancellable commitments. In a lease, the lessee acquires the right to use property owned by the lessor. Even though no legal transfer of title occurs, many leases transfer substantially all the risks and benefits of ownership. Theoretical substance governs over legal form in accounting, resulting in the lessee recording an asset and a liability for a capital lease.

NOTES: A lease may be between related parties. This occurs when one entity has significant influence over operating and financial policies of another entity.

The *date of inception* of a lease is the time of lease *agreement, or commitment,* whichever occurs first. *REQUIREMENT:* A commitment must be in writing, signed, and provide principal provisions. If any major provisions are to be negotiated later there is *no* committed agreement.

Lessee

How does the lessee account for leases?

The two methods of accounting for a lease by the lessee are the operating method and capital method.

What is an operating lease?

An operating lease is a regular rental of property.

How is recognition given to an operating lease?

• As rental payments become payable, rent expense is debited and cash and/or payables are credited.

• The lessee does not show anything on his balance sheet.

• Rent expense is reflected on a straight-line basis unless another method is more appropriate.

• Accrual basis accounting is followed.

What is a capital lease?

The lessee uses the capital lease method if any *one* of the following four criteria is met:

• The lessee obtains ownership to the property at the end of the lease term.

• There is a bargain purchase option where the lessee can either acquire the property at a nominal amount or renew the lease at nominal rental payments.

• The life of the lease is 75% or more of the life of the property.

• The present value of minimum lease payments at the inception of the lease equals or is greater than 90% of the fair market value of the property. Minimum lease payments exclude executory costs to be paid by the lessor such as maintenance, insurance, and property taxes.

NOTES: If criterion 1 or 2 is met, the depreciation period is the life of the property. If criterion 3 or 4 is satisfied, the depreciation period is the life of the lease.

Criteria 3 and 4 do not apply where the beginning of the lease term falls within the last 25% of the total economic life of the property, including earlier years of use.

What is the accounting and reporting for a capital lease?

The asset and liability are recorded at the present value of the minimum lease payments plus the present value of the bargain purchase option. The expectation is that the lessee will take advantage of the nominal purchase price.

If the present value of the minimum lease payments plus the bargain purchase option is greater than the fair value of the leased property at the time of lease inception, the asset should be capitalized at the fair market value of the property.

The discount rate used by the lessee is the *lower* of the lessee's incremental borrowing rate (the rate at which the lessee would have to borrow to be able to buy the asset) or the lessor's implicit interest rate (the rate implicit in the recovery of the fair value of the property at lease inception through the present value of minimum lease payments including the lessee's guarantee of salvage value).

The liability is broken down between current and noncurrent.

What is the MLP?

The lessee's minimum lease payments (MLP) usually includes:

• MLP over the lease term plus any residual value guaranteed by the lessee. The guarantee is the determinable amount for which the lessor has the right to require the lessee to buy the property at the lease termination. It is the stated amount when the lessee agrees to satisfy any dollar deficiency below a stated amount in the lessor's realization of the residual value.

• Any payment lessee must pay due to failure to extend or renew the lease at expiration.

NOTES: MLP includes *only* MLP over the lease term and exercise option payment, if a bargain purchase option exists.

MLP does *not* include:

- Contingent rentals
- Lessee's guarantee of lessor's debt
- Lessee's obligation for executory costs

Each minimum lease payment is allocated as a reduction of principal (debiting the liability) and as interest (debiting interest expense). The interest method is used to result in a constant periodic rate of interest. Interest expense equals the interest rate times the carrying value of the liability at the beginning of the year.

How is a capital lease shown on the balance sheet and income statement?

- BALANCE SHEET: Show the "Asset Under Lease" less "Accumulated Depreciation."

- INCOME STATEMENT: Show interest expense and depreciation expense. In the first year, the expenses under a capital lease (interest expense and depreciation) are greater than the expenses under an operating lease (rent expense).

What if the lessee buys a leased asset that has been capitalized?

Per Interpretation 26, when a lessee buys a leased asset during the lease term which has been originally capitalized, the transaction is considered an *extension* of a capital lease, not a termination. The difference between the purchase price and the carrying amount of the lease obligation recorded is an *adjustment* of the carrying amount of the asset. *NOTE: No loss recognition* is required on an *extension* of a capital lease.

EXAMPLE 5.12

On 1/1/19X1, the lessee enters into a capital lease for property. The minimum rental payment is $20,000 a year for 6 years to be made at year end. The interest rate is 5%. The present value of an ordinary annuity factor for n = 6, i = 5% is 5.0757. The journal entries for the first two years are:

1/1/19X1 Asset	101,514	
Liability		101,514
12/31/19X1		
Interest Expense	5,076	
Liability	14,924	
Cash		20,000

5% × $101,514 = $5,076

Depreciation	16,919	
Accumulated Depreciation		16,919

$$\frac{\$101,514}{6} = \$16,919$$

The liability as of 12/31/19X1 is:

Liability

12/31/19X1	14,924	1/1/19X1	101,514
		12/31/19X1	86,590

12/31/19X2		
Interest Expense	4,330	
Liability	15,670	
Cash		20,000

5% × $86,590 = $4,330

Depreciation	16,919	
Accumulated Depreciation		16,919

What footnote disclosures are necessary for leases?

Footnote disclosures under a capital lease include:

- Assets under lease by class
- Future minimum lease payments in total and for each of the next five years
- Contingent rentals (rentals based on terms other than time, e.g., sales)
- Total future sublease rentals
- Description of leasing arrangement including renewal terms, purchase options, escalation options, and restrictions in the lease agreement

Lessor

How does the lessor account for leases?

The three methods of accounting for leases by the lessor are:

- Operating method
- Direct-financing method
- Sales-type method

What is the operating method?

The operating method is a regular rental by the lessor. EXAMPLE: Avis rents automobiles.

How do I account for the operating method?

Under the operating method, the lessor records rental revenue less related expenses including depreciation and maintenance expense.

INCOME STATEMENT: Show rental revenue less expenses to obtain profit.

BALANCE SHEET: Present the asset under lease less accumulated depreciation to derive book value.

How is rental income recognized in the operating method?

Rental income is recognized as earned using the *straight-line* basis over the lease term, except if there is another preferable method.

Initial direct costs are deferred and amortized over the lease term on a prorata basis based on rental income recognized. However, the initial direct costs may be expensed if immaterial relative to the allocation amount.

EXAMPLE 5.13

Hall Corporation produced machinery costing $5,000,000 which it held for resale from January 1, 19X1 to June 30, 19X1, at a price to Travis Company under an operating lease. The lease is for four years, with equal monthly payments of $85,000 due on the first of the month. The initial payment was made on July 1, 19X1. The depreciation period is ten years with no salvage value.

Lessee's rental expense for 19X1:

$85,000 × 6	$510,000

Lessor's income before taxes for 19X1:

Rental income	$510,000
Less: Depreciation	
$\dfrac{\$5,000,000}{10} \times \dfrac{6}{12}$	250,000
Income before taxes	$260,000

What is the direct financing method?

The direct financing method satisfies one of the four criteria for a capital lease by the lessee *plus* both of the following two criteria for the lessor:

• Collectibility of lease payments is assured

• No important uncertainties exist regarding future costs to be incurred

The lessor is *not* a manufacturer or dealer. The lessor acquires the property for the sole purpose of leasing it out. EXAMPLE: A bank leasing computers.

How do I account for the direct financing method?

The carrying value and fair value of the leased property are the same at the inception of the lease.

The lessor uses as the discount rate the interest rate implicit in the lease.

Interest revenue equals the interest rate times the carrying value of the receivable at the beginning of the year. Interest income is recognized only in the financial statements over the life of the lease using the interest method. Unearned interest income is amortized as income over the lease term resulting in a constant rate of interest.

Contingent rentals are recognized in earnings as earned.

The lessor's MLP includes:

• The MLP made by the lessee (net of any executory costs together with any profit thereon)

• Any guarantee of the salvage value of the leased property, or of rental payments after the lease term, made by a third party unrelated to either party in the lease, provided the third party is financially able to satisfy the commitment.

NOTE: A guarantee by a third party related to the lessor makes the residual value unguaranteed. A guarantee by a third party related to the lessee infers a guaranteed residual value by the lessee.

What if there is a change in lease provisions?

A change in lease provisions that would have resulted in a different classification had it taken place at the beginning of the lease, mandates that the lease be considered a new agreement and be classified under the new terms.

EXCEPTIONS:

• Exercise of existing renewal options are not deemed lease changes.

• A change in estimate does not result in a new lease.

NOTE: A provision for escalation of the MLP during a construction or preacquisition period may exist. The resulting increase in MLP is considered in determining the fair value of the leased property at the lease inception. A salvage value increase resulting from an escalation clause may also exist.

What do initial direct costs include?

Initial direct costs are incurred by the lessor directly applicable to negotiating and consummating *completed* leasing transactions such as:

• Legal fees,

• Commissions,

• Document preparation and processing for new leases,

• Credit investigation,

• Relevant portion of salespersons' and other employees' compensation.

Not Included:

- Costs for *unconsummated leases*
- Supervisory, administrative, or other indirect expenses.

Initial direct costs of the lease are expensed as incurred. A portion of the unearned income equal to the initial direct costs are recognized as income in the same accounting period.

What if the lease is terminated?

If the lease agreement contains a penalty for failure to renew and the penalty becomes inoperative due to lease renewal or other extension of time, the unearned interest income account must be adjusted for the difference between the present values of the old and revised agreements. The present value of the future MLP under the new agreement should be computed using the original rate for the initial lease.

Lease termination is accounted for by the lessor through eliminating the net investment, and recording the leased property at the lower of cost or fair value. The net adjustment is then charged against earnings.

BALANCE SHEET: The lessor shows the total minimum lease payments plus salvage value of the property accruing to the lessor as the gross investment in the lease. This represents lease payments receivable. Deducted from lease payments receivable is unearned interest revenue. The balance sheet presentation follows:

Lease Payments Receivable (Principal + Interest)

Less: Unearned Interest Revenue (Interest)

Net Receivable Balance (Principal)

The income statement shows:

Interest Revenue

Less: Initial Direct Costs

Less: Executory Costs

Net Income

What footnote disclosure is necessary for the direct financing method?

Footnote disclosure should include:

- Assets leased out by category
- Future lease payments in total and for each of the next five years
- Contingent rentals
- The terms of the lease

What is the sales-type method?

The sales-type method must satisfy the same criteria as the direct financing method. The only difference is that the sales-type method involves a lessor who is a manufacturer or dealer in the leased item. Thus, a manufacturer or dealer profit results. Although legally there is no sale of the item, theoretical substance governs over legal form, and a sale is assumed to have taken place.

NOTE: The distinction between a sales-type lease and a direct financing lease affects only the lessor; as to lessee, either type would be a capital lease.

If there is a renewal or extension of an existing sales-type or financing lease, it shall *not* be classified as a sales-type lease. EXCEPTION: It may sometimes be so classified when the renewal occurs toward the end of the lease term.

How do I account for a sales-type lease?

- In a sales-type lease, profit on the assumed sale of the item is recognized in the year of lease as well as interest income over the life of the lease. The cost and fair value of the leased property are different at the inception of the lease.

- An annual appraisal should be made of the salvage value. Where necessary, reduce the net investment and recognize a loss. Do not adjust the salvage value.

- The cost of the leased property is matched against the selling price in determining the assumed profit in the year of lease. Initial direct costs of the lease are expensed.

• Except for the initial entry to record the lease, the entries are the same for the direct financing and sales-type methods.

EXAMPLE 5.14

Assume the same facts as in the capital lease example. The accounting by the lessor assuming a direct financing lease and a sales-type lease follows:

Direct Financing			*Sales-Type*		
1/1/19X1					
Receivable	120,000		Receivable	120,000	
Asset		101,514	Cost of Sales	85,000	
Unearned			Inventory		85,000
Interest			Sales		101,514
Revenue		18,486	Unearned		
			Interest		
			Revenue		18,486
12/31/19X1					
Cash	20,000				
Receivable		20,000			
Unearned					
Interest			Same entries		
Revenue	5,076				
Interest					
Revenue		5,076			
12/31/19X2					
Cash	20,000				
Receivable		20,000			
Unearned					
Interest			Same entries		
Revenue	4,330				
Interest					
Revenue		4,330			

The income statement for 19X1 presents:

Interest		Sales	$101,514
Revenue	$5,076	Less: Cost of	
		Sales	85,000
		Gross Profit	$ 16,514
		Interest	
		Revenue	5,076

EXAMPLE 5.15

Jones leased equipment to Tape Company on October 1, 19X1. It is a capital lease to the lessee and a sales type lease to the lessor. The lease is for eight years, with equal annual payments of $500,000 due on October 1 each period. The first payment was made on October 1, 19X1. The cost of the equipment to Tape Company is $2,500,000. The equipment has a life of ten years with no salvage value. The appropriate interest rate is 10%.

Tape reports the following in its income statement for 19X1:

Asset Cost ($500,000 × 5.868 = $2,934,000)		
Depreciation $\left(\dfrac{\$2,934,000}{10} \times \dfrac{3}{12}\right)$		$ 73,350
Interest Expense:		
Present value of lease payments	$2,934,000	
Less: Initial payment	500,000	
Balance	$2,434,000	
Interest Expense		60,850
$2,434,000 × 10% × 3/12		
Total Expenses		$134,200

Jones' income before tax is:

Interest revenue		$ 60,850
Gross profit on assumed sale of property:		
Selling price	$2,934,000	
Less: Cost	2,500,000	
Gross Profit		434,000
Income before tax		$494,850

Sales-Leaseback Arrangement

What is a sales-leaseback situation?

A sales-leaseback occurs when the lessor sells the property and then leases it back. The lessor may do this when he is in need of funds.

What is the accounting for a sales-leaseback arrangement?

The profit or loss on the sale is deferred and amortized as an adjustment in proportion to depreciation expense in the case of a capital lease, or in proportion to rental expense in the case of an operating lease. However, if the fair value of the property at the time of the sales-leaseback is below its book value, a loss is immediately recognized for the difference between book value and fair value.

EXAMPLE 5.16

The deferred profit on a sales-leaseback is $50,000. An operating lease is involved, where rental expense in the current year is $10,000, and total rental expense is $150,000. Rental expense is adjusted as follows:

Rental Expense	$10,000
Less: Amortization of deferred gross profit	
$50,000 \times \dfrac{\$10,000}{\$150,000}$	3,333
	$ 6,667

Subleases and Similar Transactions

What is a sublease?

There are three types of *subleases*:

• The original lessee leases the property to a third party. The lease agreement of the original parties remains intact.

• A new lessee is substituted under the original agreement. The original lessee may still be secondarily liable.

• The new lessee is substituted in a new agreement. There is a cancellation of the original lease.

What accounting is necessary by the lessor?

The original lessor continues his present accounting method if the original lessee subleases or sells to a third party. If the original lease is replaced by a new agreement with a new lessee, the lessor terminates the initial lease and accounts for the new lease in a separate transaction.

What accounting does the original lessee have to do?

In accounting by the original lessee, if the original lessee is relieved of primary obligation by a transaction other than a sublease, terminate the original lease.

• If original lease was a capital lease, remove the asset and liability, recognize a gain or loss for the difference, including any additional consideration paid or received, and accrue a loss contingency where secondary liability exists.

• If the original lease was an operating lease and the initial lessee is secondarily liable, recognize a loss contingency accrual.

If the original lessee is not relieved of *primary* obligation under a sublease, the original lessee (now sublessor) accounts in the following manner:

• If original lease met lessee criterion 1 or 2, classify the new lease per normal classification criteria by lessor. If sublease is sales-type or direct financing lease, the unamortized asset balance becomes the cost of the leased property. Otherwise, it is an operating lease. Continue to account for the original lease obligation as before.

• If original lease met only lessee criterion 3 or 4, classify the new lease using lessee criterion 3 and lessor criteria 1 and 2. Classify as a direct financing lease. The unamortized balance of the asset becomes the cost of the leased property. Otherwise, it is an operating lease. Continue to account for original lease obligation as before.

NOTE: If the original lease was an *operating lease*, account for old and new leases as operating leases.

Leveraged Leases

What is a leveraged lease?

A leveraged lease occurs when the lessor (equity participant) finances a small part of the acquisition, retaining total equity ownership. A third party (debt participant) finances the balance. The lessor maximizes his leveraged return by recognizing lease revenue and income tax shelter (e.g., interest deduction, rapid depreciation).

A leveraged lease must meet *all* of these criteria:

- It satisfies the tests for a direct financing lease. Sales-type leases are not leveraged leases.
- It involves at least three parties: lessee, long-term creditor (debt participant) and lessor (equity participant).
- The long-term creditor provides nonrecourse financing as to the general credit of the lessor. The financing is adequate to give the lessor significant leverage.
- The lessor's net investment (see below) decreases during the initial lease years, then increases in the subsequent years just before its liquidation by sale. These increases and decreases in the net investment balance may take place more than once during the lease life.

How does the lessee account for leveraged leases?

The lessee classifies and accounts for leveraged leases in the same way as for non-leveraged leases.

How does the lessor account for leveraged leases?

The lessor records investment in the leveraged lease net of the nonrecourse debt. The net of the following balances represent the initial and continuing investment:

- Rentals receivable (net of the amount applicable to principal and interest on the nonrecourse debt)
- Estimated residual value
- Unearned and deferred income

The initial entry to record the leveraged lease is:

Lease receivable

Residual value of asset

Cash investment in asset

Unearned income

• The lessor's *net investment in the leveraged lease* for computing net income is the investment in the leveraged lease less deferred income taxes.

Periodic net income is determined in the following manner employing the *net investment in the leveraged* lease:

• Determine annual cash flow equal to the following:

Gross lease rental (plus residual value of asset in last year of lease term)

Less: Loan interest payments

Less: Income tax charges (or add income tax credits)

Less: Loan principal payments

Annual Cash Flow

• Determine the return rate on the net investment in the leveraged lease. The rate of return is the one that when applied to the net investment in the years when it is positive will distribute the net income (cash flow) to those positive years.

The *net investment* will be:

• Positive in the early years (but declining rapidly due to accelerated depreciation and interest expense)

• Negative during the middle years

• Again positive in the later years (because of the declining tax shelter)

PENSION PLANS

How is a pension plan defined?

The pension plan relationship between the employer, trustee, and employee is depicted in Figure 5.2.

Figure 5.2
PENSION PLAN RELATIONSHIP

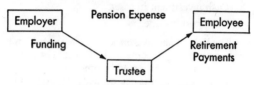

Pension Plan Assets on Books of Trustee

The two types of pension plans are:

• *Defined Contribution:* In a defined contribution plan, the employer's annual contribution amount is specified, not the benefits to be paid.

• *Defined Benefit:* In a defined benefit plan, the determinable pension benefit to be received by participants upon retirement is specified. The employer has to provide plan contributions so that sufficient assets are accumulated to pay for the benefits when due. Typically, an annuity of payments is made. *NOTES:* Pension expense applicable to administrative staff is expensed. Pension expense related to factory personnel is inventoriable.

What terminology is important for understanding pension plans?

• *Actuarial Assumptions:* Actuaries make assumptions as to variables in determining pension expense and related funding. EXAMPLES: Mortality rate, employee turnover, compensation levels, and rate of return.

• *Actuarial Cost (Funding) Method:* The method used by actuaries in determining the employer contribution to assure that sufficient funds will be available at employee retirement. The method used determines the pension expense and related liability.

• *Actuarial Present Value of Accumulated Plan Benefits:* The discounted amount of money that would be required to satisfy retirement obligations for active and retired employees.

• *Benefit Information Date:* The date the actuarial present value of accumulated benefits is presented.

• *Vested Benefits:* Employee vests when he has accumulated pension rights to receive benefits upon retirement. The employee no longer has to remain in the company to receive pension benefits.

• *Projected Benefit Obligation:* The year-end pension obligation based on *future* salaries. It is the actuarial present value of vested and nonvested benefits for services performed before a particular actuarial valuation date based on expected *future* salaries.

• *Accumulated Benefit Obligation:* The year-end obligation based on *current* salaries. It is the actuarial present value of benefits (vested and nonvested) attributable to the pension plan based on services performed before a specified date, based on *current* salary levels.

NOTE: The accumulated and projected benefit obligation figures will be the same in the case of plans having flat-benefit or non-pay-related pension benefit formulas.

• *Net Assets Available for Pension Benefits:* Net assets represents plan assets less plan liabilities. The plan's liabilities *exclude* participants' accumulated benefits.

In general, what are the accounting requirements for pension plans?

A company does not have to have a pension plan. If it does, the firm must conform to FASB and governmental rules regarding the accounting and reporting for the pension plan. FASB 87 requires accounting for pension costs on the accrual basis.

Pension expense is reflected in the service periods using a method that considers the benefit formula of the plan. On the income statement, pension expense is presented as a single amount.

Defined Contribution Pension Plan

How do I account for a defined contribution plan?

• Pension expense equals the employer's cash contribution for the year. There is no deferred charge or deferred credit arising.

• If the defined contribution plan stipulates contributions are to be made for years subsequent to an employee's rendering of services (e.g., after retirement), there should be an accrual of costs during the employee's service period.

Footnote disclosure includes:

• Description of plan including employee groups covered
• Basis of determining contributions
• Nature and effect of items affecting interperiod comparability
• Cost recognized for the period

Defined Benefit Pension Plan

What is the accounting for a defined benefit plan?

The components of pension expense in a defined benefit pension plan are:

• Service Cost
• Prior Service Cost
• Return on Plan Assets (reduces pension expense)
• Interest on Projected Benefit Obligation
• Actuarial Gain or Loss

Service cost is based on the present value of future payments under the benefit formula for employee services of the current period. It is recognized in full in the current year. The calculation involves actuarial assumptions.

Prior service cost is the pension expense applicable to services rendered before the adoption or amendment date of a pension plan. The cost of the retroactive benefits is the increase in the projected benefit obligation at the date of amendment. It involves the allocation of amounts of cost to future service years. Prior service cost determination involves actuarial considerations.

NOTE: The total pension cost is *not* booked. Rather, there are periodic charges based on actuarial determinations.

Amortization is accomplished by assigning an equal amount to each service year of active employees as of the amendment date who are expected to receive plan benefits. The amortization of prior service takes into account:

- Future service years
- Change in the projected benefit obligation
- Period employees will receive benefits
- Decrement in employees receiving benefits each year.

EXAMPLE 5.17

X Company changes its pension formula from 2% to 5% of the last three years of pay multiplied by the service years on January 1, 19X1. This results in the projected benefit obligation being increased by $500,000. Employees are anticipated to receive benefits over the next ten years.

Total Future Service Years Equals:

$$\frac{n(n+1)}{2} \times P$$

n is the number of years services are to be made

P is the population decrement each year

$$\frac{10(10+1)}{2} \times 9 = 495$$

Amortization of prior service cost in 19X1 equals:

$$\$500,000 \times \frac{10 \times 9}{495} = \underline{\$90,909}$$

- The *return on plan assets* (e.g., stocks, bonds) reduces pension expense. Plan assets are valued at the moving average of asset values for the accounting period.

- *Interest is on the projected benefit obligation* at the beginning of the year. The settlement rate, representing the rate that pension benefits could be settled for is employed.

Interest = Interest Rate × Projected Benefit Obligation at the beginning of the year

• *Actuarial gains and losses* represent the difference between estimates and actual experience. EXAMPLE: If the assumed interest rate is 10% and the actual interest rate is 12%, an actuarial gain results.

There may also be a change in actuarial assumptions regarding the future. Actuarial gains and losses are deferred and amortized as an adjustment to pension expense over future years. Actuarial gains and losses related to a single event *not* related to the pension plan and not in the ordinary course of business are immediately recognized in the current year's income statement. EXAMPLES: Plant closing and segment disposal.

NOTE: Pension expense will not usually equal the employer's funding amount. Pension expense is typically based on the unit credit method. Under this approach, pension expense and related liability is based on estimating future salaries for total benefits to be paid.

If Pension Expense > Cash Paid = Deferred Pension Liability

If Pension Expense < Cash Paid = Deferred Pension Charge

The *unit credit* method is used for flat-benefit plans (benefits are stated as a constant amount per year of service). In the case of final-pay plans, the projected unit credit method is used.

What does minimum pension liability involve?

A minimum pension liability must be recognized when the accumulated benefit obligation exceeds the fair value of pension plan assets.

CAUTION: No minimum pension asset is recognized because it violates conservatism.

When there is an accrued pension liability, an additional liability is booked up to the minimum pension liability. When an additional liability is recorded, the debit is to an intangible asset under the pension plan. NOTE: The intangible asset cannot exceed the unamortized prior service cost. If it does, the excess is reported as a separate component of stockholders' **equity** shown net of tax. While these items may be adjusted periodically, they are not amortized.

EXAMPLE 5.18

Accumulated Benefit Obligation	$500,000
Less: Fair Value of Pension Plan Assets	200,000
Minimum Pension Liability	$300,000
Less: Accrued Pension Liability	120,000
Additional Liability	$180,000

NOTE: If instead of there being an accrued pension liability, there was an accrued pension asset of $120,000, the additional liability would be $420,000.

Assume unamortized prior service cost is $100,000. The entry is:

Intangible Asset Under Pension Plan	100,000	
Stockholders' Equity	80,000	
Additional Liability		180,000

EXAMPLE 5.19

Mr. A has 6 years prior to retirement. The estimated salary at retirement is $50,000. The pension benefit is 3% of final salary for each service year payable at retirement. The retirement benefit is computed below:

Final Annual Salary	$50,000
Formula Rate	× 3%
	$ 1,500
Years of Service	× 6
Retirement Benefit	$ 9,000

EXAMPLE 5.20

On 1/1/19X1, a company adopts a defined benefit pension plan. Return rate and interest rate are both 10%. Service cost for 19X1 and 19X2 are $100,000 and $120,000, respectively. The funding amount for 19X1 and 19X2 are $80,000 and $110,000, respectively.

The entry for 19X1 is:

Pension Expense	100,000	
Cash		80,000
Pension Liability		20,000

The entry in 19X2 is:

Pension Expense	122,000	
Cash		110,000
Pension Liability		12,000
Computation:		
Service Cost	120,000	
Interest on Projected Benefit Obligation (10% × $100,000)	10,000	
Return on Plan Assets (10% × $80,000)	(8,000)	
	$122,000	

At 12/31/19X2:

Projected Benefit Obligation = $230,000 ($100,000 + $120,000 + $10,000).
Pension Plan Assets = $198,000 ($80,000 + $110,000 + 8,000).

EXAMPLE 5.21

Company X has a defined benefit pension plan for its 100 employees. On 1/1/19X1, pension plan assets have a fair value of $230,000, accumulated benefit obligation is $285,000, and the projected benefit obligation is $420,000. 10 employees are expected to resign each year for the next 10 years. They will be eligible to receive benefits. Service cost for 19X1 is $40,000. On 12/31/19X1, the projected benefit obligation is $490,000, fair value of plan assets is $265,000, and accumulated benefit obligation is $340,000. The return on plan assets and the interest rate are both 8%. No actuarial gains or losses occurred during the year. Cash funded for the year is $75,000.

Pension expense equals:

| Service Cost | $40,000 |
| Interest on Projected Benefit Obligation (8% × $420,000) | 33,600 |

Return on Plan Assets (8% × $230,000)	(18,400)
Amortization of Actuarial Gains and Losses	—
Amortization of Unamortized Prior Service Cost	34,545*
Pension Expense	$89,745
*Projected Benefit Obligation	$420,000
Fair Value of Pension Plan Assets	230,000
Initial Net Obligation	$190,000

$$\text{Amortization } \frac{\$190,000}{5.5 \text{ years}^{**}} = \$34,545$$

$$^{**}\frac{n(n + 1)}{2} \times P = \frac{10(10 + 1)}{2} \times 10 = 550$$

$$\frac{550}{100} = 5.5 \text{ years (average remaining service period)}$$

The journal entries at 12/31/19X1 follow:

Pension Expense	89,745	
Cash		75,000
Deferred Pension Liability		14,745
Intangible Asset—Pension Plan	60,255	
Additional Pension Liability		60,255

Computation follows:

Accumulated Benefit Obligation—12/31/19X1	$340,000
Fair Value of Plan Assets—12/31/19X1	265,000
Minimum Liability	$ 75,000
Deferred Pension Liability	14,745
Additional Pension Liability	$ 60,255

What information should be disclosed in the footnotes?

Footnote disclosure for a pension plan includes:

- Description of plan including benefit formula, funding policy, employee groups covered, and retirement age
- Components of pension expense
- Pension assumptions (e.g., interest rate, mortality rate, employee turnover)

- Reconciliation of funded status of plan with employer amounts recognized on the balance sheet (e.g., fair value of plan assets, projected benefit obligation, unrecognized prior service cost)
- Present value of vested and nonvested benefits
- Weighted-average assumed discount rate involved in measuring the projected benefit obligation
- Weighted-average return rate on pension plan assets
- Amounts and types of securities included in pension plan assets
- Amount of approximate annuity benefits to employees

NOTE: For analytical purposes, the excess of the projected benefit obligation over the accumulated benefit obligation represents an unrecorded liability.

When is there settlement in a pension plan?

Per FASB 88, a settlement is discharging some or all of the employer's pension benefit obligation. A settlement *must* satisfy all of the following criteria:

- Irrevocable
- Relieves pension benefit responsibility
- Materially curtails risk related to the pension obligation

Excess plan assets may revert back to the employer.

How is settlement in a pension plan handled?

The amount of gain or loss recognized in the income statement when a pension obligation is settled is limited to the unrecognized net gain or loss from realized or unrealized changes in either the pension benefit obligation or plan assets. Changes arise when actual experiences deviate from the original assumptions. All or a prorata share of the unrecognized gain or loss is recognized when a plan is settled.

• If full settlement occurs, all unrecognized gains or losses are recognized.

• If only a part of the plan is settled, a prorata share of the unrecognized net gain or loss is recognized.

EXAMPLE: When the employer furnishes employees with a lump-sum amount to give up pension rights, the gain or loss resulting is included in the current year's income statement.

When does curtailment occur in a pension plan?

Per FASB 88, a curtailment occurs when an event significantly reduces future service years of present employees or eliminates for most employees the accumulation of defined benefits for future services. EXAMPLE: A plant closing ends employee services prior to pension plan expectations.

How do I handle curtailment in a pension plan?

The gain or loss is recognized in the current year's income statement and contains these elements:

• Unamortized prior service cost attributable to employee services no longer needed

• Change in pension benefit obligation due to the curtailment

What is involved in a termination in a pension plan?

When termination benefits are offered by the employer, accepted by employees, and the amount can reasonably be determined:

• An expense and liability are recognized

• The amount of the accrual equals the down payment plus the present value of future payments to be made by the employer

• The entry is to debit loss and credit cash (down payment) and liability (future payments)

• Footnote disclosure of the arrangement should be made

Trustee Reporting for a Defined Benefit Pension Plan

What recognition is made by the trustee?

FASB 35 deals with the reporting and disclosures by the trustee of a defined benefit pension plan. GAAP must be followed. Financial statements are *not* required to be issued by the plan. If they are issued, reporting guidelines have to be followed. The prime objective is to assess the plan's capability to meet retirement benefits.

BALANCE SHEET: Present *pension assets and liabilities* as an offset. Operating assets are at book value. In determining net assets available, accrual accounting is followed. EXAMPLE: Accruing for interest earned but not received. *Investments* are shown at fair market value. An asset shown is "contributions receivable due from employer."

- In computing pension plan liability, participants' accumulated benefits are *excluded*. In effect, plan participants are equity holders rather than creditors of the plan.

Disclosure is required of:

- Net assets available for benefits
- Changes in net assets available for benefits including net appreciation in fair value of each major class of investments
- Actuarial present value of accumulated plan benefits (i.e., benefits anticipated to be paid to retired employees, beneficiaries, and present employees)
- Changes in actuarial present value of accumulated plan benefits.
- Description of the plan including amendments.
- Accounting and funding policies.

NOTE: An annuity contract may exist whereby an insurance company agrees to give specified pension benefits in return for receiving a premium.

INCOME TAX ACCOUNTING

How do I account for taxes?

According to FASB No. 96 on "Accounting for Income Taxes," temporary differences occur between book income and taxable income. The deferred tax liability or asset is measured at the tax rate under *existing law* which will be in effect when the temporary difference reverses itself. Further, the deferred tax liability or asset must be adjusted for changes in tax law or in tax rate. Thus, the *liability method* is mandated in providing for deferred income taxes. Deferred tax expense or benefit is recognized for the net change during the year in a company's deferred tax liability or asset. It is balance sheet oriented. In addition, appropriate classification of the deferred account is necessary in the balance sheet. Proper disclosures must be made regarding the accounting for income taxes to communicate information properly to financial statement readers. Comprehensive deferred tax accounting is followed where tax expense equals taxes payable plus the tax effects of *all* temporary differences.

Income taxes are accounted for on the accrual basis. Recognition is given to current and deferred taxes payable or refundable at year-end resulting from occurrences that have been reflected in the financial statements. The tax effect of an event should *not* be recognized until that occurrence is reflected in the financial statements, irrespective of the probability that the event will take place in future years. In other words, tax consequences of revenue recognition and expense incurrence applicable to *future years* are *not* anticipated for purposes of recognizing and measuring the deferred tax liability or asset for the current year's financial statements. The effects of income taxes are given only for those that arise from a company's activities during the current and prior years. Measurement of the tax effect occurs by applying the tax rules to compute taxes payable or refundable presently or in future periods.

Typically, income taxes currently payable for a specified year comprises the tax effects of most events that are recognized in the financial statements. But due to some exceptions, income taxes currently payable for a year may include the tax consequences of some events recognized in financial statements for an earlier or later year. An exception may also arise that income taxes currently payable for a year may not include the tax consequences of some other happenings recognized in the financial statements for the current year.

If tax rates are graduated based on taxable income, aggregate calculations may be made using an estimated average rate.

Note that preference taxes that cannot be carried forward to offset future tax liabilities have to be charg·d to expense.

Temporary Differences

How do I handle temporary differences?

Temporary differences may occur due to a disparity between taxable income and book income as well as the differences between the tax bases of assets or liabilities and the amounts reported in the financial statements. A temporary difference may occur between the year in which transactions affect book income versus taxable income. A deferred tax liability or asset constitutes the amount of taxes payable or refundable in future years because of temporary differences at the end of the current year.

Temporary differences may arise between book income and taxable income due to differences in the recognition and measurement of assets, liabilities, stockholders' equity, revenues, expenses, gains, and losses. For instance, a deferred tax liability is booked for temporary differences that will result in *net* taxable amounts in later years. An example is an installment sale recognized for financial reporting purposes when the sale is made but for tax purposes when cash is collected.

A difference may exist between the financial reporting and tax basis of an asset or liability in the balance sheet resulting from taxability or deducibility in some later year irrespective of future events. Examples follow:

• Revenues or gains that are taxable subsequent to being recognized for book purposes. An example is an installment sale.

• Expenses or losses that are tax deductible subsequent to being recognized for book purposes. An example is the warranty provision.

• Revenues or gains that are taxable prior to being recognized for book purposes. An example is subscriptions received in advance.

• Expenses or losses that are deductible before being reflected for financial reporting purposes. An example is using straight-line depreciation for book purposes and accelerated cost recovery system for tax purposes.

Some temporary differences cannot be identified with a specific asset or liability for financial reporting purposes. Rather, a temporary difference arises from an event recognized in the financial statements that will result in taxable or deductible amounts in later years. An example is long-term construction accounting where the percentage-of-completion method is used for book purposes while the completed contract method is employed for tax reporting.

A temporary difference may result from increases in the tax basis of assets because of indexing for inflation.

NOTE: Asset or liability recognition is given for the deferred tax effects of all temporary differences.

KEY POINT: Graduated tax brackets present a problem in computing tax because deferred taxes may be provided at one rate and reverse at another tax rate. As per the Statement, scheduled reversal differences are provided at the applicable lower tax bracket rather than the rate used to compute taxes payable. The latter rate is typically higher. When temporary differences originate in small amounts companies may have a higher effective tax provision when the temporary differences reverse.

Indefinite Reversal

What if tax is indefinitely postponed?

No tax allocation is required for the *indefinite reversal* of *undistributed* earnings of subsidiaries and corporate joint ventures. For example, if the earnings of a foreign subsidiary will be indefinitely held there, no tax allocation is needed since U.S. tax will not be paid. Further, tax allocation is not required in the case where a foreign subsidiary's earnings will be remitted tax-free. Disclosure should be given of the cumulative amount of undistributed earnings for which deferred taxes have not been provided.

Carryforward Recognition

What about carryforward losses and tax credits?

Carryforward net operating loss and tax credits (e.g., investment tax credit, alternative minimum tax credit) are recognized only to the degree that deferred tax liabilities are available to absorb them in the carryforward period and recognition is not in excess of statutory limits. Otherwise, the tax benefits of carryforwards can*not* be recognized even in the case where realization is assured beyond a reasonable doubt and the loss was from a nonrecurring situation. The later realization of a tax benefit is typically *not* to be reported as an extraordinary item.

Deferred Tax Asset

What about the recognition of a deferred tax asset?

A deferred tax asset occurs if the net deductible amounts in future years are recoverable because of a carryback refund of paid taxes in current or previous years. *Note:* In almost all cases, no recognition is given to a deferred tax asset caused by net deductible amounts in future years, i.e., deferred tax effects of expenses or losses reported later for tax purposes than for book purposes. Additionally, an asset can*not* be recognized for net operating loss (or tax credit) carryforwards.

Classification

What classification is made of deferred taxes?

The deferred tax asset or liability shall be separately classified as current and noncurrent in the balance sheet. The deferred tax effect of temporary differences scheduled to reverse during the next year is classified as current, while scheduled reversal beyond the next year is presented as noncurrent. The current amount of the deferred tax liability or asset is the *net* deferred tax effects of:

• Temporary differences that arise in net taxable or deductible amounts for the year.

• Temporary differences applicable to an asset or liability that is shown for book purposes as current.

• Temporary differences having no identifiable asset or liability related thereto.

Offset is *not* permitted for deferred tax liabilities or assets that apply to different tax jurisdictions.

Acquisitions and Mergers

What is the tax effect for a business combination accounted for as a purchase?

In a purchase combination, the net assets acquired are reflected at their gross fair values with a separate deferred tax balance for the applicable tax effects. Further, a temporary difference will occur for the difference between the financial reporting and tax basis of assets and liabilities resulting from the acquisition. If the acquired company has an operating loss or tax credit carryforward, it may be used to reduce the deferred tax liability of the acquired company and hence reduce goodwill or create negative goodwill.

Disclosures

What disclosures are required for taxes?

Disclosure should be made of the types of temporary differences that have occurred causing a material deferred tax liability or asset.

If a deferred tax liability is *not* recognized, disclosure should be made of the following:

• Description of the kinds of temporary differences for which *no* recognition has been given to a deferred tax liability and the types of events that would result in tax recognition of the temporary differences.

• Cumulative amount of each kind of temporary difference.

• Amount of unrecognized deferred tax liability for unremitted earnings if practical determination of the liability is possible. If not practical to determine, a statement should be given to that effect. In addition, there should be cited the amount of withholding taxes payable upon remittance of those earnings.

• Amount of the unrecognized deferred tax liability for temporary differences other than unremitted earnings.

Disclosure should be made of the major components of tax expense applicable to continuing operations. Included in the components are:

• Current tax expense or benefit.

• Deferred tax expense or benefit.

• Governmental grants to the degree recognized as a subtraction of income tax expense.

• Operating loss carryforward benefits.

• Adjustment of deferred tax liability or asset for changes in the tax laws or rates.

A breakdown should be given of tax expense allocated to continuing operations, discontinued operations, extraordinary items, cumulative effect of a change in accounting principle, prior period adjustments, and the like. This is referred to as intraperiod tax allocation.

A reconciliation should exist between the reported amount of tax expense and the tax expense that would have occurred using federal statutory tax rates. The reconciliation should be in terms of percentages or dollar amounts. If statutory tax rates do not exist, use the regular tax rates for alternative tax systems. Disclosure should be given of the estimated amount and the nature of each material reconciling item.

Disclosure should be made of the amounts and expiration dates of operating loss and tax credit carryforwards for financial reporting and tax reporting purposes. If material, separate disclosure should be made of net operating loss or tax credit carryforwards for which tax benefits will be applied to reduce goodwill and other noncurrent intangibles.

Disclosure should be made of the provisions of intercorporate tax sharing arrangements and tax-related balances due to or from affiliates.

EXAMPLE 5.22*

At the end of year 1, future recovery of the reported amount of an enterprise's installment receivables will result in taxable amounts totaling $240,000 in years 2–4. Also, a $20,000 liability for estimated expenses has been recognized in the financial statements in year 1, and those expenses will be deductible for tax purposes in year 4 when the liability is expected to be paid. Those temporary differences are estimated to result in net taxable amounts in future years as presented below.

	Year 2	Year 3	Year 4
Taxable amounts	$70,000	$110,000	$60,000
Deductible amount	—	—	(20,000)
Net taxable amounts	$70,000	$110,000	$40,000

This example assumes that the enacted tax rates for years 2–4 are 20 percent for the first $50,000 of taxable income, 30 percent for the next $50,000, and 40 percent for taxable income over $100,000. The liability for deferred tax consequences is measured as follows:

	Year 2	Year 3	Year 4
20 percent tax on first $50,000	$10,000	$10,000	$8,000
30 percent tax on next $50,000	6,000	15,000	—
40 percent tax on over $100,000	—	4,000	—
	$16,000	$29,000	$8,000

A deferred tax liability is recognized for $53,000 (the total of the taxes payable for years 2–4) at the end of year 1.

Source: Financial Accounting Standards Board, FASB No. 96, "Accounting for Income Taxes," Stamford, Connecticut, December 1987, p. 32. Reprinted with permission.

FOREIGN CURRENCY TRANSLATION AND TRANSACTIONS

FASB 52 applies to:

• Foreign currency transactions such as exports and imports denominated in a currency other than a company's functional currency.

• Foreign currency financial statements of branches, divisions, and other investees incorporated in the financial statements of a U.S. company by combination, consolidation, or the equity method.

What are the purposes of a translation?

The purposes of translation are to:

• Furnish data of expected impacts of rate changes on cash flow and equity

• Provide data in consolidated financial statements relative to the financial results of each individual foreign consolidated entity

FASB 52 covers the translation of foreign currency statements and gains and losses on foreign currency transactions. Translation of foreign currency statements is typically needed when the statements of a foreign subsidiary or equity-method investee having a functional currency other than the U.S. dollar are to be included in the financial statements of a domestic enterprise (e.g., through consolidation or using the equity method).

NOTES: Generally, foreign currency statements should be translated using the exchange rate at the end of the reporting year. Resulting translation gains and losses are shown as a separate item in the stockholders' equity section.

Also important is the accounting treatment of gains and losses emanating from transactions denominated in a foreign currency. These are presented in the current year's income statement.

What are important terms in foreign currency?

• *Conversion:* An exchange of one currency for another

• *Currency Swap:* An exchange between two companies of the currencies of two different countries per an agreement to re-exchange the two currencies at the same rate of exchange at a specified future date.

• *Denominate:* Pay or receive in that *same* foreign currency. It can only be denominated in one currency (e.g., pounds). It is a real account (asset or liability) fixed in terms of a foreign currency irrespective of exchange rate.

• *Exchange Rate:* Ratio between a unit of one currency and that of another at a particular time. If there is a *temporary lack of exchangeability* between two currencies at the transaction date or balance sheet date, the *first rate available* thereafter at which exchanges could be made is used.

• *Foreign Currency:* A currency other than the functional currency of a business (for instance, the dollar could be a foreign currency for a foreign entity).

• *Foreign Currency Statements:* Financial statements using as the unit of measure a functional currency that is not the reporting currency of the business.

• *Foreign Currency Transactions:* Transactions whose terms are denominated in a currency other than the entity's functional currency. Foreign currency transactions take place when a business:

- Buys or sells on credit goods or services the prices of which are denominated in foreign currency
- Borrows or lends funds, and the amounts payable or receivable are denominated in foreign currency
- Is a party to an unperformed forward exchange contract
- Acquires or disposes of assets, or incurs or settles liabilities denominated in foreign currency

• *Foreign Currency Translation:* Expressing in the reporting currency of the company those amounts that are denominated or measured in a different currency.

• *Foreign Entity:* An operation (e.g., subsidiary, division, branch, joint venture) whose financial statements are prepared in a currency other than the reporting currency of the reporting entity.

• *Functional Currency:* An entity's functional currency is the currency of the *primary economic environment* in which the business operates. It is typically the currency of the environment in which the business primarily obtains and uses cash. The functional currency of a foreign operation may be the same as that of a related affiliate in the case where the foreign activity is an essential component or extension of the related affiliate.

• *Local Currency:* The currency of a particular foreign country.

• *Measure:* Translation into a currency other than the original reporting currency. Foreign financial statements are measured in U.S. dollars by using the applicable exchange rate.

• *Reporting Currency:* The currency the business prepares its financial statements in, usually U.S. dollars.

• *Spot Rate:* Exchange rate for immediate delivery of currencies exchanged.

• *Transaction Gain or Loss:* Transaction gains or losses occur due to a change in exchange rates between the functional currency and the currency in which a foreign currency transaction is denominated. They represent an increase or decrease in (a) the actual functional currency cash flows realized upon settlement of foreign currency transactions and (b) the expected functional currency cash flows on unsettled foreign currency transactions.

• *Translation Adjustments:* Adjustments arising from translating financial statements from the entity's functional currency into the reporting one.

What are the steps in a translation?

Four steps in translating the foreign country's financial statements into U.S. reporting requirements are:

- Conform the foreign country's financial statements to U.S. GAAP.
- Determine the functional currency of the foreign entity.
- Remeasure the financial statements in the functional currency, if necessary. Gains or losses from remeasurement are includable in remeasured current net income.
- Convert from the foreign currency into U.S. dollars (reporting currency).

What accounting recognition is given to foreign currency?

Prior to translation, the foreign country figures are remeasured in the functional currency. EXAMPLE: If a company in Italy is an independent entity and received cash and incurred expenses in Italy, the Italian currency is the functional currency. However, if the Italian company is an extension of a Canadian parent, the functional currency is the Canadian currency.

The functional currency should be consistently used except if material economic changes necessitate a change.

EXCEPTION: Previously issued financial statements are not restated for an alteration in the functional currency.

Consistent use of the functional currency of the foreign entity must exist over the years except if there are changes in circumstances warranting a change. If a change in the functional currency takes place, it is accounted for as a change in estimate.

If a company's books are *not* kept in its functional currency, remeasurement into the functional currency is mandated. The remeasurement process occurs before translation into the reporting currency takes place. When a foreign entity's functional currency is the reporting currency, remeasurement into the reporting currency obviates translation. The remeasurement process is intended to generate the same result as if the entity's books had been kept in the functional currency.

How do I determine the functional currency?

Guidelines are referred to in determining the functional currency of a foreign operation.

• *Selling price.* The functional currency is the foreign currency when the foreign operation's selling prices of products or services are due primarily to local factors, e.g., government law and competition. It is *not* due to changes in exchange rate. The functional currency is the parent's currency when the foreign operation's sales prices mostly apply in the short-run to fluctuation in the exchange rate resulting from international factors, e.g., worldwide competition.

• *Market.* The functional currency is the foreign currency when the foreign activity has a strong local sales market for products or services, even though a significant amount of exports may exist. The functional currency is the parent's currency when the foreign operation's sales market is mostly in the parent's country.

• *Cash flow.* The functional currency is the foreign currency when the foreign operation's cash flows are primarily in foreign currency not directly affecting the parent's cash flow. The functional currency is the parent's currency when the foreign operation's cash flows directly impact the parent's cash flows. They are usually available for remittance via intercompany accounting settlement.

• *Financing.* The functional currency is the foreign currency if financing the foreign activity is in foreign currency and funds obtained by the foreign activity are sufficient to meet debt obligations. The functional currency is the parent's currency when financing of foreign activity is provided by the parent or occurs in U.S. dollars. Funds obtained by the foreign activity are insufficient to satisfy debt requirements.

• *Expenses.* The functional currency is the foreign currency when the foreign operation's production costs or services are usually incurred locally. However, some foreign imports may exist. The functional currency is the parent's currency when the foreign operation's production and service costs are primarily component costs obtained from the parent's country.

• *Intercompany transactions.* If there is a restricted number of intercompany transactions, the functional currency is the foreign currency—that is, when minor interrelationship occurs between the activities of the foreign entity and parent except for competitive advantages, e.g., patents. If many intercompany transactions exist, the functional currency is the parent's currency—that is, when material interrelationship exists between the foreign entity and parent.

Translation Process

What currency is used in a translation of foreign currency statements when the U.S. dollar is the functional currency?

The foreign entity's financial statement in a highly *inflationary* economy is not stable enough and should be remeasured as if the functional currency were the reporting currency. In effect, the reporting currency is used directly.

A *highly inflationary environment* is one that has cumulative inflation of about *100% or more over a three year period*. In other words, the inflation rate must be increasing at a rate of about 35% a year for three consecutive years. *NOTE:* The International Monetary Fund of Washington, D.C. publishes monthly figures on international inflation rates.

What currency is used in a translation of foreign currency statements when the foreign currency is the functional currency?

Balance sheet: Items are translated via the *current exchange rate*. For assets and liabilities, use the rate at the balance sheet date. If a current exchange rate is not available at the balance sheet date, use the first exchange rate available after that date. The *current exchange rate* is also used to translate the statement of cash flows, except for those items found in the income statement which are translated using the weighted-average rate.

Income statement: For these items (revenues, expenses, gains, and losses), use the exchange rate at the dates those items are recognized.

RECOMMENDATION: Since translation at the exchange rates at the dates the many revenues, expenses, gains, and losses are recognized is almost always impractical, use a *weighted-average exchange rate* for the period in translating *income statement items*.

Disclosure should consist of:

• A material change occurring between the date of the financial statements and the audit report date should be disclosed as a subsequent event.

• The effects on unsettled balances pertaining to foreign currency transactions.

Translation Adjustments

What are translation adjustments?

If a company's functional currency is a foreign currency, *translation adjustments* arise from translating that company's financial statements into the reporting currency. Translation adjustments are unrealized and should not be included in the income statement. They should be reported separately and accumulated in a *separate component of equity*.

EXCEPTION: If remeasurement from the recording currency to the functional currency is required before translation, the gain or loss is reflected in the income statement.

How do I handle the sale or liquidation of an investment in a foreign entity?

Upon sale or liquidation of an investment in a foreign entity, the amount attributable to that entity and accumulated in the translation adjustment component of equity is removed from the stockholders' equity section. It is considered a part of the gain or loss on sale or liquidation of the investment in the income statement for the period during which the sale or liquidation occurs.

According to Interpretation 37, sale of an investment in a foreign entity may include a partial sale of an ownership interest. In that case, a prorata amount of the cumulative translation adjustment reflected as a stockholders' equity component is includable in arriving at the gain or loss on sale. EXAMPLE: If a business sells a 40% ownership interest in a foreign investment, 40% of the translation adjustment applicable to it is included in calculating gain or loss on sale of that ownership interest.

Foreign Currency Transactions

What are foreign currency transactions?

Foreign currency transactions may result in receivables or payables fixed in terms of the amount of foreign currency to be received or paid.

A foreign currency transaction requires settlement in a currency other than the functional currency. A change in exchange rates between the functional currency and the currency in which a transaction is denominated increases or decreases the expected amount of functional currency cash flows upon settlement of the transaction.

How are foreign currency transactions accounted for?

The change in expected functional currency cash flows is a *foreign currency transaction gain or loss* that is typically included in arriving at earnings in the *income statement* for the period in which the exchange rate is altered. EXAMPLE: A transaction may result in a gain or loss when a British subsidiary has a receivable denominated in pounds from a French customer.

Similarly, a transaction gain or loss (measured from the *transaction date* or the most recent intervening balance sheet date, whichever is later) realized upon settlement of a foreign currency transaction should usually be included in determining net income for the period in which the transaction is settled.

EXAMPLE 5.23

An exchange gain or loss occurs when the exchange rate changes between the purchase date and sale date.

Merchandise is bought for 100,000 lira. The exchange rate is 4 lira to 1 dollar. The journal entry is:

Purchases	$25,000	
Accounts Payable		$25,000
100,000/4 = $25,000		

When the merchandise is paid for, the exchange rate is 5 to 1. The journal entry is:

Accounts Payable	$25,000	
Cash		$20,000
Foreign exchange gain		5,000
100,000/5 = $20,000		

The $20,000, using an exchange rate of 5 to 1, can buy 100,000 lira. The transaction gain is the difference between the cash required of $20,000 and the initial liability of $25,000.

NOTE: A foreign transaction gain or loss has to be determined at each balance sheet date on all recorded foreign transactions that have not been settled.

EXAMPLE 5.24

A U.S. company sells goods to a customer in England on 11/15/X7 for 10,000 pounds. The exchange rate is 1 pound to $.75. Thus, the transaction is worth $7,500 (10,000 pounds × .75). Payment is due 2 months later. The entry on 11/15/X7 is:

Accounts Receivable—		
England	$7,500	
Sales		$7,500

Accounts receivable and sales are measured in U.S. dollars at the transaction date employing the spot rate. Even though the accounts receivable are measured and reported in U.S. dollars, the receivable is fixed in pounds. Thus, a transaction gain or loss can occur if the exchange rate changes between the transaction date (11/15/X7) and the settlement date (1/15/X8).

Since the financial statements are prepared between the transaction date and settlement date, receivables denominated in a currency other than the functional currency (U.S. dollar) must be restated to reflect the spot rate on the balance sheet date. On December 31, 19X7 the exchange rate is 1 pound equals $.80. Hence, the 10,000 pounds are now valued at $8,000 (10,000 × $.80). Therefore, the accounts receivable denominated in pounds should be upwardly adjusted by $500. The required journal entry on 12/31/X7 is:

Accounts Receivable—		
England	$500	
Foreign Exchange Gain		$500

The income statement for the year ended 12/31/X7 shows an exchange gain of $500. Note that sales is not affected by the exchange gain since sales relates to operational activity.

On 1/15/X8, the spot rate is 1 pound = $.78. The journal entry is:

Cash	$7,800	
Foreign Exchange Loss	200	
Accounts Receivable—		
England		$8,000

The 19X8 income statement shows an exchange loss of $200.

What transaction gains and losses may be excluded from determination of net income?

Gains and losses on these foreign currency transactions are not included in earnings but rather reported as translation adjustments:

- Foreign currency transactions designated as *economic hedges* of a net investment in a foreign entity, beginning as of the designation date
- Intercompany foreign currency transactions of a *long-term investment* nature (settlement is not planned or expected in the forseeable future), when the entities to the transaction are consolidated, combined, or accounted for by the equity method in the reporting company's financial statements

A gain or loss on a forward contract or other foreign currency transaction that is intended to *hedge* an identifiable foreign currency commitment (e.g., an agreement to buy or sell machinery) should be deferred and included in the measurement of the related foreign currency transaction. *NOTE:* Losses should *not* be deferred if it is anticipated that deferral would cause losses to be recognized in subsequent periods.

A foreign currency transaction is considered a hedge of an identifiable foreign currency commitment provided both of these criteria are satisfied:

- The foreign currency transaction is designated as a hedge of a foreign currency commitment
- The foreign currency commitment is firm

Forward Exchange Contracts

What is a forward exchange contract?

A forward exchange contract is an agreement to exchange different currencies at a given future date and at a specified rate (forward rate). A forward contract is a foreign currency transaction.

How do I handle forward contracts?

A gain or loss on a forward contract that does not meet the conditions described below are includable in net income.

NOTE: Currency swaps are accounted for in a similar fashion.

• A *gain or loss on a forward contract*, except a speculative forward contract, should be computed by multiplying the foreign currency amount of the forward contract by the difference between the *spot rate* at the balance sheet date and the spot rate at the date of inception of the forward contract.

• The *discount or premium on a forward contract* (the foreign currency amount of the contract multiplied by the difference between the contracted forward rate and the spot rate at the date of inception of the contract) should be accounted for separately from the gain or loss on the contract. It should be included in computing net income over the life of the forward contract.

• A *gain or loss on a speculative forward contract* (a contract that does not hedge an exposure) should be computed by multiplying the foreign currency amount of the forward contract by the difference between the forward rate available from the remaining maturity of the contract and the contracted forward rate (or the forward rate last used to measure a gain or loss on that contract for an earlier period). *NOTE: No separate accounting recognition* is given to the discount or premium on a speculative forward contract.

Hedging

How can foreign currency transactions be hedged?

Foreign currency transactions gains and losses on assets and liabilities, denominated in a currency other than the functional currency, can be hedged if the U.S. company engages into a forward exchange contract.

A hedge can occur even if a forward exchange contract does not exist. EXAMPLE: A foreign currency transaction can serve as an economic hedge offsetting a parent's net investment in a foreign entity when the transaction is entered into for hedging purposes and is effective.

EXAMPLE 5.25

A U.S. parent completely owns a French subsidiary having net assets of $3 million in francs. The U.S. parent can borrow $3 million francs to hedge its net investment in the French subsidiary. Also assume the French franc is the functional currency, and the $3 million obligation is denominated in francs. Variability in the exchange rate for francs does not have a net impact on the parent's consolidated balance sheet, since increases in the translation adjustments balance arising from translation of the net investment will be netted against decreases in this balance emanating from the adjustment of the liability denominated in francs.

PART 2

ANALYZING FINANCIAL STATEMENTS

CHAPTER 6

FINANCIAL STATEMENT ANALYSIS

Financial statement analysis is an appraisal of a company's previous financial performance and its future potential. The CPA is often involved in analyzing the financial statements of an existing client, prospective client, or targeted company for a potential acquisition. Financial statement analysis aids the CPA in determining what areas to audit and in appraising the over-all health of the business. A "going-concern" problem may be identified. After the CPA completes his financial statement analysis, he should consult with management to discuss their plans and prospects, identify problem areas, and offer possible solutions.

This chapter covers:

- Analytical techniques to be followed in appraising the balance sheet and income statement
- Indicators of prospective business failure

Why analyze financial statements?

The CPA analyzes the financial statement of a client for a number of important reasons:

• It indicates areas requiring audit attention. The CPA can look at the percentage change in an account over the years or relative to some base year to identify inconsistencies. EXAMPLE: If promotion and entertainment expense to sales was 2% last year and shot up to 16% this year, the auditor would want to uncover the reasons. This would be especially disturbing if other companies in the industry still had a percentage relationship of 2%. The auditor might suspect that the promotion and entertainment expense account contained some personal rather than business charges. Supporting documentation for the charges would be requested and carefully reviewed by the CPA.

- It indicates the financial health of the client which is of interest to the CPA for the following reasons:
    - —A determination has to be made if the client is financially sound enough to pay the accounting fees.
    - —The CPA must ascertain whether poor financial conditions exist which may cause a going-concern problem.
    - —The CPA wants to know his potential legal exposure. If the client has a poor financial condition, corporate failure may occur resulting in lawsuits by creditors and others. If financial problems exist, the auditor would have to take proper audit and reporting steps including suitable references in the audit report.
- It provides vital information to be included in the management letter.
- It assists in identifying areas of financial problems and means of corrective action for the client.
- It aids the client in determining appropriateness of mergers and acquisitions.

A company's financial health has a bearing upon its price-earnings ratio, bond rating, cost of financing, and availability of financing. CPAs should especially watch out for "high accounting risk" companies:

- "Glamour" companies known for earnings growth
- Companies in the public eye
- Companies having difficulty obtaining financing
- Companies whose management previously committed dishonest acts

How does the CPA draw conclusions from financial analysis?

To obtain worthwhile conclusions from financial ratios, the CPA has to make two comparisons:

Industry Comparison. The CPA should compare the company's ratios to those of competing companies in the industry or with industry standards. Industry norms can be obtained from such services as:

- Dun and Bradstreet
- Robert Morris Associates
- Standard and Poor's
- Value Line

EXAMPLES: Dun and Bradstreet computes 14 ratios for each of 125 lines of business. They are published annually in *Dun's Review* and *Key Business Ratios*. Robert Morris Associates publishes *Annual Statement Studies*. Sixteen ratios are computed for more than 300 lines of business, as is a percentage distribution of items on the balance sheet and income statement (common size financial statements).

In analyzing a company, the CPA should appraise the trends in its particular industry. What is the pattern of expansion or contraction in the industry? The profit dollar is worth more if earned in a healthy, expanding industry than in a declining one.

Trend Analysis. A company's ratio may be compared over several years to identify direction of financial health or operational performance.

The optimum value for any given ratio usually varies across industry lines, through time, and within different companies in the same industry. In other words, a ratio deemed optimum for one company may be inadequate for another. A particular ratio is typically deemed optimum within a given range of values. An increase or decrease beyond this range points to weakness or inefficiency. EXAMPLE: While a low current ratio may indicate poor liquidity, a very high current ratio may indicate inefficient utilization of assets (e.g., excessive inventory) or inability to use short-term credit to the firm's advantage.

NOTE: In appraising a seasonal business, the CPA may find that year-end financial data are not representative. Thus, averages based on quarterly or monthly information may be used to level out seasonality effects.

HORIZONTAL AND VERTICAL ANALYSIS

How do horizontal and vertical analysis work?

Horizontal analysis looks at the trend in accounts over the years and aids in identifying areas of wide divergence mandating further attention. Horizontal analysis may also be presented by showing trends relative to a base year.

In *vertical analysis*, a significant item on a financial statement is used as a base value, and all other items on the financial statement are compared to it. In performing vertical analysis for the balance sheet, total assets is assigned 100%. Each asset is expressed as a percentage of total assets. Total liabilities and stockholders' equity is also assigned 100%. Each liability and stockholders' equity account is then expressed as a percentage of total liabilities and stockholders' equity. In the income statement, net sales is given the value of 100% and all other accounts are appraised in comparison to net sales. The resulting figures are then given in a common size statement.

Vertical analysis is helpful in disclosing the internal structure of the business. It shows the relationship between each income statement account and revenue. It indicates the mix of assets that produces the income and the mix of the sources of capital, whether by current or long-term liabilities or by equity funding. Besides making internal evaluation possible, the results of vertical analysis are also employed to appraise the company's relative position in the industry. Horizontal and vertical analysis point to possible problem areas to be evaluated by the CPA.

BALANCE SHEET ANALYSIS

In analyzing the balance sheet, the CPA is primarily concerned with the realizability of the assets, turnover, and earning potential. The evaluation of liabilities considers arbitrary adjustments and understatement.

Assets

How do I appraise the quality of assets?

If assets are overstated, net income will be overstated since the earnings do not include necessary charges to reduce earnings to their proper valuations. Asset quality depends on the amount and timing of the realization of assets. Therefore, assets should be categorized by risk category.

• Useful ratios are the percentage of high-risk assets to total assets and high-risk assets to sales. High asset realization risk points to poor quality of earnings due to possible future write-offs. EXAMPLE: The future realization of accounts receivable is better than that of goodwill.

• Multi-purpose assets are of better quality than single-purpose ones resulting from readier salability.

• Assets lacking separable value cannot be sold easily and as such have low realizability. EXAMPLE: Work-in-process and intangibles.

NOTES: In appraising realization risk in assets, the effect of changing government policies on the entity has to be taken into account.

Risk may exist with chemicals and other products deemed hazardous to health. Huge inventory losses may have to be taken.

EXAMPLE 6.1

Company A presents total assets of $6 million and sales of $10 million. Included in total assets are the following high risk assets as perceived by the CPA:

Deferred moving costs	$300,000
Deferred plant rearrangement costs	100,000
Receivables for claims under a government contract	200,000
Goodwill	150,000

Applicable ratios are:

$$\frac{\text{High-risk Assets}}{\text{Total Assets}} = \frac{\$750,000}{\$6,000,000} = \underline{12.5\%}$$

$$\frac{\text{High-risk Assets}}{\text{Sales}} = \frac{\$750,000}{\$10,000,000} = \underline{7.5\%}$$

Cash

Is cash proper and unrestricted?

A high ratio of sales to cash may indicate inadequate cash. This may lead to financial problems if additional financing is not available at reasonable interest rates. A low turnover ratio indicates excessive cash being held.

The CPA should determine whether part of the cash is restricted and unavailable for use. EXAMPLES: A compensating balance that does not constitute "free" cash. Cash in a politically unstable foreign country that may have remission restrictions.

Accounts Receivable

Are accounts receivables realizable?

Realization risk in receivables can be appraised by studying the nature of the receivable balance. EXAMPLES: High-risk receivables include:

- Amounts from economically unstable foreign countries
- Receivables subject to offset provisions
- Receivables due from a company experiencing severe financial problems

Companies dependent on a few customers have greater risk than those with a large number of important accounts. Receivables due from industry are usually safer than those arising from consumers. Fair trade laws are more protective of consumers.

What do increases in accounts receivable mean?

A significant increase in accounts receivable compared to the prior year may indicate increased realization risk. The firm may be selling to riskier customers. The trends in accounts receivable to total assets, and accounts receivable to sales should be evaluated.

The CPA should appraise the trends in the ratios of bad debts to accounts receivable and bad debts to sales. An unwarranted decrease in bad debts lowers the quality of earnings. This may happen when there is a decline in bad debts even though the company is selling to less creditworthy customers and/or actual bad debt losses are increasing.

A company may purposely overstate bad debts to provide accounting cushions for reporting understated profits. Also, companies may have substantial bad debt provisions in the current period because improper provisions were made in prior years distorting the earnings trend. A sudden write-off of accounts receivable may arise from prior understated bad debt provisions. Earnings may be managed by initially increasing and then lowering the bad debt provision.

Receivables are of low quality if they arose from loading customers with unneeded merchandise by giving generous credit terms. Be alert for these "red-flagged" items:

- A significant increase in sales in the final quarter of the year
- A substantial amount of sales returns in the first quarter of the next year
- A material decrease in sales for the first quarter of the next year

In a *seasonal* business, the accounts receivable turnover (credit sales/average accounts receivable) may be based on monthly or quarterly sales figures so that a proper averaging takes place.

How significant are sales returns and allowances?

The trend in sales returns and allowances is often a good reflection of the quality of merchandise sold to customers. A significant decrease in a firm's sales allowance account as a percentage of sales is not in conformity with reality when a greater liability for dealer returns exist. This will result in lower earnings quality.

EXAMPLE 6.2

Company X's sales and sales returns for the period 19X3 to 19X5 follow:

	19X5	19X4	19X3
Balance in sales returns account at year-end	$2,000	$3,800	$1,550
Sales	$240,000	$215,000	$100,000
Percentage of sales returns to sales	.0083	.0177	.0155

The reduction in the ratio of sales returns to sales from 19X4 to 19X5 indicates that less of a provision for returns is being made by the company. This is unrealistic if there is a greater liability for dealer returns and credits on an expanded sales base.

Inventory

What does an inventory buildup mean?

An inventory buildup may point to:

• *Greater realization risk.* The buildup may be at the plant, wholesaler, or retailer. A sign of buildup is when the inventory increases at a faster rate than sales.

• *A production slowdown,* when there is a reduction in raw materials coupled with an increase in work-in-process and finished goods. Further, greater obsolescence risk exists with work-in-process and finished goods due to major buildups. Raw materials have the best realizability because of greater universality and their multi-purpose nature.

What should I do in the event of inventory buildup?

Computation of the turnover rate should be made by each major inventory category and by department.

• A *low turnover rate* may indicate overstocking, obsolescence, or problems with the product line or marketing effectiveness. There are cases where a low inventory rate is appropriate. EXAMPLE: A higher inventory level may arise because of expected future increases in price.

• A *high turnover rate* may point to inadequate inventory, possibly leading to a loss in business. At the "natural year end" the turnover rate may be unusually high, because at that time the inventory balance may be very low.

The number of days inventory is held should be computed. The age of inventory should be compared to industry averages and to prior years of the company.

• *High realization risk* applies with specialized, technological, "fad," luxurious, perishable, and price sensitive merchandise. The CPA must be sure that the company has not assigned values to unsalable and obsolete merchandise. If there is a sudden inventory write-off, the CPA may be suspicious of the firm's deferral policy.

• *Low realization risk* applies to standard, staple, and necessity goods, due to their better salability.

• *Collateralized inventory* has a greater risk, because creditors can retain it in the event of nonpayment of an obligation.

• Inventory can have *political risk* associated with it.
EXAMPLE: Increased gas prices due to a shortage situation making it unfeasible to purchase large cars.

Look for inventory that is overstated due to mistakes in:

- Quantities
- Costing
- Pricing
- Valuation of work-in-process

The more technical the product and the more dependence on internally developed cost records, the greater the susceptibility of the cost estimates to misstatement.

NOTES: If adequate insurance cannot be obtained at reasonable rates due to unfavorable geographic location of the merchandise (e.g., high crime area, flood susceptibility), a problem exists.

The CPA should note the appropriateness of a change in inventory. Is it required by a new FASB pronouncement, SEC Release, or IRS tax ruling?

Investments

Are securities properly stated?

An indication of the fair value of investments may be the revenue (dividend income, interest income) obtained from them. Have decreases in portfolio market values been recognized in the accounts? Higher realization risk exists where there is a declining trend in the percentage of earnings derived from investments to their carrying value. Also check subsequent event disclosures for unrealized losses in the portfolio occurring after year-end.

EXAMPLE 6.3

Company X presents the following information:

	19X1	19X2
Investments	$50,000	$60,000
Investment Income	$ 7,000	$ 5,000

The percent of investment income to total investments decreased from 14% in 19X1 to 8.3% in 19X2, pointing to higher realization risk in the portfolio.

If a company is buying securities in other companies for diversification purposes, this will reduce overall risk. Risk in an investment portfolio can be ascertained by computing the standard deviation of its rate of return.

When an investment portfolio has a market value above cost, it constitutes an undervalued asset.

An investment portfolio of securities fluctuating widely in price is of higher realization risk than a portfolio that is diversified by industry and economic sector. But the former portfolio will show greater profitability in a bull market.

RECOMMENDATIONS: Appraise the extent of diversification and stability of the investment portfolio. There is less risk when securities are negatively correlated (price goes in opposite directions) or not correlated compared to a portfolio of positively correlated securities (price goes in same direction).

Be on guard against a dubious reclassification of a marketable security to long-term investment in order to avoid showing a future unrealized loss on the security portfolio in the income statement. The unrealized loss on a long-term portfolio is presented in the stockholders' equity section of the balance sheet.

Note cases where debt securities have a cost in excess of market value.

Fixed Assets

Are property, plant, and equipment properly maintained?

Inadequate provision for the maintenance of property, plant, and equipment detracts from the long-term earning power of the firm. If obsolete assets are not replaced and repairs not properly made, breakdowns and detracted operational efficiency will result. Failure to write down obsolete fixed assets results in overstated earnings.

RECOMMENDATIONS:

- Determine the age and condition of each major asset along with its replacement cost.
- Review the trend in fixed asset acquisitions to total gross assets. This trend is particularly revealing for a technological company that has to keep up-to-date. A decrease in the trend points to the failure to replace older assets on a timely

basis. Inactive and unproductive assets are a drain on the firm.

- Review asset efficiency by evaluating production levels, downtime, and discontinuances. Assets that have not been used for a long period of time may have to be written down.

NOTE: Pollution-causing equipment may necessitate replacement or modification to meet governmental ecology requirements.

EXAMPLE 6.4

Company T presents the following information regarding its fixed assets:

	19X1	19X2
Fixed Assets	$120,000	$105,000
Repairs and Maintenance	6,000	4,500
Replacement Cost	205,000	250,000

The company has inadequately maintained its assets as indicated by:

- The reduction in the ratio of repairs and maintenance to fixed assets from 5% in 19X1 to 4.3% in 19X2.
- The material variation between replacement cost and historical cost
- The reduction in fixed assets over the year

What does the fixed asset turnover ratio mean?

The fixed asset turnover ratio (net sales to average fixed assets) aids in appraising a company's ability to use its asset base efficiently to obtain revenue. A low ratio may mean that investment in fixed assets is excessive relative to the output generated.

When a company's rate of return on assets (e.g., net income to fixed assets) is poor, the firm may be justified in not maintaining fixed assets. If the industry is declining, fixed asset replacement and repairs may have been restricted.

A company having specialized or risky fixed assets has greater vulnerability to asset obsolescence.

EXAMPLE: Machinery used to manufacture specialized products and "fad" items.

RECOMMENDATIONS: A depreciation method should be used that most realistically measures the expiration in asset usefulness. EXAMPLE: The units-of-production method may result in a realistic charge for machinery. Unrealistic book depreciation may be indicated when depreciation for stockholder reporting is materially less than depreciation for tax return purposes.

Examine the trend in depreciation expense as a percent of both fixed assets and net sales. A reduction in the trend may point to inadequate depreciation charges for the potential obsolescence of fixed assets. Another indication of inadequate depreciation charges is a concurrent moderate rise in depreciation coupled with a material increase in capital spending.

EXAMPLE 6.5

The following information applies to X Company:

	19X1	19X2
Depreciation expense to fixed assets	5.3%	4.4%
Depreciation expense to sales	4.0%	3.3%

The above declining ratios indicate improper provision for the deterioration of assets.

NOTES: A change in classification of newly acquired fixed assets to depreciation categories different from the older assets (e.g., accelerated depreciation to straight-line) will result in lower earnings quality.

A vacillating depreciation policy will distort continuity in earnings.

If there is a reduction in depreciation expense caused by an unrealistic change in the lives and salvage values of property, plant, and equipment, there will be overstated earnings.

An inconsistency exists when there is a material decline in revenue coupled with a major increase in capital expenditures. It may be indicative of overexpansion and later write-offs of fixed assets.

Intangibles

When is there a high realization risk for intangible assets?

High realization risk is indicated when there are high ratios of:

• Intangible assets to total assets
• Intangible assets to net worth

Intangibles may be overstated compared to their market value or future earning potential. EXAMPLE: A firm's goodwill may be overstated or worthless in a recessionary environment. A forty year amortization period may be excessive. Also, intangibles acquired before 1970 may be retained on the books without amortization.

An unwarranted lengthening in the amortization period for intangibles overstates earnings. EXAMPLE: An unjustified change is when the company's reputation has been worsened due to political bribes or environmental violations.

The change in intangible assets to the change in net income should also be examined. A rising trend may mean this net income has been relieved of appropriate charges.

How do leasehold improvements affect intangibles?

Leasehold improvements are improvements made to rented property, e.g., panelling and fixtures. Leasehold improvements are amortized over the life of the rented property or the life of the improvement, whichever is shorter. Leasehold improvements have no cash realizability.

What about the goodwill value of an acquired company?

A company's goodwill account should be appraised to determine whether the acquired firm has superior earning potential to justify the excess of cost over fair market value of net assets paid for it. If the acquired company does not have superior profit potential, the goodwill has no value, because excess earnings do not exist relative to other companies in the industry. However, internally developed goodwill is expensed and not capitalized. It represents an undervalued asset, e.g., the good reputation of McDonald's.

Are patents properly valued?

Patents may be undervalued. Patents are recorded at the registration cost plus legal fees to defend them. These costs may be far below the present value of future cash flows derived from the patents.

Patents are less valuable when they may easily be infringed upon by minor alteration or when they apply to high-technology items. The company's financial condition must also be considered, since it may incur significant legal costs in defending patents. What are the expiration dates of the patents and the degree to which new patents are coming on stream?

Deferred Charges

Are deferred charges of poor quality?

Deferred expenses depend to a greater extent on estimates of future probabilities than do other assets. The estimates may be overly optimistic. Is the company deferring an item having no future benefit only to defer costs in order not to burden net income? Deferred charges are not cash realizable assets and cannot be used to meet creditor claims. EXAMPLES: Questionable deferred charges are:

- Moving costs
- Start-up costs
- Plant rearrangement costs
- Merger expenses
- Promotional costs

RECOMMENDATIONS: A company may try to hide declining profitability by deferring costs that were expensed in prior years. Be on the lookout for such a situation.

Examine the trend in deferred charges to sales, deferred charges to net income, and deferred charges (e.g., deferred promotion costs) to total expenditures. Increasing trends may be indicative of a more liberal accounting policy.

EXAMPLE 6.6

Company G presents the following information:

	19X1	19X2
Deferred charges	$ 70,000	$150,000
Total assets	500,000	590,000
Sales	800,000	845,000
Net income	200,000	215,000
Computed ratios are:		
Deferred costs to total		
assets	14%	25.4%
Deferred costs to sales	8.8%	17.8%
Deferred costs to net		
income	35%	69.8%

The higher ratios of deferred charges to total assets, to sales, and to net income indicate more realization risk in assets. Further, 19X2's earnings quality may be lower because deferred costs may include in it items that should have been expensed.

NOTE: A high ratio of intangible assets and deferred charges to total assets points to an asset structure of greater realization risk. Overstated assets in terms of realizability may necessitate later write-off.

Unrecorded Assets

Do off-balance sheet assets exist?

Unrecorded assets are positive aspects of financial position even though they are not shown on the balance sheet. EXAMPLE: Unrecorded assets include tax loss carryforward benefit and a purchase commitment where the company has a contract to buy an item at a price materially less than the going rate.

RECOMMENDATION: Note the existence of unrecorded assets representing resources of the business or items expected to have future economic benefit.

Liabilities

What is the quality of liabilities?

If liabilities are understated, net income is overstated because it does not include necessary charges to reflect the proper valuation of liabilities.

RECOMMENDATIONS: Examine trends in current liabilities to total liabilities, to stockholders' equity, and to sales. Rising trends may point to liquidity problems.

Determine whether liabilities are "patient" or "pressing." A "patient" supplier with a long relationship may postpone or modify the debt payable for a financially troubled company. "Pressing debt" includes taxes and loans payable. These have to be paid without excuse. A high ratio of "pressing liabilities" to "patient liabilities" points to greater liquidity risk.

EXAMPLE 6.7

Company A reports the following information:

Current Liabilities	19X1	19X2
Accounts payable	$ 30,000	$ 26,000
Short-term loans payable	50,000	80,000
Commercial paper	40,000	60,000
Total current liabilities	$120,000	$166,000
Total noncurrent liabilities	300,000	308,000
Total liabilities	$420,000	$468,000
Sales	$1,000,000	$1,030,000

Relevant ratios follow:

Current liabilities to total liabilities	28.6%	35.5%
Current liabilities to sales	12.0%	16.1%
"Pressing" current liabilities to "patient" current liabilities (short-term loans payable plus commercial paper/accounts payable)	3.01	5.4

The company has greater liquidity risk in 19X2 as reflected by the higher ratios of current liabilities to total liabilities, current liabilities to sales, and "pressing" current liabilities to "patient" current liabilities.

How do adjustments of estimated liabilities affect earnings?

Arbitrary adjustments of estimated liabilities should be eliminated in deriving corporate earning power. Estimated liability provisions should be realistic given the nature of the circumstances. EXAMPLE: Profits derived from a recoupment of prior year reserves may necessitate elimination.

RECOMMENDATION: If you find that reserves are used to manage earnings, add back the amounts charged to earnings and deduct the amounts credited to earnings.

A firm having an unrealistically low provision for future costs has understated earnings. EXAMPLE: It is inconsistent for a company to have a lower warranty provision when prior experience points to a deficiency in product quality.

An overprovision in estimated liabilities is sometimes made. In effect, the company is providing a reserve for a "rainy day." EXAMPLE: Profits are too high and management wants to bring them down.

NOTE: Poor earnings quality is indicated when more operating expenses and losses are being charged to reserve accounts compared to prior years.

Are some liabilities off the balance sheet?

• Unrecorded liabilities are not reported on the financial statements but do require future payment or services. EXAMPLES: Lawsuits and noncapitalized leases.

• Useful disclosures of long-term obligations are mandated by FASB 47. *RECOMMENDATION:* Review commitments applicable to unconditional purchase obligations and future payments on long-term debt and redeemable stock.

• FASB Interpretation 34 requires disclosure of indirect guarantees of indebtedness. Included are contracts in which a company promises to advance funds to another if financial problems occur, as when sales drop below a stipulated level.

• Preferred stock with a maturity date or subject to sinking fund requirements is more like debt than equity. However, convertible bonds with an attractive conversion feature are more like equity than debt since there is an expectation of conversion.

Evaluation of Liquidity

How do I analyze a firm's liquidity?

In appraising a company's liquidity, sufficient funds flow is necessary so that current assets are sufficient to meet short-term debt. Measures of funds flow include:

• *Current Ratio* equals current assets divided by current liabilities.

• *Quick Ratio* equals cash plus marketable securities plus receivables divided by current liabilities. It is a stringent test of liquidity.

• *Working Capital* equals current assets less current liabilities. A high working capital is needed when the company may have difficulty borrowing on short notice. Working capital should be compared to other financial statement items such as sales and total assets. EXAMPLE: Working capital to sales indicates if the company is optimally employing its liquid balance. To identify changes in the composition of working capital, ascertain the trend in the percentage of each current asset to total current assets. A movement from cash to inventory, for instance, points to less liquidity.

• *Sales to Current Assets*. A high turnover rate indicates inadequate working capital. Current liabilities may be due prior to inventories and receivables turning into cash.

• *Working Capital Provided From Operations to Net Income* (net income plus nonworking capital expenses minus nonworking capital revenue). Liquidity is enhanced when net income is backed up by liquid funds.

• *Working Capital Provided From Operations to Total Liabilities*. This indicates the extent to which internally generated working capital is available to meet debt.

• *Cash Plus Marketable Securities to Current Liabilities*. This indicates the immediate amount of cash available to satisfy short-term obligations.

• *Cost of Sales, Operating Expenses, and Taxes to Average Total Current Assets.* The trend in this ratio indicates the adequacy of current assets in meeting ongoing business-related expenses.

• *Quick Assets to Year's Cash Expenses.* This indicates the days of expenses the highly liquid assets could support.

• *Sales to Short-term Trade Liabilities.* This indicates whether the firm can partly finance by cost-free funds. A decline in trade credit means creditors have less faith in the financial strength of the business.

• *Net Income to Sales.* A decline in the profit margin of the business indicates financial deterioration.

• *Fixed Assets to Short-term Debt.* A company financing long-term assets with short-term obligations has a problem satisfying debt when due, because the return and proceeds from the fixed asset will not be realized prior to the maturity date of the current liabilities.

• *Short-term Debt to Long-term Debt.* A higher ratio points to greater liquidity risk because debt is of a current nature.

• *Accounts Payable to Average Daily Purchases.* This indicates the number of days required for the company to pay creditors.

• *Liquidity Index.* This indicates the days in which current assets are removed from cash.

EXAMPLE 6.8

	Amount	Days Removed From Cash	Total
Cash	$10,000 ×	—	—
Accounts receivable	40,000 ×	25	$1,000,000
Inventory	60,000 ×	40	2,400,000
	$110,000		$3,400,000

$$\text{Index} = \frac{\$3,400,000}{\$110,000} = \underline{30.9} \text{ days}$$

EXAMPLE 6.9

Company B provides the following financial information:

Current assets	$400,000
Fixed assets	800,000
Current liabilities	500,000
Noncurrent liabilities	600,000
Sales	5,000,000
Working capital provided from operations	100,000
Industry norms are:	
Fixed assets to current liabilities	4.0 times
Current liabilities to noncurrent liabilities	45.0%
Sales to current assets	8.3 times
Working capital provided from operations to total liabilities	30.5%

Company B's ratios are:

Fixed assets to current liabilities	1.6 times
Current liabilities to noncurrent liabilities	83.3%
Sales to current assets	12.5 times
Working capital provided from operations to total liabilities	9.1%

Company B's liquidity ratios are all unfavorable compared to industry standards. There is a high level of short-term debt, as well as deficiency in current assets. Also, working capital provided from operations to satisfy total debt is inadequate.

How does taking cash discounts affect a company financially?

A company's failure to take cash discounts raises a question as to management's financial astuteness, because a high opportunity cost is involved.

EXAMPLE 6.10

Company C bought goods for $300,000 on terms of 2/10, net/60. It failed to take advantage of the discount. The opportunity cost is:

$$\frac{\text{Discount foregone}}{\text{Proceeds use of}} \times \frac{360}{\text{Days Delayed}}$$

$$\frac{\$6,000}{\$294,000} \times \frac{360}{50} = \underline{14.7\%}$$

The firm would have been better off financially paying within the discount period by taking out a loan, since the prime interest rate is below 14.7%.

Appraising Corporate Solvency

How do I evaluate a firm's solvency?

Corporate solvency depends on:

- The long-term debt-paying ability of the entity to ascertain whether the firm can meet long-term principal and interest payments
- Whether long-term funds are forthcoming to meet noncurrent debt
- The long-term financial and operating structure of the business
- The magnitude of noncurrent liabilities and the realization risk in noncurrent assets
- Earning power—a company will not be able to satisfy its obligations unless it is profitable

NOTE: When practical to do so, use the market value of assets instead of book value in ratio computations; it is more representative of true worth.

Measures of long-term debt paying ability are:

- *Long-term Debt to Stockholders' Equity.* High leverage indicates risk, because it may be difficult for the company to meet interest and principal payments as well as obtain further reasonable financing. The problem is particularly acute when a company has cash problems. Excessive debt means less financial flexibility, because the entity will have more problems obtaining funds during a tight money market.

- *Cash Flow to Long-term Debt.* This evaluates the adequacy of available funds to satisfy noncurrent obligations.

- *Net Income Before Taxes and Interest to Interest (Interest Coverage Ratio).* This indicates the number of times interest expense is covered. It is a safety margin indicator that shows the degree of decline in income a company can tolerate.

• *Cash Flow Generated From Operations Plus Interest to Interest.* This ratio indicates available cash to meet interest charges. Cash *not* profit pays interest.

• *Net Income Before Taxes Plus Fixed Charges to Fixed Charges.* This ratio helps in appraising a firm's ability to meet fixed costs. A low ratio points to risk—when corporate activity falls, the company is unable to meet its fixed charges.

• *Cash Flow From Operations Plus Fixed Charges to Fixed Charges.* A high ratio indicates the ability of the company to meet its fixed charges. Further, a company with stability in operations is better able to meet fixed costs.

• *Noncurrent Assets to Noncurrent Liabilities.* Long-term debt is ultimately paid from long-term assets. A high ratio affords more protection for long-term creditors.

• *Retained Earnings to Total Assets.* The trend in this ratio reflects the firm's profitability over the years.

EXAMPLE 6.11

The following partial balance sheet and income statement data are provided for Company D:

Long-term assets	$700,000
Long-term liabilities	500,000
Stockholders' equity	300,000
Net income before tax	80,000
Cash flow provided from operations	100,000
Interest expense	20,000

Average norms taken from competitors:

Long-term assets to long-term liabilities	2.0
Long-term debt to stockholders' equity	.8
Cash flow to long-term liabilities	.3

Net income before tax plus interest
to interest   7.0

Company D's ratios are:

Long-term assets to long-term
liabilities   1.4
Long-term debt to stockholders'
equity   1.67
Cash flow to long-term liabilities   .2
Net income before tax plus interest
to interest   5.0

After comparing the company's ratios with the industry norms, it is evident that the firm's solvency is worse than its competitors' due to the greater degree of long-term liabilities in the capital structure and lower interest coverage.

What can financial management do to avoid solvency problems?

Ways for management to avoid solvency difficulties include:

- Avoid heavy debt
- Lengthen the maturity date of debt
- Assure that there is a "buffer" between actual status and compliance requirements (e.g., working capital) in connection with loan agreements
- Divest of unprofitable segments and assets
- Have adequate insurance
- Avoid operations in risky foreign areas
- Finance assets with liabilities of similar maturity
- Adjust to changes in technology
- Diversify horizontally and vertically
- Avoid long-term "fixed fee" commitments

INCOME STATEMENT ANALYSIS

The analysis of the income statement indicates a company's earning power, quality of earnings, and operating performance.

NOTES: Net income backed-up by cash is important for corporate liquidity.

The accounting policies employed should be realistic in reflecting the substance of the transactions.

Accounting changes should only be made for proper reasons.

A high degree of estimation in the income measurement process results in uncertainty in reported figures.

Earnings stability enhances the predictability of future results based on currently reported profits.

Cash Flow From Operations

How does proximity to cash realization affect the quality of earnings?

The closer a transaction is to cash, the more objective is the evidence supporting revenue and expense recognition. As the proximity to cash becomes less, the transaction becomes less objective and the interpretations become more subjective. Higher earnings quality relates to recording transactions close to cash realization.

How is cash flow from operations treated?

Cash flow from operations equals net income plus noncash expenses less noncash revenue. Net income is of higher quality if it is backed-up by cash. The trend in the ratio of cash flow from operations to net income should be evaluated.

In appraising the cash adequacy of a company, compute the following:

- Cash flow generated from operations before interest expense
- Cash flow generated from operations less cash payments to meet debt principal, dividends, and capital expenditures

EXAMPLE 6.12

A condensed income statement for A Company follows:

Sales		$1,000,000
Less: Cost of sales		300,000
Gross margin		$ 700,000
Less: Operating expenses		
Salary	$100,000	
Rent	200,000	
Telephone	50,000	
Depreciation	80,000	
Amortization expense	60,000	
Total operating expenses		490,000
Income before other items		$210,000
Other revenue and expense		
Interest expense	$70,000	
Amortization of deferred credit	40,000	
Total other revenue and expense		30,000
Net income		$ 180,000

The ratio of cash flow from operations to net income is 1.55, calculated as follows:

Cash flow from operations		$180,000
Add: Noncash expenses		
Depreciation	$80,000	
Amortization expense	60,000	140,000
Less: Noncash revenue		
Amortization of deferred credit		(40,000)
Cash flow from operations		$280,000

$$\frac{\text{Cash flow from operations}}{\text{Net income}} = \frac{\$280,000}{\$180,000} = 1.55$$

Discretionary Costs

What are discretionary costs?

Discretionary costs include:

- Advertising
- Repairs and maintenance
- Research and development

Discretionary costs may be easily changed by management. They may be decreased when a company is having problems or wants to show a stable earnings trend.

What are the effects of a change in discretionary costs?

A pull-back in discretionary costs results in overstated earnings. It has long-term negative effect because management is starving the company of needed expenses. Cost reduction programs may lower earnings quality when material cutbacks are made in discretionary costs. *NOTE:* The CPA cannot always conclude that any reduction in discretionary costs is improper. The reduction may be necessary when the prior corporate strategy is deficient or ill-conceived.

RECOMMENDATIONS: Determine if the present level of discretionary costs is in conformity with the company's prior trends and with current and future requirements. Index numbers may be used in comparing current discretionary expenditures with base year expenditures. A vacillating trend in discretionary costs to revenue may indicate the company is smoothing earnings by altering its discretionary costs. A substantial increase in discretionary costs may have a positive impact on corporate earning power and future growth.

A declining trend in discretionary costs to net sales may indicate lower earnings quality. Review the relationship of discretionary costs to the assets they apply to.

EXAMPLE 6.13

The following relationship exists between advertising and sales:

	19X1	19X2	19X3
Sales	$120,000	$150,000	$100,000
Advertising	11,000	16,000	8,000

19X1 is the most typical year.

Increasing competition is expected in 19X4.

Advertising to sales equals:

19X1	19X2	19X3
9.2%	10.7%	8%

In terms of base dollars, 19X1 is assigned 100. In 19X2, the index number is 145.5 ($16,000/ $11,000) and in 19X3 it is 72.7 ($8,000/$11,000).

The above are negative indicators regarding 19X3. Advertising is of a lower level than in previous years. In fact, advertising should have risen due to expected increased competition.

Accounting Policies

What is the nature of the company's accounting principles and estimates?

Conservatively determined net income is of higher quality than liberally determined net income. Conservatism applies to the accounting methods and estimates used.

RECOMMENDATIONS: Compare the company's accounting policies with the prevailing accounting policies in the industry. If the firm's policies are more liberal, earnings quality may be lower. Take into account the company's timing of revenue recognition and the deferral of costs relative to prevailing industry practices.

The accounting policies employed should be realistic in reflecting the economic substance of the firm's transactions. The underlying business and financial realities of the company and industry have to be taken into account. EXAMPLE: The depreciation method should most approximately measure the decline in usefulness of the asset.

The CPA may question the reasonableness of a company's accounting estimates when prior estimates have been materially different from what actually occurred. Examples of realistic accounting policies are cited in AICPA Industry Audit Guides and in accounting policy guides published by various CPA firms. If the use of realistic policies would have resulted in substantially lower earnings than the policies used, earnings quality is lower.

The artificial shifting of earnings from one year to another results in poor earnings quality. This encompasses:

- Bringing future revenue into the current year (or its converse)
- Shifting earnings from good years to bad years
- Shifting expenses and losses among the years

It is a questionable practice when a company immediately recognizes revenue even though services still have to be performed. EXAMPLE: A magazine publisher recognizes subscription income immediately when payment is received even though the subscription period may be three years.

The unrealistic deferral of revenue recognition results in poor earnings quality because profits are unjustifiably understated. When there is a reversal of previously recorded profits, question the company's revenue recognition policies.

If expenses are underaccrued or overaccrued, lower earnings quality results. EXAMPLES: An *underaccrued expense* is the failure of a computer manufacturer to provide for normal maintenance service for rented computers because they are being used by lessees.

An *overaccrued expense* is a company with high earnings deciding to accrue for possible sales returns that are highly unlikely to materialize. Try to ascertain what these normal charges are and adjust reported earnings accordingly.

Accounting changes made to conform with new FASB Statements, AICPA Industry Audit Guides, and IRS Regulations are justifiable. However, an unjustified accounting change causes an earnings increment of low quality. Unwarranted changes may be made in accounting principles, estimates, and assumptions.

RECOMMENDATION: Question whether accounting changes are being made in order to create artificial earnings growth. If there are numerous accounting changes, it will be more difficult to use current profits as a predictor for future earnings.

Degree of Certainty in Accounting Estimates

How are the estimates?

The more subjective accounting estimates and judgments are in arriving at earnings, the more uncertain is the net income figure. EXAMPLE: A firm engaged in long-term activity (e.g., a shipbuilder using the percentage of completion contract method) has more uncertainty regarding earnings due to the material estimates involved. A higher percentage of assets subject to accounting estimates (intangibles) to total assets means uncertain earnings.

RECOMMENDATIONS: Determine the difference between estimated reserves and actual losses for previous years. A significant difference between the two may point to lower earnings quality. Further, substantial gains and losses on the sale of assets may point to inaccurate depreciation estimates being originally used.

Segregate cash expenses versus estimated expenses. Trends should be determined in:

- Cash expenses to net sales
- Estimated expenses to net sales
- Estimated expenses to total expenses
- Estimated expenses to net income

EXAMPLE 6.14

The CPA assembles the following information for Company B for the period 19X1 and 19X2:

	19X1	*19X2*
Cash and near-cash (conversion period to cash is short) revenue items	$100,000	$110,000
Non-cash revenue items (long-term receivables arising from credit sales to the government, revenue recognized under the percentage of completion method)	150,000	200,000
Total revenue	$250,000	$310,000

	19X1	*19X2*
Cash and near-cash expenses (salaries, rent, telephone)	$ 40,000	$ 60,000
Non-cash expenses (depreciation, depletion, amortization, bad debts)	70,000	120,000
Total expenses	$110,000	$180,000
Net income	$140,000	$130,000

Estimated revenue items to total revenue was 60% ($150,000/$250,000) in 19X1 and 65% ($200,000/$310,000) in 19X2. Estimated revenue to net income was 107% ($150,000/$140,000) in 19X1 and 154% ($200,000/$130,000) in 19X2.

Estimated expense items to total expenses was 64% ($70,000/$110,000) in 19X1 and 67% ($120,000/$180,000) in 19X2. Estimated expenses to total revenue was 28% ($70,000/$250,000) in 19X1 and 39% ($120,000/$310,000) in 19X2. Estimated expenses to net income was 50% ($70,000/$140,000) in 19X1 and 92% ($120,000/$130,000) in 19X2.

Uncertainty exists with respect to the earnings of 19X1 and 19X2, arising from the high percentages of estimated income statement items. Also, a greater degree of estimation exists with regard to 19X2's income measurement process.

Residual Income

What are the implications of residual income?

An increasing trend in residual income to net income points to a strong degree of corporate profitability because the company is earning enough to meet its imputed cost of capital. (Residual income is discussed in more detail in Chapter 7.)

Taxable Income

What about the discrepancy between taxable income and book income?

A company having a significant deferred income tax credit account will have book profits in excess of taxable earnings. An increase in the deferred tax credit account may indicate the company is moving toward more liberal accounting policies. This is because a widening gap in the deferred tax credit account indicates a greater disparity between book earnings and taxable earnings.

A decline in the effective tax rate because of a nonrecurring source (e.g., a loss carryforward that will shortly expire) results in an earnings increment of low quality. The tax benefits will not continue in the future. However, the effective tax rate may be stable when it results from a recurring source (e.g., foreign tax credit, interest on municipal bonds).

Lower earnings quality exists if there is a high percentage of foreign earnings that will not be repatriated to the U.S. for a long time.

RECOMMENDATION: If a company reports significant stockholder earnings and a substantial tax loss, evaluate the quality of reported results.

Foreign Operations

How about foreign activities?

An erratic foreign exchange rate results in instability.

• To measure the degree of vacillation of the foreign exchange rate, determine its percentage change over time and/or its standard deviation.

• To evaluate the degree of stability, look at the trend in the ratio of foreign translation gains and losses (reported in the stockholders' equity section) to net income.

In evaluating the effect of foreign operations on the company's financial health, consider:

• Degree of intercountry transactions
• Different year-ends of foreign subsidiaries
• Foreign restrictions on the transfer of funds
• Tax structure of the foreign country
• Economic and political stability of the foreign country

Discontinued Operations

What is the analytical implication of discontinuing an operation?

Income from discontinued operations is usually of a one-time nature and should be ignored when forecasting future earnings. Further, a discontinued operation implies that a company is in a state of decline or that a poor management decision was the cause for the firm's having entered the discontinued line of business in the first place.

Stability of Earnings

Are profits of a recurring nature?

A company with an unstable earnings trend has more risk associated with it. Measures of earnings stability are:

- Average net income (e.g., five years).
- Average pessimistic earnings. This represents the average earnings based on the *worst* possible scenario for the company's operational activities. The average minimum earnings is useful in appraising a risky company.
- Standard deviation.

$$\text{S.D.} = \sqrt{\frac{\Sigma(y - \bar{y})^2}{n}}$$

where

y = reported earnings for period t,
$\bar{y}$ = average earnings,
n = number of years.

A high standard deviation means instability in profit.

- Coefficient of variation.

$$\text{C.V.} = \frac{\text{S.D.}}{\bar{y}}$$

The coefficient of variation is useful in appraising relative instability in earnings among companies. A high coefficient indicates greater risk in the earnings stream.

• Instability index of earnings.

$$I = \sqrt{\frac{\Sigma(y - y^T)^2}{n}}$$

where y^T = trend earnings for period t, and is computed by:

$$y^T = a + bt$$

where

    a = dollar intercept,
    b = slope of trend line,
    t = time period.

A simple trend equation solved by computer is used to determine trend income. The index reflects the deviation between actual profit and trend income. A high index is indicative of instability.

• Beta. Beta is computed via a computer run with the use of the following equation:

$$r_{jt} = a_j + B_j r_{Mt} + E_{jt}$$

where

    r_{jt} = return on security j for period t,
    a_j = constant
    B_j = beta for security j,
    r_{Mt} = return on a market index such as the New York Stock Exchange Index
    E_{jt} = error term

Beta is a measure of systematic or undiversifiable risk of a stock. A high beta means that the firm's stock price has vacillated more than a market index, indicating that it is a risky security.

EXAMPLE 6.15

A beta of 1.7 means that the company's stock price can rise or fall 70% faster than the market. Beta values for particular stocks may be obtained from various financial services such as Standard & Poor's.

Operating Leverage

What is operating leverage?

Operating leverage applies to the degree to which fixed costs exist in a company's cost structure.

How do I gauge operating leverage?

Measures of operating leverage are:

1. Fixed costs to total costs
2. Percentage change in operating income to the percentage change in sales volume
3. Net income to fixed costs

NOTES: An increase in (1) and (2) or decrease in (3) may point to lower earnings quality because higher fixed charges may result in greater earnings instability.

A high percentage of variable costs to total costs indicates greater earnings stability. Variable costs can be adjusted more easily than fixed costs in meeting a decline in product demand.

A high break-even company is very susceptible to economic declines.

Profitability Measures

What about profitability?

Absolute dollar profit by itself has little meaning unless it is related to its source. A company's profit margin (net income to sales) indicates how well it is being managed and provides clues to a company's pricing, cost structure, and production efficiency.

A high gross profit percent (gross profit to sales) is favorable since it indicates the company is able to control its manufacturing costs.

The return on common equity equals earnings available to common stockholders divided by average stockholders' equity. This ratio indicates the rate of return earned on common stockholders' investment.

Growth Rate

How do I compute growth rate?

Determine a company's growth rate as follows:

$$\frac{\text{EPS (end of year)} - \text{EPS (beginning of year)}}{\text{EPS (beginning of year)}}$$

Growth in dividends per share may be similarly computed:

$$\frac{\text{Change in Retained Earnings}}{\text{Stockholders' Equity (beginning of year)}}$$

Other measures of growth are the change in sales and total assets.

Market Value Measures

What indicators of market value exist?

Market value ratios apply to a comparison of the company's stock price to its earnings (or book value) per share. Also involved are dividend-related ratios. Included are:

• *Earnings per share.* This equals net income less preferred dividends divided by common stock outstanding.

• *Price-Earnings ratio.* This equals market price per share divided by earnings per share.

• *Book value per share.* This equals:

$$\frac{\text{Total stockholders'} \quad - \quad \left(\begin{array}{l}\text{liquidation value of}\\ \text{preferred stock}\\ \text{+ preferred dividends}\\ \text{in arrears}\end{array}\right)}{\text{Common stock outstanding}}$$

By comparing book value per share to market price per share, the CPA can see how investors feel about the business.

• *Dividend yield.* This equals dividends per share divided by market price per share.

• *Dividend payout.* This equals dividends per share divided by earnings per share. The investing public looks unfavorably upon lower dividends since dividend payout is a sign of the financial health of the entity.

BANKRUPTCY PREDICTION

Will the company fail?

Some key indicators to be examined by the CPA in predicting corporate bankruptcy are:

- Cash flow from operations to total liabilities
- Net income to total assets
- Total liabilities to total assets
- Quick ratio
- Current ratio
- Operating income to total assets
- Interest coverage (income before interest and taxes to interest)
- Retained earnings to total assets
- Common equity to total liabilities
- Working capital to total assets
- Debt to equity
- Fixed assets to stockholders' equity

What is the "Z-score"?

Edward Altman's "Z-score" can be used to predict bankruptcy within the short run (one or two years). The "Z-score" equals:

$$\frac{\text{Working capital}}{\text{Total assets}} \times 1.2 + \frac{\text{Retained earnings}}{\text{Total assets}} \times 1.4$$
$$+ \frac{\text{Operating income}}{\text{Total assets}} \times 3.3$$
$$+ \frac{\text{Market value of common stock and preferred stock}}{\text{Total debt}} \times .6$$
$$+ \frac{\text{Sales}}{\text{Total assets}} \times 1.$$

His scoring chart follows:

Score	Probability of short-term illiquidity
1.80 or less	Very high
1.81 to 2.7	High
2.8 to 2.9	Possible
3.0 or higher	Not likely

EXAMPLE 6.16

Company D provides the following relevant information:

Working capital	$250,000
Total assets	900,000
Total liabilities	300,000
Retained earnings	200,000
Sales	1,000,000
Operating income	150,000
Common stock:	
Book value	210,000
Market value	300,000
Preferred stock:	
Book value	100,000
Market value	160,000

The "Z-score" is:

$$\frac{\$250,000}{\$900,000} \times 1.2 + \frac{\$200,000}{\$900,000} \times 1.4$$
$$+ \frac{\$150,000}{\$900,000} \times 3.3 + \frac{\$460,000}{\$300,000} \times .6$$
$$+ \frac{\$1,000,000}{\$900,000} \times 1 = 3.225$$

The score indicates it is unlikely for business failure to occur.

Does company size bear a relationship to the probability of failure?

In a study done by Dun and Bradstreet[1], it was found that small companies had higher failure rates than large companies. Size can be measured by total assets, sales, and age.

What are indicators of financial distress?

Financial and operating deficiencies pointing to financial distress include:

- Significant decline in stock price
- Reduction in dividend payments
- Sharp increase in the cost of capital
- Inability to obtain further financing
- Inability to meet past-due obligations

[1] *The Business Failure Record—1975* (New York: Dun and Bradstreet, 1976).

- Poor financial reporting system
- Movement into business areas unrelated to the company's basic business
- Failure to keep up-to-date
- Faiure to control costs
- High degree of competition

PART 3

MANAGERIAL ACCOUNTING APPLICATIONS

CHAPTER 7

APPRAISING SEGMENTAL PERFORMANCE

Accountants typically look at budgeting and profit planning as tools for control of responsibility center operations and as facilitating factors in judging managerial performance. Accountants should be familiar with fundamental managerial accounting tools such as standard costing, flexible budgeting, and the contribution approach. Also, they should have a thorough understanding of two important issues that arise frequently with decentralized operations—divisional performance and transfer pricing.

This chapter covers measures and guidelines for internally evaluating a company's performance, including:

- Responsibility accounting and responsibility centers
- Cost center performance and standard costs
- Flexible budgets and performance reports
- Profit centers and segmented reporting
- Evaluation of divisional performance
- Transfer pricing
- Budgeting and financial planning

WHAT AND WHY OF RESPONSIBILITY ACCOUNTING

What is responsibility accounting?

Responsibility accounting is the system for collecting and reporting revenue and cost information by areas of responsibility. It operates on the premise that managers should be held responsible for their performance, the performance of their subordinates, and for all activities within their responsibility center.

What are the benefits of responsibility accounting?

Responsibility accounting, also called *profitability accounting* and *activity accounting*, has the following advantages:

• It facilitates delegation of decision making.

• It helps management promote the concept of management by objective, in which managers agree on a set of goals. The manager's performance is then evaluated based on his or her attainment of these goals.

• It provides a guide to the evaluation of performance and helps establish standards of performance which are then used for comparison purposes.

• It permits effective use of the concept of *management by exception*, which means that the manager's attention is concentrated on the important deviations from standards and budgets.

What are responsibility centers?

A well designed responsibility accounting system establishes *responsibility centers* within the organization. A responsibility center is a unit in the organization which has control over costs, revenues, and/or investment funds. Responsibility centers may be:

Cost Center

A cost center is the unit within the organization which is responsible only for costs. EXAMPLES: The production and maintenance departments of a manufacturing company, the admissions department of a university.

RECOMMENDATION: Variance analysis based on *standard costs* and *flexible budgets* would be a typical performance measure of a cost center.

Profit Center

A profit center is the unit which is held responsible for the revenues earned and costs incurred in that center. EXAMPLES: a sales office of a publishing company, an appliance department in a retail store, an auto repair center in a department store.

RECOMMENDATION: The contribution approach to cost allocation is widely used to measure the performance of a profit center.

Investment Center

An investment center is the unit within the organization which is held responsible for the costs, revenues, and related investments made in that center. EXAMPLES: The corporate headquarters, a division in a large decentralized organization.

RECOMMENDATION: Return on investment and *residual income* are two key performance measures of an investment center.

Figure 7.1 illustrates how responsibility accounting can be used within an organization and highlights profit and cost centers.

COST CENTER PERFORMANCE AND STANDARD COSTS

How do I measure the performance of a cost center?

One of the most important phases of responsibility accounting is establishing standard costs in order to evaluate performance by comparing actual costs with standard costs. The difference between the actual costs and the standard costs, called the *variance*, is calculated for individual cost centers. The variance analysis is a key tool for measuring performance of a cost center.

The standard cost is based on physical and dollar measures: it is determined by multiplying the standard quantity of an input by its standard price. Two general types of variances (price and quantity) can

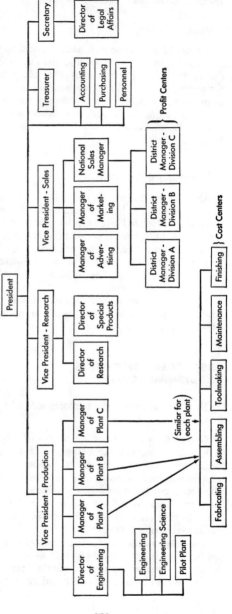

Figure 7.1
ORGANIZATION CHART COMPANY XYZ

be calculated for most cost items. The *price variance* is calculated as follows:

$$
\begin{aligned}
\text{Price} \atop \text{Variance} &= \text{Actual} \atop \text{Quantity} \times \left(\text{Actual} \atop \text{Price} - \text{Standard} \atop \text{Price} \right) \\
&= \text{AQ} \times (\text{AP} - \text{SP}) \\
&= \underset{(1)}{(\text{AQ} \times \text{AP})} - \underset{(2)}{(\text{AQ} \times \text{SP})}
\end{aligned}
$$

The *quantity variance* is calculated as follows:

$$
\begin{aligned}
\text{Quantity} \atop \text{Variance} &= \left(\text{Actual} \atop \text{Quantity} - \text{Standard} \atop \text{Quantity} \right) \times \text{Standard} \atop \text{Price} \\
&= (\text{AQ} - \text{SQ}) \times \text{SP} \\
&= \underset{(2)}{(\text{AQ} \times \text{SP})} - \underset{(3)}{(\text{SQ} \times \text{SP})}
\end{aligned}
$$

Figure 7.2 shows a general (3-column) model for variance analysis that incorporates the items (1), (2), and (3) from the above equations.

How is standard costing useful?

Standard costing has many advantages:

- Aids in cost control and performance evaluation
- "Red flags" current and future problems through the "management by exception" principle
- Improves performance by recommending paths for corrective action in cost reduction
- Fixes responsibility
- Constitutes a vehicle of communication between top management and supervisors
- Establishes selling prices and transfer prices
- Determines bid prices on contracts
- Sets business goals
- Aids in the planning and decision making processes
- Simplifies bookkeeping procedures and saves clerical costs

Standard costing is not without some drawbacks. EXAMPLES: The possible biases involved in deriving standards and the disfunctional effects of setting improper norms and standards.

Figure 7.2
A GENERAL MODEL FOR VARIANCE ANALYSIS
VARIABLE MANUFACTURING COSTS

Actual Quantity of Inputs, at Actual Price (AQ × AP) (1)	Actual Quantity of Inputs, at Standard Price (AQ × SP) (2)	Standard Quantity Allowed for Output, at Standard Price (SQ × SP) (3)
Price variance (1) - (2)		Quantity variance (2) - (3)
	Total Variance	

- Materials purchase price variance
- Labor rate variance
- Variable overhead spending variance

- Materials quantity (usage) variance
- Labor efficiency variance
- Variable overhead efficiency variance

Materials Variances

How are materials variances computed?

A *materials price variance* is isolated at the time of purchase of the material. Therefore, it is normally computed based on the actual quantity purchased. The purchasing department is responsible for any materials price variance that might occur. The *materials quantity (usage) variance* is computed based on the actual quantity used.

NOTE: The production department is responsible for any materials quantity variance that might occur.

What causes material variances?

The possible causes of *unfavorable* materials variances are:

Materials Price Variance

- Inaccurate standard prices
- Failure to take a discount on quantity purchases
- Failure to shop for bargains
- Inflationary cost increases
- Scarcity in raw material supplies resulting in higher prices
- Purchasing department inefficiencies

Materials Quantity (Usage) Variance

- Poorly trained workers
- Improperly adjusted machines
- Use of improper production method
- Outright waste on the production line
- Use of a lower grade material purchased in order to economize on price

EXAMPLE 7.1

ABC Corporation uses a standard cost system. The standard variable costs for Product J are:

Materials: 2 lb at $3.00 per lb

Labor: 1 hour at $5.00 per hour

Variable overhead: 1 hour at $3.00 per hour

During March, 25,000 pounds of material were purchased for $74,750, and 20,750 pounds of material were used in producing 10,000 units of finished product. Direct labor costs incurred were $49,896 (10,080 direct labor hours) and variable overhead costs incurred were $34,776. Using the general (3-column) model, the materials variances are:

Materials Variances

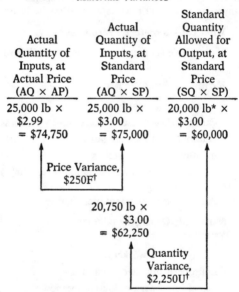

Actual Quantity of Inputs, at Actual Price (AQ × AP)	Actual Quantity of Inputs, at Standard Price (AQ × SP)	Standard Quantity Allowed for Output, at Standard Price (SQ × SP)
25,000 lb × $2.99 = $74,750	25,000 lb × $3.00 = $75,000	20,000 lb* × $3.00 = $60,000

Price Variance, $250F[†]

20,750 lb × $3.00 = $62,250

Quantity Variance, $2,250U[†]

*10,000 units actually produced × 2 lb allowed per unit = 20,000 lb. NOTE: The amount of materials purchased (25,000 lb) differs from the amount of materials used in production (20,750 lb). The materials purchase price variance was computed using 25,000 lb purchased, whereas the material quantity (usage) variance was computed using the 20,750 lb used in production. A total variance cannot be computed because of the difference.

[†]A variance represents the deviation of actual cost from the standard or budgeted cost. U and F stand for "unfavorable" and "favorable," respectively.

Alternatively, we can compute the materials variances as follows:

Materials (purchase) price variance = AQ × (AP − SP) = (AQ × AP) − (AQ × SP)
= 25,000 lb ($2.99 − $3.00) = $74,750 − $75,000 = $250F

Materials quantity (usage) variance = (AQ − SQ) × SP
= (20,750 lb − 20,000 lb) × $3.00 = $62,250 − $60,000
= $2,250U

Labor Variances

How are labor variances computed?

Labor variances are isolated when labor is used for production. They are computed in a manner similar to materials variances, except that in the 3-column model the terms "hours" and "rate" are used in place of the terms "quantity" and "price." The production department is responsible for both the "prices" paid for labor services and the "quantity" of labor services used. Therefore, the production department must explain the cause of any labor variances.

What causes labor variances?

Possible causes of unfavorable labor variances are:

- Labor price (rate) variance
  - Increase in wages
  - Poor scheduling of production resulting in overtime work
  - Use of workers commanding higher hourly rates than contemplated in the standards
- Labor efficiency variance
  - Poor supervision
  - Use of unskilled workers paid lower rates or the wrong mixture of labor for a given job
  - Use of poor quality machinery
  - Improperly trained workers
  - Poor quality of materials requiring more labor time in processing
  - Machine breakdowns
  - Employee unrest
  - Production delays due to power failure

EXAMPLE 7.2

Using the same data given in Example 7.1, the labor variances can be calculated as follows:

Labor Variances

Actual Hours of Input, at the Actual Rate (AH × AR)	Actual Hours of Input, at the Standard Rate (AH × SR)	Standard Hours Allowed for Output, at the Standard Rate (SH × SR)
10,080 hrs. × $4.95 = $49,896	10,080 hrs. × $5.00 = $50,400	10,000 hrs* × $5.00 = $50,000

Rate Variance, $504F	Efficiency Variance, $400U
Total Variance, $104F	

*10,000 units actually produced × 1 hour allowed per unit = 10,000 hrs.

NOTE: The symbols (AQ, SQ, AP, and SP) have been changed to (AH, SH, AR, and SR) to reflect the terms "hour" and "rate."

Alternatively, we can calculate the labor variances as follows:

Labor rate variance = AH × (AR − SR) = (AH × AR) − (AH × SR)
= 10,080 hrs. ($4.95 − $5.00) = $49,896 − $50,400 = $504F

Labor efficiency variance = (AH − SH) × SR
= (10,080 hrs. − 10,000 hrs.) × $5.00 = $50,400 − $50,000
= $400U

Variable Overhead Variances

How are variable overhead variances determined?

Variable overhead variances are computed in a way similar to labor variances. The production department is usually responsible for any variable overhead variance that might occur. Variances for fixed overhead are of questionable usefulness for control purposes, since these variances are usually beyond the control of the production department.

What causes unfavorable variable overhead variances?

Possible causes of unfavorable variable overhead variances are:

- Variable overhead spending variance
  - Increase in supplier prices
  - Increase in labor rates
  - Inaccurate standards
  - Waste
  - Theft of supplies
- Variable overhead efficiency variance
  - Poorly trained workers
  - Use of poor quality materials
  - Use of faulty equipment
  - Poor supervision
  - Employee unrest
  - Work interruptions
  - Poor production scheduling
  - A lack of automation and computerization in processing

EXAMPLE 7.3

Using the same data given in Example 7.1, the variable overhead variances can be computed as follows:

Variable Overhead Variances

Actual Hours of Input, at the Actual Rate (AH × AR)	Actual Hours of Input, at the Standard Rate (AH × SR)	Standard Hours Allowed for Output, at the Standard Rate (SH × SR)
10,080 hrs. × $3.45 = $34,776	10,080 hrs. × $3.00 = $30,240	10,000 hrs.* × $3.00 = $30,000

	Spending Variance, $4,536U	Efficiency Variance, $240U
	Total Variance, $4,776	

*10,000 units actually produced × 1 hour allowed per unit = 10,000 hrs.

Alternatively, we can compute the variable overhead variances as follows:

Variable overhead spending variance = AH × (AR − SR) = (AH × AR) − (AH × SR)
= 10,080 hrs. ($3.45 − $3.00) = $34,776 − $30,240 = $4,536U

Variable overhead efficiency variance = (AH − SH) × SR
= (10,080 hrs. − 10,000 hrs.) × $3.00
= $30,240 − $30,000
= $240U

Mix and Yield Variances

What about the computation of mix and yield variances?

The *material mix variance* measures the impact of the deviation from the standard mix on material costs. The *material yield variance* measures the impact on material costs of the deviation from the standard input material allowed for actual production. The *material quantity variance* is divided into a material mix variance and a material yield variance.

• Compute the material mix variance by holding the total input units constant at their actual amount.

• Compute the material yield variance by holding the mix constant at the standard amount.

The computations for labor mix and yield variances are the same as those for materials. If there is no mix, the yield variance is the same as the quantity (or usage) variance.

What causes mix and yield variances?

Possible causes of unfavorable mix variances are:

• When capacity restraints force substitution

• Poor production scheduling

• Lack of certain types of labor

• Short supply of certain materials

Possible causes of unfavorable yield variances are:

• Low quality materials and/or labor

• Faulty equipment

• Improper production methods

• Improper or costly mix of materials and/or labor

FLEXIBLE BUDGETS AND PERFORMANCE REPORTS

What are the implications of a flexible budget?

A flexible budget is an extremely useful tool in cost control. In contrast to a *static budget*, the flexible budget is:

• Geared toward a range of activity rather than a single level of activity.

• Dynamic in nature rather than static.

The static (fixed) budget is geared to only one level of activity and has problems in cost control. Flexible budgeting distinguishes between fixed and variable costs, thus allowing for a budget which can be automatically adjusted (via changes in variable cost totals) to the particular level of activity *actually* attained. By using the *cost-volume formula* (or *flexible budget formula*), a series of budgets can be easily developed for various levels of activity. Thus, variances between actual costs and budgeted costs are adjusted for volume ups and downs before differences due to price and quantity factors are computed.

NOTE: The primary use of the flexible budget is for accurate measure of performance by comparing actual costs for a given output with the budgeted costs for the *same level of output.*

EXAMPLE 7.4

To illustrate the difference between the static budget and the flexible budget, assume that the fabricating department of Company X is budgeted to produce 6,000 units during June. Assume further that the company was able to produce only 5,800 units. The budget for direct labor and variable overhead costs is as follows:

Company X
Direct Labor and Variable Overhead Budget
Fabricating Department
For the Month of June

Budgeted production	6,000 units
Actual production	5,800 units
Direct labor	$39,000
Variable overhead costs:	
Indirect labor	6,000
Supplies	900
Repairs	300
	$46,200

If a static budget approach is used the performance report will appear as follows:

Company X
Direct Labor and Variable Overhead Budget
Fabricating Department
For the Month of June

	Budget	Actual	Variance (U or F)*
Production in units	6,000	5,800	200U
Direct labor	$39,000	$38,500	$500F
Variable overhead costs:			
Indirect labor	6,000	5,950	50F
Supplies	900	870	30F
Repairs	300	295	5F
	$46,200	$45,615	$585F

These cost variances are useless; they compare oranges with apples. The problem is that the budget costs are based on an activity level of 6,000 units, whereas the actual costs were incurred at an activity level below this (5,800 units). From a control standpoint, it makes no sense to try to compare costs at one activity level with costs at a different activity level. Such comparisons would make a production manager look good as long as the actual production is less than the budgeted production. Using the cost-volume formula and generating the budget based on the 5,800 actual units gives the following performance report:

Company X
Performance Report
Fabricating Department
For the Month of June

Budgeted production	6,000 units			
Actual production	5,800 units			
	Cost-volume formula	Budget 5,800 units	Actual 5,800 units	Variance (U or F)
Direct labor	$6.50 per unit	$37,700	$38,500	$800 U

	Cost-volume formula	Budget 5,800 units	Actual 5,800 units	Variance (U or F)
Variable overhead:				
Indirect labor	1.00	5,800	5,950	150U
Supplies	.15	870	870	0
Repairs	.05	290	295	5U
	$7.70	$44,660	$45,615	$955U

Note: All cost variances are unfavorable (U), as compared to the favorable cost variance on the performance report based on the static budget approach.

PROFIT CENTERS AND SEGMENTED REPORTING

How do I evaluate business segments?

Segmented reporting is the process of reporting activities of *profit centers* of an organization such as divisions, product lines, or sales territories. The *contribution approach* is valuable for segmented reporting. It emphasizes the cost behavior patterns and the controllability of costs that are generally useful for profitability analysis of various segments of an organization. The *contribution approach* is based on the theses that:

• Fixed costs are much less controllable than variable.

• *Direct fixed costs* and *common fixed costs* must be clearly distinguished. Direct fixed costs are those fixed costs which can be identified directly with a particular segment of an organization. Common fixed costs are those costs which cannot be identified directly with the segment.

• Common fixed costs should be clearly identified as *unallocated* in the contribution income statement by segments. Any attempt to allocate these types of costs arbitrarily to the segments of the organization can destroy the value of responsibility accounting.

It would lead to unfair evaluation of performance and misleading managerial decisions.

The following concepts are highlighted in the contribution approach:

* *Contribution margin*—Sales minus variable costs

* *Contribution controllable by segment managers* —Contribution margin minus direct fixed costs controllable by segment managers. Direct fixed costs include discretionary fixed costs, e.g., certain advertising, R & D, sales promotion, and engineering.

* *Segment margin*—Contribution controllable by segment managers minus fixed costs controllable by others. Fixed costs controllable by others include tracable and committed fixed costs, e.g., depreciation, property taxes, insurance, and the segment managers' salaries.

* *Net income*—Segment margin minus unallocated common fixed costs.

EXAMPLE 7.5

Figure 7.3 illustrates two levels of segmental reporting:

* By segments defined as divisions
* By segments defined as product lines of a division

The segment margin is the best measure of the profitability of a segment. Unallocated fixed costs are common to the segments being evaluated and should be left unallocated in order not to distort the performance results of segments.

HOW TO MEASURE PERFORMANCE OF INVESTMENT CENTERS

Is the investment center healthy?

Two measurements of performance are widely used for the investment center, e.g., division of a decentralized firm: *rate of return on investment* (ROI) and *residual income* (RI).

Figure 7.3
SEGMENTAL INCOME STATEMENT

Segments Defined as Divisions

	Total	Segments	
	Company	*Division 1*	*Division 2*
Sales	$150,000	$90,000	$60,000
Variable costs:			
Manufacturing	40,000	30,000	10,000
Selling and admin.	20,000	14,000	6,000
Total variable costs	60,000	44,000	16,000
Contribution margin	$90,000	$46,000	$44,000
Less: Direct fixed costs controllable by division managers	55,000	33,000	22,000
Contribution controllable by division managers	$35,000	$13,000	$22,000
Less: Direct fixed costs controllable by others	15,000	10,000	5,000
Divisional segment margin	$20,000	$ 3,000	$17,000
Less: unallocated common fixed costs	$10,000		
Net income	$10,000		

↓

Segments Defined as Product Lines of Division 2

	Division	Segments	
	2	Deluxe Model	Regular Model
Sales	$60,000	$20,000	$40,000
Variable costs:			
Manufacturing	10,000	5,000	5,000
Selling and admin.	6,000	2,000	4,000
Total variable costs	16,000	7,000	9,000
Contribution margin	$44,000	$13,000	$31,000
Less: Direct fixed costs controllable by product line managers	22,000	8,000	14,000
Contribution controllable by product line managers	$22,000	$ 5,000	$17,000
Less: Direct fixed costs controllable by others	4,500	1,500	3,000
Product line margin	$17,500	$ 3,500	$14,000
Less: Unallocated common fixed costs	$ 500		
Divisional segment margin	$17,000		

Rate of Return on Investment (ROI)

How do I calculate ROI?

ROI relates operating income to operating assets. Specifically,

$$ROI = \frac{\text{Operating Income}}{\text{Operating Assets}}$$

ROI can be expressed as a product of the following two important factors:

$$ROI = \text{Margin} \times \text{Turnover}$$
$$= \frac{\text{Operating Income}}{\text{Sales}} \times \frac{\text{Sales}}{\text{Operating Assets}}$$
$$= \frac{\text{Operating Income}}{\text{Operating Assets}}$$

Margin is a measure of profitability or operating efficiency whereas turnover measures how well a division manages its assets.

EXAMPLE 7.6

Consider the following financial data for a division:

Operating Assets	$100,000
Operating Income	$ 18,000
Sales	$200,000

$$ROI = \frac{\text{Operating Income}}{\text{Operating Assets}} \quad \frac{\$18,000}{\$100,000} = \underline{\underline{18\%}}$$

Alternatively,

$$\text{Margin} = \frac{\text{Operating Income}}{\text{Sales}} = \frac{\$18,000}{\$200,000} = \underline{\underline{9\%}}$$

$$\text{Turnover} = \frac{\text{Sales}}{\text{Operating Assets}} = \frac{\$200,000}{\$100,000} = \underline{\underline{2 \text{ times}}}$$

Therefore,

$$ROI = \text{Margin} \times \text{Turnover} = 9\% \times 2 \text{ times}$$
$$= \underline{\underline{18\%}}$$

What are the benefits of breaking down ROI (the Du Pont formula)?

The breakdown of ROI into margin and turnover (often called the Du Pont Formula) has several advantages over the original formula in terms of profit planning:

• The importance of turnover as a key to overall return on investment is emphasized in the breakdown. In fact, turnover is just as important as profit margin.

• The importance of sales is explicitly recognized. It is not reflected in the regular formula.

• The breakdown stresses the possibility of trading one off for the other in an attempt to improve the overall performance of a division.

What effect does ROI have on the bottom line?

The breakdown of ROI into turnover and margin gives the manager of a division insight into planning for profit improvement. Generally speaking, a division manager can improve margin and/or turnover.

• *Improving margin* is a popular way of improving performance. Margins may be increased by reducing expenses, by raising selling prices, or by increasing sales faster than expenses.

• *Improving turnover* can be achieved by increasing sales while holding the investment in assets relatively constant, or by reducing assets.

• *Improving both* margin and turnover may be achieved by increasing sales revenue or by any combination of the first two.

EXAMPLE 7.7

Assume that management sets a 20% ROI as a profit target. It is currently making an 18% return on its investment.

$$\text{ROI} = \frac{\text{Operating Income}}{\text{Sales}} \times \frac{\text{Sales}}{\text{Operating Assets}}$$

$$\text{Present: } 18\% = \frac{18,000}{200,000} \times \frac{200,000}{100,000}$$

Increase margin by reducing expenses:

$$20\% = \frac{20,000}{200,000} \times \frac{200,000}{100,000}$$

Increase turnover by reducing investment in assets: '

$$20\% = \frac{18,000}{200,000} \times \frac{200,000}{90,000}$$

Increase both margin and turnover by disposing of obsolete and redundant inventories:

$$20\% = \frac{19,000}{200,000} \times \frac{200,000}{95,000}$$

Excessive investment in assets is just as much of a drag on profitability as excessive expenses. In this case, cutting unnecessary inventories also helps cut down expenses of carrying those inventories, so that both margin and turnover are improved at the same time. In practice, improving both margin and turnover is much more common than improving only one or the other.

Residual Income (RI)

What is residual income?

Residual income (RI) is the operating income which an investment center is able to earn above some minimum rate of return on its operating assets. RI, unlike ROI, is an absolute amount of income rather than a specific rate of return.

RI = Operating income − (Minimum required rate of return × Operating assets)

What are the benefits of RI?

When RI is used to evaluate divisional performance, the objective is to maximize the total amount of residual income, not to maximize the overall ROI figure.

RI is regarded as a better measure of performance than ROI because it encourages investment in projects that would be rejected under ROI. Other advantages of RI:

- The incorporation of risk by varying the minimum rate of return based on the division's risk
- Varying minimum return depending on the riskiness of a specific asset

A major disadvantage of RI is that it can't be used to compare divisions of different sizes. *Note*: RI tends to favor larger divisions due to the larger amount of dollars involved.

EXAMPLE 7.8

Using the numbers in Example 7.6, assume the minimum required rate of return is 13%. Then the residual income of the division is

$$\$18,000 - (13\% \times \$100,000)$$
$$= \$18,000 - \$13,000 = \underline{\$5,000}$$

Investment Decisions Under ROI and RI

How can I use ROI and RI?

The decision whether to use ROI or RI as a measure of divisional performance affects the manager's investment decisions.

- Under the *ROI method*, division managers tend to accept only the investments whose returns exceed the division's ROI. Otherwise, the division's overall ROI would decrease if the investment were accepted.
- Under the *RI method*, division managers would accept an investment as long as it earns a rate in excess of the minimum required rate of return. The addition of such an investment would increase the division's overall RI.

EXAMPLE 7.9

Consider the same data given in Examples 7.6 and 7.8.

Operating Assets	$100,000
Operating Income	$ 18,000
Minimum required rate of return	13%
ROI = 18% and RI = $5,000.	

Assume that the division is presented with a project that would yield 15% on a $10,000 investment. The division manager would not accept this project under the ROI approach since the division is already earning 18%. Acquiring this project will bring down the present ROI to 17.73%, as shown below:

	Present	New Project	Overall
Operating assets (a)	$100,000	$10,000	$110,000
Operating income (b)	$ 18,000	1,500*	19,500
ROI (b) ÷ (a)	18%	15%	17.73%

*$10,000 × 15% = $1,500

Under the RI approach, the manager would accept the new project since it provides a higher rate than the minimum required rate of return (15% vs. 13%). Accepting the new project will increase the overall residual income to $5,200, as shown below:

	Present	New Project	Overall
Operating assets (a)	$100,000	$10,000	$110,000
Operating income (b)	18,000	1,500	19,500
Minimum required income at 13% (c)	13,000	1,300*	14,300
RI (b) − (c)	$ 5,000	$ 200	$ 5,200

*$10,000 × 13% = $1,300

HOW TO PRICE GOODS AND SERVICES TRANSFERRED

How are transfer prices determined?

Goods and services are often exchanged between various divisions of a decentralized organization. The question then is: what monetary values should be assigned to these exchanges or transfers? Market price? Some kind of cost? Some version of either? There is no single transfer price that will please everybody—that is, top management, the selling division, and the buying division—involved in the transfer.

The choice of a transfer pricing policy (i.e., which type of transfer price to use) is normally decided by top management. The decision will typically include consideration of:

• *Goal congruence.* Will the transfer price promote the goals of the company as a whole? Will it harmonize the divisional goals with organizational goals?

• *Performance evaluation.* Will the selling division receive enough credit for its transfer of goods and services to the buying division? Will the transfer price hurt the performance of the selling division?

• *Autonomy.* Will the transfer price preserve autonomy, the freedom of the selling and buying division managers to operate their divisions as decentralized entities?

• *Other factors* such as minimization of tariffs and income taxes and observance of legal restrictions must be taken into account.

Alternative Transfer Pricing Schemes

What other factors may determine transfer prices?

Transfer prices can also be based on:

• Market price
• Cost-based price—variable or full cost
• Negotiated price
• General formula which is usually the sum of variable costs per unit and opportunity cost for the company as a whole (lost revenue per unit on outside sales)

How suitable is market price for transfers?

Market price is the best transfer price in the sense that it will maximize the profits of the company as a whole, if it meets the following two conditions:

- A competitive market price exists
- Divisions are independent of each other

If any one of these is violated, market price will not lead to an optimal economic decision for the company.

What are the pros and cons of cost-based prices?

Cost-based transfer price, another alternative transfer pricing scheme, is easy to understand and convenient to use. But there are some disadvantages:

• Inefficiencies of the selling divisions are passed on to the buying divisions with little incentive to control costs. The use of standard costs is recommended in such a case.

• The cost-based method treats the divisions as cost centers rather than profit or investment centers. Therefore, measures such as ROI and RI cannot be used for evaluation purposes.

The variable cost-based transfer price has an advantage over the full cost method because it may tend to insure the best use of the company's overall resources. The reason is that, in the short run, fixed costs do not change. Any use of facilities, without incurrence of additional fixed costs, will increase the company's overall profits.

When is a negotiated transfer price used?

A negotiated price is generally used when there is no clear outside market. A negotiated price is one agreed upon between the buying and selling divisions that reflects unusual or mitigating circumstances. NOTE: This method is widely used when no intermediate market price exists for the product transferred and the selling division is assured of a normal profit.

EXAMPLE 7.10

Company X just purchased a small company that specializes in the manufacture of Part 323.

Company X is a decentralized organization. It will treat the newly acquired company as an autonomous division called Division B with full profit responsibility. Division B's fixed costs total $30,000 per month, and variable costs per unit are $18. Division B's operating capacity is 5,000 units. The selling price per unit is $30. Division A of Company X is currently purchasing 2,500 units of Part 323 per month from an outside supplier at $29 per unit, which represents the normal $30 price less a quantity discount. Top management of the company wishes to decide what transfer price should be used.

Top management may consider the following alternative prices:

- $30 market price
- $29, the price that Division A is currently paying to the outside supplier
- $23.50 negotiated price, which is $18 variable cost plus 1/2 of the benefits of an internal transfer (($29 − $18) × 1/2).
- $24 full cost, which is $18 variable cost plus $6 ($30,000 ÷ 5,000 units) fixed cost per unit.
- $18 variable cost

We will discuss each of these prices:

- $30 would not be an appropriate transfer price. Division B cannot charge a price more than the price Division A is paying now ($29).
- $29 would be an appropriate transfer price if top management wishes to treat them as autonomous investment centers. This price would cause all of the benefits of internal transfers to accrue to the selling division, with the buying division's position remaining unchanged.
- $23.50 would be an appropriate transfer price if top management wishes to treat them as investment centers, but wishes to share the benefits of an internal transfer *equally* between them, as follows:

Variable Costs of Division B	$18.00
1/2 of the difference between the variable costs of Division B and the price Division A is paying ($29 − $18) × 1/2	5.50
Transfer price	$23.50

Note: $23.50 is just *one* example of a negotiated transfer price. The exact price depends on how they divide the benefits.

- $24 [$24 = $18 + ($30,000/5,000 units)] would be an appropriate transfer price if top management treats them like cost centers with no profit responsibility.

  All benefits from both divisions will accrue to the buying division. This will maximize the profits of the company as a whole, but adversely affect the performance of the selling division. Another disadvantage of this cost-based approach is that inefficiencies (if any) of the selling division are being passed on to the buying division.

- $18 would be an appropriate transfer price for guiding top management in deciding whether transfers between the two divisions should take place. Since $18 is less than the outside purchase price of the buying division, and the selling division has excess capacity, the transfer should take place, because it will maximize the profits of the company as a whole. However, if $18 is used as a transfer price, then all of the benefits of the internal transfer accrue to the buying division, and the performance of the selling division will be hurt.

BUDGETING AND FINANCIAL PLANNING

What is a budget?

A budget is:

- A formal statement of management's expectation regarding sales, expenses, volume, and other financial transactions of an organization for the coming period

- A set of *pro forma* (*projected* or *planned*) financial statements—income statement, balance sheet, and cash budget
- A tool for both planning and control
- At the beginning of the period, a plan or standard
- At the end of the period, a control device to help management measure its performance against the plan so that future performance may be improved

Figure 7.4 shows a simplified diagram of the various parts of the comprehensive budget, the master plan of the company.

What are the types of budgets?

Budgets are classified into two broad categories:

- *Operating budget*, reflecting the results of operating decisions
- *Financial budget*, reflecting the financial decisions of the firm

What is an operating budget?

The operating budget consists of:

- Sales budget
- Production budget
- Direct materials budget
- Direct labor budget
- Factory overhead budget
- Selling and administrative expense budget
- Pro forma income statement

What does a financial budget contain?

The financial budget consists of:

- Cash budget
- Pro forma balance sheet

Figure 7.4
COMPREHENSIVE BUDGET

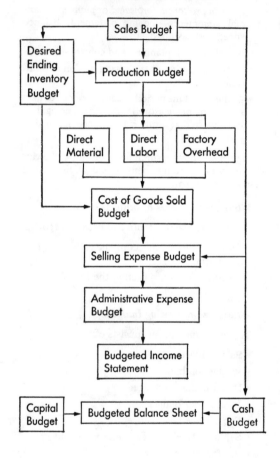

How do I prepare a budget?

The major steps in preparing the budget are:

- Prepare a sales forecast
- Determine expected production volume
- Estimate manufacturing costs and operating expenses
- Determine cash flow and other financial effects
- Formulate projected financial statements

How can I prepare a budget quickly?

In actual practice, use of a shortcut approach is widely used in formulating a budget. The approach can be summarized as follows:

Step 1: A pro forma income statement is developed using past percentage relationships between certain expense and cost items and the firm's sales. These percentages are then applied to the firm's projected sales. The income statement can be set up in a traditional or contribution format.

Step 2: A pro forma balance sheet is estimated, using the *percentage of sales method*. This involves the following steps:

- Express balance sheet items that *vary directly with sales* as a percentage of sales. Any item that does not vary with sales (such as long-term debt) is designated *not applicable* (n.a.). Multiply these percentages by the sales projected to obtain the amounts for the future period.

- Where no percentage applies (such as long-term debt, common stock, and paid-in-capital), simply insert the figures from the present balance sheet or their "desired" level in the column for the future period.

- Compute the projected retained earnings as follows:

Projected retained earnings = present retained earnings + projected net income − cash dividend to be paid

- Sum the asset accounts and the liability and equity accounts to see if there is any difference. The difference, if any, is a *shortfall*, which is the amount of financing the firm has to raise externally.

Should I use a computer to prepare budgets and do financial planning?

More and more companies are developing computer-based models for financial planning and budgeting. They use powerful, yet easy-to-use, financial modeling languages such as Execum's *Interactive Financial Planning System (IFPS)* and Social Systems' *SIMPLAN*. The models help not only build a budget for profit planning, but also explore a variety of "what-if" scenarios. The resultant calculations provide a basis for choice among alternatives under conditions of *uncertainty*. Financial modeling can be accomplished using spreadsheet programs such as Lotus 1-2-3 and SuperCalc.

CHAPTER 8

ANALYSIS OF PROJECTS, PROPOSALS, AND SPECIAL SITUATIONS

Accountants need to be equipped with various tools and techniques in order to cope with short-term and long-term decisions. Cost-volume-profit (CVP) analysis is an extremely useful tool for accountants. When used in conjunction with any spreadsheet program, it can help accountants choose a wise decision by simulating a variety of "what-if" scenarios. Analysis of short-term, special decisions typically requires such simple concepts as *contribution margin* and *relevant costs*. Long-term investment decisions, commonly called *capital budgeting*, however, require not only a good understanding of the time value concept and its application, but also a working knowledge of how to analyze and evaluate investment proposals.

This chapter covers the tools and guidelines that facilitate various short-term, nonroutine decisions and long-term investment decisions. Specifically:

- Break-even and Cost-volume-profit (CVP) analysis
- Short-term decisions, e.g., pricing decisions on special order and the make-or-buy decision
- Time value fundamentals
- Long-term investment decisions, commonly known as capital budgeting

COST-VOLUME-PROFIT AND BREAK-EVEN ANALYSIS

What are variable and fixed costs?

Not all costs behave in the same way. Certain costs, called *variable costs*, vary in proportion to change in activity. Other costs that do not change, regardless of the volume, are called *fixed costs*.

Why analyze cost behavior?

An understanding of costs by behavior is very useful:

- For break-even and cost-volume-profit (CVP) analysis
- To analyze short-term, nonroutine decisions such as the make-or-buy decision and the sales mix decision
- For appraisal of profit center performance by means of the contribution approach and for flexible budgeting (see Chapter 7)

What is cost-volume-profit and break-even analysis?

Cost-volume-profit (CVP) analysis, together with cost behavior information, helps accountants perform many useful analyses. CVP analysis deals with how profit and costs change with a change in volume. It specifically looks at the effects on profits of changes in such factors as variable costs, fixed costs, selling prices, volume, and mix of products sold. By studying the relationships of costs, sales, and net income, accountants are better able to cope with planning decisions.

Break-even analysis, a branch of CVP analysis, determines the break-even sales, which is the level of sales at which total costs equal total revenue.

How may I use CVP analysis in solving business problems?

CVP analysis tries to answer the following questions:

- What sales volume is required to break even?
- What sales volume is necessary in order to earn a desired profit?
- What profit can be expected on a given sales volume?
- How would changes in selling price, variable costs, fixed costs, and output affect profit?
- How would a change in the mix of products sold affect the break-even and target income volume and profit potential?

Contribution Margin

What does contribution margin involve?

For accurate CVP analysis, a distinction must be made between variable and fixed costs. Semivariable costs (or mixed costs) must be separated into their variable and fixed components.

To compute the break-even point and perform various CVP analyses, note the following important concepts:

- *Contribution margin (CM).* The contribution margin is the excess of sales (S) over the variable costs (VC) of the product. It is the amount of money available to cover fixed costs (FC) and to generate profits. Symbolically, CM = S − VC.

- *Unit CM.* The unit CM is the excess of the unit selling price (p) over the unit variable cost (v). Symbolically, unit CM = p − v.

- *CM ratio.* The CM ratio is the contribution margin as a percentage of sales, i.e.,

$$\text{CM Ratio} = \frac{\text{CM}}{\text{S}} = \frac{\text{S} - \text{VC}}{\text{S}} = 1 - \frac{\text{VC}}{\text{S}}$$

CM ratio can also be computed using per-unit data as follows:

$$\text{CM Ratio} = \frac{\text{Unit CM}}{p} = \frac{p - v}{p} = 1 - \frac{v}{p}$$

NOTE: The CM ratio is 1 minus the variable cost ratio. EXAMPLE: If variable costs account for 70% of the price, the CM ratio is 30%.

EXAMPLE 8.1

To illustrate the various concepts of CM, consider the following data for Company Z:

	Per Unit	Total	Percentage
Sales (1,500 units)	$25	$37,500	100%
Less: Variable cost	10	15,000	40
Contribution margin	$15	22,500	60%
Less Fixed costs		15,000	
Net income		$ 7,000	

From the data listed above, CM, unit CM, and the CM ratio are computed as:

$$CM = S - VC = \$37{,}500 - \$15{,}000 = \$22{,}500$$

$$\text{Unit CM} = p - v = \$25 - \$10 = \$15$$

$$\text{CM ratio} = \frac{CM}{S} = \frac{\$22{,}500}{\$37{,}500}$$

$$= 60\% \text{ or } 1 - \frac{VC}{S}$$

$$= 1 - .4 = .6 = 60\%$$

How can the break-even point be calculated?

The break-even point, the point of no profit and no loss, provides accountants with insights into profit planning. It can be computed in three different ways.

The *equation approach* is based on the cost-volume equation which shows the relationships among sales, variable and fixed costs, and net income.

$$S = VC + FC + \text{Net Income}$$

At the break-even volume, $S = VC + FC + 0$. Defining x = volume in *units*, the above relationship can be rewritten in terms of x:

$$px = vx + FC$$

To find the break-even point in units, simply solve the equation for x.

EXAMPLE 8.2

In Example 8.1, p = \$25, v = \$10, and FC = \$15,000. Thus, the equation is:

$$
\begin{aligned}
\$25\,x &= \$10\,x + \$15,000 \\
\$25\,x - \$10\,x &= \$15,000 \\
(\$25 - \$10)\,x &= \$15,000 \\
\$15\,x &= \$15,000 \\
x &= \$15,000/\$15 = 1,000 \text{ units}
\end{aligned}
$$

Therefore, Company Z breaks even at a sales volume of 1,000 units.

The *contribution margin approach*, another technique for computing the break-even point, is based on solving the cost-volume equation. Solving the equation px = vx + FC for x yields:

$$x_{BE} = FC / (p - v)$$

where $(p - v)$ is the unit CM by definition, and x_{BE} = break-even unit sales volume.

In words,

Break-even point in *units* = Fixed Costs/Unit CM

If the break-even point is desired in terms of dollars, then

Break-even point in *dollars* = break-even point in units *times* unit sales price

Alternatively,

Break-even point in *dollars* = Fixed Costs/CM Ratio

EXAMPLE 8.3

Using the same data given in Example 8.1, where unit CM = \$25 − \$10 = \$15 and CM ratio = 60%, we get:

Break-even point in units = \$15,000/\$15 = 1,000 units

Break even point in dollars = 1,000 units × \$25 = \$25,000

Alternatively, \$15,000/.6 = \$25,000

The *graphical approach* is based on the so-called *break-even chart* shown in Figure 8.1. Sales revenue, variable costs, and fixed costs are plotted on the vertical axis. Volume (x) is plotted on the horizontal axis. The break-even point is the point where the total sales revenue line intersects the total cost line. This chart can also effectively report profit potential for a wide range of activity.

The *profit-volume (P/V) chart* shown in Figure 8.2, focuses more directly on how profits vary with changes in volume. Profits are plotted on the vertical axis while units of output are shown on the horizontal axis. NOTE: The slope of the chart is the unit CM.

Figure 8.1
BREAK-EVEN CHART

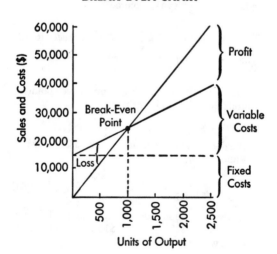

Figure 8.2
PROFIT-VOLUME (P/V) CHART

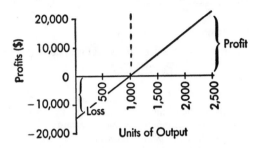

Target Income Volume and Margin of Safety

How do I determine Target Income Volume?

Besides being able to determine the break-even point, CVP analysis determines the sales required to attain a particular income level or target net income. There are two ways target net income can be expressed.

As a *specific dollar amount*, the cost-volume equation specifying target net income is:

$$px = vx + FC + \text{Target Income}$$

Solving the equation for x yields:

$$x_{TI} = \frac{FC + \text{Target Income}}{p - v}$$

where x_{TI} = sales volume required to achieve a given target income. In words,

$$\text{Target Income Sales Volume} = \frac{\text{Fixed Costs} + \text{Target Income}}{\text{Unit CM}}$$

Specifying target income as a *percentage of sales*, the cost-volume equation is:

$$px = vx + FC + \%(px)$$

Solving this for x yields:

$$x_{TI} = \frac{FC}{p - v - \%(p)}$$

In words,

Target Income Sales Volume = Fixed Costs/(Unit CM − % of unit sales price)

EXAMPLE 8.4

Using the same data given in Example 8.1 assume that Company Z wishes to attain:

As a specific dollar amount: A target income of $15,000 before tax

Target income sales volume (in units) required would be:

$$x_{TI} = \frac{FC + \text{Target Income}}{p - v}$$
$$= \frac{\$15,000 + \$15,000}{\$25 - \$10} = 2,000 \text{ units}$$

As a percentage of sales: A target income of 20% of sales

The target income volume required would be:

$$x_{TI} = \frac{FC}{p - v - \%(p)} = \frac{\$15,000}{\$15 - 20\%(\$25)}$$
$$= \frac{\$15,000}{\$15 - \$5} = 1,500 \text{ units}$$

What is the impact of income taxes on target income volume?

If target income is given on an after-tax basis, the target income volume formula becomes:

Target income volume

$$= \frac{\text{Fixed Costs} + \dfrac{\text{Target After-Tax Income}}{1 - \text{tax rate}}}{\text{Unit CM}}$$

EXAMPLE 8.5

Assume in Example 8.1 that Company Z wants to achieve an after-tax income of $6,000. Income tax is levied at 40%. Then,

$$\text{Target income volume} = \frac{\$15,000 + \dfrac{\$6,000}{1 - 0.4}}{\$15}$$

$$= \frac{\$15,000 + \$10,000}{\$15}$$

$$= 1,667 \text{ units}$$

What is the margin of safety?

The margin of safety is a measure of difference between the actual level of sales and the break-even sales. It is the amount by which sales revenue may drop before losses begin and is expressed as a percentage of budgeted sales as follows:

Margin of safety

$$= \frac{\text{Budgeted sales} - \text{break-even sales}}{\text{Budgeted sales}}$$

What is the use of the margin of safety?

The margin of safety is often used as a measure of risk. The larger the ratio, the safer the situation, since there is less risk of reaching the break-even point.

EXAMPLE 8.6

Assume Company Z projects sales of $30,000 with a break-even sales level of $25,000. The expected margin of safety is:

$$\frac{\$30,000 - \$25,000}{\$30,000} = \underline{16.7\%}$$

How is CVP analysis used in practice?

The concepts of contribution margin have many applications in profit planning and short-term decision making. Applications are illustrated in Examples 8.7 through 8.11, using the data from Example 8.1.

EXAMPLE 8.7

Recall from Example 8.1 that Z has a CM of 60% and fixed costs of $15,000 per period. Assume that the company expects sales to go up by $10,000 for the next period. How much will income increase?

Using the CM concepts, we can quickly compute the impact of a change in sales on profits. The formula for computing the impact is:

Change in net income = dollar change in sales × CM ratio

Thus, the increase in net income = $10,000 × 60% = $6,000. Therefore, the income will go up by $6,000, assuming there is no change. If we are given a change in sales in *units* instead of dollars, then the formula becomes:

Change in net income = change in unit sales × unit CM

EXAMPLE 8.8

We now compute before-tax income expected on sales of $47,500.

CM $47,500 × 60%	$28,500
Less: Fixed costs	15,000
Net income	$13,500

EXAMPLE 8.9

Company Z is considering increasing the advertising budget by $5,000, which would increase sales revenue by $8,000. Should the advertising budget be increased? The answer is no, since the increase in the CM is less than the increased cost.

Increase in CM $8,000 × 60%	$4,800
Increase in advertising	5,000
Decrease in net income	($200)

EXAMPLE 8.10

Company Z's accountant is considering a $3,000 increase in sales salaries. What additional sales are required to cover the higher cost?

The increase in fixed cost must be matched by an equal increase in CM:

$$\text{Increase in CM} = \text{increase in cost}$$
$$.60 \text{ sales} = \$3,000$$
$$\text{sales} = \underline{\underline{\$5,000}}$$

EXAMPLE 8.11

Consider the original data. Assume again that Company Z is currently selling 1,500 units per period. In an effort to increase sales, the accountant is considering cutting its unit price by $5 and increasing the advertising budget by $1,000. If these two steps are taken, the accountant feels that unit sales will go up by 60%. Should the two steps be taken?

A $5 reduction in the selling price would cause the unit CM to decrease from $15 to $10. Thus,

Proposed CM 2,400 units × $10	$24,000
Present CM 1,500 units × $15	22,500
Increase in CM	1,500
Increase in advertising outlay	1,000
Increase in net income	$500

The answer is yes. Alternatively, the same answer can be obtained by developing comparative income statements in contribution margin format:

	Present (1,500 units)	Proposed (2,400 units)	Difference
Sales	$37,500 (@25)	$48,000 (@20)	$10,500
Less: Variable cost	15,000	24,000	9,000
CM	22,500	24,000	1,500
Less: Fixed costs	15,000	16,000	1,000
Net income	$7,500	$8,000	$500

Sales Mix Analysis

What effect does the sales mix have?

Break-even and cost-volume-profit analyses require some additional computations and assumptions when a company produces and sells more than one product. Different selling prices and different variable costs result in different unit CM and CM ratios. As a result, break-even points vary with the relative proportions of the products sold, called the *sales mix*. In break-even and CVP analysis, it is necessary to:

- Predetermine the sales mix and then compute a weighted average CM
- Assume that the sales mix does not change for a specified period

The break-even formula for the company as a whole is:

Company-wide break-even in units (or in dollars)

$$= \frac{\text{Fixed Costs}}{\textit{Average} \text{ Unit CM (or } \textit{Average} \text{ CM Ratio)}}$$

EXAMPLE 8.12

Assume that Company X has two products with the following CM data:

	A	B
Selling price	$15	$10
Variable cost	12	5
Unit CM	$ 3	$ 5
Sales mix	60%	40%
Fixed costs	$76,000	

The weighted average unit CM = $3(.6) + $5(.4) = $3.80

Then the company's break-even point in units is $76,000/$3.80 = 20,000 units
   This is divided as follows:

A: 20,000 units × 60% = 12,000 units
B: 20,000 units × 40%   8,000
                        20,000 units

EXAMPLE 8.13

Assume that Company Y produces and sells three products with the following data:

	A	B	C	Total
Sales	$30,000	$60,000	$10,000	$100,000
Sales Mix	30%	60%	10%	100%
Less: VC	24,000	40,000	5,000	69,000
CM	$ 6,000	$20,000	$ 5,000	$ 31,000
CM ratio	20%	33-1/3%	50%	31%

Total fixed costs are $18,600.

The CM ratio for Company Y is $31,000/$100,000 = 31%. Therefore the break-even point *in dollars* is $18,600/.31 = $60,000.

This will be split in the mix ratio of 3:6:1 to give us the following break-even points for the individual products A, B, and C:

$$A: \$60,000 \times 30\% = \$18,000$$
$$B: \$60,000 \times 60\% = 36,000$$
$$C: \$60,000 \times 10\% = \underline{6,000}$$
$$\underline{\$60,000}$$

EXAMPLE 8.14

Assume in Example 8.13 that total sales remain unchanged at $100,000, but a shift in mix from Product B to Product C is expected:

	A	B	C	Total
Sales	$30,000	$30,000	$40,000	$100,000
Sales mix	30%	30%	40%	100%
Less: VC	24,000	20,000*	20,000	64,000
CM	$ 6,000	$10,000	$20,000	$ 36,000
CM ratio	20%	33-1/3%	50%	36%

*$20,000 = $30,000 × 66-2/3%.

Note: The shift in sales mix toward the more profitable line C has caused the CM ratio for the company as a whole to go from 31% to 36%. The new break-even point will be $18,600/.36 =

$51,667. The break-even dollar volume has decreased from $60,000 to $51,667.

What does break-even and CVP analysis assume?

The basic break-even and CVP models are subject to a number of limiting assumptions:

- The behavior of both sales revenue and expenses is *linear* throughout the entire *relevant* range of activity.
- All costs are classified as fixed or variable.
- There is only one product. In a multiproduct firm, the sales mix will not change during the planning period. If the sales mix changes, the break-even point will also change.
- Inventories do not change significantly from period to period.
- Volume is the only factor affecting variable costs.

SHORT-TERM NONROUTINE DECISIONS

What nonrecurring situations do I have to consider?

When analyzing the manufacturing and selling functions, accountants are constantly faced with the problem of choosing alternative courses of action. Typical questions include:

- What to make?
- How to make it?
- Where to sell the product or service?
- What price should be charged?

In the short run, the accountant is typically confronted with the following nonroutine, nonrecurring types of decisions:

- Acceptance or rejection of a special order
- Make or buy
- Add or drop a certain product line
- Utilization of scarce resources
- Sell or process further

What are relevant costs?

In each of the above situations, the ultimate decision rests upon cost data analysis. Cost data are important in many decisions, since they are the basis for profit calculations. However, not all costs are of equal importance in decision making, and accountants must identify the costs that are relevant to a decision. Such costs are called *relevant costs*.

Which costs are relevant in a nonroutine decision?

The relevant costs are the expected future costs which differ between the decision alternatives. Therefore:

• The *sunk costs* are *not* relevant to the decision at hand, because they are past, historical costs.

• The *incremental* or *differential* costs are relevant since they are the ones that differ between the alternatives.

EXAMPLE: In a decision on whether to sell an existing business for a new one, the cost to be paid for the new venture is relevant. However, the initial cost of the old business is not relevant to the decision because it is a sunk cost.

What is incremental analysis?

The method that uses the concept of *relevant costs* is called the *incremental approach*, also known as the *differential* or *relevant cost approach*. Under this method, the decision involves the following steps:

• Gather all costs associated with each alternative

• Drop the *sunk costs*

• Drop those costs which do not differ between alternatives

• Select the best alternative based on the remaining cost data

EXAMPLE 8.15

Assume that ABC Company is planning to expand its productive capacity. The plans consist of purchasing a new machine for $50,000 and disposing of the old machine without receiving anything. The new machine has a 5-year life. The old machine has a 5-year remaining life and a book value of $12,500. The new machine will reduce variable operating costs from $35,000 per year to $20,000 per year. Annual sales and other operating costs are shown below.

	Present Machine	New Machine
Sales	$60,000	$60,000
Variable costs	35,000	20,000
Fixed costs:		
Depreciation (straight-line)	2,500	10,000
Insurance, taxes, etc.	4,000	4,000
Net income	$18,500	$26,000

At first glance, it appears that the new machine provides an increase in net income of $7,500 per year. The book value of the present machine, however, is a sunk cost and is irrelevant in this decision. Furthermore, sales and fixed costs such as insurance, taxes, etc. are also irrelevant since they do not differ between the two alternatives being considered. Eliminating all the irrelevant costs leaves us with only the incremental costs as follows:

Savings in variable costs	$15,000	
Increase in fixed costs	10,000	(a $2,500 sunk cost is irrelevant)
Net annual cash savings arising from the new machine	$ 5,000	

When should a company accept special orders?

A company often receives a short-term, special order for its products at lower prices than usual. In normal times, the company may refuse such an order since it will not yield a satisfactory profit.

RECOMMENDATION: If times are bad or when there is idle capacity, an order should be accepted if the incremental revenue exceeds the incremental costs involved. Such a price, one lower than the regular price, is called a *contribution price.* This approach to pricing is called the *contribution approach to pricing,* also called the *variable pricing model.* This approach is most appropriate when:

- There is idle capacity
- Faced with sharp competition or in a competitive bidding situation
- Operating in a distress situation

EXAMPLE 8.16

Assume that a company with 100,000-unit capacity is currently producing and selling only 90,000 units of product each year with a regular price of $2. If the variable cost per unit is $1 and the annual fixed cost is $45,000, the income statement shows:

		Per Unit
Sales (90,000 units)	$180,000	$2.00
Less: Variable cost	90,000	1.00
Contribution margin	$ 90,000	$1.00
Less: Fixed cost	45,000	0.50
Net income	$ 45,000	$0.50

The company has just received an order that calls for 10,000 units @ $1.20, for a total of $12,000. The acceptance of this special order will not affect regular sales. Management is reluctant to accept this order because the $1.20 price is below the $1.50 factory unit cost ($1.50 = $1.00 + $0.50).

Is filling the order advisable? The answer to this question is yes. The company can add to total profits by accepting this special order even though the price offered is below the unit factory cost. At a price of $1.20, the order will contribute $0.20 (CM per unit = $1.20 − $1.00 = $0.20) toward fixed cost, and profit will increase by $2,000 (10,000 units × $0.20). Using the contribution approach to pricing, the variable cost of $1.00 will be a better guide than the full unit cost of $1.50.

NOTE: The fixed costs will not increase because of the presence of idle capacity.

What is a make-or-buy decision?

The make-or-buy decision is the decision whether to produce a component part internally or to buy it from an outside supplier. This decision involves both quantitative and qualitative factors.

• The *qualitative* considerations include ensuring product quality and the necessity for long-run business relationships with the subcontractors.

• The *quantitative* factors, dealing with cost, are best seen through *incremental analysis*.

EXAMPLE 8.17

Assume a firm has prepared the following cost estimates for the manufacture of a subassembly component based on an annual production of 8,000 units:

	Per Unit	Total
Direct materials	$ 5	$ 40,000
Direct labor	4	32,000
Variable overhead applied	4	32,000
Fixed overhead applied (150% of direct labor cost)	6	48,000
Total cost	$19	$152,000

The supplier has offered to provide the subassembly at a price of $16 each. Two-thirds of fixed factory overhead, which represents executive salaries, rent, depreciation, and taxes, continue regardless of the decision.

Should the company buy or make the product? The key to the decision lies in the investigation of those relevant costs that change between the make-or buy alternatives. Assuming that the productive capacity will be idle if not used to produce the subassembly, the analysis takes the following form:

	Per Unit		Total of 8,000 units	
	Make	Buy	Make	Buy
Purchase price		$16		$128,000
Direct materials	$5		$40,000	
Direct labor	4		32,000	
Variable overhead	4		32,000	
Fixed overhead that can be avoided by *not* making	2	—	16,000	
Total relevant costs	$15	$16	$120,000	$128,000
Difference in favor of making	$1		$8,000	

NOTE: The make-or-buy decision must be investigated in the broader perspective of available facilities. The alternatives are:

- leaving facilities idle
- buying the parts and renting out idle facilities
- buying the parts and using unused facilities for other products

How do I decide whether to add or drop a product line?

The decision whether to drop an old product line or add a new one must take into account both qualitative and quantitative factors. Ultimately, any final decision should be based on the impact the decision will have on contribution margin or net income.

EXAMPLE 8.18

The ABC grocery store has three major product lines: produce, meats, and canned goods. The store is considering dropping the meat line, because the income statement shows it is being sold at a loss. Note the income statement for these product lines:

	Produce	Meats	Canned Food	Total
Sales	$10,000	$15,000	$25,000	$50,000
Less: Variable costs	6,000	8,000	12,000	26,000
CM	$ 4,000	$ 7,000	$13,000	$24,000
Less: Fixed costs:				
Direct	2,000	6,500	4,000	12,500
Allocated	1,000	1,500	2,500	5,000
Total	$ 3,000	$ 8,000	$ 6,500	$17,500
Net income	$ 1,000	($ 1,000)	$ 6,500	$ 6,500

In this example, *direct fixed costs* are those costs that are identified directly with each of the product lines. *Allocated fixed costs* are the amount of common fixed costs allocated to the product lines using some base such as space occupied. The amount of *common fixed costs* typically continues regardless of the decision and thus cannot be saved by dropping the product line to which it is distributed.

The following calculations show the effects on the company as a whole with and without the meat line:

	Keep Meats	Drop Meats	Difference
Sales	$50,000	$35,000	($15,000)
Less: Variable cost	26,000	18,000	(8,000)
CM	$24,000	$17,000	($ 7,000)
Less: Fixed cost:			
Direct	12,500	6,000	(6,500)
Allocated	5,000	5,000	—
Total	$13,500	$11,000	($ 6,500)
Net income	$ 6,500	$ 6,000	($ 500)

From either of the two methods, we see that by dropping meats the store will lose an additional $500. Therefore, the meat product line should be kept.

CAUTION: One of the great dangers in allocating common fixed costs is that such allocations can make a product line look less profitable than it really is. Because of such an allocation, the meat line showed a loss of $1,000. In effect it contributes $500 ($7,000 − $6,500) to the recovery of the store's common fixed costs.

How do I make the best use of scarce resources?

In general, the emphasis on products with higher contribution margin maximizes a firm's total net income, even though total sales may decrease. This is not true, however, where there are constraining factors and scarce resources. The constraining factor is the factor that restricts or limits the production or sale of a given product. EXAMPLES: machine-hours, labor-hours, or cubic feet of warehouse space.

NOTE: In the presence of these constraining factors, maximizing total profits depends on getting the highest contribution margin *per unit* of the factor (rather than the highest contribution margin per unit of product output).

EXAMPLE 8.19

Assume that a company produces products **A** and B with the following contribution margins per unit.

	A		B
Sales	$8		$24
Variable costs	6		20
CM	$2		$ 4
Annual fixed costs		$42,000	

As is indicated by CM per unit, B is more profitable than A since it contributes more to the company's total profits than A ($4 vs. $2). But assume that the firm has limited capacity of 10,000 labor hours. Further, assume that A requires two labor hours to produce and B requires five labor hours.

One way to express this limited capacity is to determine the contribution margin per labor hour.

	A	B
CM/unit	$2.00	$4.00
Labor hours required per unit	2	5
CM per labor hour	$1.00	$ .80

Since A returns the higher CM per labor hour, it should be produced and B should be dropped.

TIME VALUE FUNDAMENTALS

The time value of money is a critical consideration in investment decisions. EXAMPLES: Compound interest calculations are needed to appraise future sums of money resulting from an investment. Discounting, or the calculation of present values, which is inversely related to compounding, is used to evaluate future cash flow streams associated with the investment in fixed assets, such as machinery and equipment.

What is money worth in the future?

A dollar in hand today is worth more than a dollar to be received tomorrow because of the interest it could earn from putting it into a bank account or an investment. Compounding interest means that interest earns interest. For the discussion of this and the subsequent time value concepts, let us define:

F_n = future value = the amount of money at the end of year n.

P = principal

i = annual interest rate

n = number of years

To generalize, the future value of an investment if compounded annually at a rate of i for n years is:

$$F_n = P(1 + i)^n = P.T_1(i,n)$$

where $T_1(i,n)$ is the future value interest factor for $1 (found in Table 8.1, pages 322 and 323).

EXAMPLE 8.20

Your client placed $1,000 in a savings account earning 8% interest compounded annually.

How much money will the client have in his or her account at the end of 4 years?

Substituting P = $1,000, i = .08, and n = 4 into the formula and referring to Table 8.1 gives:

F_4 = $1,000(1 + .08)^4 = $1,000
   (Table 8.1 value)
   = $1,000(1.361) = $1,361.00

What is the future value of an annuity?

An annuity is defined as a series of equal payments (or receipts) for a specified number of periods. The future value of an annuity is a compound annuity which involves depositing or investing an equal sum of money at the end of each year for a certain number of years and allowing it to grow.

It is computed as follows:

$F = A\ T_2(i,n)$

where A = the amount of an annuity and $T_2(i,n)$ = the future value interest factor for an n-year annuity compounded at i percent and can be found in Table 8.2 (see pages 324 and 325).

EXAMPLE 8.21

Your client wishes to determine the sum of money he or she will have in a savings account at the end of six years by depositing $1,000 at the end of each year for the next six years. The annual interest rate is 8%. The amount is:

$1,000 (Table 8.2 value) = $1,000(7.336) = $7,336.00

What is present value?

Present value is the present worth of future sums of money. The process of calculating present values, or *discounting* is actually the opposite of finding the compounded future value.

TABLE 8.1
FUTURE VALUE OF $1

Periods	4%	6%	8%	10%	12%	14%	20%
1	1.040	1.060	1.080	1.100	1.120	1.140	1.200
2	1.082	1.124	1.166	1.210	1.254	1.300	1.440
3	1.125	1.191	1.260	1.331	1.405	1.482	1.728
4	1.170	1.263	1.361	1.464	1.574	1.689	2.074
5	1.217	1.338	1.469	1.611	1.762	1.925	2.488
6	1.265	1.419	1.587	1.772	1.974	2.195	2.986
7	1.316	1.504	1.714	1.949	2.211	2.502	3.583
8	1.369	1.594	1.851	2.144	2.476	2.853	4.300
9	1.423	1.690	1.999	2.359	2.773	3.252	5.160
10	1.480	1.791	2.159	2.594	3.106	3.707	6.192

11	1.540	1.898	2.332	2.853	3.479	4.226	7.430
12	1.601	2.012	2.518	3.139	3.896	4.818	8.916
13	1.665	2.133	2.720	3.452	4.364	5.492	10.699
14	1.732	2.261	2.937	3.798	4.887	6.261	12.839
15	1.801	2.397	3.172	4.177	5.474	7.138	15.407
20	2.191	3.207	4.661	6.728	9.646	13.743	38.338
30	3.243	5.744	10.063	17.450	29.960	50.950	237.380
40	4.801	10.286	21.725	45.260	93.051	188.880	1469.800

Table 8.2
FUTURE VALUE OF AN ANNUITY OF $1

Periods	4%	6%	8%	10%	12%	14%	20%
1	1.000	1.000	1.000	1.000	1.000	1.000	1.000
2	2.040	2.060	2.080	2.100	2.120	2.140	2.220
3	3.122	3.184	3.246	3.310	3.374	3.440	3.640
4	4.247	4.375	4.506	4.641	4.779	4.921	5.368
5	5.416	5.637	5.867	6.105	6.353	6.610	7.442
6	6.633	6.975	7.336	7.716	8.115	8.536	9.930
7	7.898	8.394	8.923	9.487	10.089	10.730	12.916
8	9.214	9.898	10.637	11.436	12.300	13.233	16.499
9	10.583	11.491	12.488	13.580	14.776	16.085	20.799
10	12.006	13.181	14.487	15.938	17.549	19.337	25.959

11	13.486	14.972	16.646	18.531	20.655	23.045	32.150
12	15.026	16.870	18.977	21.395	24.133	27.271	39.580
13	16.627	18.882	21.495	24.523	28.029	32.089	48.497
14	18.292	21.015	24.215	27.976	32.393	37.581	59.196
15	20.024	23.276	27.152	31.773	37.280	43.842	72.035
20	29.778	36.778	45.762	57.276	75.052	91.025	186.690
30	56.085	79.058	113.283	164.496	241.330	356.790	1181.900
40	95.026	154.762	259.057	442.597	767.090	1342.000	7343.900

Recall from the future value formula:

$$F_n = P(1 + i)^n$$

Therefore,

$$P = F_n/(1 + i)^n = F_n T_3(i,n)$$

where $T_3(i,n)$ represents the present value interest factor for \$1 (given in Table 8.3, pages 328 and 329).

EXAMPLE 8.22

A client has been given an opportunity to receive \$20,000 six years from now. If the client can earn 10% on his investment, what is the most he or she should pay for this opportunity?

We compute the present worth of \$20,000 he or she will receive six years from now at a 10% rate of discount. Use Table 8.3 value as follows:

\$20,000 (Table 8.3 value) = \$20,000(.564) = \$11,280.00.

This means that the client should be indifferent to the choice between receiving \$11,280 now or \$20,000 six years from now since the amounts are time equivalent. In other words, the client could invest \$11,280 today at 10% and have \$20,000 in six years.

What is the present value of an annuity?

Interest received from bonds, pension funds, and insurance obligations all involve annuities. To compare these financial instruments, one would like to know the present value of each of these annuities. The way to find the present value of an annuity is:

$$P = A T_4(i,n)$$

where A = the amount of an annuity, and $T_4(i,n)$ = the value for the present value interest factor for a \$1 annuity at i percent for n years (found in Table 8.4, pages 330 and 331).

EXAMPLE 8.23

A client is to receive an annuity of $1,000 each year for the next three years. You are asked to compute the present value of the annuity. Use Table 8.4 for this purpose as follows:

$1,000 (Table 8.4 value) = $1,000 (2.673) = $2,673.00

CAPITAL BUDGETING

What is capital budgeting?

Capital budgeting is the process of making long-term planning decisions for investments. There are typically two types of investment decisions:

1. *Selection decisions* in terms of obtaining new facilities or expanding existing facilities.

EXAMPLES:

- Investments in long-term assets such as property, plant, and equipment
- Resource commitments in the form of new product development, market research, refunding of long-term debt, introduction of a computer, etc.

2. *Replacement decisions* in terms of replacing existing facilities with new facilities.

EXAMPLES:

- Replacing a manual bookkeeping system with a computerized system
- Replacing an inefficient lathe with one that is numerically controlled

What are the popular selection techniques?

There are several methods of evaluating investment projects:

- Payback period
- Accounting rate of return (ARR) (also called *simple rate of return*)

Table 8.3
PRESENT VALUE OF $1

Periods	4%	5%	6%	8%	10%	12%	14%	16%	18%	20%	22%	24%	26%	28%	30%	40%
1	0.962	0.952	0.943	0.926	0.909	0.893	0.877	0.862	0.847	0.833	0.820	0.806	0.794	0.781	0.769	0.714
2	0.925	0.907	0.890	0.857	0.826	0.797	0.769	0.743	0.718	0.694	0.672	0.650	0.630	0.610	0.592	0.510
3	0.889	0.864	0.840	0.794	0.751	0.712	0.675	0.641	0.609	0.579	0.551	0.524	0.500	0.477	0.455	0.364
4	0.855	0.823	0.792	0.735	0.683	0.636	0.592	0.552	0.516	0.482	0.451	0.423	0.397	0.373	0.350	0.260
5	0.822	0.784	0.747	0.681	0.621	0.567	0.519	0.476	0.437	0.402	0.370	0.341	0.315	0.291	0.269	0.186
6	0.790	0.746	0.705	0.630	0.564	0.507	0.456	0.410	0.370	0.335	0.303	0.275	0.250	0.227	0.207	0.133
7	0.760	0.711	0.665	0.583	0.513	0.452	0.400	0.354	0.314	0.279	0.249	0.222	0.198	0.178	0.159	0.095
8	0.731	0.677	0.627	0.540	0.467	0.404	0.351	0.305	0.266	0.233	0.204	0.179	0.157	0.139	0.123	0.068
9	0.703	0.645	0.592	0.500	0.424	0.361	0.308	0.263	0.225	0.194	0.167	0.144	0.125	0.108	0.094	0.048
10	0.676	0.614	0.558	0.463	0.386	0.322	0.270	0.227	0.191	0.162	0.137	0.116	0.099	0.085	0.073	0.035
11	0.650	0.585	0.527	0.429	0.350	0.287	0.237	0.195	0.162	0.135	0.112	0.094	0.079	0.066	0.056	0.025
12	0.625	0.557	0.497	0.397	0.319	0.257	0.208	0.168	0.137	0.112	0.092	0.076	0.062	0.052	0.043	0.018
13	0.601	0.530	0.469	0.368	0.290	0.229	0.182	0.145	0.116	0.093	0.075	0.061	0.050	0.040	0.033	0.013

	0.577 0.555	0.505 0.481	0.442 0.417	0.340 0.315	0.263 0.239	0.205 0.183	0.160 0.140	0.125 0.108	0.099 0.084	0.078 0.065	0.062 0.051	0.049 0.040	0.039 0.031	0.032 0.025	0.025 0.020	0.009 0.006
14 15																
16	0.534	0.458	0.394	0.292	0.218	0.163	0.123	0.093	0.071	0.054	0.042	0.032	0.025	0.019	0.015	0.005
17	0.513	0.436	0.371	0.270	0.198	0.146	0.108	0.080	0.060	0.045	0.034	0.026	0.020	0.015	0.012	0.003
18	0.494	0.416	0.350	0.250	0.180	0.130	0.095	0.069	0.051	0.038	0.028	0.021	0.016	0.012	0.009	0.002
19	0.475	0.396	0.331	0.232	0.164	0.116	0.083	0.060	0.043	0.031	0.023	0.017	0.012	0.009	0.007	0.002
20	0.456	0.377	0.312	0.215	0.149	0.104	0.073	0.051	0.037	0.026	0.019	0.014	0.010	0.007	0.005	0.001
21	0.439	0.359	0.294	0.199	0.135	0.093	0.064	0.044	0.031	0.022	0.015	0.011	0.008	0.006	0.004	0.001
22	0.422	0.342	0.278	0.184	0.123	0.083	0.056	0.038	0.026	0.018	0.013	0.009	0.006	0.004	0.003	0.001
23	0.406	0.326	0.262	0.170	0.112	0.074	0.049	0.033	0.022	0.015	0.010	0.007	0.005	0.003	0.002	
24	0.390	0.310	0.247	0.158	0.102	0.066	0.043	0.028	0.019	0.013	0.008	0.006	0.004	0.003	0.002	
25	0.375	0.295	0.233	0.146	0.092	0.059	0.038	0.024	0.016	0.010	0.007	0.005	0.003	0.002	0.001	
26	0.361	0.281	0.220	0.135	0.084	0.053	0.033	0.021	0.014	0.009	0.006	0.004	0.002	0.002	0.001	
27	0.347	0.268	0.207	0.125	0.076	0.047	0.029	0.018	0.011	0.007	0.005	0.003	0.002	0.001	0.001	
28	0.333	0.255	0.196	0.116	0.069	0.042	0.026	0.016	0.010	0.006	0.004	0.002	0.002	0.001	0.001	
29	0.321	0.243	0.185	0.107	0.063	0.037	0.022	0.014	0.008	0.005	0.003	0.002	0.001	0.001		
30	0.308	0.231	0.174	0.099	0.057	0.033	0.020	0.012	0.007	0.004	0.003	0.002	0.001	0.001		
40	0.208	0.142	0.097	0.046	0.022	0.011	0.005	0.003	0.001	0.001						

Table 8.4
PRESENT VALUE OF AN ANNUITY OF $1

Periods	4%	5%	6%	8%	10%	12%	14%	16%	18%	20%	22%	24%	26%	28%	30%	40%
1	0.962	0.952	0.943	0.926	0.909	0.893	0.877	0.862	0.847	0.833	0.820	0.806	0.794	0.781	0.769	0.714
2	1.886	1.859	1.833	1.783	1.736	1.690	1.647	1.605	1.566	1.528	1.492	1.457	1.424	1.392	1.361	1.224
3	2.775	2.723	2.673	2.577	2.487	2.402	2.322	2.246	2.174	2.106	2.042	1.981	1.868	1.816	1.816	1.589
4	3.630	3.546	3.465	3.312	3.170	3.037	2.914	2.798	2.690	2.589	2.494	2.404	2.320	2.241	2.166	1.879
5	4.452	4.330	4.212	3.993	3.791	3.605	3.433	3.274	3.127	2.991	2.864	2.745	2.635	2.532	2.436	2.035
6	5.242	5.076	4.917	4.623	4.355	4.111	3.889	3.685	3.498	3.326	3.167	3.020	2.885	2.759	2.643	2.168
7	6.002	5.786	5.582	5.206	4.868	4.564	4.288	4.039	3.812	3.605	3.416	3.242	3.083	2.937	2.802	2.263
8	6.733	6.463	6.210	5.747	5.335	4.968	4.639	4.344	4.078	3.837	3.619	3.421	3.241	3.076	2.925	2.331
9	7.435	7.108	6.802	6.247	5.759	5.328	4.946	4.607	4.303	4.031	3.786	3.566	3.366	3.184	3.019	2.379
10	8.111	7.722	7.360	6.710	6.145	5.650	5.216	4.833	4.494	4.192	3.923	3.682	3.465	3.269	3.092	2.414
11	8.760	8.306	7.887	7.139	6.495	5.988	5.453	5.029	4.656	4.327	4.035	3.776	3.544	3.335	3.147	2.438
12	9.385	8.863	8.384	7.536	6.814	6.194	5.660	5.197	4.793	4.439	4.127	3.851	3.606	3.387	3.190	2.456
13	9.986	9.394	8.853	7.904	7.103	6.424	5.842	5.342	4.910	4.533	4.203	3.912	3.656	3.427	3.223	2.468

14	10.563	9.899	9.295	8.244	7.367	6.628	6.002	5.468	5.008	4.611	4.265	3.962	3.695	3.459	3.249	2.477
15	11.118	10.380	9.712	8.559	7.606	6.811	6.142	5.575	5.092	4.675	4.315	4.001	3.726	3.483	3.268	2.484
16	11.652	10.838	10.106	8.851	7.824	6.974	6.265	5.669	5.162	4.730	4.357	4.033	3.751	3.503	3.283	2.489
17	12.166	11.274	10.477	9.122	8.022	7.120	6.373	5.749	5.222	4.775	4.391	4.059	3.771	3.518	3.295	2.492
18	12.659	11.690	10.828	9.372	8.201	7.250	6.467	5.818	5.273	4.812	4.419	4.080	3.786	3.529	3.304	2.494
19	13.134	12.085	11.158	9.604	8.365	7.366	6.550	5.877	5.316	4.844	4.442	4.097	3.799	3.539	3.311	2.496
20	13.590	12.462	11.470	9.818	8.514	7.469	6.623	5.929	5.353	4.870	4.460	4.110	3.808	3.546	3.316	2.497
21	14.029	12.821	11.764	10.017	8.649	7.562	6.687	5.973	5.384	4.891	4.476	4.121	3.816	3.551	3.320	2.498
22	14.451	13.163	12.042	10.201	8.772	7.645	6.743	6.011	5.410	4.909	4.488	4.130	3.822	3.556	3.323	2.498
23	14.857	13.489	12.303	10.371	8.883	7.718	6.792	6.044	5.432	4.925	4.499	4.137	3.827	3.559	3.325	2.499
24	15.247	13.799	12.550	10.529	8.985	7.784	6.835	6.073	5.451	4.937	4.507	4.143	3.831	3.562	3.327	2.499
25	15.622	14.094	12.783	10.675	9.077	7.843	6.873	6.097	5.467	4.948	4.514	4.147	3.834	3.564	3.329	2.499
26	15.983	14.375	13.003	10.810	9.161	7.896	6.906	6.118	5.480	4.956	4.520	4.151	3.837	3.566	3.330	2.500
27	16.330	14.643	13.211	10.935	9.237	7.943	6.935	6.136	5.492	4.964	4.525	4.154	3.839	3.567	3.331	2.500
28	16.663	14.898	13.406	11.051	9.307	7.984	6.961	6.152	5.502	4.970	4.528	4.157	3.840	3.568	3.331	2.500
29	16.984	15.141	13.591	11.158	9.370	8.022	6.983	6.166	5.510	4.975	4.531	4.159	3.841	3.569	3.332	2.500
30	17.292	15.373	13.765	11.258	9.427	8.055	7.003	6.177	5.517	4.979	4.534	4.160	3.842	3.569	3.332	2.500
40	19.793	17.159	15.046	11.925	9.779	8.244	7.105	6.234	5.548	4.997	4.544	4.166	3.846	3.571	3.333	2.500

- Net present value (NPV)
- Internal rate of return (IRR) (also called *time adjusted rate of return*)
- Profitability index (also called the *excess present value index*)

NOTE: The NPV method and the IRR method are called *discounted cash flow* (DCF) methods since they both recognize the time value of money and thus discount future cash flows. Each of the methods presented above is discussed below.

Payback Period

How do I determine the payback period?

Payback period measures the length of time required to recover the amount of initial investment. The payback period is determined by dividing the amount of initial investment by the cash inflow through increased revenues or cost savings.

EXAMPLE 8.24

Assume:

Cost of investment	$18,000
Annual cash savings	$ 3,000

Then, the payback period is:

$$\frac{\$18,000}{\$3,000} = 6 \text{ years}$$

When cash inflows are not even, the payback period is determined by trial and error. When two or more projects are considered, the rule for making a selection decision is as follows:

REQUIREMENT: Choose the project with the shorter payback period. The rationale is: the shorter the payback period, the less risky the project, and the greater the liquidity.

EXAMPLE 8.25

Consider two projects whose cash inflows are not even. Assume each project costs $1,000.

Year	A	B
1	100	500
2	200	400
3	300	300
4	400	100
5	500	—
6	600	—

Based on trial and error, the payback period of project A is 4 years ($100 + 200 + 300 + 400 = $1,000 in four years). The payback period of project B is

$$2 \text{ years} + \frac{\$100}{\$300} = 2 \text{ 1/3 years.}$$

Therefore, according to this method, choose project B over project A.

What are the pros and cons of the payback period method?

Advantages

- It is simple to compute and easy to understand.
- It handles investment risk effectively.

Disadvantages

- It does not recognize the time value of money
- It ignores the impact of cash inflows after the payback period. It is essentially cash flows after the payback period which determine profitability of an investment.

How do I not account for the time value of money?

To correct for the deficiency of not taking into account the time value of money, the *discounted* payback method may be used. In this case:

- Each year's cash inflows are expressed in present value terms
- Each year's present value is added to determine how long it takes to recoup the initial investment

Accounting (Simple) Rate of Return

What is the accounting rate of return?

Accounting rate of return (ARR) measures profitability from the conventional accounting standpoint by relating the required investment to the future annual net income. Sometimes, the former is the average investment.

EXAMPLE 8.26

Consider the investment:

Initial investment	$6,500
Estimated life	20 years
Cash inflows per year	$1,000
Depreciation by straight line	$325

Then, $\text{ARR} = \dfrac{\$1,000 - \$325}{\$6,500} = 10.4\%$

Using the *average* investment which is usually assumed to be 1/2 of the original investment, the resulting rate of return will be doubled, as shown below.

$$\text{ARR} = \frac{\$1,000 - \$325}{1/2\ (\$6,500)} = \frac{\$675}{\$3,250} = 20.8\%$$

The justification for using the average investment is that each year the investment amount is decreased by $325 through depreciation. Therefore, the average is computed as one-half of the original cost.

RECOMMENDATION: Under the ARR method, choose the project with the higher rate of return.

What are benefits and drawbacks of the ARR method?

Advantages

- The method is easily understandable, simple to compute, and recognizes the profitability factor

Disadvantages

- It fails to recognize the time value of money
- It uses accounting data instead of cash flow data

Net Present Value

What is net present value?

Net present value (NPV) is the excess of the present value (PV) of cash inflows generated by the project over the amount of the initial investment (I). Simply, NPV = PV − I. The present value of future cash flows is computed using the so-called "cost of capital" (or minimum required rate of return) as the discount rate.

RECOMMENDATION: If NPV is positive, accept the project. Otherwise, reject.

EXAMPLE 8.27

Initial investment	$12,950
Estimated life	10 years
Annual cash inflows	$ 3,000
Cost of capital (minimum required rate of return)	12%

Present value of cash inflows (PV):

$3,000 × PV of annuity of $1 for 10 years and 12% $3,000 (Table 8.4 value) = $3,000 (5.65) =	$16,950
Initial investment (I)	$12,950
Net present value (NPV = PV − I)	$ 4,000

Since the investment's NPV is positive, the investment should be accepted.

What are the pros and cons of the NPV method?

Advantages:

- Recognizes the time value of money
- Is easy to compute whether the cash flows form an annuity or vary from period to period

Disadvantage:

- Requires detailed long-term forecasts of incremental cash flow data

Internal Rate of Return (or Time Adjusted Rate of Return)

What is internal rate of return?

Internal rate of return (IRR) is defined as the rate of interest that equates I with the PV of future cash inflows. In other words, at IRR, I = PV, or NPV = 0.

RECOMMENDATION: Accept if IRR exceeds the cost of capital; otherwise, reject.

EXAMPLE 8.28

Assume the same data given in Example 8.27. We will set up the following equality (I = PV):

$12,950 = $3,000 × PV

PV = $12,950/$3,000 = 4.317, which stands somewhere between 18% and 20% in the 10-year line of Table 8.4. Using interpolation we derive the exact rate.

PV factor (Table 8.4 value)

18%	4.494	4.494
IRR		4.317
20%	4.192	
Difference	0.302	0.177

Therefore, IRR = 18% + $\dfrac{0.177}{0.302}$ (20% − 18%)

= 18% + .586 (2%)

= 18% + 1.17% = 19.17%

Since the investment's IRR is greater than the cost of capital (12%), the investment should be accepted.

What are the benefits and drawbacks of the IRR method?

Advantages:

- Considers the time value of money and is therefore more exact and realistic than ARR.

Disadvantages:

- Difficult to compute especially when the cash inflows are not even

- Fails to recognize the varying sizes of investments in competing projects and their respective dollar profitabilities

How is IRR computed by trial and error?

The trial and error method for computing IRR when cash inflows are different each year is summarized step by step, as follows:

Step 1: Compute NPV at cost of capital, denoted here as r_1,

Step 2: See if NPV is positive or negative.

Step 3: If NPV is positive, then pick another rate (r_2) much higher than r_1.
If NPV is negative, then pick another rate (r_2) much smaller than r_1. The true IRR at which NPV = 0 must be somewhere in between these two rates.

Step 4: Compute NPV using r_2.

Step 5: Use interpolation for the exact rate.

EXAMPLE 8.29

Consider the following investment whose cash flows are different from year to year:

Year	Cash Inflows
1	1,000
2	2,500
3	1,500

Assume that the amount of initial investment is $3,000 and the cost of capital is 14%.

Step 1. NPV at 14%

Year	Cash inflows	PV factor at 14%	Total PV
1	1,000	0.877	$ 877
2	2,500	0.769	1,923
3	1,500	0.675	1,013
			$3,813

Thus, NPV = $3,813 − $3,000 = $813

Step 2. We see that NPV = $813 is positive at r_1 = 14%

Step 3. Pick, say, 30% to play safe as r_2.

Step 4. Computing NPV at $r_2 = 30\%$:

Year	Cash inflows	PV factor at 30%	Total PV
1	1,000	0.769	$ 769
2	2,500	0.592	1,480
3	1,500	0.455	683
			$2,932

Thus, NPV = \$2,932 − \$3,000 = \$(68)

Step 5. Interpolate:

	NPV	
14%	$813	$813
IRR		0
30%	−68	
Difference	$881	$813

Therefore, IRR = $14\% + \dfrac{\$813}{\$881} (30\% - 14\%)$

$$= 14\% + .923 (16\%)$$
$$= 14\% + 14.76\%$$
$$= 28.76\%$$

What are the differences between NPV and IRR?

Net Present Value (NPV)

- Calculate the NPV, using the cost of capital as the discount rate.
- If the NPV is positive, accept the project; otherwise, reject the project.

Internal Rate of Return (IRR)

- Using Present Value tables, compute the IRR by trial and error interpolation.
- If this rate of return exceeds the cost of capital, accept the project; if not, reject the project.

Profitability Index (or Excess Present Value Index)

What is the profitability index?

The profitability index is the ratio of the total PV of future cash inflows to the initial investment, that is, PV/I. This index is used as a means of ranking projects in descending order of attractiveness.

RECOMMENDATION: If it is greater than 1, then accept.

EXAMPLE 8.30

Using the data in Example 8.27, the profitability index = PV/I = \$16,950/\$12,950 = 1.31. Since this project generates \$1.31 for each dollar invested (its profitability index is greater than 1), you should accept the project.

How do I choose between mutually exclusive investments?

A project is said to be *mutually exclusive* if the acceptance of one project automatically excludes the acceptance of one or more other projects. The conditions under which contradictory rankings can occur are:

- projects have different expected lives
- projects have different size of investment
- the time of the projects' cash flow differs (e.g., the cash flows of one project increase over time, while those of the other decrease)

The contradiction results from different assumptions with respect to the reinvestment rate on cash flows released from the projects.

- The NPV method discounts all cash flows at the cost of capital, thus implicitly assuming that these cash flows can be reinvested at this rate.
- The IRR method implies a reinvestment rate at IRR. Thus, the implied reinvestment rate will differ from project to project.

When one must choose between mutually exclusive investments, the NPV and IRR methods may give decision results contradictory to each other. The NPV method generally gives correct ranking, since the cost of capital is a more realistic reinvestment rate.

EXAMPLE 8.31

Assume the following:

Cash Flows

	0	1	2	3	4	5
A	(100)	120	—	—	—	—
B	(100)	—	—	—	—	201.14

Computing IRR and NPV at 10% gives the different rankings as follows:

	IRR	NPV at 10%
A	20%	9.08
B	15%	24.91

Note: The general rule is to go by NPV ranking, thus choosing project B over project A.

Limited Funds for Capital Spending

How do I deal with limited funds for capital spending?

Many firms specify a limit on the overall budget for capital spending. *Capital rationing* is concerned with the problem of selecting the mix of acceptable projects that provides the *highest overall NPV* in such a case. The profitability index is used widely in ranking projects competing for limited funds.

EXAMPLE 8.32

Projects	I	PV	Profitability index	Ranking
A	$ 70,000	$112,000	1.6	1
B	100,000	145,000	1.45	2
C	110,000	126,500	1.15	5
D	60,000	79,000	1.32	3
E	40,000	38,000	.95	6
F	80,000	95,000	1.19	4

Assume that the company's fixed budget is $250,000. Using the profitability index, we select projects A, B, and D:

	I	PV
A	$ 70,000	$112,000
B	100,000	145,000
D	60,000	79,000
	$230,000	$336,000

Therefore, NPV = $336,000 − $230,000 = $106,000

Effects of Income Tax Factors on Capital Budgeting Decisions

How do income tax factors affect capital budgeting decisions?

Income taxes make a difference in many capital budgeting decisions. The project which is attractive on a pre-tax basis may have to be rejected on an after-tax basis. Income taxes typically affect both the amount and the timing of cash flows. Since net income, not cash inflows, is subject to tax, after-tax cash inflows are not usually the same as after-tax net income.

Let us define:

S = sales
E = cash operating expenses
d = depreciation
t = tax rate

Before-tax cash inflows = $(S - E)$

Net income = $(S - E - d)$

By definition,

After-tax cash inflows = before-tax cash inflow − taxes
After-tax cash inflows = $(S - E) - (S - E - d) \times t$

Rearranging gives the *short-cut formula*:

After-tax cash inflow = $(S - E)(1 - t) + d \cdot t$

As can be seen, the deductibility of depreciation from sales in arriving at net income subject to taxes

reduces income tax payments and thus serves as a
tax shield.

Tax shield = tax savings on depreciation
$$= d \cdot t$$

EXAMPLE 8.33

Assume:

$S = \$12,000$

$E = \$10,000$

$d = \$500/year$ by straight line

$t = 40\%$

Then, after-tax cash inflow

$= (\$12,000 - \$10,000)(1 - .4) + \$500(.4)$

$= \$1,200 + \$200 = \$1,400$

NOTE: A tax shield = tax savings on depreciation
$= d \cdot t = \$500(.4) = \$200$

How is after-tax outflow determined?

After-tax cash *outflow* is computed by simply dropping "S" in the previous formula. Therefore:

After-tax cash *outflow* $= (-E)(1 - t) + d \cdot t$

EXAMPLE 8.34

Assume:

$E = \$6,000$

$d = \$800/year$ by straight line

$t = 40\%$

Then, after-tax cash *outflow*

$= (-\$6,000)(1 - .4) + \$800(.4)$

$= -\$3,600 + \$320$

$= -\$3,280$

What is the effect of accelerated depreciation on tax savings?

Since the tax shield is d × t, the higher the depreciation deduction, the higher the tax savings on depreciation. Therefore, the accelerated-depreciated methods such as the double declining balance method and the sum-of-years'-digits methods produce higher tax savings than the straight line method. They will produce higher present values for the tax savings which greatly affect investment decision. Let us look at the present values of tax shield effects of alternative depreciation methods.

EXAMPLE 8.35

Assume:

Initial investment	$100,000
Estimated life	4 years
Salvage value	0
Cost of capital after taxes	15%
Tax rate	40%

Method of depreciation	15% PV factor	PV of tax savings

Straight-Line Depreciation

Annual depreciation
($100,000 ÷ 4 =
$25,000):
Depreciation deduction
          $25,000

Multiply by
40% . . .   × 40%
Income tax savings,
  years 1–
  4 . . . . $10,000   2.855 $28,550

Sum-of-the-Years'-Digits Depreciation:

Year	Multiplier*	Depreciation deduction	Tax shield: income tax savings at 40%	15% PV factor	PV of tax savings
1	4/10	$40,000	$16,000	0.870	$13,920
2	3/10	30,000	12,000	0.756	9,072
3	2/10	20,000	8,000	0.658	5,264
4	1/10	10,000	4,000	0.572	2,288
					$30,544

*The denominator for the sum-of-the-years'-digits method is: $1 + 2 + 3 + 4 = 10$ or

$$S = \frac{n(n + 1)}{2} \quad S = \frac{4(4 + 1)}{2} = 10$$

where S = sum of the years
n = life of the asset

Double Declining Balance Depreciation:

Year	Book value	Rate** (%)	Depreciation deduction	Tax shield: income tax savings at 40%		
1	$100,000	50	$50,000	$20,000	0.870	$17,400
2	50,000	50	25,000	10,000	0.756	7,560
3	25,000	50	12,500	5,000	0.658	3,290
4	12,500	50	12,500***	5,000	0.572	2,860
						$31,110

**The percentage rate for the double-declining method is: 2 × straight-line rate = 2 × 25% = 50%.
***The asset is depreciated to zero salvage value in the 4th year.

CHAPTER 9

QUANTITATIVE APPLICATIONS AND MODELING IN ACCOUNTING

Quantitative applications and modeling in accounting have been on the rise, coupled with the advent of microcomputers and wide availability of software for various quantitative decision making tools. The accountant should make use of quantitative techniques and modeling to analyze and solve the various accounting and financial problems faced by the client or the business entity he or she is employed by. These quantitative tools allow for the consideration of a multitude of data.

STATISTICAL ANALYSIS AND EVALUATION

How do I handle large volumes of data?

In many situations, accountants have a large volume of data that needs to be analyzed. These data could be earnings, cash flows, accounts receivable balances, weights of an incoming shipment, etc. The statistics most commonly used to describe the characteristics of the data are the *mean* and the *standard deviation*. These statistics are also used to measure the return and risk in investment and financial decision making, in which the CPA may be asked to participate by the business entity.

Mean

What is a mean?

The *mean* gives us the average or central value of our data. Typically, there are three measures of central tendency:

- Arithmetic mean
- Weighted mean
- Geometric mean

What is the arithmetic mean ($\bar{x}$)?

The arithmetic mean is a simple average. To find it, we sum the values in our data and divide by the number of observations. Symbolically,

$$\bar{x} = \frac{\Sigma x}{n}$$

where n = number of observations

EXAMPLE 9.1

John Jay Lamp Company has a revolving credit agreement with a local bank. The loan showed the following ending monthly balances last year:

Jan.	$18,500
Feb.	21,000
Mar.	17,600
Apr.	23,200
May	18,600
Jun.	24,500
Jul.	60,000
Aug.	40,000
Sep.	25,850
Oct.	33,100
Nov.	41,000
Dec.	28,400

Then the mean monthly balance for the loan last year is computed as follows:

Arithmetic mean balance

$$= \frac{\begin{array}{c} \$18,500 + \$21,000 + \$17,600 \\ + \$23,200 + \$18,600 + \$24,500 \\ + \$60,000 + \$40,000 + \$25,850 \\ + \$33,100 + \$41,000 + \$28,400 \end{array}}{12}$$

$$= \frac{\$351,750}{12} = \underline{\underline{\$29,312.50}}$$

How do I determine a weighted mean?

The arithmetic mean is an unweighted average. It assumes equal likelihood of each value in one data. When observations have different degrees of importance or frequency, use the *weighted mean*. The weighted average enables us to take into account the importance of each value in the overall total. Symbolically, the formula for calculating the weighted average is:

Weighted mean = Σ w·x

where w = Weight (in percentage or in relative frequency) assigned to each observation

EXAMPLE 9.2

Consider the company that uses three grades of labor to produce a finished product. The company wants to know the average cost of labor per hour for this product.

Grade of labor	Labor hours per unit of output	Hourly wages (x)
Skilled	6	$10.00
Semiskilled	3	8.00
Unskilled	1	6.00

Using the arithmetic mean of the labor wage rates results in:

$$\text{Arithmetic mean} = \frac{\$10.00 + \$8.00 + \$6.00}{3}$$

$$= \frac{\$24.00}{3}$$

$$= \underline{\$8.00/\text{hour}}$$

This implicitly assumes the same amounts of each grade of labor were used to produce the output. More specifically,

$$\frac{\$10.00 + \$8.00 + \$6.00}{3} = \begin{array}{l} \$10.00(1/3) + \$8.00\,(1/3) \\ + \$6.00\,(1/3) \end{array}$$

$$= \underline{\$8.00/\text{hour}}$$

This is simply not true. We have to consider different amounts of each grade of labor in calculating the average cost of labor per hour. The correct way is to take a weighted average as follows:

$$\text{Weighted mean} = \begin{array}{l} \$10.00(6/10) + \$8.00(3/10) \\ + \$6.00(1/10) \end{array}$$

$$= \underline{\$9.00/\text{hour}}$$

NOTE: Weight the hourly wage for each grade by its proportion of the total labor required to produce the product.

When should the geometric mean be used?

Sometimes we are dealing with quantities that change over a period of time. In such a case, we need to know an average rate of change, such as an average rate of return on investment or an average rate of growth in earnings over a period of several years. The formula for finding the geometric mean over n periods is:

Geometric mean

$$= \sqrt[n]{(1 + x_1)(1 + x_2) \ldots \ldots (1 + x_n)} - 1$$

where x represents the percentage rate of change or percentage return on investment.

Since it is cumbersome to calculate the nth root

(although most scientific calculators have a key to compute this), we will only illustrate the two period return calculation (n = 2).

The following example shows the inadequacy of the arithmetic mean return when the price of a stock doubles in one period and then depreciates back to the original price.

EXAMPLE 9.3

	Time periods		
	t = 0	t = 1	t = 2
Price (end of period)	$80	$160	$80
Rate of return	—	100%	−50%

The rate of return for periods 1 and 2 are computed as follows:

$$\text{Period 1 } (t = 1) \quad \frac{(\$160 - \$80)}{\$80}$$

$$= \frac{\$80}{\$80} = \underline{\underline{100\%}}$$

$$\text{Period 2 } (t = 2) \quad \frac{(\$80 - \$160)}{\$160}$$

$$= \frac{-\$80}{\$160} = \underline{\underline{-50\%}}$$

Therefore, the arithmetic mean return over the two periods is the average of 100% and −50%, which is 25%, as shown below:

$$\frac{100\% + (-50\%)}{2} = \underline{\underline{25\%}}$$

As can be easily seen, the stock purchased for $80 and sold for the same price two periods later did not earn 25%. It clearly earned a *zero* return. This can be shown by computing the geometric *mean* return.

Note that n = 2, x_1 = 100% = 1, and x_2 = −50% = −.5

Geometric mean return

$$= \sqrt[2]{(1 + 1)(1 - .5)} - 1$$

$$= \sqrt[2]{(2)(.5)} - 1$$

$$= \sqrt{1} - 1 = 1 - 1 = \underline{\underline{0\%}}$$

Standard Deviation

What is the standard deviation?

The standard deviation measures the tendency of data to be spread out. Accountants can make important inferences from past data with this measure. The standard deviation, denoted with and read as *sigma*, is defined as follows:

$$\sigma = \sqrt{\frac{\Sigma(x - \bar{x})^2}{n - 1}}$$

where $\bar{x}$ is the mean.

The standard deviation can be used to measure the variation of such items as the expected contribution margin (CM) or expected variable manufacturing costs. It can also be used to assess the risk associated with investment decisions.

How do I calculate standard deviation?

The standard deviation is calculated, step-by-step, as follows:

- Subtract from the mean each value of the data
- Square each of the differences obtained in step 1
- Add together all the squared differences
- Divide the sum of all the squared differences by the number of values *minus* one
- Take the square root of the quotient obtained in step 4

EXAMPLE 9.4

One and one-half years of quarterly returns are listed for United Motors stock as follows:

Time period	x	$(x - \bar{x})$	$(x - \bar{x})^2$
1	10%	0	0
2	15	5	25
3	20	10	100
4	5	-5	25
5	-10	-20	400
6	20	10	100
	60		650

From the above table, note that x = 60/6 = 10%

$$= \sqrt{\Sigma(x - \bar{x})^2/(n - 1)} = \sqrt{650/(6 - 1)}$$
$$= \sqrt{130} = 11.40\%$$

The United Motors stock has returned on the average 10% over the last six quarters. The variability about its average return was 11.40%. The high standard deviation (11.40%) relative to the average return of 10% indicates that the stock is very risky.

REGRESSION ANALYSIS

What is regression analysis?

Regression analysis is a very popular statistical method used to project sales and earnings.

It is also used to estimate the *cost-volume formula* (also called the *flexible budget formula*), which takes the following functional form:

$$y = a + bx$$

where

> y = the semivariable (mixed) costs to be broken up
> x = any given measure of activity such as production volume, machine hours, or direct labor hours
> a = the fixed cost component
> b = the variable rate per unit of x

The regression method is a statistical procedure for estimating mathematically the average relationship between the dependent variable y and the independent variable x.

- *Simple regression* involves one independent variable (e.g., direct labor hours (DLH) or machine hours alone)
- *Multiple regression* involves two or more activity variables

(We will assume simple *linear* regression throughout this chapter, which means that we will maintain the y = a + bx relationship.)

The Method of Least Squares

How do I use least squares in making a decision?

In estimating the values of a and b, the regression method attempts to find a line of *best fit*. To find the line of best fit, a technique called the *method of least squares* is used.

To explain the least squares method, we define the error as the difference between the observed value and the estimated value of some semivariable cost and denote it with u. Symbolically,

$$u = y - y'$$

where

y = observed value of a semivariable expense
y' = estimated value based on y' = a + bx

The least-squares criterion requires that the line of best fit be such that the sum of the squares of the errors (or the vertical distance in Figure 9.1 from the observed data points to the line) is a minimum, i.e.,

$$\text{Min } \Sigma u^2 = \Sigma(y - y')^2$$

Using differential calculus we obtain the following equations, called *normal equations*:

$$\Sigma y = n \cdot a + b \cdot \Sigma x$$
$$\Sigma xy = a \cdot \Sigma x + b \cdot \Sigma x^2$$

Solving the equations for *b* and *a* yields:

$$b = \frac{n\Sigma xy - (\Sigma x)(\Sigma y)}{n\Sigma x^2 - (\Sigma x)^2}$$
$$a = \bar{y} - b\bar{x} \text{ where } \bar{y} = \Sigma y/n \text{ and } \bar{x} = \Sigma x/n$$

Figure 9.1
ACTUAL (y) VERSUS ESTIMATED (y')

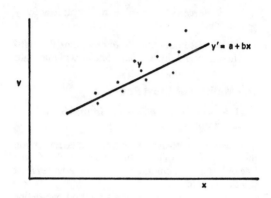

NOTE: The formula for *a* is a short cut formula, which requires the computation of *b* first. This will save a considerable amount of time.

EXAMPLE 9.5

To illustrate the computations of *b* and *a*, use the data below. All the sums required are computed and shown below:

DLH(x)	Factory Overhead (y)	xy	x²	y²
9 hours	$ 15	135	81	225
19	20	380	361	400
11	14	154	121	196
14	16	224	196	256
23	25	575	529	625
12	20	240	144	400
12	20	240	144	400
22	23	506	484	529
7	14	98	49	196
13	22	286	169	484
15	18	270	225	324
17	18	306	289	324
174 hours	$225	3,414	2,792	4,359

From the table above:

$$\Sigma x = 174$$
$$\Sigma y = 225$$
$$\Sigma xy = 3,414$$
$$\Sigma x^2 = 2,792$$
$$\bar{x} = \Sigma x/n = 174/12 = 14.5$$
$$\bar{y} = \Sigma y/n = 225/12 = 18.75$$

Substituting these values into the formula for *b* first:

$$b = \frac{n\Sigma xy - (\Sigma x)(\Sigma y)}{n\Sigma x^2 - (\Sigma x)^2}$$
$$= \frac{(12)(3,414) - (174)(225)}{(12)(2,792) - (174)^2}$$
$$= \frac{1,818}{3,228} = \underline{\underline{0.5632}}$$
$$a = \bar{y} - b\bar{x}$$
$$= (18.75) - (0.5632)(14.5) = 18.75 - 8.1664$$
$$= \underline{\underline{10.5836}}$$

NOTE: Σy^2 is not used here but rather is computed for future use.

Our final regression equation is:

$$y' = \$10.5836 + \$0.5632x$$

where
y' = estimated factory overhead
x = DLH

Use of a Spreadsheet Program for Regression

How do I use an electronic spreadsheet?

Alternatively, we can use a spreadsheet program such as *Lotus 1-2-3* in order to develop the model. This involves the following steps:

EXAMPLE 9.6

Step 1. Enter the data on x and y as shown on the following page.

x	y
DLH (00)	Factory Overhead (00)
9	15
19	20
11	14
14	16
23	25
12	20
12	20
22	23
7	14
13	22
15	18
17	18

Step 2. Press/Data Regression

Step 3. Define x and y data range

Step 4. Define output range

Step 5. Hit Go

This will produce the following regression output:

Regression Output

Constant	10.58364
Std Err of Y Est	2.343622
R Squared	0.608373
No. of Observations	12
Degrees of Freedom	10
X Coefficient(s)	0.563197
Std Err of Coef.	0.142893

The result shows:

$$y' = 10.58364 + 0.563197x$$

Trend Analysis

What is trend analysis?

Another common method for forecasting sales or earnings is the use of trend analysis, a special case of regression analysis. This method involves a regression whereby a trend line is fitted to a time series of data.

How do I apply trend analysis?

The trend line equation can be shown as:

$$y = a + bx$$

The formulas for the coefficients a and b are essentially the same as the ones for simple regression. However, for regression purposes, a time period can be given a number so that $\Sigma x = 0$. When there is an *odd* number of periods, the period in the middle is assigned a zero value. If there is an *even* number, then -1 and $+1$ are assigned the two periods in the middle, so that again $\Sigma x = 0$.

With $\Sigma x = 0$, the formula for b and a reduces to the following:

$$b = \frac{n\Sigma xy}{n\Sigma x^2}$$
$$a = \Sigma y/n$$

EXAMPLE 9.7

Case 1 (odd number)

	19x1	19x2	19x3	19x4	19x5
x =	-2	-1	0	+1	+2

Case 2 (even number)

	19x1	19x2	19x3	19x4	19x5	19x6
x =	-3	-2	-1	+1	+2	+3

In each case, $\Sigma x = 0$.

EXAMPLE 9.8

Consider ABC Company whose historical earnings per share (EPS) follow:

Year	EPS
19x1	$1.00
19x2	1.20
19x3	1.30
19x4	1.60
19x5	1.70

Since the company has 5 years' data, which is an odd number the year in the middle is assigned a zero value.

Year	x	EPS(y)	xy	x^2
19x1	-2	$1.00	-2.00	4
19x2	-1	1.20	-1.20	1
19x3	0	1.30	0	0
19x4	$+1$	1.60	1.60	1
19x5	$+2$	1.70	3.40	4
	0	$6.80	1.80	10

$$b = \frac{(5)(1.80)}{(5)(10)} = \frac{9}{50} = \underline{\underline{\$ .18}}$$

$$a = \frac{\$6.80}{5} = \underline{\underline{\$1.36}}$$

Therefore, the estimated trend equation is:

$$\hat{y} = \$1.36 + \$0.18x$$

where

$\hat{y}$ = estimated EPS
x = year index value

To project 19x6 sales, we assign $+3$ to the x value for the year 19x6. Thus,

$$\hat{y} = \$1.36 + \$.18(+3)$$
$$= \$1.36 + \$.54$$
$$= \underline{\underline{\$1.90}}$$

REGRESSION STATISTICS

Regression analysis uses a variety of statistics which tell us about the accuracy and reliability of the regression results. They include:

- Correlation coefficient (r) and coefficient of determination (r^2)
- Standard error of the estimate (s_e)
- Standard error of the regression coefficient (s_b) and t-statistic

What is the correlation between variables y and x?

The correlation coefficient, r, measures the degree of correlation between y and x. The range of values it takes on is between -1 and $+1$. More widely used, however, is the coefficient of determination, designated r^2 (read "r-squared"). Simply put, r^2 tells us how good the estimated regression equation is. In other words, it is a measure of "goodness of fit" in the regression. Therefore, the higher the r^2, the more confidence we have in the estimated cost formula.

More specifically, the coefficient of determination represents the proportion of the total variation in y that is explained by the regression equation. It has the range of values between 0 and 1.

EXAMPLE 9.9

The statement "factory overhead is a function of machine hours with $r^2 = 70\%$," can be interpreted as "70% of the total variation of factory overhead is explained by the regression equation or the change in machine hours" and "the remaining 30% is accounted for by something other than machine hours."

The coefficient of determination is computed as follows:

$$r^2 = 1 - \frac{\Sigma(y - y')^2}{\Sigma(y - \overline{y})^2}$$

In a simple regression situation, however, there is the short-cut method available:

$$r^2 = \frac{[n \cdot \Sigma xy - (\Sigma x)(\Sigma y)]^2}{[n\Sigma x^2 - (\Sigma x)^2] \cdot [n\Sigma y^2 - (\Sigma y)^2]}$$

Comparing this formula with the one for b in Example 9.5, we see the only additional information we need to compute r^2 is Σy^2.

EXAMPLE 9.10

From the table prepared in Example 9.5, $\Sigma y^2 = 4,359$. Using the short-cut method for r^2,

$$r^2 = \frac{(1{,}818)^2}{(3{,}228) \cdot [(12)(4{,}359) - (225)^2]}$$

$$= \frac{3{,}305{,}124}{(3{,}228)(52{,}308 - 50{,}625)}$$

$$= \frac{3{,}305{,}124}{(3{,}228)(1{,}683)} = \frac{3{,}305{,}124}{5{,}432{,}724}$$

$$= 0.6084 = 60.84\%$$

This means that about 60.84% of the total variation in total factory overhead is explained by DLH and the remaining 39.16% is still unexplained. A relatively low r^2 indicates that there exists a lot of room for improvement in the estimated cost-volume formula ($y' = \$10.5836 + \$0.5632x$). Machine hours or a combination of DLH and machine hours might improve r^2.

How can I compute the standard error of the estimate?

The standard error of the estimate, "s_e," is defined as the standard deviation of the regression. It is computed:

$$s_e = \sqrt{\frac{\Sigma(y - y')^2}{n - 2}} = \sqrt{\frac{\Sigma y^2 - a\Sigma y - b\Sigma xy}{n - 2}}$$

The statistics can be used to gain some idea of the accuracy of our predictions.

EXAMPLE 9.11

Going back to our example data, s_e is calculated as:

$$s_e = \sqrt{\frac{(4{,}359) - (10.5836)(225) - (0.5632)(3{,}414)}{12 - 2}}$$

$$= \sqrt{\frac{54.9252}{10}} = 2.3436$$

If a manager wants the prediction to be 95% confident, the confidence interval would be the *estimated cost* ± 2(2.3436).

More specifically, the confidence interval for

the prediction given as 10 hours of direct labor time would be:

$$\$16.2156^* \pm 2(2.3436)$$

$$= \$16.2156 \pm 4.6872, \text{ which means:}$$

$$\$11.5284 - \$20.9028$$

*$y' = \$10.5836 + \$0.5632x = \$10.5836 + \$0.5632(10)$
$= \$10.5836 + \$5.632 = \$16.2156$

What is the relationship between the standard error of the coefficient and t-statistic?

The standard error of the coefficient, "s_b," and t-statistic are closely related. s_b is calculated as:

$$s_b = \frac{s_e}{\sqrt{\Sigma(x - \overline{x})^2}}$$

or in short-cut form

$$s_b = \frac{s_e}{\sqrt{\Sigma x^2 - \overline{x}\Sigma x}}$$

s_b gives an estimate of the range in which the true coefficient "actually" is. The t-statistic shows the statistical significance of x in explaining y. It is developed by dividing the estimated coefficient, b, by its standard error, s_b. That is, t-statistic = b/s_b. Thus, the t-statistic really measures how many standard errors the coefficient is away from zero.

RECOMMENDATION: Generally, any t value greater than +2 or less than −2 is acceptable. The higher the t-value, the more significant the b is, and therefore, the greater the confidence in the coefficient as a predictor.

EXAMPLE 9.13

The s_b for our example is:

$$s_b = \frac{2.3436}{\sqrt{2,792 - (14.5)(174)}}$$

$$= \frac{2.3436}{\sqrt{2,792 - 2,523}} = \frac{2.3436}{\sqrt{269}}$$

$$= \frac{2.3436}{16.40} = .143$$

NOTE: $s_e = 2.3436$, $\Sigma x^2 = 2,792$, $\bar{x} = 14.5$, $\Sigma x = 174$.

Thus, t-statistic = $b/s_b = .5632/.143 = 3.94$

Since $t = 3.94 > 2$, we conclude that the b coefficient is statistically significant.

How can I estimate cash collection rates using regression?

Credit sales affect cash collections with time lags. In other words, there is a time lag between point of credit sale and realization of cash. More specifically, the lagged effect of credit sales and cash inflows is distributed over a number of periods as follows:

$$C_t = b_1 S_{t-1} + b_2 S_{t-2} + \ldots + b_i S_{t-i}$$

where

C_t = cash collections

S_t = credit sales made in period t

$b_1, b_2, \ldots b_i$ = collection percentages

i = # of periods lagged

By using the regression method discussed previously, we will be able to estimate these collection rates (or payment proportions). We can use /Data Regression of Lotus 1-2-3 or special packages such as STATPACK or SAS.

NOTE: The cash collection percentages (b_1, b_2, . . ., b_i) may not add up to 100% because of the possibility of bad debts. Once we estimate these percentages, we should be able to compute the bad debt percentage with no difficulty.

EXAMPLE 9.14

Figure 9.2 shows the regression results using actual monthly data on credit sales and cash inflows for a real company. Equation I can be written as follows:

$$C_t = 60.6\%(S_{t-1}) + 24.3\%(S_{t-2}) + 8.8\%(S_{t-3})$$

This result indicates that the receivables generated by the credit sales are collected at the following rates:

- First month after sale, 60.6%
- Second month after sale, 24.3%
- Third month after sale, 8.8%

The bad debt percentage is computed as 6.3% (100% − 93.7%).

CAUTION: These collection and bad debt percentages are probabilistic variables, that is, variables whose values cannot be known with precision. However, the standard error of the regression coefficient and the t-value permit us to assess a probability that the true percentage is between specified limits. The confidence interval takes the following form:

$b \pm t\, s_b$

Figure 9.2
REGRESSION RESULT FOR CASH COLLECTION (C_t)

Independent Variables	Equation I
S_{t-1}	.606*
	(.062)**
S_{t-2}	.243*
	(.085)
S_{t-3}	.088
	(.157)
S_{t-4}	
R^2	.754
Durbin-Watson	2.52***
Standard Error of the estimate (S_e)	11.63***
# of monthly observations	21
Bad Debt Percentages	.063

*Statistically significant at the 5% significance level.
**This figure in the parentheses is the standard error of the estimate for the coefficient.
***No autocorrelation present at the 5% significance level.

EXAMPLE 9.15

To illustrate, assuming $t = 2$ as a rule of thumb at the 95% confidence level, the true collection percentage from the prior month's sales will be:

$$60.6\% \pm 2(6.2\%)$$
$$= 60.6\% \pm 12.4\%$$

Turning to the estimation of cash collections and allowance for doubtful accounts, we will use the following values for illustrative purposes:

$$S_{t-1} = \$77.6$$
$$S_{t-2} = \$58.5$$
$$S_{t-3} = \$76.4$$

and forecast average monthly net credit sales = \$75.2

The forecast cash collection for period t would be:

$$C_t = 60.6\%(77.6) + 19.3\%(58.5) + 8.8\%(76.4)$$
$$= \$65.04$$

If the accountant wants to be 95% confident about this forecast value, then he or she would set the interval as follows:

$$C_t \pm t\, s_e$$

To illustrate, using $t = 2$ as a rule of thumb at the 95% confidence level, the true value for cash collections in period t will be:

$$\$65.04 \pm 2(11.63)$$
$$= \$65.04 \pm 23.26$$

The estimated allowance for uncollectible accounts for period t will be:

$$6.3\%(\$75.2) = \$4.73$$

NOTE: By using the limits discussed so far, accountants can:

- Develop flexible (or probabilistic) cash budgets, where the lower and upper limits can be interpreted as pessimistic and optimistic outcomes, respectively

- Simulate the cash budget in an attempt to determine both the expected change in cash collections each period and the variation about this value

QUANTITATIVE METHODS FOR ACCOUNTING

What types of quantitative methods are available?

The term *quantitative models*, also known as *operations research (OR)* or *management science*, describes sophisticated mathematical and statistical techniques for the solution of planning and decision making problems.

What is the definition of "quantitative models"?

In recent years, much attention has been given to use of a variety of quantitative models in accounting. Especially with the rapid development of microcomputers, accountants find them increasingly easy to use. It is becoming necessary to acquire knowledge about the use of those quantitative (mathematical and statistical) methods. The so-called Decision Support System (DSS) is in effect the embodiment of this trend. Numerous tools are available under these subject headings. We will explore six of the most important techniques which have broad applications in accounting:

- Decision making under uncertainty
- Linear programming and shadow prices
- Goal programming and multiple goals
- Learning curve
- Inventory planning and control
- Program Evaluation and Review Technique (PERT)

DECISION MAKING

What is the difference between certainty and uncertainty in decision making?

Decisions are made under *certainty* or under *uncertainty*. Decision making under certainty means that for each decision there is only one event and therefore only one outcome for each action. Decision making under uncertainty, which is more common in reality, involves several events for each action, each with its probability of occurrence.

Decision Making Under Certainty

What is an example of decision making under certainty?

An accountant is often faced with a decision situation where for each decision alternative there is only one event and therefore only one outcome for each action.

EXAMPLE 9.16

Assume there is only one possible event for the two possible actions:

- "Do nothing" at a future cost of $3.00 per unit for 10,000 units
- "Rearrange" a facility at a future cost of $2.80 for the same number of units

We can set up the following table:

Actions	Possible outcome with certainty
Do nothing	$30,000 (10,000 units × $3.00)
Rearrange	28,000 (10,000 units × $2.80)

Since there is only one possible outcome for each action (with certainty) the decision is obviously to choose the action that will result in the most desirable outcome (least cost), that is, to "rearrange."

Decision Making Under Uncertainty

What measures do I take when making a decision under uncertainty?

When decisions are made in a world of *uncertainty*, it is often helpful to make the following computations:

- Expected value
- Standard deviation
- Coefficient of variation

How do I compute expected value?

For decisions involving uncertainty, the concept of *expected value* ($\overline{A}$) provides a rational means for selecting the best course of action. The expected value of an alternative is an arithmetic mean, a weighted average using the probabilities as weights. More specifically, it is found by multiplying the probability of each outcome by its payoff.

$$\overline{A} = \Sigma A_x P_x$$

where A_x is the outcome for the xth possible event
P_x is the probability of occurrence of that outcome.

EXAMPLE 9.17

Consider two investment proposals, A and B, with the following probability distribution of cash flows in each of the next five years:

	Cash Inflows			
Probability	(.2)	(.3)	(.4)	(.1)
A	$50	200	300	400
B	$100	150	250	850

The expected value of the cash inflow in proposal A is:

$$\$50(.2) + 200(.3) + 300(.4) + 400(.1) = \$230$$

The expected value of the cash inflow in proposal B is:

$$\$100(.2) + 150(.3) + 250(.4) + 850(.1) = \$250$$

How is standard deviation determined?

The standard deviation (σ) measures the dispersion of a probability distribution. It is the square root of the mean of the squared deviations from the expected value.

$$\sigma = \sqrt{\sum_{x=1}^{n} (A_x - \overline{A})^2 \, P_x}$$

NOTE: The standard deviation is commonly used as an absolute measure of risk. The higher the standard deviation, the higher the risk.

EXAMPLE 9.18

Using the data from Example 9.17, the standard deviations of proposals A and B are computed as follows:

For A:

$$\sigma = \sqrt{\begin{array}{l}[(\$50 - 230)^2 \, (0.2) + (200 - 230)^2 \, (0.3) \\ + (300 - 230)^2 \, (0.4) + (400 - 230)^2 \, (0.1)]\end{array}}$$
$$= \underline{\$107.70}$$

For B:

$$\sigma = \sqrt{\begin{array}{l}[(\$100 - 250)^2 \, (0.2) + (150 - 250)^2 \, (0.3) \\ + (250 - 250)^2 \, (0.4) + (850 - 250)^2 \, (0.1)]\end{array}}$$
$$= \underline{\$208.57}$$

Proposal B is riskier than proposal A, because its standard deviation is greater.

How is coefficient of variation computed?

Coefficient of variation is a measure of relative dispersion, or relative risk. It is computed by dividing the standard deviation by the expected value:

$$CV = \frac{\sigma}{\overline{A}}$$

EXAMPLE 9.19

Using the data from Examples 9.17 and 9.18, we calculate the coefficient of variation for each proposal as:

For A: $107.70/$230 = <u>.47</u>

For B: $208.57/$250 = <u><u>.83</u></u>

Therefore, because the coefficient is a relative measure of risk, B is said to have a greater degree of risk.

Decision Matrix

What is a decision matrix?

Although the statistics such as expected value and standard deviation are essential for choosing the best course of action under uncertainty, the decision problem can best be approached using *decision theory*. Decision theory is a systematic approach to making decisions especially under uncertainty. Decision theory uses an organized approach such as a *payoff table* (or *decision matrix*), which is characterized by:

- The *row* representing a set of alternative *courses of action* available to the decision maker
- The *column* representing the *state of nature* or conditions that are likely to occur and the decision maker has no control over
- The *entries* in the body of the table representing the outcome of the decision (*payoffs* in the form of costs, revenues, profits or cash flows)

By computing expected value of each action, we will be able to pick the best one.

EXAMPLE 9.20

Assume the following probability distribution of daily demand for strawberries:

Daily demand	0	1	2	3
Probability	.2	.3	.3	.2

Also assume that unit cost = \$3, selling price = \$5 (i.e., profit on sold unit = \$2), and salvage value on unsold units = \$2 (i.e., loss on unsold unit = \$1). We can stock either 0, 1, 2, or 3 units.

How many units should be stocked each day? Assume that units from one day cannot be sold the next day. Then the payoff table can be constructed as follows:

State of Nature

Demand Stock (probability)	0 (.2)	1 (.3)	2 (.3)	3 (.2)	Expected value
0	\$0	0	0	0	\$0
Actions 1	-1	2	2	2	1.40
2	-2	1*	4	4	1.90**
3	-3	0	3	6	1.50

*Profit for (stock 2, demand 1) equals (no. of units sold)(profit per unit) − (no. of units unsold)(loss per unit) =
(1)(\$5 − 3) − (1)(\$3 − 2) = \$1
**Expected value for (stock 2) is: −2(.2) + 1(.3) + 4(.3) + 4(.2) = \$1.90

The optimal stock action is the one with the highest *expected monetary value*, i.e., stock 2 units.

Expected Value of Perfect Information

How is expected value computed?

Suppose the decision maker can obtain a perfect prediction of which event (state of nature) will occur. The *expected value with perfect information* (EVPI) would be the total expected value of actions selected on the assumption of a perfect forecast. The *expected value of perfect information* can then be computed as:

EVPI = Expected value with perfect information − Expected value with existing information

EXAMPLE 9.21

From the payoff table in Example 9.20, the following analysis yields the expected value *with* perfect information:

State of Nature

	Demand	0	1	2	3	Expected value
Stock		(.2)	(.3)	(.3)	(.2)	
	0	$0				$0
Actions	1		2			.6
	2			4		1.2
	3				6	1.2
						$3.00

Alternatively,

$$\$0(.2) + 2(.3) + 4(.3) + 6(.2) = \$3.00$$

With existing information, the best that the decision maker could obtain was select (stock 2) and obtain $1.90. With perfect information (forecast), the decision maker could make as much as $3. Therefore, the expected value *of* perfect information is $3.00 − $1.90 = $1.10. This is the maximum price the decision maker is willing to pay for additional information.

Decision Tree

How does decision tree analysis work?

Decision tree is another approach used in discussions of decision making under uncertainty. It is a pictorial representation of a decision situation. As in the case of the *decision matrix* approach discussed earlier, it shows decision alternatives, states of nature, probabilities attached to the states of nature, and conditional benefits and losses. The decision tree approach is most useful in a sequential decision situation.

EXAMPLE 9.22

Assume XYZ Corporation wishes to introduce one of two products to the market this year. The probabilities and present values (PV) of projected cash inflows are given on page 372.

Products	Initial investment	PV of cash inflows	Probabilities
A	$225,000		1.00
		$450,000	0.40
		200,000	0.50
		− 100,000	0.10
B	80,000		1.00
		320,000	0.20
		100,000	0.60
		− 150,000	0.20

A decision tree analyzing the two products is given on page 373.

LINEAR PROGRAMMING AND SHADOW PRICES

What is linear programming?

Linear programming (LP) addresses the problem of allocating limited resources among competing activities in an optimal manner. Specifically, it is a technique used to:

- *Maximize* a revenue, contribution margin, or profit function subject to constraints
- *Minimize* a cost function subject to constraints

Linear programming consists of two important ingredients:

- Objective function
- Constraints (including *non-negativity* constraints), which are typically inequalities

What are the applications of linear programming?

A firm may wish to:

- Find an optimal product mix so as to maximize its total contribution without violating restrictions imposed upon the availability of resources
- Determine a least cost combination of input materials while satisfying production require-

Choice A or B		Initial Investment (1)	Probability (2)	PV of Cash Inflow (3)	PV of Cash Inflow (2 × 3) = (4)
	Product A	$225,000	0.40	$450,000	$180,000
			0.50	$200,000	100,000
			0.10	–$100,000	10,000
			Expected PV of Cash Inflows		$270,000
	Product B	$ 80,000	0.20	$320,000	$ 64,000
			0.60	$100,000	60,000
			0.20	–$150,000	30,000
			Expected PV of Cash Inflows		$ 94,000

For Product A:
Expected NPV = expected PV − I = $270,000 − $225,000 = $45,000
For Product B:
Expected NPV = $94,000 − $80,000 = $14,000

Based on the expected net present value, the company should choose product A over product B.

ments, maintaining required inventory levels, staying within production capacities, and using available employees

Other managerial applications include:

- Selecting an investment mix
- Blending chemical products
- Scheduling flight crews
- Assigning jobs to machines
- Determining transportation routes
- Determining distribution or allocation pattern

How do I formulate a linear programming problem?

To formulate the LP problem:

- *Step 1*: Define the *decision variables* you are trying to solve for.
- *Step 2*: Express the objective function and constraints in terms of these decision variables.

NOTE: As the name *linear* programming implies, all the expressions must be of *linear* form.

EXAMPLE 9.23

A firm produces two products, A and B. Both products require time in two processing departments, Assembly Department and Finishing Department. Data on the two products are as follows:

	Products		Available
Processing	*A*	*B*	*Hours*
Assembly	2	4	100 hrs.
Finishing	3	2	90
Contribution Margin			
Per Unit	$25	$40	

The firm wants to find the most profitable mix of these two products.

Step 1: Define the decision variables as follows:

A = the number of units of product A to be produced

B = the number of units of product B to be produced

Step 2: The objective function to maximize total contribution margin (CM) is expressed as:

Total CM = $25A + $40B

Then, formulate the constraints as inequalities:

2A + 4B ≤ 100	(Assembly constraint)
3A + 2B ≤ 90	(Finishing constraint)

Do not forget to add the non-negativity constraints:

A, B ≥ 0

Our LP model is:

maximize	Total CM = 25A + 40B
subject to	2A + 4B ≤ 100
	3A + 2B ≤ 90
	A, B ≥ 0

How are LP problems solved?

There are solution methods available to solve LP problems. They include:

- The simplex method
- The graphical method

What is the simplex method?

The *simplex* method is the technique most commonly used to solve LP problems. It is an algorithm, which is an iteration method of computation, moving from one solution to another until it reaches the best solution. Virtually all computer software for LP uses this method of computation.

What is the graphical method?

The graphical solution is easier to use but limited to the LP problems involving two (or at most three) decision variables. The graphical method follows the steps:

Step 1: Change inequalities to equalities.

Step 2: Graph the equalities.

Step 3: Identify the correct side for the original inequalities.

Step 4: After all this, identify the feasible region, the area of feasible solutions. *Feasible solutions* are values of decision variables that satisfy all the restrictions simultaneously.

Step 5: Determine the contribution margin at all of the corners in the feasible region.

EXAMPLE 9.24

Using the data from Example 9.23, follow steps 1 through 4. We obtain the following feasible region (shaded area).

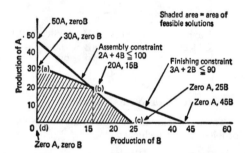

Then we evaluate all of the corner points in the feasible region in terms of their CM, as follows:

Corner Points		Contribution Margin
A	*B*	$25A + $40B
(a) 30	0	$25(30) + $40(0) = $ 750
(b) 20	15	25(20) + 40(15) = 1,100
(c) 0	25	25(0) + 40(25) = 1,000
(d) 0	0	25(0) + 40(0) = 0

The corner, 20A, 15B produces the most profitable solution.

Shadow Prices (Opportunity Costs)

What are shadow prices?

An accountant who has solved an LP problem might wish to know whether it pays to add capacity in hours in a particular department. He or she might be interested in the monetary value to the firm of adding an hour per week of assembly time. This monetary value is the additional contribution margin that could be earned. This amount is called the *shadow price* of the given resource. A shadow price is in a way an opportunity cost, the contribution margin that would be lost by not adding an additional hour of capacity. To justify a decision in favor of a short-term capacity expansion, the accountant must be sure that the shadow price (or opportunity cost) exceeds the actual price of that expansion.

How are shadow prices determined?

Shadow prices are computed as follows:

Step 1: Add one hour (preferably, more than an hour to make it easier to show graphically) to the constraint under consideration.

Step 2: Resolve the problem and find the maximum CM.

Step 3: Compute the difference between CM of the original LP problem and the CM determined in step (2), which is the shadow price.

Other methods, e.g., using the dual problem, are available to compute shadow prices.

EXAMPLE 9.25

Using the data in Example 9.23, compute the shadow price of the assembly capacity. To make it easier to show graphically, add 8 hours of capacity to the assembly department, rather than one hour. The new assembly constraint is shown in the graph on the following page:

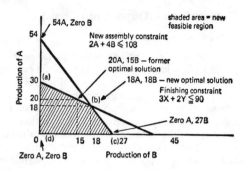

Corner Points		Contribution Margin
A	B	$25A + $40B
(a)	30	0	$25(30) + $40(0) = $ 750
(b)	18	18	25(18) + 40(18) = 1,170
(c)	0	27	25(0) + 40(27) = 1,080
(d)	0	0	25(0) + 40(0) = 0

The new optimal solution of 18A, 18B has total CM of $1,170 per week. Therefore, the shadow price of the assembly capacity is $70 ($1,170 − $1,100 = $70). The firm would be willing to pay up to $70 to obtain an additional 8 hours per week, or $8.75 *per hour* per week.

Can the computer be used for LP problem solving?

We can use a computer LP software package, e.g., LINDO (Linear Interactive and Discrete Optimization), to quickly solve an LP problem. Figure 9.3 shows a computer output by an LP program for our LP model set up in Example 9.23.

NOTE: The printout shows the following optimal solution:

A   = 20
B   = 15
CM = $1,100

Figure 9.3
COMPUTER PRINTOUT FOR LP

•• INFORMATION ENTERED ••

NUMBER OF CONSTRAINTS	2
NUMBER OF VARIABLES	2
NUMBER OF <= CONSTRAINTS	2
NUMBER OF = CONSTRAINTS	0
NUMBER OF >= CONSTRAINTS	0

MAXIMIZATION PROBLEM

$$25 \times 1 \quad + 40 \times 2$$

SUBJECT TO

$$2 \times 1 \quad + 4 \times 2 \quad <= 100$$
$$3 \times 1 \quad + 2 \times 2 \quad <= 90$$

Note:
$x_1 = A$
$x_2 = B$

•• RESULTS ••

VARIABLE	VARIABLE VALUE	ORIGINAL COEFF.	COEFF. SENS.
× 1	20	25	0
× 2	15	40	0

Solution:
$x_1 = A = 20$
$x_2 = B = 15$

CONSTRAINT NUMBER	ORIGINAL RHS	SLACK OR SURPLUS	SHADOW PRICE
1	100	0	8.75
2	90	0	2.5

**Figure 9.3
(continued)**

OBJECTIVE FUNCTION VALUE : <u>1100</u> = CM

SENSITIVITY ANALYSIS

OBJECTIVE FUNCTION COEFFICIENTS

VARIABLE	LOWER LIMIT	ORIGINAL COEFFICIENT	UPPER LIMIT
$\times 1$	20	25	60
$\times 2$	16.67	40	50

RIGHT HAND SIDE

CONSTRAINT NUMBER	LOWER LIMIT	ORIGINAL VALUE	UPPER LIMIT
1	60	100	180
2	50	90	150

GOAL PROGRAMMING AND MULTIPLE GOALS

What is goal programming?

In the previous section, we saw how to develop an optimal program (or product mix) using LP. However, LP has one important drawback; it is limited primarily to solving problems where the objectives of management can be stated in a single goal, e.g., profit maximization or cost minimization. But management must now deal with multiple goals, which are often incompatible and in conflict with each other. Goal programming (GP) gets around this difficulty. In GP, unlike LP, the objective function may consist of multiple, incommensurable, and conflicting goals. Rather than maximizing or minimizing the objective criterion, the deviations from these set goals are minimized, often based on the priority factors assigned to each goal. The fact that management has multiple goals that are in conflict with each other means that management will look for a *satisfactory* solution rather than an *optimal* solution.

What are some examples of multiple conflicting goals?

Consider an investor who desires investments that will have a maximum return and minimum risk. These goals are generally incompatible and therefore unachievable. Other examples of multiple conflicting goals can be found in businesses that want to:

- Maximize profits and increase wages paid to employees
- Upgrade product quality and reduce product costs
- Pay larger dividends to shareholders and retain earnings for growth
- Increase control of channels of distribution and reduce working-capital requirements
- Reduce credit losses and increase sales

How is a goal programming problem solved?

EXAMPLE 9.26

In Example 9.23, the company during this planning period is facing a major organizational change and feels that maximizing contribution margin is not a realistic objective. However, it would like to achieve some satisfactory level of profit during this difficult period. Management feels that a CM of $750 would be satisfactory.

The GP problem is to determine, given the production time and material constraints, the product mix that would yield this rate of profit contribution.

To incorporate the $1,500 profit contribution into the GP model, we first define the following *deviational* variables:

$d-$ = underachievement of the target profit

$d+$ = overachievement of the target profit

This profit goal is now written into the model as a goal constraint,

$25A + 40B + d- - d+ = \$750$ (profit goal constraint)

Then our GP model is as follows:

$$\text{Min } D = d- + d+$$

subject to	$2A + 4B$		<100
	$3A + 2B$		< 90
	$25A + 40B + d- - d+$	$= 750$
	$A, B, d-, d+$	> 0

The solution is shown in Figure 9.4.

Figure 9.4
COMPUTER PRINTOUT FOR GP

MINIMIZATION PROBLEM

$0 \times 1 \quad + 0 \times 2 \quad + 1 \times 3 \quad + 1 \times 4$

SUBJECT TO

$2 \times 1 \quad + 4 \times 2 \quad + 0 \times 3 \quad + 0 \times 4$
$\quad\quad\quad\quad\quad\quad <= 100$

$3 \times 1 \quad + 2 \times 2 \quad + 0 \times 3 \quad + 0 \times 4$
$\quad\quad\quad\quad\quad\quad <= 90$

$25 \times 1 \quad + 40 \times 2 \quad + 1 \times 3 \quad - 1 \times 4$
$\quad\quad\quad\quad\quad\quad = 750$

Note:
$x_1 = A$
$x_2 = B$
$x_3 = d-$
$x_4 = d+$

** RESULTS **

VARIABLE	VARIABLE VALUE	ORIGINAL COEFF.	COEFF. SENS.
× 1	0	0	0
× 2	18.75	0	0
× 3	0	1	1
× 4	0	1	1

Solution:
$x_1 = A = 0$
$x_2 = B = 18.75$
$x_3 = d- = 0$
$x_4 = d+ = 0$

Figure 9.4
(continued)

CONSTRAINT NUMBER	ORIGINAL RHS	SLACK OR SURPLUS	SHADOW PRICE
1	100	25	0
2	90	52.5	0
3	750	0	0

OBJECTIVE FUNCTION VALUE : 0

SENSITIVITY ANALYSIS

OBJECTIVE FUNCTION COEFFICIENTS

VARIABLE	LOWER LIMIT	ORIGINAL COEFFICIENT	UPPER LIMIT
× 1	0	0	NO LIMIT
× 2	−40	0	40
× 3	0	1	NO LIMIT
× 4	0	1	NO LIMIT

RIGHT HAND SIDE

CONSTRAINT NUMBER	LOWER LIMIT	ORIGINAL VALUE	UPPER LIMIT
1	75	100	NO LIMIT
2	37.5	90	NO LIMIT
3	0	750	1000

The GP solution is:

$$A = 0, B = 18.75, d- = 0, d+ = 0$$

This means that the company should make 18.75 units of product B (drop product A) in order to fully achieve the target profit of \$750.

NOTE: One further step might be considered when formulating the GP model. The goal can be ranked according to "preemptive" priority factors. The deviational variables at the same priority level may be given different weights in the objective function so that the deviational variables within the same priority have the different cardinal weights. (This topic is not treated here and should be referred to in an advanced text).

LEARNING CURVE

What is the learning curve?

The *learning curve* is based on the proposition that labor hours decrease in a definite pattern as labor operations are repeated. More specifically, it is based on the statistical findings that as the cumulative output doubles, the cumulative average labor input time required per unit will be reduced by some constraint percentage, ranging between 10% and 40%. The curve is usually designated by its complement. If the rate of reduction is 20%, the curve is referred to as an *80% learning curve.* (See Figure 9.5.)

EXAMPLE 9.27

The following data illustrate the 80% learning curve relationship:

Quantity (in units)		Time (in hours)	
Per lot	Cumulative	Total (Cumulative)	Average time per unit
15	15	600	40.0
15	30	960	32.0(40.0 × 0.8)
30	60	1,536	25.6(32.0 × 0.8)
60	120	2,460	20.5(25.6 × 0.8)
120	240	3,936	16.4(20.5 × 0.8)

As can be seen, as production quantities double, the average time per unit decreases by 20% of its immediately preceding time.

Figure 9.5
LEARNING CURVE

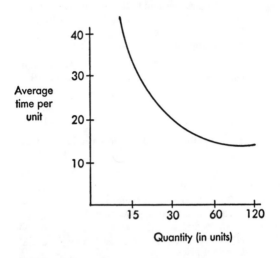

Quantity (in units)

What are some applications of the learning curve?

Applications of learning curve theory include:

• Scheduling labor requirements
• Capital budgeting decisions
• Setting incentive wage rates

EXAMPLE 9.28

Stanley Electronics Products, Inc. finds that new-product production is affected by an 80% learning effect. The company has just produced 50 units of output at 100 hrs. per unit. Costs were as follows:

Materials @ $20	$1,000
Labor and labor-related costs:	
Direct labor—100 hrs. @ $8	800
Variable overhead—100 hrs. @ $2	200
	$2,000

The company has just received a contract calling for another 50 units of production. It wants to add a 50% markup to the cost of materials and labor and labor-related costs. Determine the price for this job as follows:

Building up the table yields:

Quantity	Total Time (in hours)	Average time (per unit)
50 units	100 hours	2 hours
100	160	1.6 (80% × 2 hrs.)

Thus, for the new 50 unit job, it takes 60 hours total.

Materials @ $20	$1,000
Labor and labor-related costs:	
Direct labor—60 hrs. @ $8	480
Variable overhead—60 hrs. @ $2	120
	$1,600
50 percent markup	800
Contract price	$2,400

INVENTORY PLANNING AND CONTROL

How do I plan and control inventory?

One of the most common problems which faces managerial accountants is that of inventory planning and control. Inventory usually represents a sizable portion of a firm's total assets. Excess funds tied up in inventory is a drag on profitability. The purpose of inventory planning and control is to develop policies which will achieve an optimal investment in inventory. This objective is achieved by determining the optimal level of inventory necessary to minimize inventory related costs.

What types of inventory costs are there?

Inventory costs fall into three categories:

• *Order costs* include all costs associated with preparing a purchase order.

• *Carrying costs* include storage costs for inventory items plus opportunity cost (i.e., the cost incurred by investing in inventory).

• *Shortage (stockout) costs* include those costs incurred when an item is out of stock. These include the lost contribution margin on sales plus lost customer goodwill.

What are the basic types of inventory models?

There are many inventory planning and control models available which try to answer the following basic questions:

• How much to order?

• When to order?

They include the:

• Basic economic order quantity (EOQ) model

• Reorder point

• Determination of safety stock

Economic Order Quantity (EOQ)

What is the optimal amount to order?

The EOQ model determines the order size that minimizes the sum of carrying and ordering costs.

• Demand is assumed to be a fixed amount and constant throughout the year

• Order cost is assumed to be a fixed amount

• Unit carrying costs are assumed to be constant

NOTE: Since demand and lead time are assumed to be determinable, there are no shortage costs.

EOQ is computed as:

$$\text{EOQ} = \sqrt{\frac{2(\text{annual demand})(\text{ordering cost})}{\text{carrying cost per unit}}}$$

EXAMPLE: If the carrying cost is expressed as a percentage of average inventory value (e.g., 12% per year to hold inventory), then the denominator value in the EOQ formula would be 12% times the price of an item.

EXAMPLE 9.29

ABC Store buys sets of steel at $40 per set from an outside vendor. ABC will sell 6,400 sets evenly throughout the year. ABC desires a 16% return on investment (cost of borrowed money) on its inventory investment. In addition, rent, taxes, etc. for each set in inventory is $1.60. The ordering cost is $100 per order.

The carrying cost per dozen is 16% ($40) + $1.60 = $8.00. Therefore,

$$EOQ = \sqrt{\frac{2(6,400)(\$100)}{\$8.00}} = \sqrt{160,000} = 400 \text{ sets}$$

$$\begin{aligned}
\text{Total} \\
\text{inventory} \\
\text{costs}
\end{aligned} = \begin{aligned} \text{Carrying cost} \\ \text{per unit} \end{aligned} \times \frac{EOQ}{2}$$

$$+ \begin{aligned} \text{Order cost} \\ \text{per order} \end{aligned} \times \frac{\text{Annual demand}}{EOQ}$$

$$= (\$8.00)(400/2) + (\$100)(6,400/400)$$
$$= \$1,600 + \$1,600 = \$3,200$$

Total number of orders per year
= Annual demand/EOQ
= 6,400/400
= 16 orders

How is the EOQ model applied?

The EOQ model described here is appropriate for a pure inventory system, i.e., for single-item, single-stage inventory decisions for which joint costs and constraints can be ignored. EOQ assumes that both lead time and demand rates are constant and known with certainty. *CAUTION*: This may be unrealistic. Nevertheless, these models have proven useful in inventory planning for many firms.

Many situations exist where such an assumption holds or nearly holds. *EXAMPLES*: Subcontractors who must supply parts on a regular basis to a primary contractor face a constant demand. Even where demand varies, the assumption of uniform usage is not unrealistic. For an auto dealer, demand for automobiles varies from week to week, but over a season the weekly fluctuations cancel each other out so that seasonal demand can be assumed constant.

How does EOQ handle quantity discounts?

The economic order quantity (EOQ) model does not take into account quantity discounts. This makes it unrealistic in many real life cases. Usually, the more you order, the lower the unit price you pay. Quantity discounts are price reductions for large orders offered to buyers to induce them to buy in large quantities. If quantity discounts are offered, the buyer must weigh the potential benefits of reduced purchase price and fewer orders that will result from buying in large quantities against the increase in carrying costs caused by higher average inventories. Hence, the buyer's goal is to select the order quantity which will minimize total cost, where total cost is the sum of carrying cost, ordering cost, *and* purchase cost:

$$\frac{\text{Total}}{\text{cost}} = \frac{\text{Carrying}}{\text{cost}} + \frac{\text{Ordering}}{\text{cost}} + \frac{\text{Purchase}}{\text{cost}}$$

$$= C \times (Q/2) + O\,(D/Q) + PD$$

where

C = carrying cost per unit
O = ordering cost per order
D = annual demand
P = unit price
Q = order quantity

How do I calculate EOQ with quantity discounts?

To find the EOQ *with* quantity discounts:

Step 1: Compute the *economic order quantity* (EOQ) ignoring price discounts; and compute the corresponding costs using the new cost formula given above. NOTE: EOQ = $\sqrt{2OD/C}$.

Step 2: Compute the costs for those quantities greater than the EOQ at which price reductions occur.

Step 3: Select the value of Q which will result in the lowest total cost.

EXAMPLE 9.30

Using the data from Example 9.29, assume that ABC was offered the following price discount schedule:

Order quantity (Q)	Unit price (P)
1 to 499	$40.00
500 to 999	39.90
1000 or more	39.80

Step 1: The EOQ with no discounts is computed as follows:

$$EOQ = \sqrt{2(6,400)(100)/8.00} = \sqrt{160,000}$$
$$= 400 \text{ sets.}$$
$$\text{Total cost} = \$8.00(400/2) + \$100(6,400/400)$$
$$+ \$40.00(6,400) = \$1,600 + 1,600$$
$$+ 256,000 = \$259,200$$

Step 2: The value which minimized the sum of the carrying cost and the order cost but not the purchase cost was EOQ = 400 sets. As can be seen in Figure 9.6, the further we move from the

Figure 9.6
INVENTORY COST AND QUANTITY

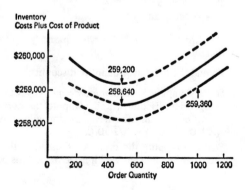

point 400, the greater the sum of the carrying and ordering costs is. Thus, 400 is obviously the only candidate for the minimum total cost value within the first price range. Q = 500 is the only candidate within the $39.90 price range, and Q = 1,000 is the only candidate within the $39.80 price bracket.

Step 3: These three quantities are evaluated in Table 9.1 and illustrated in Figure 9.6. The EOQ *with* price discounts is 500 sets. Hence, ABC is justified in going to the first price break, but the extra carrying cost of going to the second price break more than outweighs the savings in ordering and in the cost of the product itself.

What are the pros and cons of quantity discounts?

Buying in large quantities has some favorable and some unfavorable features for a firm. The advantages are:

- Lower unit costs.
- Lower ordering costs.
- Fewer stockouts.
- Lower transportation costs.

The disadvantages are:

- Higher inventory carrying costs.
- Greater capital requirement.
- Higher probability of obsolescence and deterioration.

Reorder Point (ROP)

When is the best time to place an order?

Reorder point (ROP), which answers *when* to place a new order, requires a knowledge of the *lead time*, the interval between placing an order and receiving delivery. ROP is calculated as follows:

Reorder point = average usage per unit of lead time × lead time + safety stock

Table 9.1
ANNUAL COSTS WITH VARYING ORDER QUANTITIES

Order Quantity	400	500	1,000
Ordering cost			
$100 × (6,400/order quantity)	$ 1,600	$ 1,280	$ 640
Carrying cost			
$8 × (order quantity/2)	1,600	2,000	4,000
Purchase cost			
Unit price × 6,400	256,000	255,360	254,720
Total cost	$259,200	$258,640	$259,360

Step 1: Multiply average daily (or weekly) usage by the lead time in days (or weeks) yielding the lead time demand.

Step 2: Add safety stock to this to provide for the variation in lead time demand.

NOTE: If average usage and lead time are both certain, no safety stock is necessary and should be dropped from the formula.

EXAMPLE 9.31

Using the data in Example 9.29, assume lead time is constant at one week, and there are 50 working weeks in a year.

Step 1: Reorder point is 128 sets = (6,400 sets/ 50 weeks) × 1 week. Therefore, when the inventory level drops to 128 sets, the new order should be placed.

Step 2: Suppose, however, that the store is faced with variable usage for its steel and requires a safety stock of 150 additional sets to carry. Then the reorder point will be 128 sets *plus* 150 sets, or 278 sets.

Figure 9.7 shows this inventory system when the order quantity is 400 sets and the reorder point is 128 sets.

Figure 9.7
BASIC INVENTORY SYSTEM WITH EOQ AND REORDER POINT

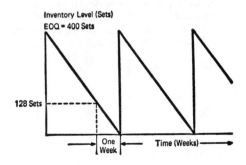

Safety Stock and Reorder Point

At what level should inventory be ordered?

When lead time and demand are not certain, the firm must carry extra units of inventory called *safety stock* as protection against possible stockouts. Stockouts can be quite expensive. *EXAMPLES*: Lost sales and disgruntled customers are external costs. Idle machine and disrupted production scheduling are internal costs.

The probability approach is used to show how the optimal stock size can be determined in the presence of stockout costs.

EXAMPLE 9.32

Using the data from Examples 9.29 and 9.30, assume that the total usage over a one-week period is expected to be:

Total usage	Probability
78	.2
128	.4
178	.2
228	.1
278	.1
	1.00

Further assume that a stockout cost is estimated at $12.00 per set. Recall that the carrying cost is $8.00 per set.

The computation shows that the total costs are minimized at $1,200, when a safety stock of 150 sets is maintained. Therefore, the reorder point is: 128 sets + 150 sets = 278 sets.

Computation of Safety Stock

Safety stock levels in units	Stock out and probability	Average stockout in units	Average stockout costs	No. of orders	Total annual stockout costs	Carrying costs	Total
0	50 with .2 100 with .1 150 with .1	35[1]	$420[2]	16	$6,720[3]	0	$7,140
50	50 with .1 100 with .1	15	180	16	2,880	400[4]	3,280
100	50 with .1	5	60	16	960	800	1,760
150	0	0	0	16	0	1,200	1,200

[1]50(.2) + 100(.1) + 150(.1) = 10 + 10 + 15 = 35 units
[2]35 units × $12.00 = $420
[3]$420 × 16 times = $6,720
[4]50 units × $8.00 = $400

PROGRAM EVALUATION AND REVIEW TECHNIQUE (PERT)

What is PERT?

Program Evaluation and Review Technique (PERT) is a useful management tool for planning, scheduling, costing, coordinating, and controlling complex projects such as

- Formulation of a master budget
- Construction of buildings
- Installation of computers
- Scheduling the closing of books
- Assembly of a machine
- Research and development activities

Questions to be answered by PERT include:

- When will the project be finished?
- What is the probability that the project will be completed by any given time?

How do I schedule a project?

The PERT technique involves the diagrammatic representation of the sequence of activities comprising a project by means of a *network*. The network:

- Visualizes all of the individual tasks (activities) to complete a given job or program.
- Points out interrelationships.
- Consists of activities (represented by arrows) and events (represented by circles).

In Figure 9.8:

- *Arrows.* Arrows represent "tasks" or "activities" which are distinct segments of the project requiring time and resources.

- *Nodes (circles).* Nodes symbolize "events" or milestone points in the project representing the completion of one or more activities and/or the initiation of one or more subsequent activities. An event is a point in time and does not consume any time in itself as does an activity.

Figure 9.8
NETWORK DIAGRAM

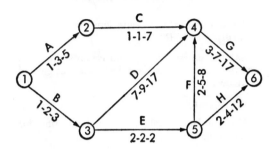

When will the project be finished?

In a real world situation, estimates of activity completion times will seldom be certain.

NOTE: To cope with the uncertainty in activity time estimates, the PERT proceeds by estimating *three* possible duration times for each activity. As shown in Figure 9.8, the numbers appearing on the arrows represent the three time estimates for activities needed to complete the various events. These time estimates are:

- the most optimistic time, "a"
- the most likely time, "m"
- the most pessimistic time, "b"

EXAMPLE 9.33

For activity B:

- The optimistic time for completing activity B is 1 day
- The most likely time is 2 days
- The pessimistic time is 3 days

The next step is to calculate an expected time, which is determined as follows:

t_e (expected time) = $(a + 4m + b)/6$

For activity B, the expected time is

$$t_e = (1 + 4(2) + 3)/6 = 12/6 = 2 \text{ days}$$

What quantitative calculations are involved in PERT?

As a measure of variation (uncertainty) about the expected time, the standard deviation is calculated as follows:

$$\sigma = (b - a)/6$$

The standard deviation of completion time for activity B is:

$$\sigma = (3 - 1)/6 = 2/6 = .33 \text{ days}$$

Expected activity times and their standard deviations are computed in this manner for all of the activities of the network and arranged in the tabular format as shown below:

Activity	Predecessors	a	m	b	t_e	σ
A	None	1	3	5	3.0	.67
B	None	1	2	3	2.0	.33
C	A	1	1	7	2.0	1.00
D	B	7	9	17	10.0	1.67
E	B	2	2	2	2.0	0.00
F	E	2	5	8	5.0	.67
G	C,D,F	3	7	17	8.0	2.33
H	E	2	4	12	5.0	1.67

What is a critical path?

To answer the first question—when will the project be finished—we need to determine the network's *critical path*. A path is a sequence of connected activities. In Figure 9.8, 1-2-4-6 is a path. The critical path for a project is the path that takes the longest time. The sum of the estimated activity times for all activities on the critical path is the total time required to complete the project. These activities are "critical," because any delay in their completion causes a delay in the project.

The critical path is also the minimum amount of time needed for the completion of the project. Thus, the activities along this path must be shortened in order to speed up the project. Activities not on the critical path are not critical; they will be worked on simultaneously with critical path activities, and their completion could be delayed up to a point without delaying the project as a whole.

How do I find the critical path?

An easy way to find the critical path involves the following two steps:

- Identify all possible paths of a project and calculate their completion times.
- Pick the one with the longest completion time; this is the critical path.

NOTE: When the network is large and complex, a more systematic and efficient approach is needed. Refer to an advanced management science text.

EXAMPLE 9.34

Given the data in Example 9.33, we have:

Path	Completion time
A-C-G	13 days (3 + 2 + 8)
B-D-G	20 days (2 + 10 + 8)
B-E-F-G	17 days (2 + 2 + 5 + 8)
B-E-H	9 days (2 + 2 + 5)

The critical path is B-D-G, which means it takes 20 days to complete the project.

What is the probability that the project will be completed on time?

The next important information to obtain is the probability of the project being completed within a contract time. To obtain this information, use the standard deviation of total project time around the expected time, as follows:

Standard deviation (project)

$$= \sqrt{\begin{array}{l}\text{the sum of the squares of the standard} \\ \text{deviations of all critical path activities}\end{array}}$$

Using the standard deviation and table of areas under the normal distribution curve (Table 9.2), the probability of completing the project within any given time period can be determined.

Table 9.2
NORMAL DISTRIBUTION TABLE

AREAS UNDER THE NORMAL CURVE

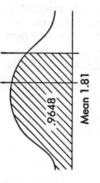

Z	0	1	2	3	4	5	6	7	8	9
.0	.5000	.5040	.5080	.5120	.5160	.5199	.5239	.5279	.5319	.5359
.1	.5398	.5438	.5478	.5517	.5557	.5596	.5636	.5675	.5714	.5753
.2	.5793	.5832	.5871	.5910	.5948	.5987	.6026	.6064	.6103	.6141
.3	.6179	.6217	.6255	.6293	.6331	.6368	.6406	.6443	.6480	.6517
.4	.6554	.6591	.6628	.6664	.6700	.6736	.6772	.6808	.6844	.6879
.5	.6915	.6950	.6985	.7019	.7054	.7088	.7123	.7157	.7190	.7224
.6	.7257	.7291	.7324	.7357	.7389	.7422	.7454	.7486	.7517	.7549
.7	.7580	.7611	.7642	.7673	.7703	.7734	.7764	.7794	.7823	.7852
.8	.7881	.7910	.7939	.7967	.7995	.8023	.8051	.8078	.8106	.8133
.9	.8159	.8186	.8212	.8238	.8264	.8289	.8315	.8340	.8365	.8389

1.0	8413	8438	8461	8485	8508	8531	8554	8577	8599	8621
1.1	8643	8665	8686	8708	8729	8749	8770	8790	8810	8830
1.2	8849	8869	8888	8907	8925	8944	8962	8980	8997	9015
1.3	9032	9049	9066	9082	9099	9115	9131	9147	9162	9177
1.4	9192	9207	9222	9236	9251	9265	9278	9292	9306	9319
1.5	9332	9345	9357	9370	9382	9394	9406	9418	9430	9441
1.6	9452	9463	9474	9484	9495	9505	9515	9525	9535	9545
1.7	9554	9564	9573	9582	9591	9599	9608	9616	9625	9633
1.8	9641	9648	9656	9664	9671	9678	9686	9693	9700	9706
1.9	9713	9719	9726	9732	9738	9744	9750	9756	9762	9767
2.0	9772	9778	9783	9788	9793	9798	9803	9808	9812	9817
2.1	9821	9826	9830	9834	9838	9842	9846	9850	9854	9857
2.2	9861	9864	9868	9871	9874	9878	9881	9884	9887	9890
2.3	9893	9896	9898	9901	9904	9906	9909	9911	9913	9916
2.4	9918	9920	9922	9925	9927	9929	9931	9932	9934	9936
2.5	9938	9940	9941	9943	9945	9946	9948	9949	9951	9952
2.6	9953	9955	9956	9957	9959	9960	9961	9962	9963	9964
2.7	9965	9966	9967	9968	9969	9970	9971	9972	9973	9974
2.8	9974	9975	9976	9977	9977	9978	9979	9979	9980	9981
2.9	9981	9982	9982	9983	9984	9984	9985	9985	9986	9986
3.	.9987	.9990	.9993	.9995	.9997	.9998	.9998	.9999	.9999	1.0000

EXAMPLE 9.35

Using the formula above and information in Table 9.2, the standard deviation of completion time (the path B-D-G) for the project is as follows:

$$\sqrt{(.33)^2 + (1.67)^2 + (2.33)^2}$$
$$= \sqrt{.1089 + 2.7889 + 5.4289}$$
$$= \sqrt{8.3267} = 2.885 \text{ days}$$

Assume the expected delivery time is 21 days.

• *Step 1*: Compute z, the number of standard deviations from the mean represented by our given time of 21 days. The formula for z is:

z = (delivery time − expected time)/standard deviation

Therefore, z = (21 days − 20 days)/2.885 days = .35

• *Step 2*: Find the probability associated with the calculated value of z by referring to a table of areas under a normal curve (Table 9.2).

From Table 9.2 we see the probability is .63683, which means there is close to a 64% chance that the project will be completed in less than 21 days. To summarize:

• The expected completion time of the project is 20 days.

• There is a better than 60% chance of finishing before 21 days. The chances of meeting any other deadline can also be obtained, if desired.

• Activities B-D-G are on the critical path; they must be watched more closely than the others. If they fall behind, the whole project falls behind.

What other considerations are there with critical path?

If extra effort is needed to finish the project on time or before the deadline, borrow resources (such as money and labor) from any activity *not* on the critical path.

It is possible to reduce the completion time of one or more activities. This will require an extra expenditure of cost. The benefit from reducing the total completion time of a project by accelerated efforts on certain activities must be balanced against this extra cost. A related problem is determining which activities must be accelerated in order to reduce the total project completion time. Critical Path Method (CPM), also known as PERT/COST, is widely used to deal with this subject.

CAUTION: PERT is a technique for project management and control.

- It is *not* an optimizing decision model, since the decision to undertake a project is initially assumed.
- It won't evaluate an investment project according to its attractiveness or the time specifications observed.

PART 4

AUDITING, COMPILING, AND REVIEWING FINANCIAL STATEMENTS

CHAPTER 10

AUDITING PROCEDURES

The financial statement audit, commonly referred to as the *attest function*, involves (1) the examination of the financial statements through the gathering of sufficient competent evidential matter and (2) the expression of an opinion on the fairness of the presentation of the financial statements in conformity with generally accepted accounting principles (or another comprehensive basis of accounting).

In planning a financial statement audit, the practitioner should develop an overall strategy for:

- Considering a client's internal control structure
- Performing substantive tests

This strategy should be documented in the audit work papers.

INTERNAL CONTROL STRUCTURE

What are the elements of an internal control structure?

A client's internal control structure consists of management's policies and procedures which are designed to provide reasonable, but not absolute, assurance that specific entity objectives will be achieved.

A client's internal control structure consists of three elements:

- The control environment
- The accounting system
- Control procedures

What is the control environment?

The control environment considers the overall attitude, awareness, and actions of senior management and the owners of the entity. Factors to consider in assessing the client's control environment include:

- Management's philosophy and operating style, such as management's attitude and actions concerning financial statement assertions
- The client's organizational structure
- The entity's audit committee, if applicable
- Practices pertaining to the delegation of authority and responsibility, such as specific employee job descriptions
- Management control methods including an internal audit function, budgeting, and variance analysis, as well as forecasting
- Personnel policies and practices regarding hiring, termination, review of employee performance, advancement, and compensation
- External influences, such as enforcement of policies established by regulatory agencies

What should I understand about the client's accounting system?

An accounting system enables the identification, assembly, analysis, classification, recording, and reporting of an entity's transactions as well as the maintenance of accountability for the related assets and liabilities. An effective accounting system should provide reasonable assurance that transactions are (1) valid, (2) authorized, (3) valued properly, (4) complete, (5) posted and summarized in the correct amounts and time period, and (6) classified appropriately.

What is meant by control procedures?

Control procedures represent policies and procedures in addition to the control environment and accounting system that management has adopted in order to provide reasonable assurance that the specific objectives of the entity will be attained. Control procedures should provide for:

- Authorized execution of transactions
- Limited access to assets
- Comparison of recorded amounts with assets in existence
- Recording of transactions in a manner that reflects the substance of the transactions
- Well-trained, competent personnel
- Segregation of incompatible functions that would enable employees to both perpetrate and conceal errors and irregularities

To what extent must I consider the client's internal control structure?

The practitioner must obtain a sufficient understanding of the internal control structure to enable the proper planning of the audit. Whether policies or procedures have been placed in operations is of prime importance. Operating effectiveness is not to be judged by the practitioner. The understanding of the internal control structure should (1) provide a basis for identifying types of potential misstatements, (2) enable the assessment of the risk that such misstatements will occur, and (3) enable the auditor to design substantive tests.

What are the procedures used to obtain an understanding of the internal control structure?

Ordinarily, a combination of the following procedures is used in obtaining a sufficient understanding of the internal control structure:

- Previous experience with the client
- Inquiry of appropriate client personnel
- Observation of client activities
- Reference to prior year working papers
- Inspection of client-prepared descriptions, such as organization charts and accounting manuals

How should I document my understanding of the internal control structure?

The auditor must exercise professional judgment in determining the methods and extent of documentation. The most frequently used methods of documentation are:

- Flowcharts
- Questionnaires
- Narrative memos (written descriptions)

How are flowcharts helpful?

A flowchart is a pictorial representation of the flow of transactions. Flowcharts use standardized symbols and enable the auditor to visualize strengths and weaknesses in the internal control structure. (See Figures 10.1A and 10.1B and 10.2A–D).

How are questionnaires used?

A questionnaire is a series of questions designed to elicit a yes or no response as to whether a control, policy, or procedure exists. A no response, indicating a lack of the control, policy, or procedure, should prompt the auditor to pose another question in order to ascertain the existence of a compensating control, policy, or procedure. Questionnaires are useful because they can be tailored to fit a particular client. (See Figure 10.3.)

What is meant by assessing control risk?

The assessment of control risk is a process of evaluating the effectiveness of a client's internal control structure in preventing or detecting material misstatements in the financial statements.

How do I assess control risk?

If the auditor concludes, based on his or her understanding of the internal control structure, that policies and procedures are likely to be ineffective or that evaluation of their effectiveness would be inefficient, then the auditor may assess control risk at the maximum level for some or all financial statement assertions.

If specific policies and procedures are likely to prevent or detect material misstatements and the auditor performs tests of controls in order to evaluate the effectiveness of the policies and procedures

Figure 10.1A

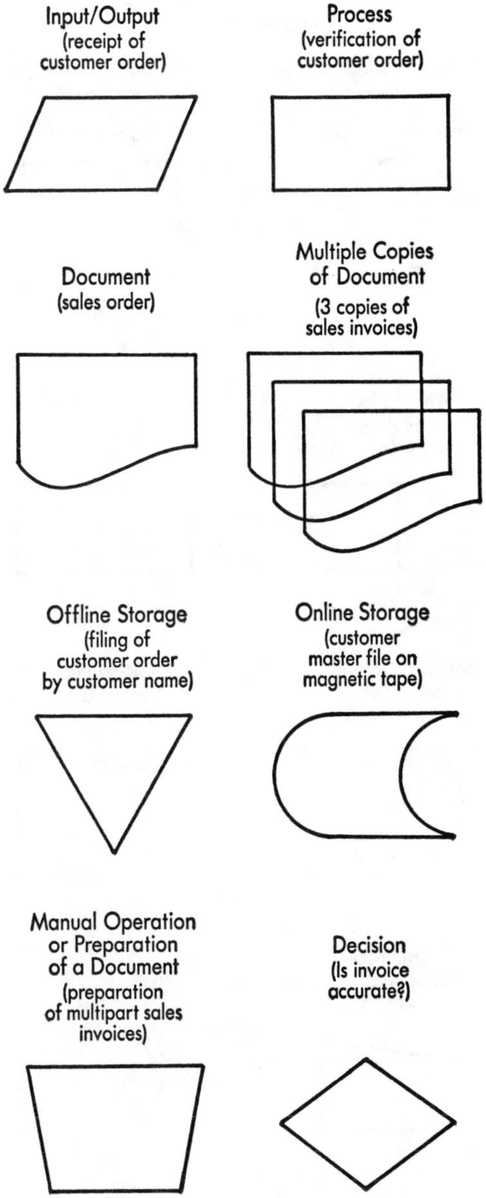

Input/Output
(receipt of
customer order)

Process
(verification of
customer order)

Document
(sales order)

**Multiple Copies
of Document**
(3 copies of
sales invoices)

Offline Storage
(filing of
customer order
by customer name)

Online Storage
(customer
master file on
magnetic tape)

**Manual Operation
or Preparation
of a Document**
(preparation
of multipart sales
invoices)

Decision
(Is invoice
accurate?)

Figure 10.1B

Onpage Connector
(transfer of
customer order to
the credit dept.)

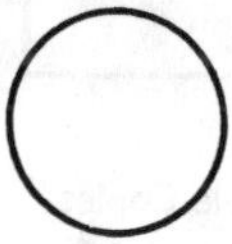

Offpage Connector
(mailing of
sales invoice
to customer)

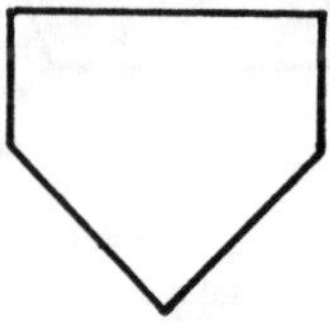

Annotation
(used to describe
or note an activity)

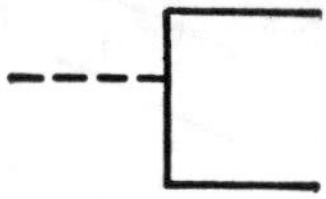

Punched Card
(method of
computer input)

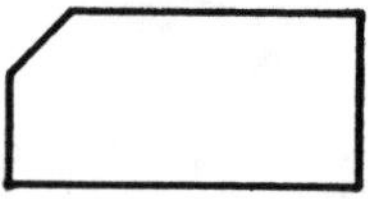

Magnetic Tape
(method of
computer input)

Punched Tape
(method of
computer input)

Manual Input
(keyboard
entry of data)

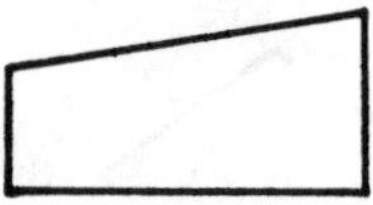

Figure 10.2A
FLOWCHART FOR A TYPICAL PURCHASING AND CASH DISBURSEMENT SYSTEM

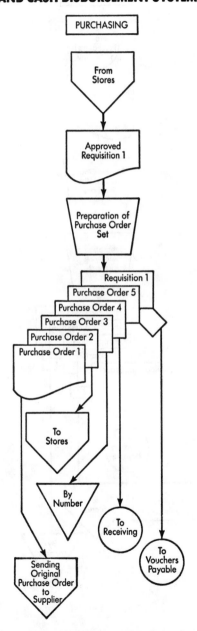

Figure 10.2B

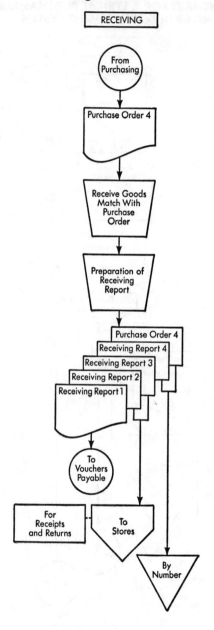

Figure 10.2C

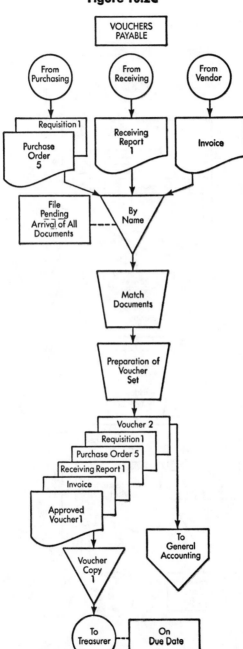

Figure 10.2D

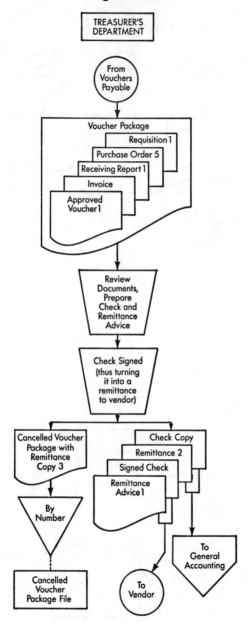

Figure 10.3
THE MAKE A MILLION DOLLARS COMPANY
SAMPLE INTERNAL CONTROL
QUESTIONNAIRE FOR INVESTMENTS

Authorized Execution of Transactions

	YES	NO	BASIS FOR ANSWER	COMMENTS
1. Are investment transactions approved by the board of directors, the treasurer, or other responsible officer?				
2. Is authorization required for access to vaults or safe-deposit boxes?				
3. Is there proper documentation for initiation and approval of transactions?				

417

Figure 10.3 (continued)

Limited Access to Assets

	YES	NO	BASIS FOR ANSWER	COMMENTS
1. Are investment securities kept in safe-deposit boxes or vaults?				
2. If not, is a bonded custodian utilized?				
3. Are securities, other than bearer bonds, registered in the name of the company?				
4. Does the company require two authorized signatures for access to the securities?				

Figure 10.3 (continued)

Comparison of Recorded Amounts with Assets in Existence

	YES	NO	BASIS FOR ANSWER	COMMENTS
1. Is there periodic inspection of investment securities?				
2. Is there periodic comparison of recorded amounts with actual investment certificates?				
3. Is there periodic review of worthless securities for possible realization?				

Figure 10.3 (continued)

Recording of Transactions

	YES	NO	BASIS FOR ANSWER	COMMENTS
1. Is an investment ledger maintained?				
2. Are general ledger control totals compared to subsidiary investment ledgers?				
3. Does management record investments using the lower-of-cost-or-market-value method?				
4. Are investment transactions classified between current and long-term?				
5. Is the cost or equity method being utilized?				

Figure 10.3 (continued)

Technically Trained and Competent Personnel

	YES	NO	BASIS FOR ANSWER	COMMENTS
1. Are employees involved in the custody function bonded?				
2. Are employees involved in the custody function subjected to polygraph tests?				
3. Does the company maintain a prior work-experience requirement for all employees involved in custody and recording of transactions?				

Figure 10.3 (continued)

Segregation of Incompatible Functions

	YES	NO	BASIS FOR ANSWER	COMMENTS
1. Are the following functions segregated:				
a. Custody of investment securities?				
b. Maintenance of subsidiary records?				
c. Journalizing transactions?				
d. Posting to general ledger accounts?				
e. Authorization for acquiring and disposing of investments?				
f. Execution of authorized transactions?				
g. Cash transactions?				

identified, then assessment of control risk below the maximum level is permissible.

What are tests of controls?

SAS 55 defines tests of controls as tests directed toward the design or operation of an internal control structure policy or procedure to assess its effectiveness in preventing or detecting material misstatements in a financial statement assertion. Inquiry of company personnel, inspection of client documents and records, observation of client activities, and reperformance of control procedures represent some of the procedures used in performing tests of controls.

In performing tests of controls, the auditor seeks answers to the following questions:

- Who performed the policy or procedure?
- When was the policy or procedure performed?
- How was the policy or procedure performed?
- Was the policy or procedure consistently applied?

What is the relationship between the assessed level of control risk and substantive testing?

Since the auditor's determination of the nature, extent, and timing of substantive tests is dependent on detection risk, the assessed level of control risk must be considered in conjunction with inherent risk (see SAS 47). There is an inverse relationship between detection risk and the assurances to be provided from substantive tests. Accordingly, as detection risk decreases, the auditor should consider the following:

- Utilize more effective substantive tests
- Perform substantive tests at year-end rather than at interim dates
- Increase the amount of substantive testing

Do I have to document the assessed level of control risk?

The assessed level of control risk must be documented in the working papers in every audit engagement. If the control risk is assessed at the maximum level, documentation may be limited to a statement to that effect. The basis for the auditor's conclusion is not required when control risk is assessed at the maximum level. If the control risk is assessed at below the maximum level, documentation must include the assessed level and the basis for the auditor's conclusion.

How do cycles figure in assessing control risk?

The second fieldwork standard under Generally Accepted Auditing Standards (GAAS) requires that the auditor obtain a sufficient understanding of the internal control structure in order to plan the audit and to determine the nature, extent, and timing of tests to be performed.

RECOMMENDATION: The auditor should use the cycle approach, whereby broad areas of activity are selected and specific classes of transactions are identified. The main cycles and their related classes of transactions are:

- *Revenue Cycle:* revenue and accounts receivable (order processing, credit approval, shipping, invoicing and recording) and cash receipts
- *Expenditure Cycle:* purchasing, receiving, accounts payable, payroll and cash disbursements
- *Production or Conversion Cycle:* inventories, cost of sales, and property, plant, and equipment
- *Financing Cycle:* notes receivable and investments, notes payable, debt, leases, and other obligations and equity accounts
- *External Reporting:* accounting principles and preparation of financial statements

Can I use statistical methods in performing tests of control?

To save time and money in performing tests of controls, auditors can use statistical sampling, in the form of attribute sampling. The following steps should prove useful in this regard:

Step 1: Determine the objective of the test, namely to obtain reasonable assurance that a particular control is in place (e.g., mathematical accuracy of invoices is verified by an individual other than the preparer of the invoice).

Step 2: Define the deviation condition. A deviation condition is a departure from a prescribed control (sometimes referred to as an attribute), such as the failure to initial an invoice that was mathematically verified. *WARNING*: Deviation conditions increase the likelihood of, but do not necessarily result in, errors and irregularities.

Step 3: Define the population:

• Define the period covered. If interim testing is performed, consider (a) inquiring about the period after testing and through the end of the year, and (b) the nature and amount of transactions and balances, and the length of the remaining period.

• Define the sampling unit. The sampling unit represents the item to be tested, e.g., a document, a journal page, a transaction, a line item.

• Determine the completeness of the population. The sample drawn must be representative of the population.

EXAMPLE: In testing purchase transactions, the population should include unpaid as well as paid invoices.

Step 4: Determine the selection technique:

• Random number selection provides assurance that each and every item in the population has a chance of being picked.

• Systematic selection involves picking every nth item from the population. The nth item, often referred to as the skip interval, is determined by dividing the population size by the sample size. EXAMPLE: If the population size is 10,000 and the sample size is 50, the skip interval is 200. Thus, the auditor would pick every 200th item, beginning with a blind start.

Step 5: Determine the sample size by using the appropriate table.

• Select an acceptable level of risk of overreliance on internal control. Practically speaking, auditors select either a 5% or a 10% risk. These levels will provide the auditor 95% and 90% confidence, respectively, that the sample is representative of the population. NOTE: The lower the risk the auditor selects, the bigger the sample size will be.

• Select the tolerable rate. This is the maximum rate of deviation the auditor is willing to tolerate while still being able to reduce assessed control risk. The tolerable rate is dependent on professional judgment and the planned degree of reliance on the control or procedure.

Planned degree of reliance	Tolerable rate
Substantial	2–7%
Moderate	6–12%
Little	11–20%

• Assess the expected population deviation rate. This may be based on (a) reference to actual deviation rates of the prior year, adjusted for current-year implementation of prior-year recommendations; (b) communication with prior-year accountants; or (c) a preliminary sample of 50 items.

Step 6: Select the sample and perform tests of controls.

Step 7: Interpret the sample results.

• Calculate the sample deviation rate—divide the actual number of deviations by the sample size.

• Determine the upper occurrence limit by using the appropriate table. Essentially the upper occurrence limit takes the sample deviation rate and adjusts it upward to reflect the fact that the population is likely to contain a greater rate of deviations.

• Determine whether the deviations are a result of errors (unintentional) or irregularities (intentional).

• Accept or reject the sample as representative of the population:

  • If the sample deviation is greater than the tolerable rate, no reliance may be placed on the control.
  • If the upper occurrence limit is less than the tolerable rate, reliance may be placed upon the control.
  • If the upper occurrence limit is greater than the tolerable rate, no reliance should be placed

on the control or procedure. In this case, the auditor might perform tests of control on another control or procedure or proceed to substantive testing without modification.

EXAMPLE 10.1

In determining whether the credit department is performing properly, Margie Scott, CPA, utilizes attribute sampling in testing controls over sales orders. Scott determines:

- The deviation condition is the absence of the credit manager's initials on a sales order
- The population consists of the duplicate sales orders for the entire fiscal year
- The sampling unit is the sales order itself
- Random number selection will be utilized
- A 5% risk of overreliance on internal control will be utilized
- The tolerable rate of deviation is 6%
- The expected population deviation rate is 2%

Using Table 10.1, the sample size will be 127. Scott uses a random number table (Table 10.5) to select the sample. Since the population consists of sales orders numbered 1 to 500, Scott decides to use the first 3 digits of items selected from the random number table. Using a blind start at column 5, line 6, Scott selects the following sales orders:

Number

277
188
174
496
482
312
.
.
.

Statistical Sample Sizes for Tests of Controls (for large populations)

Table 10.1
5 PERCENT RISK OF OVERRELIANCE

Expected Population Deviation Rate	TOLERABLE OCCURRENCE RATE								
	2%	3%	4%	5%	6%	7%	8%	9%	10%
0.00%	149	99	74	59	49	42	36	32	29
.50	•	157	117	93	78	66	58	51	46
1.00	•	•	156	93	78	66	58	51	46
1.50	•	•	192	124	103	66	58	51	46
2.00	•	•	•	181	127	88	77	68	46
2.50	•	•	•	•	150	109	77	68	61
3.00	•	•	•	•	195	129	95	84	61
4.00	•	•	•	•	•	•	146	100	89
5.00	•	•	•	•	•	•	•	158	116
6.00	•	•	•	•	•	•	•	•	179

Table 10.2
10 PERCENT RISK OF OVERRELIANCE

Expected Population Deviation Rate	TOLERABLE OCCURRENCE RATE								
	2%	3%	4%	5%	6%	7%	8%	9%	10%
0.00%	114	76	57	45	38	32	28	25	22
.50	194	129	96	77	64	55	48	42	38
1.00	•	176	96	77	64	55	48	42	38
1.50	•	•	132	105	64	55	48	42	38
2.00	•	•	198	132	88	75	48	42	38
2.50	•	•	•	158	110	75	65	58	52
3.00	•	•	•	•	132	94	65	58	52
4.00	•	•	•	•	•	149	98	73	65
5.00	•	•	•	•	•	•	160	115	78
6.00	•	•	•	•	•	•	•	182	116

•Sample size is too large to be cost effective.

Statistical Sample Results Evaluation Table for Tests of Controls

Upper Occurrence Limit
(for large populations)

Table 10.3
5 PERCENT RISK OF OVERRELIANCE

Sample Size	ACTUAL NUMBER OF OCCURRENCES FOUND								
	0	1	2	3	4	5	6	7	8
25	11.3	17.6	•	•	•	•	•	•	•
30	9.5	14.9	19.5	•	•	•	•	•	•
35	8.2	12.9	16.9	•	•	•	•	•	•
40	7.2	11.3	14.9	18.3	•	•	•	•	•
45	6.4	10.1	13.3	16.3	19.2	•	•	•	•

50	5.8	9.1	12.1	14.8	17.4	19.9	•	•	•
55	5.3	8.3	11.0	13.5	15.9	18.1	•	•	•
60	4.9	7.7	10.1	12.4	14.6	16.7	18.8	•	•
65	4.5	7.1	9.4	11.5	13.5	15.5	17.4	19.3	•
70	4.2	6.6	8.7	10.7	12.6	14.4	16.2	18.0	19.7
75	3.9	6.2	8.2	10.0	11.8	13.5	15.2	16.9	18.4
80	3.7	5.8	7.7	9.4	11.1	12.7	14.3	15.8	17.3
90	3.3	5.2	6.8	8.4	9.9	11.3	12.7	14.1	15.5
100	3.0	4.7	6.2	7.6	8.9	10.2	11.5	12.7	14.0
125	2.4	3.7	4.9	6.1	7.2	8.2	9.3	10.3	11.3
150	2.0	3.1	4.1	5.1	6.0	6.9	7.7	8.6	9.4
200	1.5	2.3	3.1	3.8	4.5	5.2	5.8	6.5	7.1

Table 10.4
10 PERCENT RISK OF OVERRELIANCE

Sample Size	ACTUAL NUMBER OF OCCURRENCES FOUND								
	0	1	2	3	4	5	6	7	8
20	10.9	18.1	•	•	•	•	•	•	•
25	8.8	14.7	19.9	•	•	•	•	•	•
30	7.4	12.4	16.8	•	•	•	•	•	•
35	6.4	10.7	14.5	18.1	•	•	•	•	•
40	5.6	9.4	12.8	15.9	19.0	•	•	•	•
45	5.0	8.4	11.4	14.2	17.0	19.6	•	•	•
50	4.5	7.6	10.3	12.9	15.4	17.8	•	•	•

55	4.1	6.9	9.4	11.7	14.0	16.2	18.4	•	•
60	3.8	6.3	8.6	10.8	12.9	14.9	16.9	18.8	•
70	3.2	5.4	7.4	9.3	11.1	12.8	14.6	16.2	17.9
80	2.8	4.8	6.5	8.3	9.7	11.3	12.8	14.3	15.7
90	2.5	4.3	5.8	7.3	8.7	10.1	11.4	12.7	14.0
100	2.3	3.8	5.2	6.6	7.8	9.1	10.3	11.5	12.7
120	1.9	3.2	4.4	5.5	6.6	7.6	8.6	9.6	10.6
160	1.4	2.4	3.3	4.1	4.9	5.7	6.5	7.2	8.0
200	1.1	1.9	2.6	3.3	4.0	4.6	5.2	5.8	6.4

•over 20%

Table 10.5
RANDOM NUMBER TABLE

Line	(1)	(2)	(3)	(4)	(5)	(6)	(7)	(8)	(9)	(10)	(11)	(12)	(13)	(14)
1	10480	15011	01536	02011	81647	91646	69179	14194	62590	36207	20969	99570	91291	90700
2	22368	46573	25595	85393	30995	89198	27982	53402	93965	34095	52666	19174	39615	99505
3	24130	48360	22527	97265	76393	64809	15179	24830	49340	32081	30680	19655	63348	58629
4	42167	93093	06243	61680	07856	16376	39440	53537	71341	57004	00849	74917	97758	16379
5	37570	39975	81837	16656	06121	91782	60468	81305	49684	60672	14110	06927	01263	54613
6	77921	06907	11008	42751	27756	53498	18602	70659	90655	15053	21916	81825	44394	42880
7	99562	72905	56420	69994	98872	31016	71194	18738	44013	48840	63213	21069	10634	12952
8	96301	91977	05463	07972	18876	20922	94595	56869	69014	60045	18425	84903	42508	32307
9	89579	14342	63661	10281	17453	18103	57740	84378	25331	12566	58678	44947	05585	56941
10	85475	36857	53342	53988	53060	59533	38867	62300	08158	17983	16439	11458	18593	64952
11	28918	69578	88231	33276	70997	79936	56865	05859	90106	31595	01547	85590	91610	78188
12	63553	40961	48235	03427	49626	69445	18663	72695	52180	20847	12234	90511	33703	90322

13	09429	93969	52636	92737	88974	33488	36320	17617	30015	08272	84115	27156	30613	74952
14	10365	61129	87529	85689	48237	52267	67689	93394	01511	26358	85104	20285	29975	89868
15	07119	97336	71048	08178	77233	13916	47564	81056	97735	85977	29372	74461	28551	9070;
16	51085	12765	51821	51259	77452	16308	60756	92144	49442	53900	70960	63990	75601	40719
17	02368	21382	52404	60268	89368	19885	55322	44819	01188	63255	64835	44919	05944	55157
18	01011	54092	33362	94904	31273	04146	18594	29852	71585	85030	51132	01915	92747	64951
19	52162	53916	46369	58586	23216	14513	83149	98736	23495	64350	94738	17752	35156	35749
20	07056	97628	33787	09998	42698	06691	76988	13602	51851	46104	88916	19509	25625	58104
21	48663	91245	85828	14346	09172	30168	90229	04734	59193	22178	30421	61666	99904	32812
22	54164	58492	22421	74103	47070	25306	76468	26384	58151	06646	21524	15227	96909	44592
23	32639	32363	05597	24200	13363	38005	94342	28728	35806	06912	17012	64161	18296	22851
24	29334	27001	87637	87308	58731	00256	45834	15398	46557	41135	10367	07684	36188	18510
25	02488	33062	28834	07351	19731	92420	60952	61280	50001	67658	32586	86679	50720	94953
26	81525	72295	04839	96423	24878	82651	66566	14778	76797	14780	13300	87074	79666	95725
27	29676	20591	68086	26432	46901	20849	89768	81536	86645	12659	92259	57102	80428	25280
28	00742	57392	39064	84673	40027	32832	61362	98947	96067	64760	64584	96096	98253	
29	05366	04213	25669	26422	44407	44048	37937	63904	45766	66134	75470	66520	34693	90449
30	91921	26418	64117	94305	26766	25940	39972	22209	71500	64568	91402	42416	07844	69618

435

Table 10.5 (continued)

Line	(1)	(2)	(3)	(4)	(5)	(6)	(7)	(8)	(9)	(10)	(11)	(12)	(13)	(14)
31	00582	04711	87917	77341	42206	35126	74087	99547	81817	42607	43808	76655	62028	76630
32	00725	69884	62797	56170	86324	88072	76222	36086	84637	93161	76038	65855	77919	88006
33	69011	65795	95876	55293	18988	27354	26575	08625	40801	59920	29841	80150	12777	48501
34	25976	57948	29888	80604	67917	48708	18912	82271	65424	69774	33611	54262	85963	03547
35	09763	83473	73577	12908	30883	18317	28290	35797	05998	41688	34952	37888	38917	80050
36	91567	42595	29758	30134	04024	86385	29880	99730	55536	84855	29080	09250	79656	73211
37	17955	56349	90999	49127	20044	59931	06115	20542	18059	02008	73708	83517	36103	42791
38	46503	18584	18845	49618	02304	51038	20655	58727	28168	15475	56942	53389	20562	87338

39	92157	89634	94824	78171	84610	82834	09922	25417	44137	48413	25555	21246	35509	20468
40	14577	62765	35605	81263	39667	47358	56873	56307	61607	49518	89656	20103	77490	18062
41	98427	07523	33362	64270	01638	92477	66969	98420	04880	45585	46565	04102	46880	45709
42	34914	63976	88720	82765	34476	17032	87589	40836	32427	70002	70663	88863	77775	69348
43	70060	28277	39475	46473	23219	53416	94970	25832	69975	94884	19661	72828	00102	66794
44	53976	54914	06990	67245	68350	82948	11398	42878	80287	88267	47363	46634	06541	97809
45	76072	29515	40980	07391	58745	25774	22987	80059	39911	96189	41151	14222	60697	59583
46	90725	52210	83974	29992	65831	38857	50490	83765	55657	14361	31720	57375	56228	41546
47	64364	67412	33339	31926	14883	24413	59744	92351	97473	89286	38931	04110	23726	51900
48	08962	00358	31662	25388	61642	34072	81249	35648	56891	69352	48373	45578	78547	81788
49	95012	68379	93526	70765	10592	04542	76463	54328	02349	17247	28865	14777	62730	92277
50	15664	10493	20492	38391	91132	21999	59516	81652	27195	48223	46751	22923	32261	85653

After performing the sampling plan, Scott finds that 4 sales orders are missing the credit manager's signature (apparently an error on the part of the credit manager). The sample deviation rate is therefore 4/127 or 3.1%. The upper occurrence limit, determined by using Table 10.3 is 7.2. (The sample size of 125 is used for conservative results.) Since the upper occurrence limit is greater than the tolerable rate of 7%, Scott rejects the control and attempts to identify a compensating control for additional testing.

SUBSTANTIVE TESTING

What is the purpose of substantive testing?

To form the basis of an opinion on the fairness of the financial statements, the third generally accepted fieldwork standard requires the gathering of sufficient competent evidential matter. Substantive tests are the procedures by which auditors gather this matter.

While the nature, extent, and timing of substantive tests is a matter of professional judgment, effective client internal control structure is a positive influence. Accordingly, the auditor may decide to decrease the amount of substantive testing, omit certain procedures, and/or schedule interim testing. Conversely, weak internal control structure will likely result in increased substantive testing, the need for additional audit procedures and/or scheduling testing at or after year-end.

What is involved in substantive testing?

In general, substantive tests include:

- Tests of transactions
- Tests of details of account balances
- Analytical procedures

In *testing transactions*, the auditor is concerned with tests of:

- Omitted transactions and account understatement (tracing source documents to the books of entry)

- Invalid or unsupported transactions and account overstatement (tracing recorded transactions to source documents)

Tests for omitted Transactions
and Account
Understatement

Documents ⟵————————————————→ Books

Tests for Invalid or
Unsupported Transactions
and Account Overstatement

In analyzing *details of account balances,* auditors use professional judgment in determining which accounts to scrutinize. Some of the accounts commonly requiring scrutiny are:

- Repairs and maintenance
- Fixed assets
- Officers' salaries
- Contributions
- Travel and entertainment
- Income tax provisions

Analytical procedures include the study and comparison of the relationships between data. This involves the comparison of current period financial information with:

- Prior-period information
- Expected results
- Predictable pattern information
- Intra-industry information
- Nonfinancial information

How do I construct an audit program?

To facilitate the examination, audit work programs should be developed for each account subject to examination. Audit work programs are easily developed by considering:

- The auditor's objectives
- Generally accepted accounting principles
- Required actions or procedures

What are the audit objectives?

The following audit objectives provide the framework for any audit program a particular engagement may demand:

- *Presentation and disclosure*: Do the financial statements include all relevant footnote disclosures and are the statements appropriately classified?
- *Valuation or allocation*: Do accounts accurately reflect appropriate amounts?
- *Completeness*: Do accounts reflect all transactions executed in the accounting period?
- *Existence or occurrence*: Do recorded amounts of assets and liabilities actually exist? Have recorded transactions actually occurred in the accounting period?
- *Rights and obligations*: Does the entity maintain rights to its assets? Are the entity's liabilities its own obligations?
- *Related income statement effects*: Are there any income statement implications?

What else is needed in preparing an audit program?

The next steps in developing an audit work program are identifying the flow of transactions in the accounting process and developing an understanding of relevant generally accepted accounting principles.

Finally, you must select the appropriate audit procedures from among the following general procedures:

- Inspection of related documents
- Observation of procedures
- Confirmation of account balances and existence of assets, liabilities and transactions
- Inquiry of company personnel
- Retracing of transactions from books to records
- Recalculation of extensions and footings
- Vouching of documents to verify propriety and validity

- Counting of tangible assets
- Scanning ("eyeballing") of documents, schedules and accounts
- Scrutinizing of documents, schedules and accounts
- Reading or reviewing documents, minutes of board meetings and financial statements
- Comparing perpetual records with physical assets
- Analyzing account balances

(See Figure 10.4.)

Figure 10.4
SAMPLE AUDIT WORK PROGRAMS

I. *Substantive Tests of Cash Balances*

A. *Presentation and Disclosure*

1. Read or review the financial statements to verify proper classification.
2. Read or review the financial statements to verify disclosures such as those relating to compensating balances.
3. Determine the conformity with GAAP.

B. *Valuation or Allocation*

1. Simultaneously count cash on hand and negotiable securities.
2. Confirm directly with the bank:
    a. Account balances
    b. Direct liabilities to bank
    c. Contingent liabilities to bank
    d. Letters of credit
    e. Security agreements under the Uniform Commercial Code
    f. Authorized signatures
3. Count petty cash fund and reconcile with vouchers.

Figure 10.4 (continued)

C. *Completeness*

1. Obtain bank cutoff statement and determine propriety of year-end outstanding checks and deposits-in-transit.

2. Examine or prepare year-end bank reconciliation.

3. Prepare a proof of cash.

4. Perform analytical procedures.

D. *Existence or Occurrence* (See Valuation or Allocation.)

E. *Rights and Obligations*

1. Read minutes of the board of directors' meetings.

2. Determine existence of compensating balances, levies, etc.

3. Verify names on accounts through confirmation requests.

F. *Related Income Statement Effects*—not truly relevant

II. *Substantive Tests of Receivable Balances*

A. *Presentation and Disclosure*

1. Determine appropriate classification of account balances.

2. Read or review the financial statements in order to verify disclosure of
   a. Restrictions—pledging, factoring and discounting
   b. Related party transactions

3. Trace amounts on trial balance to general ledger control accounts and subsidiary ledger totals.

B. *Valuation or Allocation*

1. Confirm account balances where reasonable and practicable using positive and/or negative confirmation requests.

Figure 10.4 (continued)

2. Examine collections in the subsequent period cash receipts journal.
3. Examine and verify amortization tables.
4. Examine aging schedules.
5. Review adequacy of allowance for doubtful accounts.
6. Review collectibility by checking credit ratings (e.g., Dunn and Bradstreet ratings).
7. Verify clerical accuracy and pricing of sales invoices.
8. Foot daily sales summaries and trace to journals.
9. Perform tests for omitted and invalid (or unsupported) transactions with respect to subsidiary ledger account balances.

C. *Completeness*

1. Perform sales and sales return cutoff tests.
2. Perform analytical procedures.
3. Test for omitted transactions.

D. *Existence or Occurrence*

1. Inspect note agreements.
2. Confirm accounts receivable and notes receivable balances.
3. Review client documentation.

E. *Rights and Obligations*

1. Read minutes of board of directors' meetings.
2. Read leases for pledging agreements.
3. Determine pledging and contingent liabilities to bank by using a standard bank confirmation.

F. *Related Income Statement Effects*

1. Review installment sales profit recognition.
2. Verify accuracy of sales discounts and term discounts.
3. Review bad debt expense computations.
4. Recalculate interest income on notes receivable.

Figure 10.4 (continued)

III. *Substantive Tests of Inventory*

   A. *Presentation and Disclosure*

       1. Read or review the financial statements to verify footnote disclosure of:

          a. Valuation method and inventory flow, e.g., lower-of-cost-or-market value, first-in-first-out

          b. Pledged inventory

          c. Inventory in or out on consignment

          d. Existence of and terms of major purchase commitments.

   B. *Valuation or Allocation*

       1. Verify the correct application of lower-of-cost-or-market value.

       2. Recalculate inventory valuation under the full absorption costing method.

       3. Verify the quality of inventory items.

       4. Vouch and test inventory pricing.

       5. Perform analytical procedures.

       6. Verify the propriety of inventory flow.

       7. Consider using the services of a specialist to corroborate the valuation of inventory (e.g., a gemologist to corroborate the valuation of precious stones).

   C. *Completeness*

       1. Perform cutoff tests for purchases, sales, purchase returns and sales returns.

       2. With respect to tagged inventory, perform tests for omitted transactions and tests for invalid transactions.

       3. Verify the clerical and mathematical accuracy of inventory listings.

       4. Reconcile physical inventory amounts with perpetual records.

       5. Reconcile physical counts with general ledger control totals.

Figure 10.4 (continued)

D. *Existence or Occurrence*

1. Observe client inventory counts.
2. Confirm inventory held in public warehouses.
3. Confirm existence of inventory held by others on consignment.

E. *Rights and Obligations*

1. Determine existence of collateral agreements.
2. Read consignment agreements.
3. Review major purchase commitment agreements.
4. Examine invoices for evidence of ownership.
5. Review minutes of the board of directors' meetings.

F. *Related Income Statement Effects*

1. Verify that ending inventory on the balance sheet is identical to ending inventory in the Cost of Goods Sold section.

IV. *Substantive Tests for Fixed Assets*

A. *Presentation and Disclosure*

1. Read the financial statements in order to verify:
   a. Disclosure of historical cost
   b. Disclosure of depreciation methods under GAAP
   c. Financial statement classification
   d. Disclosure of restrictions

B. *Valuation or Allocation*

1. Examine invoices.
2. Inspect lease agreements and ascertain the proper accounting treatment (e.g., capital vs. operating lease).
3. Analyze repairs and maintenance accounts.

Figure 10.4 (continued)

   4. Analyze related accumulated depreciation accounts.
   5. Vouch entries in fixed asset accounts.
   6. Test extensions and footings on client-submitted schedules.

C. *Completeness*

   1. Perform analytical procedures.
   2. Inspect fixed assets.
   3. Examine subsidiary schedules.
   4. Reconcile subsidiary schedules with general ledger control.

D. *Existence or Occurrence*

   1. Inspect fixed assets.
   2. Examine supporting documentation.

E. *Rights and Obligations*

   1. Inspect invoices.
   2. Inspect lease agreements.
   3. Inspect insurance policies.
   4. Inspect title documents.
   5. Inspect personal property tax returns.
   6. Read minutes of the board of directors' meetings.

F. *Related Income Statement Effects*

   1. Recalculate depreciation expenses.
   2. Recalculate gain or loss on disposal of fixed assets.

AUDIT REPORTS

How does the auditor report?

After the auditor gathers sufficient competent evidential matter, pursuant to the fourth generally accepted reporting standard, he or she must form an opinion on the fairness of the presentation of the financial statements, or disclaim an opinion.

The auditor's standard unqualified opinion can be modified when warranted.

EXAMPLE 10.2

A STANDARD REPORT

Independent Auditor's Report

I (we) have audited the accompanying balance sheet of [company name] as of (at) [date] and the related statements of income, retained earnings, and cash flows for the year then ended. These financial statements are the responsibility of the Company's management. My (our) responsibility is to express an opinion on these financial statements based on my (our) audit.

I (we) conducted my (our) audit in accordance with generally accepted auditing standards. Those standards require that I (we) plan and perform the audit to obtain reasonable assurance about whether the financial statements are free of material misstatement. An audit includes examining, on a test basis, evidence supporting the amounts and disclosures in the financial statements. An audit also includes assessing the accounting principles used and significant estimates made by management, as well as evaluating the overall financial statement presentation. I (we) believe that my (our) audit provides a reasonable basis for my (our) opinion.

In my (our) opinion, the financial statements referred to above present fairly, in all material respects, the financial position of [company name] as of (at) [date], and the result of its operations and its cash flows for the year then ended in conformity with generally accepted accounting principles.

Date—completion of
    the fieldwork

Signature of CPA

How may the standard report be modified?

Using the auditor's standard report as a guideline, the practitioner can easily make modifications depending upon the circumstances. These modifications can be classified by the type of report being issued. They are:

- Unqualified opinion
- Qualified opinion
- Disclaimer of opinion
- Adverse opinion

Unqualified Opinion

When does a division of responsibility apply?

A division of responsibility occurs, for instance, when the auditor of a consolidated group of companies is unable to examine one of the subsidiaries included in the group. Another auditor, however, is able to conduct that examination. The principal auditor has the choice of referring to the other auditor if he or she:

- Is satisfied as to the professional reputation of the other auditor
- Has obtained a representation letter from the other auditor confirming his or her independence
- Is satisfied that the other auditor is familiar with generally accepted auditing standards and generally accepted accounting principles
- Coordinates the audit activities of the two auditors

REQUIREMENT: If reference is to be made, then all paragraphs are modified to reflect the division of responsibility. The introductory paragraph should indicate the magnitude or the size of the portion of the financial statements examined by the other auditor. This may be accomplished through the use of dollars or percentages of total assets and revenues.

EXAMPLE 10.3

Independent Auditor's Report

I (we) have audited the consolidated balance sheets of HJB Company as of (at) December 31, 19XX, and the related consolidated statements of income, retained earnings, and cash flows for the year then ended. These financial statements are the responsibility of the Company's management. My (our) responsibility is to express an opinion on these financial statements based on my (our) audit. I (we) did not audit the financial statements of KJB Company, a wholly owned subsidiary, which statements reflect total assets of $_____ as of December 31, 19XX and total revenues of $_____ for the year then ended. Those statements were audited by other auditors whose report has been furnished to me (us), and my (our) opinion, insofar as it relates to the amounts included for KJB Company, is based solely on the report of the other auditors.

I (we) conducted my (our) audit in accordance with generally accepted auditing standards. Those standards require that I (we) plan and perform the audit to obtain reasonable assurance about whether the financial statements are free of material misstatement. An audit includes examining, on a test basis, evidence supporting the amounts and disclosures in the financial statements. An audit also includes assessing the accounting principles used and significant estimates made by management, as well as evaluating the overall financial statement presentation. I (we) believe that my (our) audit and the report of the other auditors provide a reasonable basis for my (our) opinion.

In my (our) opinion, based on my (our) audit and the report of other auditors, the consolidated financial statements referred to above present fairly, in all material respects, the financial position of HJB as of (at) December 31, 19XX, and the results of its operations and its cash flows for the year then ended in conformity with generally accepted accounting principles.

How may I emphasize a disclosure?

The practitioner, in his or her report, may emphasize a matter which is already disclosed and properly accounted for in the financial statements. Emphasis of a matter, such as a type II subsequent event (discussed later), should be made in a separate paragraph between the scope and opinion paragraphs. No modification should be made to either the scope or the opinion paragraph.

Qualified Opinion

How do I handle breaks in consistency?

When financial statements reflect a change in accounting principles, the auditor must modify the audit report by adding an explanatory paragraph following the opinion paragraph:

EXAMPLE 10.4

As discussed in Note X to the financial statements, the company changed its method of computing depreciation in 19X2.

Caution: In general, if the year of change is reported on in subsequent years, the additional paragraph must be presented.

When is the consistency modification required?

Changes in accounting principles requiring the consistency modification include a change:

- From one generally accepted accounting principle (GAAP) or method to another
- In reporting entity

- From a non-GAAP method to a method or principle that is generally accepted
- In principle which is inseparable from a change in accounting estimate

Changes in the following, however, do not require consistency modifications:

- Accounting estimates
- Correction of an error not involving a principle
- Financial statement classification, format and terminology

When is the scope of the examination limited?

A scope limitation arises when the auditor is unable to do one or more of the following:

- Gather enough evidential matter to afford the expression of an unqualified opinion
- Apply a required auditing procedure
- Apply one or more auditing procedures considered necessary under the circumstances

What if the limitation is not a serious one?

When the scope limitation is not severe enough to warrant the expression of a disclaimer of an opinion, an "except for" qualified opinion should be issued. The necessary modifications to the report include:

- Adding the phrase "Except as discussed in the following paragraph" to the beginning or end of the second sentence of the scope paragraph
- Adding a paragraph before the opinion paragraph that explains the nature of the scope limitation
- Modifying the opinion paragraph for the possible effects of the scope limitation on the financial statements

EXAMPLE 10.5

The following is a report modified to indicate a scope limitation.

Independent Auditor's Report

I (we) have audited the accompanying balance sheet of SMR Company as of (at) December 31, 19XX, and the related statements of income, retained earnings, and cash flows for the year then ended. These financial statements are the responsibility of the Company's management. My (our) responsibility is to express an opinion on these financial statements based on my (our) audit.

Except as discussed in the following paragraph, I (we) conducted my (our) audit in accordance with generally accepted auditing standards. Those standards require that I (we) plan and perform the audit to obtain reasonable assurance about whether the financial statements are free of material misstatement. An audit includes examining, on a test basis, evidence supporting the amounts and disclosures in the financial statements. An audit also includes assessing the accounting principles used and significant estimates made by management, as well as evaluating the overall financial statement presentation. I (we) believe that my (our) audit provides a reasonable basis for my (our) opinion.

I was (we were) unable to obtain audited financial statements supporting the Company's investment in a foreign affiliate stated at $_____ at December 31, 19XX, or its equity in earnings of that affiliate of $_____, which is included in net income for the year then ended as described in Note X to the financial statements; nor was I (were we) able to satisfy myself (ourselves) as to the carrying value of the investment in the foreign affiliate or the equity in its earnings by other auditing procedures.

In my (our) opinion, except for the effects of such adjustments, if any, as might have been determined to be necessary had I (we) been able to examine evidence regarding the foreign affiliate investment and earnings, the financial statements referred to in the first paragraph above present fairly, in all material respects, the financial position of SMR Company as of (at) December 31, 19XX, and the results of its operations and its cash flows for the year then ended in conformity with generally accepted accounting principles.

How do I handle a departure from GAAP?

When financial statements contain a departure from GAAP, and the client refuses to make the necessary modifications, the auditor will express a qualified opinion, unless the effects of the departure warrant the issuance of an adverse opinion. Departures from GAAP include the lack of adequate disclosure (e.g., the omission of the summary of significant accounting policies) as well as the use of an accounting method that does not reflect the substance of a particular transaction (e.g., the failure to capitalize lease obligations).

The necessary modifications to the report include:

- Adding an explanatory paragraph between the scope and opinion paragraphs describing the departure, the treatment required under GAAP, and the principal effects on the financial statements (or, if not practicable, a statement so indicating).
- Modifying the opinion paragraph by adding the phrase "except for" and including a reference to the explanatory paragraph

EXAMPLE 10.6

The following is a report modified to disclose a departure from GAAP:

Independent Auditor's Report

I (we) have audited the accompanying balance sheet of SR Company as of (at) December 31, 19XX and the related statements of income, retained earnings, and cash flows for the year then ended. These financial statements are the responsibility of the Company's management. My (our) responsibility is to express an opinion on these financial statements based on my (our) audit.

I (we) conducted my (our) audit in accordance with generally accepted auditing standards. Those standards require that I (we) plan and perform the audit to obtain reasonable assurance about whether the financial statements are free of material misstatement. An audit includes examining, on a test basis, evidence supporting the amounts and disclosures in the financial statements. An audit also includes assessing the accounting principles used and significant estimates made by management, as well as evaluating the overall financial statement presentation. I (we) believe that my (our) audit provides a reasonable basis for my (our) opinion.

The Company has excluded from property and debt in the accompanying balance sheet certain lease obligations, which in my (our) opinion should be capitalized in order to conform with generally accepted accounting principles. If these lease obligations were capitalized, property would be increased (decreased) by $_____, long-term debt by $_____, and retained earnings by $_____ as of December 31, 19XX, and net income and earnings per share would be increased (decreased) by $_____ and $_____ respectively for the year then ended.

In my (our) opinion, except for the effects of not capitalizing certain lease obligations as discussed in the preceding paragraph, the financial statements referred to above present fairly, in all material respects, the financial position of SR Company as of (at)

December 31, 19XX, and the results of its operations and its cash flows for the year then ended in conformity with generally accepted accounting principles.

NOTE: If the departure from GAAP is adequately disclosed in the notes to the financial statements, the explanatory paragraph may be shortened by referring to the applicable note (see Example 10.7).

EXAMPLE 10.7

As more fully described in Note X to the financial statements, the Company has excluded certain lease obligations from property and debt in the accompanying balance sheet. In my (our) opinion, generally accepted accounting principles require that such obligations be included in the balance sheet.

What if a material uncertainty exists?

Uncertainties include:

- Litigation.
- Income tax audits.
- Financial problems which raise a question as to the ability of the company to continue in existence (i.e., a going-concern problem).

If, prior to the issuance of the financial statements, management is unable to reasonably estimate an item or disclosure, then the auditor should consider the likelihood of a material loss resulting from the resolution of the uncertainty. The CPA must use professional judgment in determining whether or not to modify his or her request.

How do I modify the audit report for a material uncertainty?

If the audit report is to be modified due to a material uncertainty, an explanatory paragraph in which the uncertainty is described should be added after the opinion paragraph.

EXAMPLE 10.8

The following is an example of an explanatory paragraph describing an uncertainty involving litigation:

> As discussed in Note X to the financial statements, the Company is a defendant in a lawsuit alleging infringement of certain patent rights and claiming royalties and punitive damages. The Company has filed a counteraction, and preliminary hearings and discovery proceedings on both actions are in progress. The ultimate outcome of the litigation cannot presently be determined. Accordingly, no provision for any liability that may result upon adjudication has been made in the accompanying financial statements.

CAUTION: The addition of an explanatory paragraph to describe a material uncertainty does not result in a qualification to the audit report—an unqualified opinion is to be expressed.

Disclaimer of Opinion

When is a disclaimer of opinion issued?

When a severe scope limitation exists and the auditor does not wish to express a qualified opinion, a disclaimer of opinion is warranted. A disclaimer of opinion indicates the practitioner's inability to form an opinion on the fairness of the financial statements.

The necessary modifications to the report are as follows:

- Modify the introductory paragraph
- Omit the scope (second) paragraph of the standard report
- Add an explanatory paragraph describing the reasons why the audit was not in conformity with generally accepted auditing standards
- In lieu of an opinion paragraph, draft a disclaimer paragraph which includes wording to the effect that "I (we) do not express an opinion on these financial statements."

EXAMPLE 10.9

The following audit report contains a disclaimer of opinion:

Independent Auditor's Report

I was (we were) engaged to audit the accompanying balance sheet of Harold Corporation as of (at) December 31, 19XX, and the related statements of income, retained earnings, and cash flows for the year then ended. These financial statements are the responsibility of the Company's management.

The Company did not make a count of its physical inventory in 19XX, stated in the accompanying financial statements at $...... Further, evidence supporting the cost of property and equipment acquired prior to December 31, 19XX, is no longer available. The Company's records do not permit the application of other auditing procedures to inventories or property and equipment.

Since the Company did not take physical inventories and I was (we were) not able to apply other auditing procedures to satisfy myself (ourselves) as to inventory quantities and the cost of property and equipment, the scope of my (our) work was not sufficient to enable me (us) to express, and I (we) do not express, an opinion on these financial statements.

CAUTION: In disclaiming an opinion, never identify the audit procedures that were actually performed.

Adverse Opinion

When is an adverse opinion warranted?

An adverse opinion should be expressed when financial statements do *not* present fairly in conformity with GAAP an entity's

- Financial position
- Results of operations
- Retained earnings
- Cash flows

Issued when financial statements are misleading, the adverse opinion should include the following modifications:

• Add a paragraph between the scope and opinion paragraphs disclosing all of the substantive reasons for the issuance of the adverse opinion as well as the principal effects on the financial statements. If the principal effects cannot be reasonably determined, the report should so state.

• Modify the opinion paragraph to indicate that the statements are not presented fairly in conformity with generally accepted accounting principles.

EXAMPLE 10.10

The following report reflects the auditor's adverse opinion:

Independent Auditor's Report

I (we) have audited the accompanying balance sheet of X Company as of (at) December 31, 19XX and the related statements of income, retained earnings, and cash flows for the year then ended. These financial statements are the responsibility of the Company's management. My (our) responsibility is to express an opinion on these financial statements based on my (our) audit.

I (we) conducted my (our) audit in accordance with generally accepted auditing standards. Those standards require that we plan and perform the audit to obtain reasonable assurance about whether the financial statements are free of material misstatement. An audit includes examining, on a test basis, evidence supporting the amounts and disclosures in the financial statements. An audit also includes assessing the accounting principles used and significant estimates made by management, as well as evaluating the overall financial statement presentation. I (we) believe that my (our) audit provides a reasonable basis for my (our) opinion.

As discussed in Note X to the financial statements, the Company carries its property, plant and equipment accounts at appraisal values, and provides depreciation on the basis of such values. Further, the Company does not provide for income taxes with respect to differences between financial income and taxable income arising because of the use, for income tax purposes, of the installment method of reporting gross profit from certain types of sales. Generally accepted accounting principles, in my (our) opinion, require that property, plant and equipment be stated at an amount not in excess of cost, reduced by depreciation based on such amount, and that deferred income taxes be provided. Because of the departures from generally accepted accounting principles identified above, as of December 31, 19XX, inventories have been increased $...... by inclusion in manufacturing overhead of depreciation in excess of that based on cost; property, plant and equipment, less accumulated depreciation, is carried at $...... in excess of an amount based on the cost to the Company; and allocated income tax of $...... has not been recorded; resulting in an increase of $...... in retained earnings and in appraisal surplus of .... For the year ended December 31, 19XX, cost of goods sold has been increased $...... because of the effects of the depreciation accounting referred to above and deferred income taxes of $...... have not been provided, resulting in an increase in net income and earnings per share of $...... and $...... respectively.

In my (our) opinion, because of the effects of the matters discussed in the preceding paragraph, the financial statements referred to above do not present fairly, in conformity with generally accepted accounting principles, the financial position of X Company as of December 31, 19XX, or the results of its operations and its cash flows for the year then ended.

CHAPTER 11

COMPILATION, REVIEW, AND OTHER REPORTING SERVICES

A practitioner whose client's stock is not publicly traded is often requested to compile or review financial statements. When an accountant is involved in the compilation or review of a client's financial statements, he or she is required to issue a report at the conclusion of the engagement. It is no longer permissible to present financial statements to a client, as an accommodation, without the issuance of a report.

Compilation and review services represent two types of engagements that practitioners face daily. This chapter will explain these services and the reporting practices associated with them, in addition to special reports generally associated with audit engagements.

Engagements involving prospective financial statements and attestation services are relatively new. They should be viewed by the practitioner as an important area for practice expansion.

COMPILATION OF FINANCIAL STATEMENTS

What is a compilation of financial statements?

A compilation of financial statements is limited to presenting in the form of financial statements information that is the representation of management or owners. A key characteristic of a compilation is that *no opinion* or any other form of assurance is expressed on the fairness of the presentation of the financial statements.

How is a compilation conducted?

Inasmuch as a compilation engagement does not result in the expression of any assurance, the procedures to be performed are quite limited.

RECOMMENDATION: To facilitate the compilation engagement and to demonstrate that due care has been exercised, the practitioner should consider the following checklist:

Step 1: Obtain an engagement letter.

Step 2: Research the accounting principles and practices applicable to the client's industry.

Step 3: Obtain a general understanding of the flow and nature of the transactions underlying the client's financial records.

Step 4: Obtain a general understanding of the client's accounting records.

Step 5: Inquire about the stated qualifications of the client's accounting personnel.

Step 6: Determine the basis of accounting used—GAAP or another comprehensive basis of accounting (e.g., cash basis, modified cash basis, income tax basis, etc.).

Step 7: Determine the necessity of performing the following accounting services:

- Adjustment of client books

- Consultation with appropriate personnel regarding accounting-related matters

- Bookkeeping services when the client's manual or automated bookkeeping does not produce financial statements as the end result

Step 8: Although it is not required to verify or corroborate representations made by management and personnel, obtain satisfaction as to representations that appear incorrect, incomplete or otherwise unsatisfactory.

Step 9: When financial statements depart from the basis of accounting in use, and the client refuses to make the necessary adjustments, modify the accountant's report to disclose this fact.

Step 10: Read the financial statements to confirm that the statements are free from obvious errors. (*EXAMPLES*: Mathematical mistakes, omission of relevant disclosures, and departures from relevant accounting principles.)

Step 11: If a higher level of service was performed (e.g., a review or an audit), issue the report that relates to the highest level of service performed.

Step 12: If the accountant is not independent with respect to the client, indicate this fact, but not the reasons therefor, in the compilation report.

What reports may be issued on a compilation engagement?

At the conclusion of a compilation engagement, the accountant must issue a report that includes the following:

- An identification of the financial statements
- A statement that the compilation was performed in accordance with standards established by the American Institute of Certified Public Accountants
- The definition of a compilation, stating that a compilation is limited to presenting in the form of financial statements information that is the representation of management (owners)
- A statement that the financial statements have not been subjected to an audit or a review and accordingly, no opinion or any other form of assurance on them is provided
- The date of the report, which should coincide with the date on which the compilation was completed
- The accountant's signature

RECOMMENDATIONS: Each page of the financial statements must be labeled "See accountant's compilation report." If desired, expand the label to include "and the Notes to the Financial Statements," since the notes are an integral part of the financial statements.

In order to avoid misinterpretation, mark each page of the financial statements "unaudited."

EXAMPLE 11.1

The following is a standard compilation report:

> I (We) have compiled the accompanying balance sheet of Debit Company as of (at) December 31, 19XX, and the related statements of income, retained earnings, and cash flows for the year then ended, in accordance with standards established by the American Institute of Certified Public Accountants.
>
> A compilation is limited to presenting in the form of financial statements information that is the representation of management (owners). I (We) have not audited or reviewed the accompanying financial statements and, accordingly, do not express an opinion or any other form of assurance on them.

NOTE: It is permissible to compile and report on only one of the financial statements normally included in the complete set.

When should the standard compilation report be modified?

The following circumstances warrant modification of the standard compilation report:

• *Omission of substantially all disclosures.* When financial statements which purport to be in conformity with generally accepted accounting principles (or another comprehensive basis of accounting) lack the necessary disclosures (e.g., notes to the financial statements, parenthetical comments on the face of the statements, etc.), the accountant should add the following paragraph immediately after the standard two paragraph report:

> Management has elected to omit substantially all of the disclosures required by generally accepted accounting principles. If the omitted disclosures were included in the financial statements, they might influence the user's conclusions about the company's financial posi-

tion, results of operations, and cash flows. Accordingly, these financial statements are not designed for those who are not informed about such matters.

• *Selected information presented.* When notes to the financial statements include only a few matters, the presentation of this information should be labeled "Selected Information—Substantially all of the Disclosures Required by Generally Accepted Accounting Principles Are Not Included." The compilation report should include the additional paragraph stated above.

• *Omission of the statement of cash flows.* See the first departure above. Modify the first sentence of the additional paragraph to reflect the omission of either the statement of cash flows alone or the statement of cash flows and substantially all of the disclosures required by GAAP:

Management has elected to omit the statement of cash flows (and substantially all of the disclosures) required by generally accepted accounting principles . . .

NOTE: Financial statements, which are prepared using a comprehensive basis of accounting other than GAAP, do not *require* presentation of a statement of cash flows.

• *Lack of independence.* While an accountant who is not independent with respect to a client's financial statements *may* issue a compilation report, he or she must state in the report that, "I am (we are) not independent with respect to Debit Company."

CAUTION: The accountant should not disclose the reasons as to why it is believed that independence is lacking.

• *Departure from generally accepted accounting principles.* Although the accountant is under no obligation to search for departures from GAAP, such departures, if uncovered and not corrected, must be disclosed in the accountant's report. This is accomplished by adding to the standard report a middle explanatory paragraph, which either discloses the effects of the departure or states that the effects of such departure have not been determined.

• *Financial statements are based on a comprehensive basis of accounting other than generally accepted accounting principles.* If a client uses a comprehensive basis of accounting other than GAAP it is necessary to appropriately modify the titles of the financial statements, and disclose the basis of accounting used if the financial statements do not include the necessary disclosure.

EXAMPLE 11.2

The following is a compilation report on cash basis financial statements with omission of substantially all disclosures:

I (we) have compiled the accompanying statement of assets and liabilities arising from cash transactions of Credit Incorporated as of (at) December 31, 19XX, and the related statement of revenue collected and expenses paid for the year then ended, in accordance with standards established by the American Institute of Certified Public Accountants. The financial statements have been prepared on the cash basis of accounting which is a comprehensive basis of accounting other than generally accepted accounting principles.

A compilation is limited to presenting in the form of financial statements information that is the representation of management (owners). I (We) have not audited or reviewed the accompanying financial statements and, accordingly, do not express an opinion or any other form of assurance on them.

Management has elected to omit substantially all of the informative disclosures ordinarily included in financial statements. If the omitted disclosures were included in the financial statements, they might influence the user's conclusions about the Company's assets, liabilities, equity, revenue and expenses. Accordingly, these statements are not designed for those who are not informed about such matters.

REVIEW OF FINANCIAL STATEMENTS

What constitutes a review of financial statements?

A review is a step up in the level of service from a compilation engagement, since some form of assurance on the financial statements will be expressed.

A review consists principally of inquiry of company personnel and analytical procedures applied to financial data. These provide the accountant with a reasonable basis for expressing *limited assurance* that no material modifications need be made to the financial statements in order for them to be in conformity with generally accepted accounting principles (or another comprehensive basis of accounting).

Since review procedures do not include consideration of the client's internal control structure or the gathering of competent evidential matter, an opinion may not be expressed. In a review, the practitioner may identify matters that significantly affect the financial statements. However, the review engagement may not be relied upon to disclose all significant matters that would surface in an audit.

What are the steps in a review engagement?

Step 1: Obtain an engagement letter.

Step 2: Obtain a satisfactory level of knowledge of the accounting principles, methods and practices of the industry in which the client operates.

Step 3: Obtain a general understanding of:

- The client's organization
- The client's operating characteristics
- The nature of the client's assets, liabilities, equity, revenues and expenses
- The client's production, distribution and compensation methods

- The types of products and services offered
- The client's operating locations
- Any material related-party transactions

Step 4: Perform the following inquiry and analytical procedures:

- Obtain satisfaction as to independence from the client.
- Inquire about the client's basis of accounting and the related accounting principles, methods and practices.
- Inquire about the client's procedures for recording, classifying, and summarizing transactions and presenting informative disclosures.
- Inquire about results of stockholder meetings.
- Inquire about results of board of directors' meetings.
- Consider reading the minutes of the meetings of the board of directors.
- To confirm conformity with GAAP (or other comprehensive basis of accounting), read the financial statements (including related notes).
- If another accountant is involved in the review of a significant component of the entity (e.g., subsidiary or other investee), obtain reports from the other accountants.
- Inquire about changes in business activities, accounting methods, principles and practices.
- Resolve matters that were considered to be incomplete, inaccurate, or otherwise questionable.
- If desired, obtain a client representation letter.
- Document the review procedures in the work papers.
- Prepare the review report.

RECOMMENDATION: To identify significant fluctuations in financial data, consider performing the following analytical procedures:

- Compare current-period financial information with that of prior periods.

- Compare current-period financial information with anticipated results. *EXAMPLE*: Budgeted and forecasted amounts.
- Study and analyze current-period financial information that is expected to conform to predictable patterns. *EXAMPLE*: Changes in purchases and accounts payable.
- Compare current-period financial information with nonfinancial information. *EXAMPLE*: Inventory quantities with the square footage of storage areas.

Are illustrative inquiries available?

The *Appendix to Statement on Accounting and Review Services No. 1* contains guidance on the inquiries applicable to review engagements.

The list of illustrative inquiries presented in Figure 11.1 (by permission of the American Institute of Certified Public Accountants) should not be construed as a mandatory work program or all-inclusive checklist. The practitioner must be guided by professional judgment in tailoring inquiries and procedures to the needs of the client given all facts and circumstances.

Figure 11.1

1. General

    a. What are the procedures for recording, classifying, and summarizing transactions (relates to each section discussed below)?

    b. Do the general ledger control accounts agree with subsidiary records (for example, receivables, inventories, investments, property and equipment, accounts payable, accrued expenses, non-current liabilities)?

    c. Have accounting principles been applied on a consistent basis?

Figure 11.1 (continued)

2. Cash

   a. Have bank balances been reconciled with book balances?

   b. Have old or unusual reconciling items between bank balances and book balances been reviewed and adjustments made where necessary?

   c. Has a proper cutoff of cash transactions been made?

   d. Are there any restrictions on the availability of cash balances?

   e. Have cash funds been counted and reconciled with control accounts?

3. Receivables

   a. Has an adequate allowance been made for doubtful accounts?

   b. Have receivables considered uncollectible been written off?

   c. If appropriate, has interest been reflected?

   d. Has a proper cutoff of sales transactions been made?

   e. Are there any receivables from employees and related parties?

   f. Are any receivables pledged, discounted, or factored?

   g. Have receivables been properly classified between current and noncurrent?

4. Inventories

   a. Have inventories been physically counted? If not, how have inventories been determined?

   b. Have general ledger control accounts been adjusted to agree with physical inventories?

   c. If physical inventories are taken at a date other than the balance sheet date, what procedures were used to record changes in inventory between the date of the physical inventory and the balance sheet date?

Figure 11.1 (continued)

    d. Were consignments in or out considered in taking physical inventories?

    e. What is the basis of valuation?

    f. Does inventory cost include material, labor, and overhead where applicable?

    g. Have write-downs for obsolescence or cost in excess of net realizable value been made?

    h. Have proper cutoffs of purchases, goods in transit, and returned goods been made?

    i. Are there any inventory encumbrances?

5. Prepaid Expenses

    a. What is the nature of the amounts included in prepaid expenses?

    b. How are these amounts amortized?

6. Investments, Including Loans, Mortgages, and Intercorporate Investments

    a. Have gains and losses on disposal been reflected?

    b. Has investment income been reflected?

    c. Has appropriate consideration been given to the classification of investments between current and noncurrent, and the difference between the cost and market value of investments?

    d. Have consolidation or equity accounting requirements been considered?

    e. What is the basis of valuation of marketable equity securities?

    f. Are investments unencumbered?

7. Property and Equipment

    a. Have gains or losses on disposal of property or equipment been reflected?

    b. What are the criteria for capitalization of property and equipment? Have such criteria been applied during the fiscal period?

Figure 11.1 (continued)

    c. Does the repairs and maintenance account only include items of an expense nature?

    d. Are property and equipment stated at cost?

    e. What are the depreciation methods and rates? Are they appropriate and consistent?

    f. Are there any unrecorded additions, retirements, abandonments, sales, or trade-ins?

    g. Does the entity have material lease agreements? Have they been properly reflected?

    h. Is any property or equipment mortgaged or otherwise encumbered?

8. Other Assets

    a. What is the nature of the amounts included in other assets?

    b. Do these assets represent costs that will benefit future periods? What is the amortization policy? Is it appropriate?

    c. Have other assets been properly classified between current and noncurrent?

    d. Are any of these assets mortgaged or otherwise encumbered?

9. Accounts and Notes Payable and Accrued Liabilities

    a. Have all significant payables been reflected?

    b. Are all bank and other short-term liabilities properly classified?

    c. Have all significant accruals, such as payroll, interest, and provisions for pension and profit-sharing plans been reflected?

    d. Are there any collateralized liabilities?

    e. Are there any payables to employees and related parties?

Figure 11.1 (continued)

10. Long-Term Liabilities

    a. What are the terms and other provisions of long-term liability agreements?

    b. Have liabilities been properly classified between current and noncurrent?

    c. Has interest expense been reflected?

    d. Has there been compliance with restrictive covenants of loan agreements?

    e. Are any long-term liabilities collateralized or subordinated?

11. Income and Other Taxes

    a. Has provision been made for current and prior-year federal income taxes payable?

    b. Have any assessments or reassessments been received? Are there tax examinations in process?

    c. Are there temporary differences? If so, have deferred taxes been reflected?

    d. Has provision been made for state and local income, franchise, sales, and other taxes payable?

12. Other Liabilities, Contingencies, and Commitments

    a. What is the nature of the amounts included in other liabilities?

    b. Have other liabilities been properly classified between current and noncurrent?

    c. Are there any contingent liabilities, such as discounted notes, drafts, endorsements, warranties, litigation, and unsettled asserted claims? Are there any unasserted potential claims?

    d. Are there any material contractual obligations for construction or purchase of real property and equipment and any commitments or options to purchase or sell company securities?

Figure 11.1 (continued)

13. Equity
    a. What is the nature of any changes in equity accounts?
    b. What classes of capital stock have been authorized?
    c. What is the par or stated value of the various classes of stock?
    d. Do amounts of outstanding shares of capital stock agree with subsidiary records?
    e. Have capital stock preferences, if any been disclosed?
    f. Have stock options been granted?
    g. Has the entity made any acquisitions of its own capital stock?
    h. Are there any restrictions on retained earnings or other capital?

14. Revenue and Expenses
    a. Are revenues from the sale of major products and services recognized in the appropriate period?
    b. Are purchases and expenses recognized in the appropriate period and properly classified?
    c. Do the financial statements include discontinued operations or items that might be considered extraordinary?

15. Other
    a. Are there any events that occurred after the end of the fiscal period that have a significant effect on the financial statements?
    b. Have actions taken at stockholder, board of directors, or comparable meetings that affect the financial statements been reflected?
    c. Have there been any material transactions between related parties?
    d. Are there any material uncertainties? Is there any change in the status of material uncertainties previously disclosed?

Reports on Reviewed Financial Statements

What should the review report contain?

The accountant's review report should include:

- An identification of the financial statements

- A statement that a review was performed in accordance with standards established by the American Institute of Certified Public Accountants

- A statement that all the information included in the financial statements is the representation of management (or owners)

- The definition of a review stating that a review consists principally of inquiries of company personnel and of analytical procedures applied to financial data

- A statement that a review is substantially less in scope than an audit, the objective of which is the expression of an opinion on the financial statements taken as a whole, and that no such opinion is expressed

- If warranted, the issuance of limited assurance; i.e., a statement that the accountant is not aware of any material modifications that should be made to the financial statements in order for them to be in conformity with generally accepted accounting principles (or other comprehensive basis of accounting)

- Disclosure of any material modifications, if any, that should be made to the financial statements for them to be in conformity with generally accepted accounting principles (or other comprehensive basis of accounting)

- The date of the report, which should coincide with the completion of the inquiries and analytical procedures

- The accountant's signature

RECOMMENDATIONS: Each page of the reviewed financial statements must be labeled "See Accountant's Review Report." If desired expand the label to include "and the Notes to the Financial Statements." It is also permissible to label each page of the financial statements as "unaudited."

What does a standard review report look like?

EXAMPLE 11.3

I (We) have reviewed the accompanying balance sheet of Credit Corporation as of (at) December 31, 19XX, and the related statements of income, retained earnings, and cash flows for the year then ended, in accordance with standards established by the American Institute of Certified Public Accountants. All information included in these financial statements is the representation of the management (owners) of Credit Corporation.

A review consists principally of inquiries of company personnel and analytical procedures applied to financial data. It is substantially less in scope than an examination in accordance with generally accepted auditing standards, the objective of which is the expression of an opinion regarding the financial statements taken as a whole. Accordingly, I (we) do not express such an opinion.

Based on my (our) review, I am (we are) not aware of any material modifications that should be made to the accompanying financial statements in order for them to be in conformity with generally accepted accounting principles.

What should I be cautious about in review engagements?

If the practitioner is precluded from performing review procedures that he or she considers necessary, then a review report should *not* be issued. In such circumstances, the accountant might consider issuing a compilation report. *CAUTION:* Professional judgment must be exercised in considering the circumstances which precluded the review report.

Independence is a requirement for the issuance of a review report.

An accountant may undertake an engagement to review less than a complete set of financial statements. EXAMPLE: The practitioner may accept an engagement to review only a client's balance sheet.

Under certain circumstances, a client may request that an accountant, who was engaged to perform an examination under GAAS, change the engagement to a lower level of service, namely a change to a compilation or a review. Before undertaking the step down, the accountant should take into consideration:

- The client's reasons for the step down, including any client-imposed scope limitations
- The extent of any additional procedures to complete the audit engagement
- The cost to the client of performing the additional auditing procedures

When justification exists for the step down, as in the case of a client who no longer requires an audit report to secure a bank loan because alternative financing was arranged, the accountant's report should not refer to the step down nor to the application of any audit procedures performed. Accordingly, the standard compilation or review report is appropriate.

CAUTION: If the accountant is precluded from discussing litigation, claims, and assessments with the client's legal counsel because the client refuses to authorize the communication or the client refuses to furnish a representation letter, then the situation is tantamount to a scope limitation sufficient to preclude the issuance of an opinion. Such scope limitations similarly preclude the accountant from issuing a review or compilation report on the financial statements.

When must the standard report be modified?

Departures from Generally Accepted Accounting Principles. When the accountant becomes aware of a material departure from generally accepted accounting principles, it is necessary to modify the standard report by:

- Beginning the third paragraph with wording such as "Based on my (our) review, with the exception of the matter(s) described in the following paragraph(s), I am (we are) not aware of any material modifications. . . ."
- Presenting an additional paragraph in order to disclose the effects of the departure.

In situations where the principal effects of the departure cannot reasonably be determined, the practitioner should state this in the report.

Supplementary Information. When the basic financial statements are accompanied by additional information, such as a supporting schedule of selling, general and administrative expenses, the accountant should indicate the responsibility he or she is taking with respect to this supplementary information. This may be accomplished by presenting either of two reports:

- One report that covers both the basic financial statements and the supplementary information
- Separate reports on the basic financial statements and the supplementary information.

Whichever approach is followed, the report should include a statement that the additional information is presented for the purpose of analysis only and was or was not subjected to the review procedures applicable to the review of the basic financial statements.

NOTE: If the additional information was reviewed, the report should contain the expression of limited assurance; i.e., that the accountant is not aware of any material modifications that should be made to the additional information. On the other hand, if the practitioner did not review the supplementary information, the report should state this fact. In this circumstance, it would be appropriate to state that the additional information was compiled from information that is the representation of management, without audit or review, and that no opinion or any other form of assurance is being expressed.

REPORTS ON PROSPECTIVE FINANCIAL STATEMENTS

What are prospective financial statements?

Prospective financial statements encompass financial forecasts and financial projections. Pro forma financial statements and partial presentations are specifically excluded from this category.

Financial forecasts are prospective financial statements that present, to the best of the responsible party's knowledge and belief, an entity's expected financial position, results of operations, and cash flows. They are based on assumptions about conditions *actually* expected to exist and the course of action expected to be taken.

Financial projections are prospective financial statements that present, to the best of the responsible party's knowledge and belief, an entity's expected financial position, results of operations and cash flows. They are based on assumptions about conditions expected to exist and the course of action expected to be taken, given one or more *hypothetical* (i.e., "what if") assumptions.

Responsible parties are those who are responsible for the underlying assumptions. While the responsible party is usually management, it may be a third party. EXAMPLE: If a client is negotiating with a bank for a large loan, the bank may stipulate the assumptions to be used. Accordingly, in this case, the bank would represent the responsible party.

What are my reporting responsibilities regarding prospective financial statements?

Statement on Standards for Accountants' Services on Prospective Financial Information specifically precludes an accountant from compiling, examining or applying agreed-upon procedures to prospective financial statements that fail to include a summary of significant assumptions. The practice standards in the *Statement* are *not* applicable:

- To engagements involving prospective financial statements that are restricted to internal use
- To those used solely in litigation support services (e.g., in circumstances where the practitioner is serving as an expert witness)
- When budgets are presented with interim period financial statements

How are prospective financial statements used?

The intended use of an entity's prospective financial statements governs the type of prospective financial statements to be presented.

• When an entity's prospective financial statements are for *general use*, only a financial forecast is to be presented. "General use" means that the statements will be used by persons not negotiating directly with the responsible party. EXAMPLE: In a public offering of a tax shelter interest.

• When an entity's prospective financial statements are for *limited use* either a financial forecast or a financial projection may be presented. "Limited use" refers to situations where the statements are to be used by the responsible party alone or by the responsible party and those parties negotiating directly with the responsible party. EXAMPLE: If a client is negotiating directly with a bank, either a forecast or a projection is appropriate.

How do I compile prospective statements?

Compilation procedures applicable to prospective financial statements are not designed to provide any form of assurance on the presentation of the statements or the underlying assumptions.

They are essentially the same as those applicable to historical financial statements. Additional procedures:

- Inquire of the responsible party as to the underlying assumptions developed.

- Compile or obtain a list of the underlying assumptions and consider the possibility of obvious omissions or inconsistencies.
- Verify the mathematical accuracy of the assumptions.
- Read the prospective financial statements in order to identify departures from AICPA presentation guidelines.
- Obtain a client representation letter in order to confirm that the responsible party acknowledges its responsibility for the prospective statements (including the underlying assumptions).

CAUTION: An accountant is precluded from compiling forecasts and projections which do not present the summary of significant assumptions. Furthermore, the practitioner should not compile a projection that fails to identify the underlying hypothetical assumptions or describe the limitations on the utility of the projection.

What do I include in a compilation report on prospective statements?

The accountant's report on compiled prospective financial statements should include:

- An identification of the prospective financial statements presented
- A statement as to the level of service provided and that the prospective financial statements were compiled in accordance with standards established by the AICPA
- A statement describing the limited scope of a compilation and the fact that no opinion or any other form of assurance is being expressed
- A warning that the prospective results may not materialize
- A statement that the accountant is under no responsibility to update his or her report for conditions occurring after the compilation report is issued
- The date of the report, which should coincide

with the completion of the compilation procedures

- In the case of a projection, a separate middle paragraph describing the limitations on the utility of the statements

- A separate paragraph when the statements present the expected results in the form of a range of values

- If the accountant is not independent, a statement as to this fact. (No disclosure should be made as to the reasons why the accountant feels that he or she is not independent)

- A separate explanatory paragraph when the prospective statements contain a departure from AICPA presentation guidelines or omit disclosures unrelated to the significant assumptions

EXAMPLE 11.4

The following is a standard report on compiled forecasts:

I (we) have compiled the accompanying forecasted balance sheet, statement of income, retained earnings, and cash flows of Future Corporation as of (at) December 31, 19XX, and for the year then ending, in accordance with standards established by the American Institute of Certified Public Accountants.

A compilation is limited to presenting in the form of a forecast information that is the representation of management (or other responsible party) and does not include evaluation of the support for the assumptions underlying the forecast. I (we) have not examined the forecast and, accordingly, do not express an opinion or any other form of assurance on the accompanying statements or assumptions. Furthermore, there will usually be differences between the forecasted and actual results, because events and circumstances frequently do not occur as expected, and those differences may be material. I (we) have no responsibility to update this report for events and circumstances occurring after the date of this report.

EXAMPLE 11.5

The following is a standard report on compiled projections:

I (we) have compiled the accompanying projected balance sheet, statements of income, retained earnings, and cash flows of Future Corporation as of December 31, 19XX, and for the year then ending, in accordance with standards established by the American Institute of Certified Public Accountants.

The accompanying projection, and this report, were prepared for [state special purpose, for example, "the Takeover Corporation for the purpose of negotiating a buyout of the Company,"] and should not be used for any other purpose.

A compilation is limited to presenting in the form of a projection information that is the representation of management (or other responsible party) and does not include evaluation of the support for the assumptions underlying the projection. I (we) have not examined the projection and, accordingly, do not express an opinion or any other form of assurance on the accompanying statements or assumptions. Furthermore, even if [describe hypothetical assumption, for example, "the buyout is consummated"] there will usually be differences between the projected and actual results, because events and circumstances frequently do not occur as expected, and those differences may be material. I (we) have no responsibility to update this report for events and circumstances occurring after the date of this report.

EXAMPLE 11.6

The following additional paragraph should be included in statements containing a range of values:

> As described in the summary of significant assumptions, management of Future Corporation (or another responsible party) has elected to portray forecasted (or projected) [describe financial statement element(s) for which expected results of one or more assumptions fall within a range, and identify the assumptions expected to fall within a range, for example, "revenue at the amounts of $XXX,XXX and $YYY,YYY, which is based on a buyout purchase price of X% of 19XX net income and Y% of 19XY net income,"] rather than as a single point estimate. Accordingly, the accompanying forecast (projection) presents forecasted (projected) financial position, results of operations, and cash flows [describe assumption(s) expected to fall within a range, for example, "at such buyout rates"]. However, there is no assurance that the actual results will fall within the range of [describe assumption(s) expected to fall within a range, for example, "buyout rates"] presented.

EXAMPLE 11.7

An explanatory paragraph should be included when the prospective financial statements depart from AICPA presentation guidelines. For example:

> Management (or another responsible party) has elected to omit the summary of significant accounting policies required by the guidelines for presentation of a financial forecast (or projection) established by the American Institute of Certified Public Accountants. If the omitted disclosures were included in the forecast (projection), they might influence the user's conclusions about

the Company's financial position, results of operations, and cash flows for the forecasted (projected) period. Accordingly, this forecast (projection) is not designed for those who are not informed about such matters.

What is involved in an examination of prospective financial statements?

An examination (formerly called a review) of prospective financial statements evaluates:

- The preparation of the statements
- The support of the related underlying assumptions
- The conformity of the statements with AICPA presentation guidelines

The practitioner's report should contain an opinion as to whether:

- The statements are presented in conformity with the AICPA guidelines
- The underlying assumptions provide a reasonable basis for the forecast
- The underlying assumptions provide a reasonable basis for the projection in light of the hypothetical assumptions

How do I conduct an examination of prospective financial statements?

In performing an examination of prospective financial statements, the practitioner should:

Step 1: Assess inherent and control risk as well as limit his or her detection risk.

Step 2: Consider the sufficiency of external sources (such as government and industry publications) and internal sources (such as management-prepared budgets) of information supporting the underlying assumptions.

Step 3: Determine the consistency of the assumptions and the sources from which they are predicated.

Step 4: Determine the consistency of the assumptions themselves.

Step 5: Determine the reliability and consistency of the historical financial information used.

Step 6: Evaluate the preparation and presentation of the prospective financial statements:

- Does the presentation reflect the underlying assumptions?

- Are the assumptions mathematically accurate?

- Do the assumptions reflect an internally consistent pattern?

- Do the accounting principles in use reflect those expected to be in effect in the prospective period?

- Are the AICPA presentation guidelines followed?

- Is there adequate disclosure of the assumptions?

Step 7: Obtain a client representation letter to confirm that the responsible party acknowledges its responsibility for the presentation of the prospective financial statements *and* the underlying assumptions.

What is included in examination reports on prospective statements?

The accountant's report on examined prospective financial statements should include:

- An identification of the prospective financial statements presented

- A statement to the effect that an examination (including an appropriate description) was performed in accordance with standards established by the AICPA

- An opinion on the presentation of the prospective financial statements in terms of their conformity with AICPA presentation guidelines

- An opinion as to whether the underlying assumptions provide a reasonable basis for the prospective financial statements

- A warning that the prospective results may not materialize
- A statement that the accountant is under no responsibility to update his or her report for conditions occurring after the examination report is issued
- The date of the report, which should coincide with the completion of the examination procedures

EXAMPLE 11.8

The following is a sample standard report on examined forecasts:

I (we) have examined the accompanying forecasted balance sheet, statements of income, retained earnings, and cash flows of Jeanne Corporation as of (at) December 31, 19XX, and for the year then ending. My (our) examination was made in accordance with standards for an examination of a forecast established by the American Institute of Certified Public Accountants and, accordingly, included such procedures as I (we) considered necessary to evaluate both the assumptions used by management and the preparation and presentation of the forecast.

In my (our) opinion, the accompanying forecast is presented in conformity with guidelines for presentation of a forecast established by the American Institute of Certified Public Accountants, and the underlying assumptions provide a reasonable basis for management's forecast. However, there will usually be differences between the forecasted and actual results, because events and circumstances frequently do not occur as expected, and those differences may be material. I (we) have no responsibility to update this report for events and circumstances occurring after the date of this report.

EXAMPLE 11.9

The following is a sample standard report on examined projections:

I (we) have examined the accompanying projected balance sheet, statement of income, retained earnings and cash flows of Purchase Corporation as of December 31, 19XX, and for the year then ending. My (our) examination was made in accordance with standards for an examination of a projection established by the American Institute of Certified Public Accountants and, accordingly, included such procedures as I (we) considered necessary to evaluate both the assumptions used by management (or other responsible party) and the preparation and presentation of the projection.

The accompanying projection and this report were prepared for [state special purpose, for example, "the Takeover Corporation for the purpose of negotiating a buyout of the Company,"] and should not be used for any other purpose.

In my (our) opinion, the accompanying projection is presented in conformity with guidelines for presentation of a projection established by the American Institute of Certified Public Accountants, and the underlying assumptions provide a reasonable basis for management's (or other responsible party's) projection [describe the hypothetical assumption, for example, "assuming the buyout is consummated"]. However, even if [describe hypothetical assumption, for example, "the buyout is consummated"], there will usually be differences between the projected and actual results, because events and circumstances frequently do not occur as expected, and those differences may be material. I (we) have no responsibility to update this report for events and circumstances occurring after the date of this report.

When should the standard examination report be modified?

Range of Values. When prospective financial statements contain a range of values, the report should contain an additional paragraph clearly indicating this. The explanatory paragraph should be similar to the one added to compilation reports on prospective financial statements containing a range of values.

Departure from AICPA Presentation Guidelines. When the prospective financial statements contain a departure from the AICPA presentation guidelines, issue either an "except for" qualified opinion or an adverse opinion. An "except for" qualified opinion should contain an explanatory middle paragraph which describes the departure. The opinion paragraph should specifically refer to the explanatory middle paragraph.

> "In my (our) opinion, except for [describe the departure, for example, the omission of the disclosures of the reasons for significant variation in the relationship between income tax expense and pretax accounting income as discussed in the preceding paragraph,] ...

NOTE: The issuance of an adverse opinion is mandated if the prospective financial statements fail to disclose the significant underlying assumptions.

Significant Assumption Does Not Provide Reasonable Basis. When the accountant believes that one or more significant assumptions (including hypothetical assumptions) do not provide a reasonable basis for the prospective financial statements, the issuance of an adverse opinion is justified. NOTE: The examination report should include a middle paragraph which discloses all of the substantive reasons for the issuance of the adverse opinion. The opinion paragraph should specifically refer to the middle explanatory paragraph.

EXAMPLE 11.10

The following paragraph should be used in an adverse opinion report:

In my (our) opinion, the accompanying forecast is not presented in conformity with guidelines for presentation of a financial forecast established by the American Institute of Certified Public Accountants because management's (or another responsible party's) assumptions, as discussed in the preceding paragraph, do not provide a reasonable basis for management's (or another responsible party's) forecast. I (we) have no responsibility to update this report for events or circumstances occurring after the date of this report.

Scope Limitation. When the accountant is unable to perform one or more examination procedures considered necessary for the particular engagement, a disclaimer of an opinion should be expressed. The disclaimer should clearly describe the scope limitation in a separate explanatory paragraph. NOTE: The scope paragraph of the examination report should be modified to indicate the existence of a scope limitation and the explanatory middle paragraph. EXAMPLE: "Except as explained in the following paragraph, . . ." The disclaimer paragraph should also refer to the explanatory paragraph.

EXAMPLE 11.11

The following is a sample disclaimer:

Because, as described in the preceding paragraph, I am (we are) unable to evaluate management's (or another responsible party's) assumptions regarding income from an equity investee and other assumptions depend thereon, I (we) express no opinion with respect to the presentation of or the assumptions underlying the accompanying forecast. I (we) have no responsibility to update this report for events and circumstances occurring after the date of this report.

Emphasis of a Matter. The accountant may emphasize a matter in a separate paragraph while simultaneously expressing an unqualified opinion. This is accomplished in a manner similar to emphasizing a matter already disclosed in historical financial statements.

Division of Responsibility. When another auditor is involved and the principal auditor wishes to divide the responsibility for the overall examination report, the principal auditor should modify the report in a manner similar to the modifications pertinent to historical financial statements.

Agreed-Upon Procedures

When may I undertake an engagement with agreed-upon procedures?

It is permissible to undertake an engagement involving the application of agreed-upon procedures to prospective financial statements provided that:

- The practitioner is independent
- The users of the prospective financial statements have participated in determining the scope and nature of the engagement
- Only specified users will receive the report
- A summary of significant assumptions is included in the prospective financial statements

How do I report on the results of applying agreed-upon procedures?

The accountant's report on prospective financial statements subjected to agreed-upon procedures should include:

- An identification of the prospective financial statements presented
- A statement that the accountant's report is for specified users only and that the report is limited in use
- A listing of the specific procedures performed and a statement that the procedures were performed pursuant to arrangements made with the specific users of the report
- When the scope of the engagement is less than that in an examination, a statement that the

application of the agreed-upon procedures is less in scope than an audit

- A disclaimer of opinion
- A statement as to the findings of the accountant
- A warning that the prospective financial results may not materialize
- A statement that the accountant is under no responsibility to update his or her report for conditions occurring after the report is issued
- A statement that no representation is made with respect to the sufficiency of the procedures performed for the designated purpose

CAUTION: While the accountant's report issued in connection with the application of agreed-upon procedures normally expresses negative assurance, the practitioner should not express any form of negative assurance on the prospective financial statements as a whole. The negative assurance that is provided should be limited to the areas covered by the arrangements made with the specified users.

EXAMPLE 11.12

The following is a typical report after applying agreed-upon procedures:

Nick Andrews, Trustee
Generosity Incorporated

At your request, we performed the agreed-upon procedures enumerated below with respect to the forecasted balance sheet, statements of income, retained earnings and cash flows of Generosity, Incorporated as of December 31, 19XX, and for the year then ending. These procedures, which were specified by Nick Andrews, Trustee and Generosity Incorporated, were performed solely to assist you, and this report is solely for your information and should not be used by those who did not participate in determining these procedures.

a. We assisted the management of Generosity Incorporated in assembling the prospective financial statements.

b. We read the prospective financial statements for compliance of the format with the presentation guidelines established by the American Institute of Certified Public Accountants for presentation of a forecast.

c. We subjected the financial forecast to tests for mathematical and clerical accuracy.

Because the procedures described above do not constitute an examination of prospective financial statements in accordance with standards established by the American Institute of Certified Public Accountants, we do not express an opinion on whether the prospective financial statements are presented in conformity with AICPA guidelines or on whether the underlying assumptions provide a reasonable basis for the presentation.

In connection with the procedures referred to above, no matters came to our attention that caused us to believe that the format of the forecast should be modified or that the forecast is mathematically inaccurate. Had we performed additional procedures or had we made an examination of the forecast in accordance with standards established by the American Institute of Certified Public Accountants, matters might have come to our attention that would have been reported to you. Furthermore, there will usually be differences between forecasted and actual results, because events and circumstances frequently do not occur as expected, and those differences might be material. We have no responsibility to update this report for events and circumstances occurring after the date of this report.

What are the minimum items to be included in prospective financial statements?

Financial forecasts and financial projections may be in the form of either complete basic financial statements or financial statements containing the following minimum items:

- Sales or gross revenues
- Gross profit or cost of sales
- Unusual or infrequently occurring items
- Provision for income taxes
- Discontinued operations or extraordinary items
- Income from continuing operations
- Net income
- Primary and fully diluted earnings per share
- Significant changes in financial position
- Management's (or another responsible party's) intent as to what the prospective statements present, a statement indicating that management's (or another responsible party's) assumptions are predicated on facts and circumstances in existence when the statements were prepared, and a warning that the prospective results may not materialize.
- Summary of significant assumptions
- Summary of significant accounting policies

CAUTION: A partial presentation (omitting one or more of the first nine items) is not appropriate for general use. Such a partial presentation is not subject to the provisions of the *Statement on Standards for Accountants' Services on Prospective Financial Information.* Presentations omitting only the last three items are not considered partial presentations. Accordingly, in such circumstances, the practitioner must adhere to the requirements of the *Statement.*

ATTESTATION ENGAGEMENTS

What is an attestation engagement?

An *attestation engagement* is when an accountant is requested to issue or does issue a written statement that expresses a conclusion as to the reliability of a written assertion (representation) made by another party. EXAMPLES: Assertions that may require attestation engagements include:

- A client write-up computer program is capable of generating a monthly, quarterly and year-to-date payroll ledger without the need for a separate payroll module
- The value of stocks and bonds in a particular mutual fund have grown at the rate of 48% over the last two years

Attestation engagements may involve examinations, reviews or the application of agreed-upon procedures.

When should I not undertake an attestation engagement?

The practitioner should not accept an attestation engagement when requested to provide assurance on assertions that are so subjective that two or more practitioners would not derive substantially the same estimate or measurement. EXAMPLE: The practitioner should not accept an engagement to examine, review or apply agreed-upon procedures to the assertion that Floppy Corporation's accounting software is the best product available on the market.

CAUTION: Should the practitioner find that he or she cannot issue a report in connection with an attestation engagement, he or she should withdraw from the current engagement.

How do I conduct an attestation engagement?

In performing an attestation engagement, the practitioner must:

- Possess sufficient knowledge of the subject matter of the assertion.
- Only perform engagements if the assertion is capable of evaluation (or measurement) against reasonable criteria, *and* the assertion can be consistently estimated or measured.
- Be independent in fact (i.e., possess independence in mental attitude).

- Exercise due professional care.
- Plan the engagement and supervise any assistants.
- Obtain sufficient competent evidence in order to express the written conclusion.

What is contained in the attestation engagement report?

The report of the attestation engagement must include:

- An identification of the nature of the engagement and the assertion
- The accountant's conclusion as to the conformity of the assertion with the established or stated criteria used to evaluate the assertion
- A description of the accountant's significant reservations, if any, about the presentation of the assertion or the engagement itself
- When applicable, a statement limiting the use of the report if issued in connection with engagements to apply agreed-upon procedures or when the assertion has been prepared in conformity with agreed-upon criteria

Examination Engagements

What is the aim of an examination engagement?

The purpose of an examination engagement is to express a "positive" opinion as to whether the presentation of the assertion is in conformity with established or stated criteria. If necessary, the practitioner may express a qualified opinion or a disclaimer of an opinion. *NOTE*: The practitioner may modify the report in order to emphasize a matter.

The accountant's report should contain a statement limiting the use of the report to specified parties when the assertions are based on specified criteria agreed upon by the user of the report and the party making the assertion(s). If applicable, indicate that the presentation is different from that which would have resulted had criteria for general distribution been followed.

EXAMPLE 11.13

The following is the standard report for an examination engagement:

I (we) have examined the accompanying [identify the presentation of assertion(s)—for example, Statement of Investment Performance Statistics of Reap the Benefits Fund for the year ended December 31, 19YY]. My (our) examination was made in accordance with standards established by the American Institute of Certified Public Accountants and, accordingly, included such procedures as I (we) considered necessary in the circumstances.

[If desired, the practitioner may present additional paragraphs to emphasize matters pertaining to the engagement or the presentation of the assertion(s).]

In my (our) opinion, the [identify the presentation of the assertion(s), for example, Statement of Investment Performance Statistics] referred to above presents [identify assertion(s); for example, the investment performance of Reap the Benefits Fund for the year ended December 31, 19YY] in conformity with [identify stated or established criteria, or the measurement and disclosure criteria discussed in Note X].

Review Engagements

What is the objective of a review engagement?

The purpose of a review engagement is to express *negative* assurance, that is, a statement as to whether anything came to the attention of the accountant indicating that the assertions are not presented in conformity with stated or established criteria.

What should be in the review report?

The review report should include:

- A statement that a review is substantially less in scope than an examination, the objective of which is the expression of an opinion on the presentation of the assertions

- A disclaimer of opinion
- A statement limiting the use of the report to specified parties when the assertions are based on specific criteria agreed upon by the user of the report and the party making the assertions
- If applicable, a statement that the presentation is different from one which would have resulted had criteria for general distribution been followed.

EXAMPLE 11.14

The following text gives the standard report for a review:

I (we) have reviewed the accompanying [identify the presentation of assertion(s), for example, Statement of Investment Performance Statistics of Reap the Benefits Fund for the year ended December 31, 19YY]. My (our) review was conducted in accordance with standards established by the American Institute of Certified Public Accountants.

A review is substantially less in scope than an examination, the objective of which is the expression of an opinion on the [identify the presentation of assertion(s), for example, Statement of Investment Performance Statistics]. Accordingly, I (we) do not express such an opinion.

[If desired, the practitioner may present additional paragraphs to emphasize matters pertaining to the engagement or the presentation of the assertion(s).]

Based on my (our) review, nothing came to my (our) attention that caused me (us) to believe that the accompanying [identify the presentation of assertion(s), for example, Statement of Investment Performance Statistics] is not presented in conformity with [identify the established or stated criteria, for example, the measurement and disclosure criteria set forth in Note X].

Engagements to Apply Agreed-Upon Procedures

How do I report when applying agreed-upon procedures to an assertion?

The conclusions expressed upon completion of an engagement to apply agreed-upon procedures should be in the form of a summary of findings, negative assurance, or both. The practitioner's report should include:

- A statement limiting the use of the report to specified parties
- An enumeration of, or reference to, the procedures performed

EXAMPLE 11.15

The following is the standard report used when applying agreed-upon procedures to an assertion.

To Matthew Corporation and We Deliver Dividends Fund

I (we) have applied the procedures enumerated below to the accompanying [identify the presentation of assertion(s), for example, Statement of Investment Performance Statistics of We Deliver Dividends Fund for the year ended August 31, 19BB]. The procedures, which were agreed to by Matthew Corporation and We Deliver Dividends Fund, were performed solely to assist you in evaluating [identify the assertion(s), for example, the investment performance of We Deliver Dividends Fund]. This report is intended solely for your information and should not be used by those who did not participate in determining the procedures.

[Include a paragraph to enumerate or refer to the procedures and findings.]

These agreed-upon procedures are substantially less in scope than an examination, the objective of which is the expression of an opinion on the [identify the presentation of assertion(s), for example, Statement of Investment Performance Statistics]. Accordingly, I (we) do not express such an opinion.

Based on the application of the procedures referred to above, nothing came to my (our) attention that caused me (us) to believe that the accompanying [identify the presentation of assertions, for example, Statement of Investment Performance Statistics] is not presented in conformity with [identify the established, stated, or agreed-upon criteria, for example, the measurement and disclosure criteria set forth in Note X]. Had I (we) performed additional procedures or had I (we) made an examination of the [identify the presentation of assertion(s), for example, Statement of Investment Performance Statistics], other matters might have come to my (our) attention that would have been reported to you.

PERSONAL FINANCIAL STATEMENTS INCLUDED IN WRITTEN PERSONAL FINANCIAL PLANS

What are my responsibilities when personal financial statements are included in a financial plan?

When the accountant prepares personal financial statements that are included in a written personal financial plan, the accountant may:

- Follow the compilation standards applicable to compilation engagements involving historical basic financial statements

- Issue the compilation report specified in *Statement on Standards for Accounting and Review Services 6.*

In order to make use of the exemption provided in SSARS 6, the accountant must reach an understanding with the client that the personal financial statements:

- Are prepared only to assist in the development of goals and objectives pertaining to the client's personal finances
- Will not be used in securing credit.

CAUTION: If the accountant, during the engagement, discovers that the personal financial statements *are* to be used to obtain credit or for some purpose other than to develop a financial strategy, the accountant may not utilize the exemption from SSARS 1.

EXAMPLE 11.16

The following is the standard report for personal financial statements in financial plans based on exemption from SSARS 1:

The accompanying Statement of Financial Condition of Karen B, as of December 31, 19XX, was prepared solely to help you develp your personal financial plan. Accordingly, it may be incomplete or contain other departures from generally accepted accounting principles and should not be used to obtain credit or for any other purposes other than developing your financial plan. I (we) have not audited, reviewed, or compiled the statement.

What must I do when examining personal financial statements?

Engagements to examine personal financial statements are subject to the standards applicable to examinations of historical financial statements. Accordingly, the auditor must gather sufficient competent evidential matter to form the basis of his or her opinion. While the accountant normally expresses the opinion on a statement of financial condition, the accountant may report on:

- A statement of changes in net worth
- Comparative financial statements

NOTE: If warranted, the practitioner may express a qualified opinion, an adverse opinion or a disclaimer of opinion on personal financial statements.

EXAMPLE 11.17

The following is the standard report for personal financial statements.

I (we) have examined the statement of financial condition of Marc and Susan Janes as of December 31, 19XX, and the related statement of changes in net worth for the year then ended. My (our) examination was made in accordance with generally accepted auditing standards and, accordingly, included such tests of the accounting records and such other auditing procedures as I (we) considered necessary in the circumstances.

In my (our) opinion, the financial statements referred to above present fairly the financial condition of Marc and Susan Janes as of December 31, 19XX, and the changes in their net worth for the year then ended, in conformity with generally accepted accounting principles applied on a basis consistent with that of the preceding year.

REPORTING ON COMPARATIVE STATEMENTS

What are the reporting requirements for comparative statements?

Guidance for reporting on audited comparative financial statements is provided in *Statement on Auditing Standards 58*.

The practitioner may report on financial statements of one or more prior periods that are presented with financial statements of the current period.

If the accountant is the *continuing auditor* having performed the examination of the current period and immediately preceding period(s), he or she has the responsibility of updating the report on the financial statements of the prior period(s).

NOTES: In updating the audit report, the practitioner should either re-express a previous opinion or express an opinion different from the one previously expressed. The latter circumstance may arise when, for example, prior-period financial statements are subsequently restated.

EXAMPLE 11.18

The following is the text of a continuing auditor's standard report on comparative financial statements.

Independent Auditor's Report

I (we) have audited the accompanying balance sheets of M Corporation as of (at) December 31, 19X2 and 19X1, and the related statements of income, retained earnings, and cash flows for the years then ended. These financial statements are the responsibility of the Company's management. My (our) responsibility is to express an opinion on these financial statements based on my (our) audits.

I (we) conducted my (our) audits in accordance with generally accepted auditing standards. Those standards require that I (we) plan and perform the audit to obtain reasonable assurance about whether the financial statements are free of material misstatement. An audit includes examining, on a test basis, evidence supporting the amounts and disclosures in the financial statements. An audit also includes assessing the accounting principles used and significant estimates made by management, as well as evaluating the overall financial statement presentation. I (we) believe that my (our) audits provide a reasonable basis for my (our) opinion.

In my (our) opinion, the financial statements referred to above present fairly, in all material respects, the financial position of M Corporation as of (at) December 31, 19X2

and 19X1, and the results of its operations
and its cash flows for the years then ended
in conformity with generally accepted accounting principles.

How may the continuing auditor's standard report be modified?

The practitioner may issue a report that contains
differing opinions. EXAMPLE: A qualified opinion
on the current year's financial statements and an
unqualified opinion on the prior year's financial
statements.

If the practitioner deems it necessary to modify
the opinion expressed on prior-period financial
statements, he or she should include an explanatory
paragraph (preceding the opinion paragraph) in the
updated report. The explanatory paragraph should
disclose:

- Date of the original audit report
- Type of the original report (e.g., unqualified, qualified)
- Reasons for the change in the type of report
- Statement that the updated report is different from the report previously expressed

EXAMPLE 11.19

The following presents the framework for the
explanatory paragraph added when the standard
report needs to be modified:

In my (our) report dated April 3, 19X2, I
(we) expressed an opinion that the 19X1
financial statements did not present fairly
financial position, results of operations, and
cash flows in conformity with generally accepted accounting principles because of two
departures from such principles: (1) the
Company carried its property, plant, and
equipment at appraisal values, and provided for depreciation on the basis of such
values, and (2) the Company did not provide
for deferred income taxes with respect to

differences between income for financial reporting purposes and taxable income. As described in Note X, the Company has changed its method of accounting for these items and restated its 19X1 financial statements to conform with generally accepted accounting principles. Accordingly, my (our) present opinion on the 19X1 financial statements, as presented herein, is different from that expressed in my (our) previous report.

When may I reissue a report on prior-period statements?

If a client requests that a predecessor auditor reissue a report on prior-period financial statements, he or she must first:

- Read the current-period financial statements.
- Compare the original prior-period financial statements with the statements to be presented.
- Obtain a representation letter from the successor auditor. *NOTE*: The representation letter should disclose events and circumstances that came to the successor's attention which might have a significant effect on the predecessor's report or on the prior-period financial statements.
- If events and circumstances arose after the original report was issued, perform inquiry and other necessary procedures.

NOTE: The date of a reissued report should coincide with the date of the original report. However, if the predecessor revises his or her report, or if the financial statements of the prior period need to be restated, the practitioner should utilize dual dating in the report.

What if the predecessor auditor's report is not with the successor's?

When the report of the predecessor auditor is not presented with the report of the successor auditor, add the following to the introductory paragraph of the successor auditor's report:

- A statement that another auditor audited the financial statements of the prior period(s)
- The date of the predecessor's report
- A statement as to the type of opinion expressed by the predecessor
- If the predecessor's report was not standard, a statement of the substantive reasons for the type of opinion

EXAMPLE 11.20

When the predecessor modified his or her report, the introductory paragraph of the successor's report may contain the following additional wording:

> The financial statements of KJB Company as of December 31, 19X1 were audited by other auditors whose report, dated April 1, 19X2, on those statements included an explanatory paragraph that described the litigation discussed in Note X to the financial statements.

How do I compile and review comparative statements?

If a client requests that the practitioner report on comparative financial statements of a nonpublicly traded entity, the practitioner should be guided by the provisions of SSARS 2. Accordingly, the accountant must reissue or update the report issued in connection with the financial statements of the prior period.

SAME LEVEL OF SERVICE: When a continuing accountant performs the same level of service for each of the comparative periods (e.g., compilation for all periods or review for all periods), the accountant's report is modified by merely including the comparative dates.

HIGHER LEVEL OF SERVICE: When the continuing accountant is requested to step up the level of service, the resulting report must be modified to reflect the levels of service provided and the responsibility the practitioner is taking.

Guideline: If the prior period involved a compilation and the current period involves a review, the report should contain the standard wording of a review report for the current period and the following additional paragraph as shown in Example 11.21:

EXAMPLE 11.21

The accompanying 19X1 financial statements of SJD Corporation were compiled by me (us). A compilation is limited to presenting in the form of financial statements information that is the representation of management (owners). I (we) have not audited or reviewed the 19X1 financial statements and, accordingly, do not express an opinion or any other form of assurance on them.

LOWER LEVEL OF SERVICE: The accountant may be involved in a step-down in the level of service provided. Accordingly, the accountant may perform an audit with respect to the financial statements of one period and a review or compilation in a subsequent period.

In a step-down *from an audit to a compilation or a review*, the practitioner should issue the appropriate compilation or review report with respect to the statements of the current period. An additional paragraph should:

- Describe the responsibility assumed for the prior periods
- Indicate the date of the previous report
- State the type of opinion expressed in the audit report
- State that subsequent to the date of the audit report no additional auditing procedures have been performed

Similarly, if an engagement involves a step-down *from a review to a compilation*, the comparative report should contain the standard compilation report and an additional paragraph that:

- Describes responsibility for the prior period
- Indicates the date of the review report
- Provides the limited assurance normally expressed in a standard review report
- States that no additional review procedures have been performed subsequent to the date of the review report

EXAMPLE 11.22

Sample wording to be added to the comparative report when there is a step-down to a compilation might be:

The accompanying 19X1 financial statements of SJD Company were previously reviewed by me (us), and my (our) report dated April 1, 19X2, stated that I was (we were) not aware of any material modifications that should be made to those statements in order for them to be in conformity with generally accepted accounting principles. I (we) have not performed any procedures in connection with that review engagement after the date of my (our) report on the 19X1 financial statements.

SPECIAL REPORTS

What is a special report?

SAS 14 states that a special report is an auditor's report issued in connection with any of the following:

- Financial statements based on a comprehensive basis of accounting other than GAAP
- Specified elements, accounts, or items contained in a basic set of financial statements
- Compliance with contractual agreements or regulations related to financial statements subjected to an audit
- Financial information included in prescribed forms

What constitutes a comprehensive basis of accounting other than GAAP?

A comprehensive basis of accounting other than generally accepted accounting principles includes:

- The cash basis of accounting, which recognizes income when collected and expenses when paid

- The modified cash basis of accounting, which recognizes income when collected and expenses when paid, except for the capitalization of fixed assets and the recognition of depreciation expense, which is a noncash item

- A basis of accounting that follows the requirements of a regulatory agency

- Any basis of accounting that uses a definite set of criteria having substantial support, such as the price-level basis of accounting

NOTE: With respect to financial statements based on a comprehensive basis of accounting other than GAAP, an auditor may perform an examination in conformity with generally accepted auditing standards.

What should a special report include?

The report issued at the conclusion of the audit engagement should include:

- An identification of the financial statements examined and a statement as to whether the examination was performed in accordance with generally accepted auditing standards.

- An opinion on the fairness of presentation of the financial statements. "Fairness of presentation" is considered in light of the comprehensive basis of accounting used. The opinion should specifically refer to the consistent application of the comprehensive basis of accounting.

An additional paragraph should:

- Identify (or refer to the note to the financial statements that identifies) the basis of accounting utilized.

- Refer to the note to the financial statement that

describes the difference between the basis of accounting used and GAAP.

• State that the financial statements are not intended to be in conformity with GAAP.

RECOMMENDATION: Change the titles of financial statements based on a comprehensive basis of accounting other than GAAP. EXAMPLE: In the cash basis of accounting, use "statement of assets and liabilities arising from cash transactions" instead of "balance sheet."

EXAMPLE 11.23

The following is a sample report for cash basis financial statements:

I (we) have examined the statement of assets and liabilities arising from cash transactions of Nickel and Dime Corporation as of (at) December 31, 19XX, and the related statement of revenue collected and expenses paid for the year then ended. My (our) examination was made in accordance with generally accepted auditing standards and, accordingly, included such tests of the accounting records and such other auditing procedures considered necessary in the circumstances.

As described in Note X to the financial statements, it is the Corporation's policy to prepare its financial statements on the basis of cash receipts and disbursements; consequently, certain revenue and the related assets are recognized when received rather than when earned, and certain expenses are recognized when paid rather than when the obligation is incurred. Accordingly, the accompanying financial statements are not intended to be in conformity with generally accepted accounting principles.

In my (our) opinion, the financial statements referred to above present fairly the assets and liabilities arising from cash transactions of Nickel and Dime Corporation as of (at) December 31, 19XX, and the revenue collected and expenses paid during the year then ended, on the basis of accounting described in Note X, which has been applied in a manner consistent with that of the preceding year.

What about the statement of cash flows?

The presentation of a statement of cash flows is required under GAAP. Accordingly, when financial statements are intended to be in conformity with a comprehensive basis of accounting other than GAAP, a statement of cash flows need not be presented.

Specific Elements, Accounts, or Items in a Basic Set of Financial Statements

What should I do when asked to evaluate specific elements or items?

With respect to specific elements, accounts or items (such as rentals, royalties, and the provision for income tax expense) contained in a basic set of financial statements, an accountant may undertake an engagement to:

- Express an opinion
- Apply agreed-upon procedures

What is included in a report on specific items?

The report issued in connection with an engagement to express an opinion on specified elements, accounts or items of a financial statement should include:

- An identification of the specific elements, accounts, or items subjected to the auditor's examination
- A statement (if applicable) that the basic financial statements were examined and whether the examination was performed in accordance with generally accepted auditing standards
- The date of the audit report

- If the basic financial statements were not examined, a statement as to whether the examination of the specified element, account or item was performed in accordance with generally accepted auditing standards
- An identification of the basis on which the elements, items or accounts are presented
- The source of significant interpretations represented by the client
- An opinion (including, if applicable, a reference to consistency) on the fairness of presentation of the specified element, account or item

EXAMPLE 11.24

The following is a sample report for a specific element in the basic set of financial statements, namely the adequacy of provision for income taxes.

I (we) have examined the financial statements of Franchise Corporation for the year ended October 31, 19XX, and have issued my (our) report thereon dated December 15, 19XY. My (our) examination was made in accordance with generally accepted auditing standards and, accordingly, included such tests of the accounting records and such other auditing procedures considered necessary in the circumstances.

In the course of my (our) examination, I (we) examined the provision for federal, state and city income taxes for the year ended October 31, 19XX, included in the Company's financial statements referred to in the preceding paragraph. I (we) also reviewed the federal, state and city income tax returns filed by the Company that are subject to examination by the respective taxing authorities.

In my (our) opinion, the Company has paid or has provided adequate accruals in the financial statements referred to above for the payment of all federal, state and city income taxes, and has provided for related deferred income taxes, applicable to fiscal 19XX, and prior fiscal years, that could be reasonably estimated at the time I (we) examined the financial statements of Franchise Corporation for the year ended October 31, 19XX.

May agreed-upon procedures be used on specific items?

An engagement to apply agreed-upon procedures to specific elements, accounts, or items is more limited in scope than an examination that leads to the expression of an opinion. Accordingly, the practitioner should issue a disclaimer of opinion.

CAUTION: Engagements involving the application of agreed-upon procedures may be accepted provided that:

- An understanding between the accountant and client has been reached regarding the specific procedures to be performed
- The accountant's report is to be distributed only to the named parties involved

What should the report include when agreed-upon procedures are used?

The accountant's report issued in connection with the application of agreed-upon procedures should include:

- An identification of the specified elements, accounts, or items which were subjected to the agreed-upon procedures
- The intended report distribution
- A list of the specific procedures performed
- A statement of the accountant's findings
- A disclaimer of opinion
- A statement that no association should be made between the report and the financial statements of the entity

NOTE: The following statements may be added:

"In connection with the procedures referred to above, no matters came to my (our) attention that caused me (us) to believe that the [list the specified elements, accounts or items] should be adjusted."

"Had I (we) performed additional procedures or had I (we) made an examination of the financial statements in accordance with generally accepted auditing standards, matters might have come to my (our) attention that would have been reported to you."

Compliance With Contracts or Regulations Relating to Audited Financial Statements

What are my responsibilities regarding compliance with contracts?

Clients sometimes request an independent accountant to issue a report concerning compliance with contractual agreements or regulations. EXAMPLE: A report on compliance with the terms, provisions and covenants of bond indentures. Such a report should express the requisite negative assurance either in a separate report or as part of the audit report on the basic financial statements.

In either reporting situation, the report should specifically state that the negative assurance is being expressed in connection with the examination (of the financial statements).

NOTE: The practitioner has the option of stating that the "examination was not directed primarily toward obtaining knowledge of such noncompliance."

What should the separate report contain?

If the accountant elects to issue a separate report, the following items should be included:

- A statement that the financial statements were examined
- The date of the audit report
- An indication as to whether the examination was made in accordance with generally accepted auditing standards

EXAMPLE 11.25

The following sample (separate) report deals with compliance with contractual provisions:

> I (We) have examined the balance sheet of Matthew Corporation as of December 31, 19XX, and the related statements of income, retained earnings, and cash flows for the year then ended, and have issued my (our) report thereon dated March 3, 19XY. My (Our) examination was made in accordance with generally accepted auditing standards and, accordingly, included such tests of the accounting records and such other auditing procedures considered necessary in the circumstances.
>
> In connection with my (our) examination, nothing came to my (our) attention that caused me (us) to believe that the Company was not in compliance with any of the terms, covenants, provisions, or conditions of Section XX to YY, inclusive, of the Indenture dated June 26, 19XW, with Moneypenny Bank. However, it should be noted that my (our) examination was not directed primarily toward obtaining knowledge of such noncompliance.

NOTE: If the practitioner issues negative assurance as part of the audit report, he or she should add the second paragraph of the sample report above to the standard audit report.

Financial Information Included in Prescribed Forms

What are the requirements for financial information in prescribed forms?

Accountants often accept engagements to audit financial information included in prescribed forms. EXAMPLE: The accountant may be requested to certify the financial information presented in forms prescribed by the United States Government for the reimbursement of expenses paid by health care facilities.

In such circumstances, the practitioner must be satisfied that the form prescribed for the auditor's report adheres to relevant reporting standards. When the prescribed audit report contains inappropriate or unacceptable wording, the practitioner should either modify the wording or attach a separate report that conforms to the relevant reporting standards.

CHAPTER 12

STATEMENTS ON AUDITING STANDARDS

This chapter provides the practitioner with a handy reference guide to the major practical provisions of the Statements on Auditing Standards (SAS) not previously covered.

Statements on Auditing Standards set forth authoritative guidance for properly conducting an audit. In applying the substantive material of these Statements, the practitioner must exercise professional judgment and due professional care.

SAS 1—Codification of Auditing Standards and Procedures

This statement covers the material contained in Statements on Auditing Procedures 33 through 54. While much of SAS 1 has been superseded by subsequent pronouncements, the information presented below remains in effect.

What are subsequent events?

Subsequent events are events that occur after the balance sheet date but before the issuance of the financial statements and the auditor's report. They provide additional information about conditions or circumstances:

- Existing at or before the balance sheet date (Type I)
- Arising after the balance sheet date (Type II)

How should subsequent events be handled?

• Type I subsequent events require adjustment of the financial statements.

• Type II subsequent events may require disclosure in the financial statements in order to prevent readers from being misled.

EXAMPLE 12.1

The following is a Type I subsequent event:

A client has advised you that one of their accounts receivable is deemed to be uncollectible as of the balance sheet date. Accordingly, the client has made an adjusting entry to record the bad debt expense and to remove the account receivable from the subsidiary ledger. However, while examining the cash receipts of the period subsequent to the balance sheet date you find a partial collection of the receivable. Accordingly, the practitioner should suggest to the client that an adjusting entry be made to properly reflect the receivable at its net realizable value.

EXAMPLE 12.2

The following is a Type II subsequent event:

Fifteen days after the end of the year, a client's building is completely destroyed in a fire. Since the building was in existence as of the balance sheet date, no adjusting entry is necessary. In order to prevent the readers from being misled, the casualty should be disclosed in the notes to the financial statements.

How do I handle the subsequent discovery of facts existing at the date of the auditor's report?

Subsequent discovery of facts existing at the date of the auditor's report differs from subsequent events in that the audit report is already issued in the case of subsequent discovery of facts.

In such a case, the auditor should:

- Determine the reliability of the facts and verify their existence as of the date of the audit report

- Ascertain whether the audit report would have been affected had the facts been known at the date of the report

- Determine whether readers of the financial statements might be materially influenced

- Advise the client that disclosure is necessary through revised financial statements

The audit report may need to be modified, especially if the client refuses to make the necessary disclosures. In such circumstances, the practitioner should withdraw from the engagement and take steps to recall the financial statements.

SAS 2—Reports on Audited Financial Statements

Superseded by SAS 58.

SAS 3—The Effects of EDP on the Auditor's Study and Evaluation of Internal Control

Superseded by SAS 48.

SAS 4—Quality Control Considerations for a Firm of Independent Auditors

Superseded by SAS 25.

SAS 5—The Meaning of "Present Fairly in Conformity with Generally Accepted Accounting Principles" in the Independent Auditor's Report

The phrase "present fairly" contained in the opinion paragraph of the auditor's report should be applied within the framework of generally accepted accounting principles.

When is a principle, method, or practice in accordance with GAAP?

In deciding whether an accounting principle, practice or method is in conformity with GAAP, the practitioner should consider whether:

1. The accounting principle, practice or method has general acceptance. To determine general acceptance, the auditor should refer to:
- APB Opinions
- FASB Statements and Interpretations
- AICPA Research Bulletins
- Sources of generally accepted accounting principles, such as AICPA Industry Audit Guides and AICPA Statements of Position. EXAMPLE: The accelerated cost recovery system of depreciation, used for tax purposes, is not considered generally accepted for financial statement purposes, since the estimated useful life of the asset is not considered; rather, shorter recovery periods are used.

2. The accounting principle, practice or method is appropriate in the circumstances. The rule of thumb is "substance over form." EXAMPLE: If a client's lease (of machinery) provides for a bargain purchase price (e.g., $1) at the expiration of the lease, the lease should be treated as a capital lease, not an operating lease.

3. The financial statements are informative. Accordingly, the accountant must gain assurance that the financial statements include all of the disclosures, including notes, necessary to prevent the reader from being misled.

4. The financial statements are classified and summarized.

5. The information contained in the financial statements is presented within limits. The cost/benefit relationship should prevail. As such, the benefit of presenting the information must exceed the cost of providing it.

SAS 6—Related Party Transactions

Superseded by SAS 45.

SAS 7—Communication Between Predecessor and Successor Auditor

What should I do as a successor auditor?

Before undertaking an audit of a prospective client whose financial statements were examined by a predecessor auditor who has resigned or one whose services have been terminated, the successor auditor should communicate with the predecessor in order to determine if there are any reasons why the engagement should not be accepted.

REQUIREMENT: The successor auditor must obtain the prospective client's permission to contact the predecessor, and the prospective client should authorize the predecessor to respond promptly and fully.

The successor should seek to identify any facts that bear on the integrity of management. Accordingly, the successor is interested in:

- Reasons for the change in auditors
- Any disagreements the predecessor may have had with the client regarding application of generally accepted accounting principles and/or generally accepted auditing standards
- Any phases of the predecessor's audit which required an unusually large amount of time

In their communication before acceptance of the engagement, the successor may request that the predecessor make available information contained in the workpapers of prior engagements. If the client authorizes the release of this information, the predecessor should promptly comply with the request.

SAS 8—Other Information in Documents Containing Audited Financial Statements

When other information is presented in client-prepared documents containing audited financial statements (e.g., annual reports), the auditor's responsibility is to read *all* of the information contained in the document. In doing so, the practitioner's objective is to identify material inconsistencies between the information in the document and the information presented in the audited financial statements.

The auditor has the responsibility of notifying the client of any material inconsistencies. The auditor should request that the client appropriately modify the "other information."

If the client refuses to do so, the auditor should consider modifying the audit report by adding an explanatory paragraph which describes the material inconsistency. The inclusion of this explanatory paragraph generally does not affect the opinion expressed on the financial statements.

CAUTION: Depending upon the materiality of the inconsistency, the auditor may consider withholding the use of the audit report in the document and/or withdrawing from the current engagement.

SAS 9—The Effect of an Internal Audit Function on the Scope of the Independent Auditor's Examination

What is required of me as an independent auditor?

The work performed by a client's *internal* auditors may affect the nature, extent and timing of the *independent* auditor's procedures. Internal auditors may provide direct assistance to the independent auditor. Accordingly, the practitioner should review the competency and objectivity of the internal auditors as well as evaluate their work.

• *Competency* of the internal auditors may be evaluated in light of their education and work experience.

• In judging *objectivity*, the independent auditor should consider the organizational level to which the internal audit reports are sent. Furthermore, the recommendations contained in the reports is an index of objectivity.

• In *evaluating the work* of the internal auditors,

the practitioner should test check the work performed by the internal auditors. The independent auditor should *never* subordinate his or her judgment to that of the internal auditors.

CAUTION: The practitioner should never allow internal auditors to gather evidence which the independent auditor cannot corroborate. EXAMPLE: The practitioner should not allow the internal auditors to prepare and mail the accounts receivable confirmations. It would, however, be acceptable for the internal auditors to prepare a listing of the receivable balances in the subsidiary ledger. The independent auditor could easily verify the balances by inspecting the subsidiary ledger.

SAS 10—Limited Review of Interim Financial Information

Superseded by SAS 24 and later superseded by SAS 36.

SAS 11—Using the Work of a Specialist

How is a specialist used?

During the course of an examination, the independent auditor may need to employ a specialist. A specialist has expertise in an area other than accounting or auditing. Matters which might require the use of a specialist include:

- Valuation of assets. EXAMPLE: A gemologist may be consulted in valuing inventories consisting of diamonds or other precious stones.

- Determination of physical characteristics. EXAMPLE: A specialist may be consulted in connection with mineral reserves.

- Determination or verification of amounts derived through use of specialized methods and techniques. EXAMPLE: An actuary may be consulted in order to corroborate a client's accrual for contributions to a defined benefit pension plan.

- Interpretation of technical requirements, regulations or agreements. EXAMPLE: An attorney may be consulted in connection with contracts or other legal documents.

What must be considered before using a specialist?

If the auditor wants to use the services of a specialist, he or she should:

- Consider the professional competency and reputation of the specialist
- Weigh the relationship of the specialist to the client. (Independence of the specialist from the client is not required, but lack of independence warrants additional auditing procedures)
- Understand the accounting assumptions and data being used by the specialist

NOTE: It is the independent auditor's responsibility to determine whether the findings of the specialist support the representations or assertions made by management.

Does using a specialist affect reporting requirements?

If the findings of the specialist support the representations or assertions made by management, the auditor could appropriately express an unqualified opinion. In such circumstances, the auditor should not refer to the use of the specialist.

The auditor may make reference to and identify the specialist if he or she decides to either:

- Qualify his or her opinion because the findings of the specialist do not corroborate the representations or assertions made by management
- Disclaim an opinion because of the inability to obtain sufficient competent evidential matter regarding a material client representation or assertion. EXAMPLE: when a difference of opinion exists among specialists and the auditor cannot perform alternate auditing procedures

SAS 12—Inquiry of a Client's Lawyer Concerning Litigation, Claims, and Assessments

The independent auditor must obtain sufficient competent evidential matter concerning the existence of a possible loss from litigation, claims, and assessments. In this connection, he or she should identify the period in which the underlying cause occurred, the probability of an unfavorable outcome, and an estimate of the potential loss.

The auditing procedures to be performed by the independent auditor include:

- Inquiry of management personnel
- Obtaining a client-prepared description of litigation, claims, and assessments
- Examination of documents in the possession of the client
- Obtaining written assurance from management as to the disclosure and proper accounting of all unasserted claims
- Reading the minutes of the board of directors meetings
- Reading contracts, loan agreements, leases, and correspondence with governmental agencies and legal counsel

How do I corroborate information furnished by the client?

The auditor's primary means of corroborating information provided by the client concerning litigation, claims, and assessments is a letter of audit inquiry sent to the client's legal counsel. The client's legal counsel, after obtaining the permission of the client to respond, is expected to respond promptly and fully. The client's lawyer, however, may limit his or her response to the matters to which he or she has devoted substantial attention.

EXAMPLE 12.3

(Prepared on client's letterhead—See Note A)

Date (See Note B)

(Name of lawyer)
(Address of lawyer)

Dear . . . . :

In connection with an examination of our financial statements at (balance sheet date) and for the (period) then ended, management of the Company has prepared, and furnished to our auditors (name and address of auditors), a description and evaluation of certain contingencies, including those set forth below involving matters with respect to which you have been engaged and to which you have devoted substantive attention on behalf of the Company in the form of legal consultation or representation. These contingencies are regarded by management of the Company as material for this purpose (management may indicate a materiality limit if an understanding has been reached with the auditor). Your response should include matters that existed at (balance sheet date) and during the period from that date to the date of your response.

Pending or Threatened Litigation
(excluding unasserted claims)

> [Ordinarily the information would include the following: (1) the nature of the litigation, (2) the progress of the case to date, (3) how management is responding or intends to respond to the litigation (for example, to contest the case vigorously or to seek an out-of-court settlement), and (4) an evaluation of the likelihood of an unfavorable outcome and an estimate, if one can be made, of the amount or range of potential loss.]

Please furnish to our auditors such explanation, if any, that you consider necessary to supplement the foregoing information, including an explanation of those matters as to which your views may differ from those stated and an identification of the omission of any pending or threatened litigation, claims, and assessments or a statement that the list of such matters is complete.

Unasserted Claims and Assessments

(considered by management to be probable of assertion, and that, if asserted, would have at least a reasonable possibility of an unfavorable outcome)

> [Ordinarily management's information would include the following: (1) the nature of the matter, (2) how management intends to respond if the claim is asserted, and (3) an evaluation of the likelihood of an unfavorable outcome and an estimate, if one can be made, of the amount or range of potential loss.]

Please furnish to our auditors such explanation, if any, that you consider necessary to supplement the foregoing information, including an explanation of those matters as to which your views may differ from those stated.

We understand that whenever, in the course of performing legal services for us with respect to a matter recognized to involve an unasserted possible claim or assessment that may call for financial statement disclosure, if you have formed a professional conclusion that we should disclose or consider disclosure concerning such possible claim or assessment, as a matter of professional responsibility to us, you will so advise us and will consult with us concerning the question of such disclosure and the applicable requirements of Statement of Financial Accounting Standards No. 5. Please specifically confirm to our auditors that our understanding is correct.

Please specifically identify the nature of and reasons for any limitation on your response.

[The auditor may request the client to inquire about additional matters, for example, unpaid or unbilled charges or specified information on certain contractually assumed obligations of the company, such as guarantees of indebtedness of others.]

Very truly yours,

(Authorized signature for client)

NOTES TO USER:

(A) Auditors should carefully consider the provisions of SAS No. 12 in drafting this letter.

(B) Sending of this letter should be timed so that the lawyer's response is dated as close to the auditor's opinion date as practicable. However, the auditor and client should consider early mailing of a draft inquiry as a convenience for the lawyer in preparing a timely response to the formal inquiry letter.

What if the lawyer does not respond to the inquiry?

The lawyer's refusal to respond to the letter of audit inquiry is tantamount to a scope limitation sufficient to preclude the issuance of an unqualified opinion.

SAS 13—Reports on a Limited Review of Interim Financial Information

Superseded by SAS 24 and subsequently superseded by SAS 36.

SAS 14—Special Reports

See Chapter 11.

SAS 15—Reports on Comparative Financial Statements

Superseded by SAS 58.

SAS 16—The Independent Auditor's Responsibility for the Detection of Errors or Irregularities

Superseded by SAS 53.

SAS 17—Illegal Acts by Clients

Superseded by SAS 54.

SAS 18—Unaudited Replacement Cost Information

Withdrawn by the Auditing Standards Board.

SAS 19—Client Representations

What type of representations do I need from the client?

At the conclusion of an audit, the independent auditor must obtain from the client a representation letter confirming oral representations or assertions made by the client during the course of the audit. The representation letter, to be addressed to the auditor, is usually signed by the chief executive officer and chief financial officer. It should be dated as of the conclusion of the fieldwork.

What should the letter of representation include?

The items included in the client representation letter will vary depending on the engagement. Some commonly included items are:

- Management's acknowledgment of its responsibility for the fair presentation in the financial statements
- A statement that management has made all financial records and data available
- An assertion that the minutes of all board and stockholder meetings are complete and have been made available
- A statement that the financial statements do not contain errors and that there are no unrecorded transactions

- Information pertaining to related party transactions
- Information pertaining to Type I and Type II subsequent events
- Information concerning irregularities perpetrated by management and other employees
- Any plans or intentions affecting the carrying value of assets
- Disclosure of compensating balances or other cash-restricting arrangements
- Information pertaining to inventory valuation, such as reduction of obsolete inventory to its net realizable value
- Satisfactory title to assets, any liens, or collateral agreements pertaining to such assets
- Losses from sales or purchase commitments
- Violations of law which warrant disclosure in the financial statements
- The proper accounting of gain or loss contingencies
- Information pertaining to litigation, claims, and assessments

Can a representation letter replace audit procedures?

While the management representation letter is a form of evidential matter, it is not a substitute for the application of audit procedures.

CAUTION: Management's refusal to issue the representation letter to the auditor is tantamount to a scope limitation sufficient to preclude the issuance of an unqualified opinion. The refusal to issue the representation letter ordinarily will lead the auditor to doubt the integrity of management. As a result, the auditor should reconsider his or her ability to rely on other management assertions or representations. This will usually result in a disclaimer of opinion.

EXAMPLE 12.4

ILLUSTRATIVE REPRESENTATION LETTER

(Prepared on client's letterhead)

(Date of Auditor's Report)

(To Independent Auditor)

In connection with your examination of the (identification of financial statements) of (name of client) as of (date) and for the (period of examination) for the purpose of expressing an opinion as to whether the (consolidated) financial statements present fairly the financial position, results of operations, and cash flows of (name of client) in conformity with generally accepted accounting principles (other comprehensive basis of accounting), we confirm, to the best of our knowledge and belief, the following representations made to you during your examination.

1. We are responsible for the fair presentation in the (consolidated) financial statements of financial position, results of operations, and cash flows in conformity with generally accepted accounting principles (other comprehensive basis of accounting).

2. We have made available to you all—

   a. Financial records and related data.

   b. Minutes of the meetings of stockholders, directors, and committees of directors, or summaries of actions of recent meetings for which minutes have not yet been prepared.

3. There have been no—

   a. Irregularities involving management or employees who have significant roles in the internal control structure.

b. Irregularities involving other employees that could have a material effect on the financial statements.

c. Communications from regulatory agencies concerning noncompliance with, or deficiencies in, financial reporting practices that could have a material effect on the financial statements.

4. We have no plans or intentions that may materially affect the carrying value or classification of assets and liabilities.

5. The following have been properly recorded or disclosed in the financial statements:

a. Related party transactions and related amounts receivable or payable, including sales, purchases, loans, transfers, leasing arrangements, and guarantees.

b. Capital stock repurchase options or agreements or capital stock reserved for options, warrants, conversions, or other requirements.

c. Arrangements with financial institutions involving compensating balances or other arrangements involving restrictions on cash balances and line-of-credit or similar arrangements.

d. Agreements to repurchase assets previously sold.

6. There are no—

a. Violations or possible violations of laws or regulations whose effects should be considered for disclosure in the financial statements or as a basis for recording a loss contingency.

b. Other material liabilities or gain or loss contingencies that are required to be accrued or disclosed by Statement of Financial Accounting Standards No. 5 [AC section C59].

7. There are no unasserted claims or assessments that our lawyer has advised us are probable of assertion and must be disclosed in accordance with Statement of Financial Accounting Standards No. 5 [AC section C59].

8. There are no material transactions that have not been properly recorded in the accounting records underlying the financial statements.

9. Provision, when material, has been made to reduce excess or obsolete inventories to their estimated net realizable value.

10. The company has satisfactory title to all owned assets, and there are no liens or encumbrances on such assets nor has any asset been pledged.

11. Provision has been made for any material loss to be sustained in the fulfillment of, or from inability to fulfill, any sales commitments.

12. Provision has been made for any material loss to be sustained as a result of purchase commitments for inventory quantities in excess of normal requirements or at prices in excess of the prevailing market prices.

13. We have complied with all aspects of contractual agreements that would have a material effect on the financial statements in the event of noncompliance.

14. No events have occurred subsequent to the balance sheet date that would require adjustment to, or disclosure in, the financial statements.

....
(Name of Chief Executive
Officer and Title)

....
(Name of Chief Financial
Officer and Title)

SAS 20—Required Communication of Material Weaknesses in Internal Accounting Control

Superseded by SAS 60.

SAS 21—Segment Information

What must I do with respect to segment information?

Under Statement of Financial Accounting Standards 14, *Financial Reporting for Segments of a Business Enterprise*, certain entities are required to present segment information in their financial statements.

• The auditor is not required to apply auditing procedures necessary to enable the expression of a separate opinion on the segment information.

• Unless the required segment information is misstated, omitted, or incomplete, the auditor should not refer to the segment information in the standard (unqualified) audit report.

What if the segment information is flawed?

When the segment information is *materially misstated or incomplete*, the auditor should issue a qualified opinion. The *complete omission* of required segment information warrants the expression of a qualified opinion, due to lack of adequate disclosure.

What if I cannot determine the adequacy of segment information?

If the auditor is unable to reach a conclusion as to whether the presentation of segment information is in conformity with the provisions of Statement of Financial Accounting Standards 14, then a scope limitation has resulted, and a qualified opinion should be expressed.

SAS 22—Planning and Supervision

How do I develop an audit work program?

This statement provides guidance in planning the audit (including supervision of assistants) as required by the first standard of field work.

The nature, extent, and timing of planning depends on the size and complexity of the client organization and the auditor's prior experience with the organization and business. The audit examination should be based on an audit work program. This is a detailed listing of the procedures to be performed during the course of the engagement.

The following are considerations for developing an audit work program:

- Matters which pertain to the client's business and type of industry. EXAMPLES: types of products and services offered by the client, the client's capital structure, the existence of related parties, the location of the client's facilities, and any pertinent governmental regulations
- The accounting policies, procedures, and methods used by the client
- The auditor's understanding of the client's internal control structure and the auditor's assessment of control risk
- The auditor's preliminary estimates of materiality levels
- Items included in the financial statements likely to require adjustment or modification
- Circumstances which may need extensive or additional auditing procedures
- The report expected to be issued in connection with the engagement

The actual procedures for planning an audit engagement should be based on professional judgment. Some common procedures are:

- A review of prior years' working papers, financial statements and audit reports
- A discussion about matters affecting the audit with firm personnel responsible for non-audit services. EXAMPLES: Management advisory services and tax services
- Inquiry about current business developments
- Reading and reviewing interim financial statements of the current year
- A discussion with client management, the board

of directors, or audit committee concerning the
type, scope, and timing of the audit engagement

- Determining the effect of related auditing and
accounting promulgations
- Determining staff requirements and assigning
audit personnel
- Determining the timing of specific audit procedures
- Considering the use of outside consultants, specialists, and internal auditors
- Coordinating the assistance of client personnel
in the data preparation process

How are the auditor's assistants to be supervised?

With respect to the supervision of assistants, the
auditor with final responsibility should:

- Instruct the assistants
- Review their work at every critical level of su-
pervision
- Resolve any differences of opinion

Differences of opinion concerning auditing and
accounting matters, when resolved, should be documented in the audit work papers.

SAS 23—Analytical Review Procedures

Superseded by SAS 56.

SAS 24—Review of Interim Financial Information

Superseded by SAS 36.

SAS 25—The Relationship of Generally Accepted Auditing Standards to Quality Control Standards

Am I responsible for quality control?

When performing an audit, the independent auditor is responsible for complying with generally accepted auditing standards.

When conducting an audit practice, an independent auditor (or firm of independent auditors) is responsible for complying with quality control standards in order to provide assurance of compliance with generally accepted auditing standards.

NOTE: Refer to Quality Control Statement 1 for guidance in establishing an effective system of quality control.

SAS 26—Association with Financial Statements

When am I considered associated with financial statements?

An accountant is deemed to be associated with financial statements when:

- He or she has consented to the use of his or her name in a report, document, or any written communication containing the financial statements.
- The accountant has prepared or assisted in the preparation of the financial statements, even though his or her name is not on the financial statements.

NOTE: This statement applies to association with *audited or unaudited* financial statements of a public entity.

RECOMMENDATION: The practitioner engaged to compile or review unaudited financial statements of a nonpublic entity should comply with Statements on Standards for Accounting and Review Services.

May I use a disclaimer?

When the practitioner is associated with unaudited financial statements of a public entity, it is appropriate to issue a disclaimer of opinion. Such a disclaimer may be in the form of a report on the financial statements, or the disclaimer may be placed directly on the statements. In addition to providing the disclaimer of opinion, the practitioner should clearly mark every page of the financial statements "unaudited."

SAS 27–28—Supplementary Information Required by the Financial Accounting Standards Board; Supplementary Information on the Effects of Changing Prices

SAS 27 is superseded by SAS 52. SAS 28 was withdrawn by the Auditing Standards Board.

SAS 29—Reporting on Information Accompanying the Basic Financial Statements in Auditor-Submitted Documents

Must I report on information accompanying the statements?

When an independent auditor submits to a client or other third party a document that includes information in addition to the basic financial statements, he or she must report on all information contained in that document.

What information must the report cover?

The auditor's report covering the information accompanying the basic financial statements should:

• State that the examination was for the purpose of forming an opinion on the basic financial statements taken as a whole.

• Identify the accompanying information. This may be by descriptive title, such as "Supporting Schedule —Administrative Expenses," or by reference to the page number of the document.

• State that the information accompanying the basic financial statements is presented for analysis purposes and is not part of the basic financial statements.

• Express an opinion as to whether the accompanying information is presented fairly in all material respects in relation to the basic financial statements taken as whole. If the accompanying information was not subjected to auditing procedures, a disclaimer of opinion should be expressed.

NOTE: The report on the accompanying information may be included as part of the opinion on the basic financial statements or presented as a separate report in the auditor-submitted document.

EXAMPLE 12.5

The following is a sample report on audited information:

My (our) examination was made for the purpose of forming an opinion on the basic financial statements taken as a whole. The [identify accompanying information] is presented for purposes of additional analysis and is not a required part of the basic financial statements. Such information has been subjected to the auditing procedures applied in the examination of the basic financial statements and, in my (our) opinion, is fairly stated in all material respects in relation to the basic financial statements taken as a whole.

EXAMPLE 12.6

The following text provides the framework for a disclaimer on all accompanying information:

My (our) examination was made for the purpose of forming an opinion on the basic financial statements taken as a whole. The [identify accompanying information] is presented for purposes of additional analysis and is not a required part of the basic financial statements. Such information has not been subjected to the auditing procedures applied in the examination of the basic financial statements, and, accordingly, I (we) express no opinion on it.

SAS 30—Reporting on Internal Accounting Control

Modified by SAS 55 and SAS 60.

SAS 31—Evidential Matter

What constitutes evidential matter?

Evidential matter consists of:

- Underlying accounting data (e.g., books of original entry)
- Related accounting manuals and informal worksheets supporting computations
- Corroborating evidential matter (e.g., client-prepared documents, minutes of board meetings, and information obtained through inquiry, observation, inspection, and confirmation)

How much evidential matter is enough?

Professional judgment must be exercised in determining the nature, extent and timing of substantive tests the auditor should perform in gathering sufficient competent evidential matter needed to enable the expression of an opinion.

When is evidential matter competent?

Evidential matter is deemed to be competent if it is valid and relevant.

SAS 32—Adequacy of Disclosure in Financial Statements

How much disclosure is enough?

If the independent auditor concludes that the audited financial statements omit information required by GAAP, the auditor should express either a qualified opinion or an adverse opinion.

RECOMMENDATION: If practicable, present the omitted information in an explanatory paragraph of the audit report. "Practicable" means that the information is obtainable from the client's records and the auditor is not put in the position of being the preparer of the information.

SAS 33—Supplementary Oil and Gas Reserve Information

Superseded by SAS 45.

SAS 34—The Auditor's Considerations When a Question Arises About an Entity's Continued Existence

Superseded by SAS 59.

SAS 35—Special Reports: Applying Agreed-Upon Procedures to Specified Elements, Accounts, or Items of a Financial Statement

See Chapter 11.

SAS 36—Review of Interim Financial Information

This statement applies to reviews of financial statements of a publicly traded entity.

NOTE: The review procedures and reporting requirements contained in this statement are essentially the same as those applicable to reviews of financial statements of nonpublicly traded entities governed by Statements on Standards for Accounting and Review Services (discussed in Chapter 11). However, with respect to a review of interim financial information of a publicly traded entity, each page of the financial statements *must* be labeled "unaudited."

SAS 37—Filings Under Federal Securities Statutes

What are my responsibilities in filings under Federal Securities Statutes?

The accountant involved in filings under the Federal Securities Statutes is considered to be an expert. Therefore, the accountant's responsibility is based on the "reasonable man standard."

The "subsequent events" period is extended from

the date of the audit report to the effective date of the filing under the Federal Securities Statutes. In addition, if the accountant finds that any unaudited information is not in conformity with generally accepted accounting principles, he or she should insist that an appropriate revision be made.

SAS 38—Letters for Underwriters

Superseded by SAS 49.

SAS 39—Audit Sampling

What risks are involved in statistical sampling?

This statement provides guidance in situations where the independent auditor decides to utilize statistical or nonstatistical sampling plans or approaches in performing tests of controls or substantive tests or both.

While sampling plans create uncertainty, the uncertainty is justified due to the cost/benefit relationship since a well-designed sample is presumed to be representative of a population.

In performing sampling plans, the auditor should assess and control *sampling risk*, which is the risk that a sample may not be representative of a population and therefore cause the auditor to draw an invalid conclusion.

• In *substantive testing*, sampling risk involves the risk of incorrect acceptance and the risk of incorrect rejection.

• In *tests of controls*, it includes the risk of over-reliance on internal control and the risk of under-reliance on internal control.

Nonsampling risk should also be controlled. Non-sampling risk includes the risk that the auditor will fail to detect errors and irregularities due to non-application of a required procedure or the application of a procedure inconsistent with a given audit objective. EXAMPLE: The audit objective is the detection of unrecorded liabilities and the audit procedure is the confirmation of recorded account balances.

Ultimate audit risk is a combination of sampling and nonsampling risks.

SAS 40—Supplementary Mineral Reserve Information

Withdrawn by the Auditing Standards Board.

SAS 41—Working Papers

What is the purpose of working papers?

Working papers are the means of documenting the audit procedures performed, the evidential matter gathered from those procedures, and the judgments and evaluations made throughout the audit. Working papers are usually written, but they may also be in another form, such as on tape or film.

What should working papers contain?

The auditor should use professional judgment when deciding the content of working papers. Factors in this determination include:

- The nature of the engagement
- The type of audit report expected to be issued
- The condition of the client's financial records
- The auditor's understanding of the client's internal control structure and his or her assessment of control risk

To whom do working papers belong?

Since the auditor prepares the working papers, he or she is the owner of them and is responsible for their custody.

SAS 42—Reporting on Condensed Financial Statements and Selected Financial Data

What about client-prepared documents?

This statement is applicable to reporting on a client-prepared document containing:

- Condensed financial statements that are derived from audited financial statements.
- Selected financial data derived from audited financial statements.

NOTE: The practitioner should refer to SAS 29 when reporting on an auditor-submitted document that contains condensed financial statements or selected financial data.

Condensed Financial Statements

What should be in the report on condensed financial statements?

The auditor's report on condensed financial statements should contain:

- A statement that the auditor has examined, in accordance with generally accepted auditing standards, the complete set of financial statements
- An indication that an opinion has been expressed on the complete set of financial statements
- The date of the auditor's report on the complete set of financial statements
- The type of opinion expressed on the complete set of financial statements
- An opinion as to whether the information contained in the condensed financial statements is presented fairly in all material respects in relation to the complete set of financial statements

CAUTION: To prevent readers from being misled, condensed financial statements should be so marked.

EXAMPLE 12.7

The typical wording of a report on condensed financial statements is as follows:

I (we) have examined, in accordance with generally accepted auditing standards, the consolidated balance sheet of Mat Corporation as of December 31, 19X0, and the related statements of income, retained earnings, and cash flows for the year then ended (not presented herein); and in my (our) report dated March 2, 19X1, I (we) expressed an unqualified opinion on those financial statements. In my (our) opinion, the information set forth in the accompanying condensed financial statements is fairly stated in all material respects in relation to the financial statements from which it has been derived.

Selected Financial Data

Since selected financial data are not a required part of the basic financial statements, the auditor's report on such data should be limited to data that are derived from financial statements subjected to an audit.

What should be in the report on selected financial data?

The auditor's report on selected financial data should include:

- A statement that the auditor has examined, in accordance with generally accepted auditing standards, the complete set of financial statements
- An indication that an opinion has been expressed on the complete set of financial statements
- The type of opinion expressed on the complete set of financial statements
- An opinion as to whether the information contained in the selected financial data is presented fairly in all material respects in relation to the complete set of financial statements

EXAMPLE 12.8

The following is the typical wording of the additional paragraph to be added to the auditor's standard report (in this case, on comparative financial statements):

I (we) have also previously examined, in accordance with generally accepted auditing standards, the balance sheets as of December 31, 19X3, 19X2, and 19X1, and the related statements of income, retained earnings, and cash flows for the years ended December 31, 19X3, 19X2, and 19X1 (none of which are presented herein); and I (we) expressed unqualified opinions on those financial statements. In my (our) opinion, the information set forth in the selected financial data for each of the five years in the period ended December 31, 19X5, appearing on page xx, is fairly stated in all material respects in relation to the consolidated financial statements from which it has been derived.

SAS 43—Omnibus Statement on Auditing Standards

This statement amends parts of selected Statements on Auditing Standards. These amendments have been incorporated into the summaries of the pertinent Statements.

SAS 44—Special-Purpose Reports on Internal Accounting Control at Service Organizations

What is the effect of service organizations used by the client?

A service organization may have an internal control structure that interacts with the client's internal control structure. EXAMPLE: A payroll processing company which is independent of a client entity.

Auditors of clients that employ a service organization should obtain, from the auditor of the service organization, a special purpose report on the service organization's internal control structure. The report should cover the design and compliance of the internal control structure. This is an essential procedure because of the effect the controls (at the service organization) may have upon the client's execution and recording of transactions.

SAS 45—Omnibus Statement on Auditing Standards—1983

This statement amends parts of selected Statements on Auditing Standards.

Substantive Tests Prior to the Balance-Sheet Date

How do I control incremental audit risk?

Auditors may perform substantive tests prior to the balance-sheet date. However, interim testing increases the likelihood that errors and irregularities will occur between the interim-testing date and the balance-sheet date. Accordingly, the auditor should assess the difficulty in controlling this risk ("incremental audit risk"). In order to control this risk, the auditor should consider whether:

- Business conditions have changed in the remaining period to such an extent that management would be more likely to perpetrate irregularities
- Accounts selected for interim testing are expected to adhere to predictable patterns

RECOMMENDATION: The auditor should design substantive tests which will enable the extension of interim conclusions to the balance-sheet date. Accordingly, the auditor should consider:

- Comparing interim results with those at the balance-sheet date
- Performing other types of analytical procedures
- Performing substantive tests of details

Any significant fluctuations between interim results and those as of the balance-sheet date warrant investigation.

Related Parties

How do I handle related party transactions?

With respect to related party transactions, the auditor should be aware that the substance of a particular transaction could be significantly different than its legal form. Whenever a client transacts business with another entity at terms more favorable than would be afforded under usual circumstances, it is possible that a related party relationship exists.

RECOMMENDATION: The auditor should design substantive tests in order to identify the existence and terms of related party transactions. This is crucial, since FASB Statement 57 requires that related party information be disclosed in financial statements.

How do I identify related party transactions?

In order to identify transactions with related parties, the auditor should review:

- The minutes of meetings of the board of directors
- Transactions with major customers, suppliers, borrowers, and lenders
- Large, unusual, and nonrecurring transactions

Once identified, related party transactions should be examined in order for the auditor to gain satisfaction as to the purpose, extent, and nature of the transactions. Additionally, the practitioner must be satisfied with the related party disclosures contained in the financial statements.

SAS 46—Consideration of Omitted Procedures After the Report Date

What if one or more procedures were omitted?

Under certain circumstances, such as peer review, the auditor may conclude, after the issuance of an audit report, that he or she omitted one or more auditing procedures. In these situations, the auditor has the responsibility of assessing the importance of the omitted procedures to his or her present ability to support the previously-expressed opinion. In making this assessment, the auditor should consider any alternate auditing procedures performed.

If the auditor still feels that the omitted procedures impairs the present ability to support the audit report, he or she should undertake to apply the omitted or alternate procedures. If the auditor is unable to apply the necessary procedures, he or she should contact legal counsel in order to discuss the appropriate course of action.

SAS 47—Audit Risk and Materiality in Conducting an Audit

What constitutes audit risk?

The risk that the independent auditor may unknowingly fail to modify his or her audit opinion on materially misstated financial statements is known as *audit risk*.

In considering audit risk, the auditor must be aware of the following:

• *Inherent risk* is the "built in" susceptibility of an account balance or class of transactions to errors, regardless of the internal control structure. EXAMPLE: Cash has a high inherent risk due to its liquidity.

• *Control risk* is the risk that an account balance or class of transactions will contain errors which will not be detected or prevented by the client's internal control structure.

• *Detection risk* is the risk that the auditor will fail to identify material errors.

NOTE: There should be an inverse relationship between detection risk and inherent and control risks. In other words, the greater the inherent and control risk, the less the detection risk the auditor can and should accept.

RECOMMENDATION: The auditor can control detection risk by applying the appropriate auditing procedures. On the other hand, it is management's responsibility to minimize control risk by establishing and maintaining an effective internal control structure.

What is materiality?

Materiality relates to the financial importance of an item or group of items in the financial statements.

There is no quantitative definition of materiality; rather, materiality is qualitatively defined.

CRITERION: An item (or group of items) should be considered material if the inclusion or omission of the item (or group of items) will affect the reader of the financial statements.

What must I do with respect to audit risk and materiality?

Both audit risk and materiality must be considered in planning an audit and expressing an opinion on the financial statements. Needless to say, the auditor should limit audit risk to a relatively low level.

Additionally, audit risk and materiality are inversely related. Accordingly, the risk that an account may be materially misstated may be low, although the risk that an account may be misstated by a small amount may be very high.

SAS 48—The Effects of Computer Processing on the Examination of Financial Statements

What effect does automation have on an audit?

An auditor should consider the following in planning an engagement to audit an entity that records its transactions by computer:

- The extent of electronic data processing
- The complexity of the electronic data processing operations
- The organizational structure of the electronic data processing department
- The availability of financial data
- The application of computer-assisted audit techniques
- The need for a specialist to explain the effects of electronic data processing

How do automated and manual systems differ?

When considering a client's internal control structure in an electronic data processing environment, the auditor should consider the characteristics that distinguish computer processing from manual recording:

• *Transaction trails*: Audit trails in a computerized environment are either nonexistent or short lived.

• *Uniform Processing of Transactions*: If a computer handles a particular type of transaction correctly, then it will handle all subsequent transactions of the same type in the same manner. CAUTION: The converse is also true. If a transaction is handled incorrectly, all subsequent similar transactions processed will also be incorrectly handled.

• *Segregation of functions*: Since many functions are performed internally by the computer, there is an inherent lack of segregation of functions in a computerized environment. To compensate for this situation, job functions should be segregated within the electronic data processing activities.

• *Potential for errors and irregularities*: The potential for errors and irregularities in a computerized environment depends on the human involvement in the computerized applications and the extent of the segregation of functions.

• *Potential for Increased Management Supervision*: Given that a computer can generate data more quickly than manual preparation, financial information is provided on a more timely basis. This enables management to use information before it outlives its utility.

• *Initiation or Subsequent Execution of Transactions by Computer*: Authorization for initiation or subsequent execution of transactions is built into the computer. Documentation for this authorization is therefore not always apparent.

• *Dependence of Other Controls on Controls Over Computer Processing*: The output derived from computer processing is often useful in performing manual control procedures.

SAS 49—Letters for Underwriters

What is the purpose of a comfort letter?

A CPA may issue a letter for an underwriter, called a *comfort letter*. A comfort letter may refer to one or more of the following:

- The accountant's independence
- Compliance of the financial statements included in the registration statement with the Securities Act of 1933
- Unaudited financial statements
- Changes in financial statement items after the date of the financial statements included in the registration statements
- Tables and statistics

NOTE: A comfort letter usually includes negative assurance as opposed to the expression of an opinion.

SAS 50—Reports on the Application of Accounting Principles

When might I have to report on the application of accounting principles?

An accountant may be requested to prepare a written report on:

- The application of accounting principles to specified transactions
- The type of opinion that may be expressed on an entity's financial statements
- The application of accounting principles not involving facts or circumstances of a particular principle, as in a hypothetical transaction

What should be in a report on the application of accounting principles?

The accountant's report on the application of accounting principles should include:

- The appropriate address (it should be addressed to the principal to the transaction or to the intermediary)
- A statement describing the type of engagement
- An indication that the engagement was performed in accordance with the relevant standards of the American Institute of Certified Public Accountants

- A description of the transaction and its related facts, circumstances, and assumptions (including their source)
- An identification of the principals to the transaction
- A description of the relevant accounting principles
- A statement fixing the responsibility for the proper accounting treatment with the preparers of the financial statements, who should consult with their continuing accountants
- A warning that the report may change if differences of facts, circumstances, or assumptions arise

EXAMPLE 12.9

Typical wording for a report on accounting applications follows:

I (we) have been engaged to report on the appropriate application of generally accepted accounting principles to the specific (hypothetical) transaction described below. This report is being issued to the Karen Company (DBA Intermediaries) for assistance in evaluating accounting principles for the described specific (hypothetical) transaction. My (our) engagement has been conducted in accordance with standards established by the American Institute of Certified Public Accountants.

The facts, circumstances, and assumptions relevant to the specific (hypothetical) transaction as provided to me (us) by the management of the Karen Company (DBA Intermediaries) are as follows:

[Description of Transaction]

[Description of Appropriate Accounting Principles]

The ultimate responsibility for the decision on the appropriate application of generally accepted accounting principles for an actual transaction rests with the preparers of financial statements, who should consult with their continuing accountants. My (our) judgment on the appropriate application of generally accepted accounting principles for the described specific (hypothetical) transaction is based solely on facts provided to me (us) as described above; should these facts and circumstances differ, my (our) conclusion may change.

SAS 51—Reporting on Financial Statements Prepared for Use in Other Countries

When reporting on financial statements for overseas use, what should I do?

Generally accepted auditing standards as developed in the United States should be adhered to when examining financial statements of a U.S. entity prepared in conformity with accounting principles accepted in another country. Under certain circumstances the auditor may also have to adhere to the auditing standards of the foreign country.

If the financial statements are for use *only* in a foreign country, the auditor may issue:

- A U.S.-style report modified for reporting on the foreign country's accounting principles
- A report based on the foreign country's standards

EXAMPLE 12.10

The following is a sample U.S.-style report modified for use in a foreign country:

I (we) have examined the balance sheet of Transcontinental Company as of December 31, 19XX, and the related statements of income, retained earnings, and cash flows for the year then ended, which, as described in Note X, have been prepared on the basis of accounting principles generally accepted in [name of country]. My (our) examination was made in accordance with auditing standards generally accepted in the United States (and in [name of country]) and, accordingly, included such tests of the accounting records and such other auditing procedures as I (we) considered necessary in the circumstances.

In my (our) opinion, the financial statements referred to above present fairly the financial position of Transcontinental Company at December 31, 19XX, and the results of its operations and cash flows for the year then ended, in conformity with accounting principles generally accepted in [name country] applied on a basis consistent with that of the preceding year.

SAS 52—Omnibus Statement on Auditing Standards—1987

Essentially modified SAS 5 to recognize various publications of the Government Accounting Standards Board (GASB) as a source of generally accepted accounting principles.

This pronouncement also (a) recognizes supplementary information required by the GASB and (b) reflects changes in light of the issuance of FASB Statement 89, Financial Reporting and Changing Prices, which no longer makes it mandatory to disclose supplementary information pertaining to the effects of changing prices.

Since supplementary information required by the FASB or GASB is not a required part of the basic financial statements, the auditor is not required to modify his or her audit report to refer to the supplementary information unless:

- It is omitted
- Its measurement or presentation is not in conformity with prescribed guidelines
- The auditor is unable to apply prescribed procedures
- The auditor is precluded from removing sub-

stantial doubt as to the conformity with prescribed guidelines

RECOMMENDATION: The auditor's opinion
should not be modified due to the circumstances
described above. Accordingly, even though the auditor may deem it necessary to add an explanatory
paragraph, the auditor may still issue an unqualified
opinion.

SAS 53—The Auditor's Responsibility to Detect and Report Errors and Irregularities

What constitutes an error or irregularity?

- An error is an unintentional misstatement or omission from the financial statements
- An irregularity is an intentional misstatement or omission from the financial statement

EXAMPLES: Errors include:

- Clerical and/or mathematical mistakes in the preparation of sales invoices
- Misinterpretation of facts

EXAMPLES: Irregularities include:

- Management fraud
- Misappropriation of company assets (i.e., de-falcations)
- The intentional failure to record transactions

What is my responsibility for the detection of errors and irregularities?

1. The auditor must assess the risk that errors
and irregularities may result in material misstatement of the financial statements.

2. Based on this assessment, the auditor should
design his or her audit procedures in a manner that
will provide reasonable, but not absolute, assurance
that he or she will detect those errors and irregularities that have a material effect on the financial
statements.

3. Plan and perform the audit with an attitude of professional skepticism.

4. Consider the quantitative and qualitative aspects of errors and irregularities.

What factors enter into the consideration of audit risk?

In addition to the internal control structure, the auditor should consider the following:

- Management characteristics, such as an overly aggressive attitude
- Operating and industry characteristics, such as a rapid change in the industry in which a client operates
- Engagement characteristics, such as the presence of many complex accounting issues
- The size and complexity of the entity
- Ownership characteristics

What should I do if I detect an irregularity that does not have a material effect on the financial statements?

Even though the irregularity does not have a material effect on the financial statements, the irregularity should be reported to management at least one level above those involved. Further, the auditor must be satisfied that there are no other related audit implications to be considered.

What should I do if I detect an irregularity that could be material or I cannot evaluate its potential materiality?

In these situations, the auditor should

1. Consider the audit implications of the irregularity.

2. Discuss with management, at least one level above those involved, the approach to further investigating the matter.

3. Seek sufficient evidence to enable determination of the irregularity's existence and materiality.

4. If the circumstances warrant, suggest that the client seek legal counsel.

Do irregularities have an effect on the audit report?

If an irregularity has a material effect on the financial statements, the auditor should insist that the client revise the financial statements. If the client refuses to comply with the auditor's suggestion, either a qualified or an adverse opinion should be issued. The qualified or adverse opinion should disclose all substantive reasons for the issuance of such opinion.

If a scope limitation arises with respect to irregularities, then a qualified opinion or disclaimer of opinion would be appropriate.

Are there circumstances that warrant withdrawal from the engagement?

If the client fails to modify the financial statements and refuses to accept the modified auditor's report, the auditor should withdraw.

Does the audit committee have to be informed about errors and irregularities?

Yes, the audit committee (or others with equivalent authority and responsibility) must be adequately informed about irregularities, other than those that are inconsequential. Under certain circumstances, the auditor should disclose an irregularity to outsiders, as when the client reports a change in auditors under the Federal Securities Statutes.

SAS 54—Illegal Acts by Clients

What is an illegal act?

An illegal act is a violation of law or government regulations by the client.

CAUTION: The auditor should seek legal counsel when determining what is an illegal act.

What is my responsibility for the detection and reporting of illegal acts?

The auditor's responsibility is essentially the same as his or her responsibility to detect and report errors and irregularities (as discussed in SAS 53).

NOTE: The auditor is concerned with the illegal act's effect on the financial statements as opposed to the illegality itself.

What if I detect an illegal act that does not have a material effect on the financial statements?

If the client refuses to take appropriate action with respect to *any* illegal act, material or otherwise, the auditor should consider withdrawing from the engagement.

SAS 55—Consideration of the Internal Control Structure in a Financial Statement Audit

Refer to Chapter 10.

SAS 56—Analytical Procedures

Analytical procedures must be performed in the planning and overall review stages of all audits. Because analytical procedures enable identification of unusual relationships and fluctuations, the auditor can better determine the nature and extent of substantive tests.

NOTE: Analytical procedures do not have to be used in substantive testing. This is a matter of professional judgment.

What are analytical procedures?

Analytical procedures include comparison of recorded amounts, or ratios based on recorded amounts, to expectations derived by the auditor. Accordingly, analytical procedures include comparison of current period financial information with

- Prior period information
- Expected results

- Predictable pattern information
- Intra-industry information
- Nonfinancial information

SAS 57—Auditing Accounting Estimates

What is meant by an accounting estimate?

An accounting estimate is an approximation of a financial statement element, item, or account.
EXAMPLES:

- Net realizable values of inventory
- Pension and warranty expenses
- Obsolete inventories
- Amount of a probable loss contingency

What is my responsibility with respect to accounting estimates?

While management is responsible for developing accounting estimates, the auditor is responsible for evaluating the reasonableness of such estimates.

The auditor must evaluate accounting estimates in order to obtain reasonable assurance that (a) all material accounting estimates have been developed, (b) the accounting estimates are reasonable, (c) the accounting estimates are in conformity with GAAP, and (d) the accounting estimates are properly disclosed in the financial statements.

How do I evaluate the reasonableness of accounting estimates?

The auditor should review and test the process employed by management in developing a particular accounting estimate. Further, the auditor should develop an independent expectation of the estimate to corroborate the reasonableness of the client's estimate. Finally, the auditor should review subsequent events.

SAS 58—Reports on Audited Financial Statements

Refer to Chapter 10.

SAS 59—The Auditor's Consideration of an Entity's Ability to Continue as a Going Concern

The auditor is responsible for evaluating whether there is substantial doubt about the entity's ability to continue as a going concern for a reasonable time period, not to exceed one year beyond the date of the audited financial statements.

What conditions and events may indicate a going-concern problem?

The following might be considered indicative of a going-concern problem:

- *Negative trends*—such as a poor current working capital ratio
- *Indicators of possible financial trouble*—such as defaults on note agreements
- *Internal matters*—such as a strike by employees
- *External matters*—pending or actual litigation or legislation

CAUTION: The auditor should consider mitigating circumstances by evaluating management's plans. For example, management may be planning to restructure its debt in a manner that will increase equity ownership.

Do going-concern problems affect financial statements?

Certain informative disclosures might be necessary if the client is experiencing a going-concern problem. These disclosures include:

- The conditions and events causing the going-concern problem
- The possible effects of such conditions
- Management's evaluation of the significance of those conditions and events along with any mitigating factors
- The possible cessation of operations
- Management's plans for overcoming the going-concern problem
- Significant information regarding the recoverability or classification of assets and liabilities

What is my reporting responsibility?

If the auditor concludes that there is substantial doubt about the entity's ability to continue as a going concern for a reasonable time period, then the audit report should be modified to include an additional paragraph (to be inserted after the opinion paragraph) that reflects the auditor's conclusion.

EXAMPLE: The following represents sample wording of such an additional paragraph:

> The accompanying financial statements have been prepared assuming that the Company will continue as a going concern. As discussed in Note X to the financial statements, the Company has suffered recurring losses from operations and has a net capital deficiency that raise substantial doubt about its ability to continue as a going concern. Management's plans in regard to these matters are also described in Note X. The financial statements do not include any adjustments that might result from the outcome of this uncertainty.

CAUTION: A going-concern problem should not result in a qualified opinion. It would still be appropriate to issue an unqualified opinion.

SAS 60—Communication of Internal Control Structure Related Matters Noted in an Audit

While performing an audit, an auditor is under no obligation to search for reportable conditions (i.e., matters pertaining to significant deficiencies in the client's internal control structure that could have an adverse affect on the recording, processing, summarizing, and reporting of financial data).

What is my responsibility if I do identify reportable conditions?

If reportable conditions are identified, the auditor should communicate with the audit committee (or its equivalent). Such communication may be oral or written, although the latter is preferable.

What should be included in a report issued on reportable conditions?

A report on reportable conditions should:

- Include a statement that the purpose of the audit was to report on the financial statements and not to provide assurance relating to the internal control structure
- Define reportable conditions
- Describe the reportable conditions identified
- Restrict the distribution of the report

EXAMPLE: The typical wording of a report on reportable conditions follows:

In planning and performing my (our) audit of the financial statements of the ABC Corporation for the year ended December 31, 19XX, I (we) considered its internal control structure in order to determine my (our) auditing procedures for the purpose of expressing my (our) opinion on the financial statements and not to provide assurance on the internal control structure. However, I (we) noted certain matters involving the internal control structure and its operation that I (we) consider to be reportable conditions under standards established by the American Institute of Certified Public Accountants. Reportable conditions involve matters coming to my (our) attention relating to significant deficiencies in the design or operation of the internal control structure that, in my (our) judgment, could adversely affect the organization's ability to record, process, summarize, and report financial data consistent with the assertions of management in the financial statements.

[Include paragraph(s) to describe reportable conditions noted.]

This report is intended solely for the information and use of the audit committee (board of directors, board of trustees, or owners in owner-managed enterprises), management, and others within the organization (or specified regulatory agency or other specified third party).

CAUTION: Never issue a report containing a representation that no reportable conditions were noted during the audit.

RECOMMENDATION: The CPA should exercise professional judgment in determining when to communicate reportable conditions. Interim communication may be warranted.

What if I identify a material weakness?

A material weakness in the internal control structure is a reportable condition in which the design or operation of the internal control structure elements do not reduce to a relatively low level the risk that material errors or irregularities may occur and go undetected by employees in the normal course of performing their assigned functions.

The auditor is not responsible for separately identifying and reporting material weaknesses.

Since material weaknesses are reportable conditions, the auditor may communicate them as such.

SAS 61—Communication with Audit Committees

Certain matters pertaining to an audit must be communicated to the audit committee (or those having responsibility for oversight of the financial reporting process).

What matters are to be included in a communication with the audit committee?

Some of the matters to be communicated concern:

- The auditor's responsibility for internal control structure
- The auditor's responsibility for the audited financial statements
- The significant accounting policies of the entity
- Management judgments and accounting estimates

- Significant audit adjustments
- Other information in documents containing audited financial statements
- Disagreements with management
- Client consultations with other accountants
- Major issues discussed with management prior to retention
- Difficulties encountered in performing the audit

PART 5

TAXATION

CHAPTER 13

TAX RESEARCH

One of the greatest assets for an accountant is the ability to conduct tax research. Whether the accountant is attempting to solve an existing tax problem or formulating suggestions for proposed tax transactions, the practitioner should be familiar with the many sources of tax information.

SOURCES OF TAX LAW

What is the Internal Revenue Code?

The Internal Revenue Code represents the tax law. Amendments to the Internal Revenue Code must be approved by both the House of Representatives and the Senate before the president signs them into law.

How are committee reports helpful?

The legislative intent of the law may be found in the committee reports of the House Ways and Means Committee, the Senate Finance Committee, and the Joint Conference Committee. Committee reports often provide examples which may closely approximate your client's transactions and proposals.

When defending positions in court, the use of congressional intent is quite forceful. Each section in the Code includes a reference to the legislative history of the law, that is, a reference to *Revenue Acts* and their years of enactment. Standard tax services, such as those published by Prentice-Hall, reprint congressional committee reports upon issuance. Another source for the committee reports is the *Cumulative Bulletin* issued twice a year by the Internal Revenue Service (IRS). The *Cumulative Bulletin* is the hardbound version containing 26 weekly *Internal Revenue Bulletins*.

What is the importance of Treasury Department regulations?

Treasury Department regulations represent the government's interpretation of the Internal Revenue Code. Regulations are issued in three forms:

• *Proposed Regulations* are not authoritative since their adoption has not been finalized.

• *Temporary Regulations*, although not in their final form, do represent an authoritative source for the practitioner.

• *Final Regulations* are completely authoritative and are published in the *Federal Register*.

What is a Revenue Ruling?

• *Revenue Rulings*, which are interpretive in nature, are issued by the National Office of the Internal Revenue Service in Washington, D.C. They are published weekly in the *Internal Revenue Bulletin* and are reprinted in the semi-annual *Cumulative Bulletin*.

• A *letter ruling* is issued in response to a taxpayer's request for a ruling on a particular transaction. If the IRS feels that the substance of the ruling could affect the public, it converts the letter ruling into a revenue ruling.

What should you know about revenue procedures?

Revenue procedures offer guidance on practices and procedures of the IRS. EXAMPLE: A revenue procedure may instruct the practitioner on how to apply for a ruling on a particular type of tax transaction.

Revenue Procedures are published in the same manner as Revenue Rulings.

What is the purpose of Treasury Decisions?

Published in the weekly *Internal Revenue Bulletin* and the semi-annual *Cumulative Bulletin*, *Treasury Decisions* are issued to:

- Promulgate new regulations.
- Amend current regulations.
- Announce the Treasury's position relative to certain court decisions.

How are Technical Information Releases useful?

This source of tax information is used to locate announcements of various publications.

How about Technical Advice Memoranda?

Technical Advice Memoranda represent responses to requests made by auditors of the IRS. *Technical Advice Memoranda* are not published officially and may not be cited or used as precedent since they are applicable to specific audit situations.

THE COURT SYSTEM

What should I know about the Tax Court?

Taxpayers may wish to seek relief in the Tax Court since it only hears cases involving tax law. Therefore, the Tax Court specializes in tax matters.

While most Tax Court cases are ruled upon by one of 19 judges, all 19 judges will rule upon a case ("*sit en banc*") when novel issues are of concern. Furthermore, Tax Court judges travel around the country in order to hear cases.

Decisions issued by the Tax Court are either regular decisions or memorandum decisions.

- The *Regular* decisions involve new issues never before resolved by the Court. They are published in semi-annual volumes of *Tax Court of the United States Reports*.

- *Memorandum Decisions* involve only the application of existing doctrines of law. They are published only in mimeograph form.

An important distinction between regular and memorandum decisions is that with respect to regular decisions the IRS will publicly announce, in its

Internal Revenue Bulletin, its decision as to whether it will or will not acquiesce. Acquiescence means that the Internal Revenue Service has agreed to follow the Tax Court's Decision in all subsequent cases.

NOTES: Taxpayers do not have to pay tax assessments before they bring suit in the Tax Court. Suits of $10,000 or less are the jurisdiction of the Small Claims Division of the U.S. Tax court.

How does U.S. Claims Court differ from Tax Court?

The U.S. Claims Court, like the U.S. Tax Court, is a court of original jurisdiction. The U.S. Claims Court may rule upon any claim against the United States that involves constitutional law, Congressional Acts, or executive department regulations. Accordingly, the decisions of the U.S. Claims Court are not restricted to tax matters.

NOTE: To bring suit in the U.S. Claims Court, taxpayers must first pay the tax assessed.

What is the role of U.S. District Courts?

District Court cases are ruled upon by only one judge. A minimum of one District Court is found in every state. Like the U.S. Claims Court, the District Courts rule upon nontax matters.

A distinguishing characteristic of a District Court is that a jury trial is available in cases involving only questions of fact. Questions of law must be decided by a judge. Decisions of District Courts are only valid in the court's geographic jurisdiction.

NOTE: To bring suit in a U.S. District Court, a taxpayer must first pay the deficiency assessed by the government.

How do I appeal a court decision?

When a taxpayer loses a case in either U.S. Tax Court or U.S. District court, an appeal may be made to a Regional Circuit of the U.S. Court of Appeals. Losses in the U.S. Claims Court may be appealed by seeking relief in the Court of Appeals for the Federal Circuit.

Trial courts (District Courts, the Tax Court and

the Claims Court) are bound by the decisions established by the Court of Appeals having jurisdiction. A Court of Appeals, however, does not have to follow the decisions handed down by a Court of Appeals in a different jurisdiction.

Can a tax case go to the Supreme Court?

The U.S. Supreme Court represents the highest appellate court. The U.S. Supreme Court decides which cases it will hear by granting a *Writ of Certiorari*. Although the U.S. Supreme Court will not usually hear cases involving tax matters, it will agree to resolve conflicts between Courts of Appeals.

NOTE: All courts must abide by the decisions of the U.S. Supreme Court.

Which court should be used in a particular case?

The decision to use a particular court for tax litigation depends upon many factors, including:

- The expertise in tax matters possessed by the judges
- The ability to request a jury trial
- The requirement that the assessed tax be paid before legal action may be taken

Index

573